Extraterrestrial Contact

Extraterrestrial Contact

The Evidence and Implications

Steven M. Greer, M.D

Crossing Point, Inc.
Publications
Afton, Virginia

Publisher's Cataloging-in-Publication
(Provided by Quality Books, Inc.)

Greer, Steven M., 1955-
Extraterrestrial contact : the evidence and implications / Steven M. Greer. -- 1st ed.
p. cm.
ISBN: 0-9673238-0-0
1. Life on other planets. 2. Human-alien encounters.
3. Unidentified flying objects--Sightings and encounters. I. Title.
QB54.G74 1999 001.94
QBI99-500437

Cover Artwork
Ron Russell
P.O. Box 460760
Aurora, CO 80046

Manuscript editors: Brian Crissey, Emily Greer

Printed in the United States of America.

Address all inquiries to:
Crossing Point, Inc.
Post Office Box 265
Crozet, VA 22932

Produced by
Granite Publishing, LLC
Post Office Box 1429,
Columbus, NC 28722 U.S.A.
828-894-3088

living gently on the Earth

Dedication

This book is dedicated to our children—
and to our children's children's children.

Acknowledgments

There are so many people to thank and acknowledge that an even partial listing would go on for much too long.

But of all those to thank and acknowledge, first must be my wife Emily who has done so much behind the scenes to support my work and the work of CSETI. Without her, truly none of this would have been possible. Selflessly and with dedication, she is always there.

The people in CSETI who have worked to move disclosure forward and who have labored to establish peaceful contact with extraterrestrial (ET) life forms are certainly numbered in the hundreds. But preeminent among them is Shari Adamiak, who for 6 years was my most trusted colleague and a true lioness for truth. Without her extraordinary efforts our accomplishments would have been impossible. Indeed, she lived—and gave her life—to see that the day would come when the truth would be known and universal peace could be established.

She helped research and write many of the case reports found in this book, and was present at nearly every major CSETI expedition/ET contact event. Her labors were Promethean in nature; she never flinched—and until she could no longer walk or move, she worked to advance our efforts.

And there are so many others: Tony Craddock, our website administrator and a first rate field researcher; Debbie Foch and Linda Willetts, who have taken on key roles in getting the work of CSETI done; Dr. Ted Loder, who has ably taken on the task of liaison with the scientific community; Marty Keller who has worked for over 5 years to network with the mainstream media; Dr. Richard Haines, who has methodically documented human interactive contact with ETs in his new book CE-5; Jan Harzan who has worked to network our disclosure efforts to top political leaders; and my key military, national security and political advisors (you know who you are) without whose support and advise the historic events of the past 5 years could not have been possible.

And to all of the CSETI supporters—the thousands of field researchers, donors and advocates: thank you. Let us continue to work to draw that good future towards us. For it is those of us who live upon the Earth today who must achieve world peace, universal peace and a new civilization which coexists with the Earth and with others in harmony.

A Tribute

Shari Adamiak passed on to the world of Light today, January 20, 1998 at 9:50 A.M. MST. Shari made her transition in the presence of friends and loved ones, peacefully and without pain. I ask that everyone pause to say a prayer for Shari and the progress of her soul in the presence of God. What words can contain our sense of loss and of the love we all shared with Shari?

Since 1991, when we first met at a lecture in Los Angeles, Shari has been a pillar of strength and support, an indefatigable colleague, a true friend, an intrepid fellow explorer, an irreplaceable confidant and a fearless lioness without whose dedication CSETI could not have realized its many historic achievements.

She has been my right hand and trusted assistant for over six years. Whether braving the dangers of the remote parts of Latin America or assisting with meetings at the offices of the Joint Chiefs of Staff in the Pentagon, Shari was there with me—and for all of us. She never faltered and she never gave up.

Unfazed by the barbs of critics or the machinations of relentless covert operations, she resolutely worked for a time of peace—a peace universal, for the Earth and for countless worlds beyond.

How many wonders did we witness together? From walking in the shadow of some of the world's largest volcanos with ET spacecraft floating silently above us, to watching a dozen top-secret military witnesses tell an assemblage of Congressmen the truth about UFOs, Shari and I saw events unfold of such great significance. And through it all, Shari was filled with a joy, an excitement and energy, an almost childlike curiosity and wonder at the mysteries of creation and the astonishing potential of these times.

Even as her body began to fail her, she evinced a spirit of such grace, courage and love that all those who knew her were amazed and blessed by her example.

Just two months ago, in November of 1997, she journeyed to Joshua Tree wilderness in California with me. There she experienced what she loved most: the oneness with the stars, the universe and the communication with those peoples from other planets visiting our turbulent world. Fighting weakness, pain and increasing paralysis of her right arm and leg, Shari went into the desert each night, undeterred by the growing obstacles posed by her physical condition. And there, through the crossing point of light, we saw the depths of space and the people and spacecraft from other worlds, who await our own coming of age as a people. Nothing would keep her from this purpose.

Now, a great light has gone from this world, but it shines forever brightly in the realms of eternity. I know Shari was ready for this great journey: Precisely seven mornings before the morning of her passing, we crossed over together to the other side, if only for a while. Awestruck, we witnessed a Light—a Presence—so beautiful, emanating from the center of creation. No words can depict it; it was beyond anything the intellect can grasp. An infinite brilliance, golden white in the center and becoming more peach, pink and magenta as it expanded infinitely before us, suffused us in a sea of love, joy and beauty unlike any experience of my life. It was the experience of the consciousness of God—pure light, unspeakable love and peace. And permeating that Spot were millions of voices joining as one, singing a melody too sweet to recall. And the refrain was: "We are all One in Spirit."

Knowing her time was near, I came to Denver yesterday to see her to the other side. Last night while saying prayers, she emerged from the coma, and with a look of great joy on her face, opened her eyes. I told her all was ready for her transition to the world of Light, and that she should go when she was ready. I could hear her acknowledge these words, and a large tear welled up in her eyes as she knew that our time together in this world was nearly over.

This morning, we were called to her bedside. As we gathered, we said prayers and prepared her spiritually for the transition. As lights and a breath of great spirit filled the room, we saw it was time, and I said: "Shari, go into the eternal light." With that, she took her final breath and ascended to Providence.

Even while knowing the joy and love of her present state, the loss is nonetheless severe. but let us remember her thus: She lived in the world of Light, joyous, and she would want us to continue the work to which she dedicated her life—the establishment of Universal Peace, and the creation of a cosmic civilization.

And we find hope in the knowledge that those who have passed on to the next world become the leaven which raises this world of existence. Shari and I discussed her future work, from beyond the veil of light, which would advance the cause of peace and enlightenment in all the realms of God. I have no doubt that she will serve well from her new home in the eternal and become one with the angels of peace.

Without peace, there can be no progress on this Earth. So let us work for peace with hearts filled with love. For when we pass from this world, all we really take with us is love—endless, infinite love.

—Steven M. Greer, M.D., 20 January 1998

Table of Contents

Introduction

On December 13, 1993, my wife and I flew to Washington, D.C., to meet with President Clinton's first CIA Director, James Woolsey. The cover story for this meeting was simply a small dinner party consisting of CIA Director Woolsey and his wife, Dr. Sue Woolsey (Chief Operating Officer of the National Academy of Sciences) and our host and his wife. Shortly before the meeting, we learned that I was to be the first person to brief the Director of Central Intelligence on the subject of UFOs and extraterrestrial (ET) intelligence: Woolsey had made inquiries but had received no information on the subject from any official government channels.

Naturally, I came prepared with a large brief case filled with case evidence, witness testimony, photographs and video footage of UFOs, government documents and the like. After a few introductions and pleasantries, we got right to business.

I learned that the CIA Director and his wife had actually seen one of these UFOs in New Hampshire in the late 1960s, in broad daylight. So after about 10 or 15 minutes of presenting the evidence, Mr. Woolsey said, in effect, 'Yes, I know they exist. Now talk to me about what all of this means'.

This book is all about what does all of this mean. While this book certainly presents some compelling case evidence, smoking gun government documents and photographs, the core of this book is really about meaning. Any open-minded person can peruse a handful of these cases, government documents and authenticated photographs and conclude, as Mr. Woolsey did, that there is something very real going on here. But now for the interesting part: Why are they here, how has the secrecy been maintained, what are the implications to our society, and what will disclosure of these facts mean? How do these devices travel through interstellar space and get someplace in a life form's natural life time and how can you communicate in real time through many light years of space, and....

Presented here, then, are a collection of papers which attempt to elucidate these and many other critical issues. The evidence is really the easy part: making some sense of it is what is truly challenging. This book is just such an attempt, one which I offer with the caveat that this is only an initial attempt to unravel one of the greatest mysteries of all time. It is a work in progress. And as we stand on the eve of the next millennium, we can only peer dimly into a reality that is showing us our future.

And so it was that on that night in December 1993, we spent two and a half hours with the CIA Director and the Chief Operating Officer of the National Academy of Sciences discussing the meaning behind the mysteries. I remember discussing geopolitical implications of disclosing this matter fully to the public. I remember elucidating the implications of disclosing ET technologies which could replace all of the sources of pollution in the world. I remember discussing how religious figures might react to such a disclosure. But one of my fondest memories is of Dr. Sue Woolsey asking, "But how do they communicate through the great distances of space?" I swallowed hard and for an instance contemplated not telling her the truth. But then quickly I realized that if she was perceptive enough to ask the question, perhaps she was ready for the answer. Whereupon I said to her: "Their communications systems are technologies which interface with aspects of reality closely associated with what we would call mind and thought, and this spectrum of reality bypasses linear time and space totally...". And to my astonishment, Dr. Woolsey smiled and said, "I thought it had to be something like that."

She got it. And I am sure that you will too.

Steven M. Greer, M.D.
February 1999
Albemarle County, Virginia

Part I

Meaning and Implications

This section of the book presents the "big picture": What does the UFO and ET phenomenon mean? In this section, discussions of geopolitics and interplanetary relations are followed by a comprehensive look at the nature of reality and how space, time and mind are all inter-related.

The reader may find it odd that this section precedes the section which follows which is on the evidence. But the overview of the meaning read first will bring the evidence to life.

Once you understand the meaning and implications of this subject, the evidence and the research results of CSETI becoming relevant: This subject is not only about whether or not we are alone in the universe. More deeply, it is about what does it mean, and how do we make some sense of it all. This section of the book presents the 'big picture': What does the UFO and ET phenomenon mean? In this section, discussions of geopolitics and interplanetary relations are followed by a comprehensive look at the nature of reality and how space, time and mind are all inter-related.

And most important of all: How do we relate to these life forms coming to us from the depths of space and time? Are they "alien"— or are they really us—humanoids who are awake, conscious and with whom we deeply share the roots of being?

1

Implications of an Extraterrestrial Disclosure

1996

In a recent conversation with a retired Air Force General, we were discussing a major disclosure on the existence of extraterrestrial (ET) life forms. This gentleman, who had known the UFOs were real and were ET in origin since 1946, asked me, "But Steve, what would a disclosure mean?"

It was clear that he had real uncertainty regarding the implications of such a disclosure, even though the General was wholly in favor of the truth coming out now. It occurred to me that it is now necessary to elaborate, to the extent possible, what the implications of disclosure would be to humanity. For nearly four years, I have been having this discussion with national security think tanks, business leaders, CIA officials, UN figures and various world leaders. We need to begin contemplating a future which includes the existence of ET life forms, and the early stages of inter-planetary relations.

Lest the more pragmatic among us question the timeliness of such a discussion, let me state here unequivocally that we are about 50 years late in this deliberation. For half a century, it has been known that we are not alone, and the long-delayed discussion of the meaning and implications of contact with advanced ET civilizations is long over-due, not premature.

However, before any such discussion can begin, we must first consider the nature, atmosphere and framework of a disclosure. The implications are very different if the disclosure is militaristic, alarmist, xenophobic and frightening, versus one which is calm, scientific, evidence-driven and hopeful. That is, the message, images, framework and atmosphere surrounding a disclosure will largely determine its immediate implications. A disclosure can be one of the greatest galvanizing and transcendent moments in human history, if handled wisely... or it can be terror in the aisles.

Given current media, entertainment and UFO subculture treatment of the subject, there is reason for concern here. Because if this disclosure is in any way linked to the mind-set of "space invaders," victims of alien "abduction" and other disinformation, paranoid or fantasy-driven perspectives, then we are in real trouble. However, the CSETI Project Starlight disclosure effort is aimed 180 degrees away from such xenophobic concepts, and envisions a rational, evidence-driven event which will simply convey the following facts:

- There is substantial scientific and witness evidence for the existence of ET life forms in proximity to the Earth
- While the specific motives of these life forms may not be totally understood, there is no evidence that they are hostile, and there is no reason for fear or alarm
- The world community needs to establish an open discussion on this matter and take constructive steps to ensure a peaceful, sustainable relationship with these life forms.

Of course, this sounds simple, but we are competing with the fear-mongering and paranoiac leanings of the pop culture. Nevertheless, the prevailing madness in the media and entertainment fields should not be allowed to deter us from a disclosure of the simple truth that we are not alone. But we must be prepared to calmly distance this disclosure from the histrionics of those who would have us scream "the sky is falling..."

The remaining discussions, then, will assume a framework of disclosure which is calm, scientific and hopeful. And regardless of the immediate din of alarmist proclamations from certain quarters, there will be fundamental implications which will be the focus of our deliberations here. These implications are so profound and far-reaching that no aspect of life on Earth will remain unaffected. From theology to technology, from geopolitics to economics, from the environment to the future exploration of space, nearly every field of human endeavor will eventually be touched by such a disclosure.

Immediate Implications

The near-term implications of a high-level disclosure on the existence of ET life forms range from the geopolitical to the philosophical. The most pronounced immediate effect of such a disclosure will be that of altering the fundamental paradigm of how we view ourselves, the world of humanity and the universe. While the full effect of this will take some decades, if not centuries, to manifest fully, there will be an immediate realization that we are really all one people on the homeland of Earth, among many worlds inhabited by other intelligent life forms.

This realization will alter not only our view of ourselves and the Earth, but I believe it will impact the current state of geopolitical fractionalization. In the post-Cold War era, the world is becoming increasingly "Balkanized," precisely at the time when one would hope for increasing world unity and coherence. The definitive disclosure that we are not alone in the universe, and that, more importantly, these advanced life forms are landing on *terra firma*, will provide significant impetus to the as-yet incomplete process of forming a truly global civilization. This disclosure will complete the galvanizing effect which the space program provided as it sent back to the Earth photographs of this beautiful blue sphere floating in space, which we all call home.

As the global community contemplates the immediate and future reality of Earth coming into contact with other advanced civilizations, all of the usual preoccupations with the endless internecine battles among nations and peoples on Earth will suddenly appear in quite a different light. The differences and conflicts between various racial, religious, ethnic and national identities will be seen in a new perspective as we begin to contemplate the reality of Earth evolving into an inter-planetary civilization. The world will increasingly quicken the pace of globalization and integration into a functional peaceful civilization.

This can—and must—be done without either demonizing or deifying these ET peoples. The ingrained xenophobic response of today and yesteryear will need to give way to a new paradigm motivated by hope, understanding and tolerance of diversity.

Even the process of coming to grips with the post-disclosure reality of an ET presence will force humanity to evolve in terms of the moral, spiritual, psychological and physical capacity to effectively meet the challenges of the situation. So the immediate impact will include the rapid development of a functional global capability *vis-a-vis* an ET presence. No single nation can achieve this; no superpower, however well-meaning, can think and act on behalf of the entire world as it adjusts to the early challenges of inter-planetary relations. This, then, will provide both the practical and philosophical setting for the development of a world civilization.

While people will no doubt retain their various national, ethnic and religious identities, there will be added to these the over-arching identity of being "from Earth." Beyond this, an awareness will grow that all conscious, intelligent life forms have in common the intangible but real link of awareness, of consciousness, and the early stages of universal citizenship will dawn. That is, we will experience, first inwardly and later in practical life, the awareness of the universality of life.

Governments around the world will immediately be affected in several inter-related ways. There will be an examination of covert, previously unacknowledged "black" projects in the military/intelligence/industrial sector, and these projects will be moved back to the public domain and to conventional oversight and control. Currently, these projects officially "do not exist," and as such pose a serious threat to governmental integrity, especially in constitutional democracies such as the United States. A disclosure will set in motion governmental and social pressures to restore constitutional chain of command and control over this matter, and senior government leaders will no longer be able to avoid responsibility for this issue by claiming "plausible deniability." In short, a disclosure on the existence of ET life forms in proximity to the Earth will reverse the excesses of secrecy which developed in the post-World War II era and Cold War.

Academic, scientific and governmental institutions and agencies will quickly focus on the meaning, implications and requirements of a newly-ordered global paradigm, which suddenly includes the existence of ET civilizations visiting Earth. From international policy think-tanks, to various academies of science around the world, this issue will become a prime focus of discussion, study and debate. In an academic sense, no field of study will be untouched by such a disclosure: history, anthropology, philosophy, geopolitics, exo-biology, theology, philosophy, the arts, science and technology, business and economics—all will be immediately galvanized by and preoccupied with such a disclosure. The vast and profound implications inherent to the fact that we are not alone in the universe, and are already being visited by advanced ET life forms, will indeed be of unparalleled significance in the history of the human species.

Theological and philosophical implications will immediately be discussed among the world's religions and religious leaders, as they come to terms with a universe in which humans are no longer the only intelligent, sentient children of God. In this respect, concepts of God, creation, life and religious meaning will evolve in the direction of accommodating the existence of intelligent life elsewhere in the universe, and this will cause an increasing "universalization" of God and religious meaning. Additionally, there will likely be an unfortunate yet predictable reactionary segment from various religions around the world which will place such a disclosure into a strictly eschatological framework, or worse. Already, among fringe elements in the civilian sector, we see attempts to either demonize or deify these ET visitors. Such reactivity and fanaticism, while predictable, will eventually give way to a more reasoned and mature response and the world's religions will adopt an understanding of intelligent life which is universal, and which will, I believe, redound to the appreciation of an infinite Creator whose glory is not confined to the Earth.

Intermediate and Long-Term Implications

The length and scope of this paper obviously does not permit a thorough analysis of the immediate ramifications of such a disclosure, much less the intermediate and long-term implications. However, it is important to review a few of the highlights of these more distant implications, because it is here that we will see a literal transformation of human society.

This cannot be appreciated fully without also appreciating a central fact of the past 50 years of UFO/ET secrecy: that covert human projects have possessed advanced ET technologies and have been "reverse-engineering" them for decades. This means that in the post-disclosure era, there will be the opportunity to eventually apply these technologies to the problems of human society. The elaboration of the mechanisms of advanced energy, propulsion, communications and other ET technologies will have an extraordinary impact on current Earth technologies, including energy generation, transportation, communications, education, manufacturing, medicine and more. Aside from our science, physics, mathematics and technology textbooks being rewritten, the practical applications of these technologies will completely transform the face of human society.

There is, however, a disturbing side to this, and that is the long history of humans using every breakthrough in technology to build a better war machine. The proliferation of nuclear, chemical and biological weapons of mass destruction should give us some pause as we contemplate what the destructive uses of such advanced ET technologies might be. (Moreover, we should be quite concerned already about the implications of such technological breakthroughs resting in the hands of "black" projects which do not answer to the people or the chain of command mechanisms of government.) For this reason, it is extremely important that such applied technologies not be propagated until the world has established a more stable international setting and attained a lasting international peace.

The pessimists and cynics will say that humans will never reach a state of stable international peace, but I hold the opposing view that we will, because we will have to. Humans have many faults and foibles, but when all is said and done, we are survivors—and adapt extraordinarily well to circumstances threatening our survival. Certainly, the current situation of weapons of mass destruction proliferating into the hands of every unstable dictatorship is such a circumstance. While there may yet be disastrous consequences, these will only serve to galvanize humans into doing what must be done to survive: adapt and evolve into a peaceful, stable global civilization.

Putting this debate aside for now, let us contemplate a "down-loading" of these advanced ET technologies in a setting of international stability and peace.

These technologies are not polluting fossil fuels or radioactive nuclear power, but are completely revolutionary energy systems which are non-linear, zero-point type technologies. That is, there is a background source of limitless energy which is omnipresent in the universe, even in deep space, and these devices tap into this energy. The result is vast amounts of energy generated, and, in defiance of the law of thermodynamics, more energy is obtained than is put into the system.

Without going into a long discussion of propulsion systems which propel vehicles at beyond the speed of light (allegedly impossible according to 20th century physics), of "bending" space-time, of negating the effects of gravity and mass inertia, or of non-linear communications systems which interface directly with mind or thought, or a myriad other considerations related to advanced ET technology, let us simply state that these technologies are many quanta ahead of current technologies on Earth.

What are the implications of such technologies being applied around the world?

- The Earth's environment, which is being degraded at an alarming rate primarily due to the burning of fossil fuels and the relative scarcity of energy, would be greatly assisted, if not saved by the widespread application of such technology. For the most part, the Earth is still in the 1800s as far as energy generation, transportation and related technologies are concerned. The internal combustion engine reigns supreme, as do gas, oil and coal as sources of energy. Aside from being the chief sources of air and water pollution, their relative scarcity results in a further cost and efficiency-related inability to remove other sources of pollution from chemical processing, manufacturing and the like. Such inefficiencies, scarcity and intrinsically polluting qualities of the current world energy system are literally killing the Earth. The application of advanced ET energy systems would completely reverse this situation.
- When it takes only minutes—instead of 12-14 hours—to go from Asia to New York, the world will truly be a global village. Indeed, the need for vast, inefficient and dehumanizing metropolises will no longer exist, since both communications and transportation will allow small towns and villages to have access to each other instantly. This will result in a transformation in the nature and function of society unequaled in recorded history.
- The relative scarcity of energy, and hence of resources generally, has resulted in a vast inequality among the poor and rich nations of the world. The application of these ET technologies will alter this situation radically, and eventually abundance and an economic equilibrium will emerge. This will alter the world socio-economic situation and mitigate the economic pressures and inequalities which create so much strife and conflict in the world. With zero-point and related technologies in every village and every home, the consciousness of scarcity and a "zero-sum game" will give way to one of abundance. The human race will be freed from the oppressive mentality of material acquisitions and survival to a larger vision of developing the full potential of each human.
- Public health and medical advances will result both directly and indirectly from these new technologies. For example, imagine a world where abundance of clean water and energy removes the specter of famine and disease from the entire Earth.

- Space exploration will be a viable activity, since these energy and propulsion systems permit transport through space effectively at many times the speed of light. The economic and sociological implications of this possibility are incalculable.

In addition to these technological and environmental implications, there are the long-term implications related to the world coming to grips with an open relationship with various ET civilizations. What might be the effects of an open dialogue with advanced life forms on world culture, art, music, philosophy, science and so forth? Only when we have stopped denying the existence of these other civilizations and disclosed the truth can we move in the direction of a sustainable global and inter-planetary society.

Volumes can—and no doubt will—be written on the meaning of contact with advanced ET civilizations. But of this we are sure: The first step is to achieve an honest disclosure. The implications of this disclosure are truly world-encompassing and far reaching. At present, we do not have a sustainable civilization on this planet, but one which is morally, technologically and socially moribund. As the old Chinese proverb says, "Unless we change directions, we are likely to end up where we are going."

Indeed, to borrow from Al Gore's book title, Earth is in the balance. The evolution of a sustainable global civilization and the further development of the capacity to become an inter-planetary civilization are dependent on an honest disclosure regarding the existence of ET civilizations, and our development into a peaceful world civilization. Only then can we enter an era of sustainable technology, a sustainable economy, and a lasting culture. Only then can we on Earth take our place among the stars as members of a growing universal civilization.

2

The CSETI Comprehensive Assessment Of The UFO/ETI Phenomenon—May 1991

A comprehensive analysis of the UFO phenomenon, as well as original research and experiences of members of the CSETI CE-5 Initiative Working Group, has enabled us to make some specific conclusions about UFOs, ET intelligence and their motives. The summation of this analysis, which follows, is intended to assist both groups and individuals in their efforts to understand this complex subject. We have recorded only those conclusions for which we have a high level of certainty.

General Conclusions

- Some UFOs are Extraterrestrial Spacecraft (ETS) which are piloted by ET biological entities (EBEs) who originate on another planet, and most likely another star system.
- More than one ET civilization is represented in the current activities involving Earth.
- These ET civilizations are working in concert and not competitively, although there is some specialization in function and activities for the various groups. This indicates that there exists an emerging or well established organization for these groups.
- These beings have bases within this solar system and may maintain temporary bases on Earth, particularly under water.
- While various reports and speculations exist, we cannot at this time definitely state which planets or star systems are the home bases for these beings. Any specific information on this subject is very likely to be incorrect due to the security considerations of these beings. That is, given current human tendencies towards war, aggression and violence, open disclosure of their planets of origin would put these planets at potential risk should human military interests unravel the energy and propulsion technology of their craft.

- The variety in sizes and shapes of ETS observed is due to:
  - a) varying civilizations of origin, and more importantly;
  - b) specializations of functions, which include general reconnaissance, medical research and intelligence, Earth environmental research, central command and base operations, energy generation and transfer, and human technology, military and space program research and reconnaissance.
- Sudden and fully open contact with human civilization has been avoided because of a number of interrelated factors, including:
  - a) The need to avoid an untimely disruption of Earth civilization, including military, political, geopolitical, cultural, economic, technological and religious upheaval;
  - b) Risks to their own civilization and "people" as well as overall mission, given human xenophobia and tendencies towards violent, armed reactions.
  - c) Up to this time, such massive and open contact has not been necessary, and has not been consonant with their overall long-term mission and purpose (see "The Question Of Intent" on page 15), since their purpose is not acquisition-oriented or disruptive.
- A plan is in place to allow for gradually broader and deeper contact with human society and individuals so that humans may become accustomed to the reality of other intelligent beings in the universe, and so that needed research and observations may take place on both sides. Limited but increasing opportunities for bilateral and human-initiated contact will occur in the reasonably near future.
- Sudden and large scale contact will occur only in the event of a significant worldwide emergency (man-made or natural).
- While ETI observations and interaction with Earth is probably an ancient as opposed to purely modern phenomenon, the marked increase in activity coinciding with World War II and the dawning of the "nuclear age" indicates that ETI are quite concerned about this transitional stage of human social evolution. They are particularly concerned about human nuclear weapons and technology, and potential threat to ETI, although this is nominal. These beings are further concerned with our peaceful transition to a world society, international peace, and the establishment of a just, effective

and representative world government, expected to occur within 10 to 15 years or less.

- ETI technology is strictly guarded by both ETI and covert human agencies because of its potential for military applications which would greatly threaten world security. It is imperative that this technology not find significant human applications until such time as the Earth attains international peace and an effective world government.
- The US government, at least at the level of a highly compartmentalized above top secret group, has known about the reality of these ETS and their occupants since at least 1946. A strict secrecy and a worldwide cover-up of these facts have been maintained due to:

  a)fear of public panic and social disruption;

  b)security issues surrounding possible military and technology applications of ETI technology, especially in the setting of a world beset with Cold War tensions and competing interests;

  c)uncertainty and mistrust regarding ETI motives and ultimate intentions;

  d)embarrassment and loss of face resulting from disclosures concerning how this matter has been handled, such as the harassment and ridicule of innocent civilians and military personnel, the withholding of information from the public and Congress, etc.
- The US government possesses several ETS and the deceased bodies of several EBEs. While there is evidence to strongly suggest that these agencies are attempting to reverse-engineer these craft, such efforts have not been functionally successful, although a number of secondary and partial "discoveries" have resulted from this research.
- The nature of "reality" of these craft and the beings has been incorrectly characterized by some as belonging to "another dimension or reality" from this dimension. Unfortunately, these statements are made without fully considering what "this reality" is. A more correct understanding is that the Full Spectrum of Reality is a singular, integrated one which may be perceived wholly or in its various aspects, such perception being entirely dependent on the level of consciousness of the perceiver. The various aspects of "dimensions"

of this reality, which are limitless in number, are not restricted to or by time and space as we know it commonly. These beings and their craft belong to the same Reality as humans; however, their advancement in the realms of physical science and the science of consciousness have given them competence in a broader aspect of the Full Spectrum of Reality than is usually experienced by humans. The differences are not insurmountable, nor are they truly fundamental; in fact, they are relative and only temporary. While these beings are utilizing and experiencing a broader aspect of the Full Spectrum of Reality, so too can and will humans, for we are as "interdimensional" by nature as they...

- ETS energy and "propulsion" (or space transfer) systems utilize principles and laws of the physical universe not yet fully appreciated by human science, and include:
  - a) gravity/anti-gravity and electromagnetic/gravity technology;
  - b) space energy and so-called hyper-dimensional energy systems;
  - c) matter/energy interchangeable technologies; and
  - d) possible Consciousness Assisted Technology (CAT) and Technology Assisted Consciousness (TAC).
- Some if not all EBEs have advanced mental capabilities which include telepathy, precognition, remote viewing and others, indicating that they have developed the "science of consciousness" to a degree which parallels or surpasses their advanced physical technologies. Humans also possess these capabilities, but these remain largely undeveloped by most humans.
- EBEs are more developed or advanced than humans in a number of respects, but are not superior to humans as beings. Our point of unity and equality with EBEs is in our mutual existence as conscious, intelligent beings.
- While these various EBEs may have values and priorities which are different from those of some 20th century humans, their motives and ultimate intentions are non-hostile and do not include the acquisition or subjugation of the Earth or its peoples (see "The Case For Non-hostility" on page 48).
- The establishing of a lasting world peace and just and effective world government is essential to the long-term ETI/human relationship.

The Question Of Intent

While not minimizing the strange and startling aspects of this phenomenon which some humans have experienced, our assessment of these visitors' motives and ultimate intentions is that they are decidedly non-hostile. Their primary operations and activities center around:

- General reconnaissance of Earth and her societies
- Military (especially nuclear) observations and assessment
- Human social and psychological study and observation
- Observation and assessment of human mental and spiritual development
- Earth ecology research and documentation, including documentation of Earth life systems, and mineral, plant and animal specimens
- Observation of human technology and technological developments
- Observation, active monitoring and, if necessary, limitation of human space programs, particularly those directed towards the nationalistic colonization of space
- Careful interaction with humans to convey certain information about themselves and to accustom humans to their presence.

Our assessment is that these activities are derived from several ultimate motives which include:

1. Pure study and research of a rapidly developing intelligent species (humans) during a time of transition to a world community.
2. A needed increase in ETI knowledge of world societies and human nature preparatory to future significant interaction, which will be mutual in nature, and which will eventually culminate in the introduction of Earth civilization into an interplanetary network (this may require several centuries to complete).
3. Preparatory activities for continued readiness in the event that intervention is required during a major world emergency, such as a large-scale nuclear war. Such interventions would be in the form of:
    a) interception and destruction of Intercontinental Ballistic Missiles (ICBMs);
    b) alteration of missile coordinates and readiness; and

c) emergency Earth-based activities when and where warranted.

The minimum intervention necessary would be used, with the intention being the preservation of Earth as an inhabitable planet with adequate human resources remaining to sustain intelligent life here.

4. Emergency intervention in the event of an environmental or geological catastrophe of worldwide dimensions.
5. Preservation of Earth species, including human genetic preservation and/or augmentation as a precaution in the event of a worse-case scenario (see above).
6. Protection of space from hostile or military utilization by human national interests.
7. ETI self-protective interests, insofar as humans have a strong recent history of coupling marked aggressiveness with rapid technological development; in this setting, monitoring and perhaps even limiting human capabilities may be important to ETI security -- human evolution to world peace, non-aggression and world government would remove this motive as well as several of the motives listed above.
8. ETI short- and long-term goals related to the attainment of a significant human paradigm shift from one of fragmentation/separation to one of unity, to include the unity of science and religion, world political and eventual spiritual unity, and universal unity. This paradigm shift is dependent on the development of human consciousness, which is of particular interest to ETI; and
9. The preservation and advancement of intelligent life in the universe.

3

One Universe, One People

1992

One of the greatest tasks humanity has faced throughout history is the establishment of peace and unity among differing and diverse peoples. Superficial, external and cultural distinctions such as gender, race, ethnic origin, nationality, religion and so forth have long divided humanity and been the cause of much warfare and social turmoil. It is only in the last 100 or so years that humans have seriously begun to explore worldwide our points of unity and begun to overcome the barriers which have separated humanity. Central to this evolutionary process has been the dynamic of at once accepting and celebrating diversity while simultaneously seeing the fundamental oneness which all humans share. This dynamic of unity—seeing with the eye of oneness—is the essential foundation for lasting world peace and prosperity, and will be the motivating principle of the next millennium. The long and painful process of overcoming prejudice and embracing humanity's essential oneness, while by no means yet complete, has brought us to the dawn of a true world-encircling community of one people. The recognition that mankind is one, that race, nationality, gender, religion and so on are secondary to our shared humanness, may well be the crowning achievement of the 20th century.

But what does it mean to be human, essentially human, apart from a purely biological definition? Our deepest point of unity transcends race, culture, gender, profession, life roles, even level of intelligence or emotional make-up, since all these attributes vary widely among people. Rather, the foundation of human oneness is consciousness itself, the ability to be conscious, self-aware, intelligent sentient beings. All other human qualities arise from this mother of all attributes. Conscious intelligence is the root essence from which all other human qualities emanate. It is the universal and fundamentally pure canvas on which the dazzling array of human life manifests. The firmest, most enduring and transcendent foundation on which human unity is based then is consciousness itself; for we are all sentient beings, conscious, self-aware and intelligent. No matter how diverse two people or two cultures may be, this foundation of consciousness will enable unity to prevail, as it is the simplest yet most profound common ground which all humans share.

As great as the challenges to unity have been and continue to be for humans, how much greater this might be for the emerging and embryonic relationship between humans and ET civilizations. The superficial and cultural differences between, say, an American and a Kenyan tribesman may pale before it! If disunity and conflict arise when we look only to the differences between humans, how much greater will the potential disunity and conflict be if we are able only to focus on the points of difference between humans and ET beings. The failed and disastrous ways of the past—of seeing only differences and foreign qualities—must give way to a new way of seeing—of seeing with the eye of oneness. This eye of oneness must be directed not only towards our fellow humans, but towards ET people as well, for the same fundamental basis for unity which exists among humans also exists for the relationship between humans and ETs.

The term Extraterrestrial Intelligence (ETI), so curiously nondescript, wonderfully lends itself to these concepts of unity. Regardless of planet, star system or galaxy of origin, and no matter how diverse, ETs are essentially intelligent, conscious, sentient beings. We are, essentially, one. On this basis, we may speak of one people inhabiting one universe, just as we now envision one people as children of one planet. Differences are always a matter of degree, but true unity established in consciousness is absolute. The beings currently visiting Earth from other planets, while no doubt different from humans in both superficial and more profound ways, are nevertheless conscious intelligent beings. Consciousness is the basis for both human and ET existence and is therefore the foundation for unity and communication between the various people of the universe. Beliefs may vary, biological processes may vary, assorted capacities may vary, social systems and technology may vary—but the simple thread of conscious intelligence which runs through all peoples elegantly weaves our unity. This essential unity is not subject to the trials of diversity, for it is pure, immutable and fundamental to the existence of intelligent life itself.

The challenges of establishing unity among the peoples of the universe is a grand extension of the challenge of establishing unity and peace among people of the Earth. Diversity, distinction and differences must be met with mutual respect, acceptance and even celebration, while the deeper foundations of unity are held steadily in view. The eye of oneness does not exclude or reject the diversity among peoples but relates this diversity to a paradigm of universality based in consciousness. The development of this capability, of this kind of awareness, is the most important prerequisite for not only peace and unity among humans, but also for the peace and unity between humans and other intelligent life in the universe. We must hope and pray that the errors and shortcomings humanity has manifested in its long and, as yet, incomplete march to world unity will serve as well-remembered lessons as we face the task of peacefully interacting with ET peoples. The endless diversity which so astounding a universe can present will only be endured by minds established in the calmness of universal consciousness. In the coming decades, centuries and millennia, it will be increasingly realized that the success of humanity's existence will be dependent on the development of consciousness more than on any outward progress.

As there is one God which manifests one creation, so there is one God which is the source of all conscious beings, whether on Earth or elsewhere. The great Universal Intelligence has sent a ray of this light of consciousness throughout all conscious beings, and we are united to God and to one another through its subtle and all-pervading effect. It is for these reasons that I state that the reality of man and the reality of other ET peoples are one. Viewed with the eye of differences, we are diverse and unrelated; but viewed with the eye of oneness, we are more alike than dissimilar, more kindred than alien. And so it is that we must look to our inner reality to find not only our oneness with other intelligent life in the universe as well. While ephemeral differences may confound us, our essential oneness in consciousness will never fail us. For there is one universe inhabited by one people, and we are they.

4

The Foundations of Interplanetary Unity

1993

The evidence that Earth is being visited by at least one ET civilization is extensive both in scope and detail. In its totality, it comprises a body of evidence which at the very least supports the general assessment that ET life has been detected, and that a vigorous program of research and serious diplomatic initiatives is warranted.

Consider the following overview of facts:

- There are numerous daytime and nighttime photographs and videotapes of clearly non-human spacecraft from all over the world; these films and videotapes have been evaluated and deemed authentic by competent experts in optical physics and related fields.
- There are over 3500 military and commercial aircraft pilot reports of encounters worldwide; many cases have corroborating radar documentation and multiple witnesses both on the ground and in the air.
- There are over 4000 landing trace cases from around the world.
- There are hundreds of electromagnetic cases where spacecraft have been observed by police, military personnel and civilians to affect car engines, radios and other electric devices.
- There are over 100 first- and second-hand witnesses to the retrieval of an ET spacecraft and at least four ET bodies from a crash which occurred in July, 1947, 75 miles northwest of Roswell New Mexico; written and videotaped testimony from several first-hand witnesses who are respected military officers have been obtained.
- There are hundreds of credible reports, many with multiple witnesses, of humanoids in association with landed spacecraft.

- There are several multiple-witnessed events where humans have been taken on board spacecraft.
- CSETI (The Center for the Study of Extraterrestrial Intelligence) has in the past 18 months succeeded in intentionally establishing contact with ET spacecraft, on two occasions at very close range, and with multiple witnesses present.
- Various polls have indicated that approximately 10% of Americans (25 million people) have seen them at close range so that details of the structure of the object can be discerned.
- Numerous U.S. Government documents exist which indicate that these objects are real and have been involved with observing Earth for several decades.

It is an understatement to say that the time has arrived for a serious and open international dialogue regarding the possibility of future interplanetary relations. In no other area of human experience has so much evidence existed for so long, and yet been attended by such a paucity of serious research and analysis—at least in the civilian domain. I was once asked at a conference what was the most astounding aspect of this subject, and I replied that, while the subject matter itself is extraordinary, it is the absence of a serious human response to it that is most extraordinary.

Indeed, the true barriers to the furtherance of this field of study are neither scientific nor evidential, rather they are political, psychological, social, spiritual, and "paradigmatic." Admittedly, it takes real courage for a person, otherwise respected in his or her profession and community, to stand up and speak the truth about a subject which has been the stuff of sensational tabloid claims, crackpots, and the "cottage industry" in the UFO subculture. The social stigma and opprobrium associated with this subject is a formidable barrier to the serious treatment it deserves, and yet if only a 10% probability exists that we have detected ET life which is already visiting Earth—this being one of the most profound discoveries in human history—we must find the inner fortitude to go forward.

To the sincere person who remains skeptical, consider this: Absolute proof is not needed before serious research begins on a subject. In no other field of human endeavor is proof required *before* serious study and research begins; on the contrary, proof is the result of this research. In this regard, the subject of ET studies is being held to an irrational requirement of proof before serious research can begin, on the one hand, and denounced as an area of spurious interest because no proof exists, on the other!

This, then, is not a function of scientific reason or evidence, but is the result of a political, social and psychological reaction to a subject which causes most serious scientists to blush. Our collective temerity is driven in part by fear of the unknown, in part by fear of ridicule, and in part by faint-heartedness. The evidence, however, is so profound, the implications so vast, and the consequences of doing nothing so dire that we have reached the point where we must find the fortitude to respond to this subject in a mature and responsible way.

To any impartial observer, the evidence which exists certainly supports a greater than 10% probability that we are being visited by advanced ET civilizations. Indeed, to most people who have seen the data in its entirety, the probability is in excess of 90%. Having spoken to several government officials who have held Top Secret clearances on this subject, and who have confirmed to me that the U.S. Government has in its possession several objects and bodies of ET origin, my own personal assessment approaches certainty. Beyond this, I have personally been present when these spacecraft have approached the CSETI research teams within a few hundred feet, and have then signaled repeatedly to us. Frankly, there is very little doubt in my mind that we are dealing with at least one ET civilization, and that they are non-hostile.

However, for argument sake, let us state that all of the evidence available to us in the civilian domain constitutes only a 10% probability of contact with ET intelligence. Does this not constitute adequate evidence to initiate a serious scientific and diplomatic mission? Certainly in medicine a 10% probability of finding a cure for cancer would warrant an all out effort in the cancer research community. For it is generally true that when the stakes are very high, the probability of success need not be, prior to initiating a research project. Without question, the stakes are so high in this area that even a 10% probability is adequate to mount one of the most extensive worldwide research initiatives in history.

This question, however, is not limited to the realm of science alone, for as soon as one makes the assessment, however tentative, that we are being visited by advanced ET life forms, the larger question of interplanetary (and inter-species) relations becomes preeminent. This is, then, the ultimate diplomatic challenge. And to find our common ground with intelligent life forms which are not even human may prove to be the most extraordinary task humanity has ever faced.

For witness how difficult it has been for humanity to come together in peace among the diverse peoples of the world. Notwithstanding the fact that we are all human, living on the one homeland called Earth, yet wars, prejudices and enmity have repeatedly submerged the world into chaos and destruction. As the world moves, in fits and starts, towards a true world civilization, and the people of the world increasingly realize their essential unity as humans, the potential for increasingly open contact between humans and other intelligent life-forms is likely to increase exponentially.

However, before we can entertain this concept, we must first ask ourselves some basic questions:

- What global developments must occur before full open contact can take place?
- How will communication occur, and what should be communicated?
- Prior to full, open contact, what form of contact and communication is possible, in a pioneering or preliminary framework?
- And most importantly, what are the fundamental points of unity between humans and other intelligent life forms in the universe? What is our universal common ground?

Regarding this last question, we cannot assume that ET life forms who are thinking, sentient beings, and who by definition have evolved under conditions different from those on Earth, are likely to be much like humans, at least superficially. Their level of intelligence, fund of knowledge, emotional nature, social and political structures, ethical, moral and religious systems—and more—are likely to be quite different from that of humans. We must therefore find a deeper point of unity, what I call our highest common denominator.

This consideration, however abstract it may seem to some, is really central to establishing a sense of common ground between intelligent species. And without common ground, we can have no relationship.

I hold that this common ground is so obvious, and yet hidden, so near, and yet so overlooked, that it is easily missed altogether. It is at once simple and profound, proximal and yet hard to grasp. It is really the universal constant found in every intelligent life form: It is conscious intelligence.

Pure "awakeness" or conscious intelligence is what every conscious, sentient being in the universe *is*, in its essential nature. The universal—or non-anthropocentric—aspect of human consciousness is that highest common denominator on which a sustainable relationship between diverse life forms can be based. As humans, we are conscious, awake; other higher life forms are conscious and awake. We may share very little else in common, but this universal constant is shared, by definition, by all intelligent, conscious beings, whether human or ET.

Consciousness, or universal conscious intelligence, then is the first cornerstone of the foundation of interplanetary unity.

Having realized the essential oneness which all intelligent higher life forms share, we are then faced with the practical challenge of formulating an approach to interplanetary and inter-species relations which is peaceful, sustainable and mutually beneficial. Here are a few of the principles which appear to be essential to the successful, sustained engagement of ET civilizations:

- Any successful approach will incorporate a global perspective, and not one driven by nationalistic or strictly national security imperatives. The motive behind any attempt at contact and communication should clearly be globally based, and any benefits resulting from contact must benefit all the peoples of the world, and not just one nation or culture. The evolution of the world into a true global civilization will certainly facilitate this type of relationship. This entire matter, then, should be the focus of the international community. One of the hallmarks of the maturation of the human race is the attainment of a true world civilization and the establishing of a just and representative world government, which should be empowered to respond to the challenge of interplanetary relations. Until such a body is effectively functioning, any group attempting such contact should be operating within this global perspective.
- The motivation of such contact and relations should be based in the principle of mutual benefit, and be free of exploitative motives and unilateral acquisition-oriented goals. Until a permanent world peace and order can be achieved on Earth, the acquisition of ET technology, which most likely would be used for unilateral military application, should be avoided.
- While the precise motives for current ET involvement with this planet may not be fully known, there is no evidence that they are motivated by any net hostile intentions. Until proven otherwise,

therefore, it should be assumed that any such visitors are non-hostile and approachable. It is critical that humans avoid making anthropocentric assumptions regarding ET motives, since it is likely that their ethical, moral, social and political concepts vary from those of many Earth-based cultures. Recognizing the human tendency towards xenophobia, prejudice and fear of the unknown, we must evaluate ET motives cautiously, and, to the extent possible, from an interplanetary perspective.

- The attainment of a healthy and appropriate collective self-esteem for humans is essential for an appropriate relationship to evolve between humans and any other ET species. Individuals and organizations involved with interplanetary contact should avoid the common tendency to swing between viewing advanced technological beings as intrinsically superior or inferior. It is more sustainable to view such variations as simply differences which are the product of diverse evolutionary paths, and that on the level of conscious intelligence, all sentient beings are essentially equal. Here, equality does not require sameness.
- It should be realized that until the world achieves the level of maturity described above, that any direct contact and relationship which develops may be limited, preliminary, and by nature pioneering. Given recent CSETI successes in this regard, we can make the initial assessment that such contact is likely, and will progress as the world becomes increasingly a genuine global civilization.
- The knowledge of any contact and evolving relationship should be shared with all the peoples of the world to the fullest extent possible, and in a timely fashion. Secret or covert contact should be viewed as intrinsically dysfunctional and should be avoided to the fullest extent possible.
- A multi-disciplinary and multi-cultural approach to any contact, relationship, or exchange should be used. Communication itself may proceed verbally, electronically, "symbolically/archetypically" or even telepathically.
- A very broad view must be maintained in evaluating the manifestations of an advanced ET civilization, since their technological development may be thousands to hundreds of thousands—and conceivably millions—of years more advanced than Earth's. The manifestations of such an advanced technology may appear magical to humans, even as a hologram, TV, or laser would appear mag-

ical to people of the 17th century. The tendency to pronounce such manifestations as "supernatural" or magical should be avoided.

Are we alone in the universe, and have other intelligent life forms found their way to our small part of the galaxy? The best available evidence suggest that, no, we are not alone, and yes, they have already found us. The real question at this point may be "what are we going to do about it?" We must come together to search for answers to this and even more difficult questions, for nothing less than the future of Planet Earth may hang in the balance. If we are wrong, and all of the existing evidence points to some other phenomenon, then the attempt to contact whatever that phenomenon is may prove extremely enlightening. But if we are correct in our assessment, and we are being visited by advanced ET civilizations, then the risks of doing nothing are immense, and the benefits of acting wisely will change the world as we know it.

In either case, the time has come to act.

5

National Security Implications of the UFO/ETI Subject

A Brief Summary, 30 August 1995

National Security Implications of the UFO/ETI subject are profound and far-reaching, albeit currently largely unrecognized.

These implications may be considered in separate but related aspects: those intrinsic to ET activity and those arising from current covert management of the issue.

Historical Background

Early National Security considerations dealt with concern over public panic arising from the detection of near Earth and Earth-landed ET spacecraft (ETS)and from the technological implications of advanced ET material as it may impact the arms race and cold war. Additional concerns were related to the impact on religious belief systems, the political order and economic systems.

Importantly, once actual ETS were retrieved in 1947, thereby allowing ET hardware to be studied and back- engineered for possible human military applications, the need for *complete* secrecy regarding the matter was deemed paramount by authorities at that time. Given the tensions of the early atomic era and the mounting "cold war" with the USSR, it is understandable that the introduction of ET technology was thought to be destabilizing to an already dangerous situation. Moreover, given the history of technological secrets related to atomic and hydrogen weapons being stolen by agents of the USSR, there was understandable concern that any technological breakthrough related to ET technology might find its way into Soviet hands. If such an event enabled the USSR to produce actual military applications before the US, obviously this would have placed the US military capability in a *potentially* catastrophic disadvantage.

Since the 1970's, we have reason to believe that a degree of cooperation on this matter has evolved with the USSR and the US and perhaps other nations. Certainly the end of the cold war has largely removed earlier concerns vis a vis technological breakthroughs and the fear of Soviet aggression.

Moreover, the psychological reasons for secrecy related to public panic are not valid today. At least 57% of the population accept that UFOs are real and are of ET origin. And 30-40 years of space exploration by human society has prepared the population for the possible existence of other ET civilizations capable of space travel. In short, the previous concerns motivating secrecy are not relevant today.

Intrinsically, there is no reason to believe that the ET presence poses a threat to the national or world security. If hostility and aggression were related to their purpose here, it is likely that events congruent with hostility would have transpired long before now. It is our assessment that the ETs are not hostile, but are very concerned with human capability related to warfare and the militarization of space. Activity by ET assets related to the neutralization of ICBM facilities and to containing military oriented space exploration should be understood in light of their concern over a known history of human aggression which has been coupled with the advent of weapons of mass destruction and space exploration. Indeed, given the past history of human military assets focusing on and pursuing ET Spacecraft, we believe the ETs have responded with remarkable restraint.

Ironically, the threat to national security exists not with the ET presence, but the *current covert management of the subject.* In the absence of ET hostility over 50 *years*, current secrecy cannot be justified on the basis of fear of ET aggression. A disclosure related to the ET presence, if calmly and rationally presented, will not cause public panic in the US or elsewhere. 1995 is not 1945, and world society has evolved to the point where this information can be assimilated in a positive fashion.

In contrast, the covert and apparently extra-constitutional management of this matter is a real threat to national and world security, and undermines constitutional freedom and democracy. Unless it is terminated, this covert management will greatly harm US national security and the chances of a lasting world peace.

It is our assessment that the current covert management of this issue involves the following elements which are a direct, immediate and ongoing threat to the national security:

1. The continued denial of the ET presence creates a situation where a sudden, undeniable, public ET event could induce panic, since proactive disclosure efforts which could ameliorate public fears are non-existent. It is likely that such a public ET event will transpire within the next 2-10 years or sooner. Therefore secrecy and denial are a real threat to national and world security.

2. The current covert management of this issue appears to be operating independently and outside of the constitutional chain of command. The group controlling these operations, which involve reconnaissance, ET technology reverse-engineering, and space-based targeting of ETS (among others) is non-responsive to congressional or executive branch oversight and control. This constitutes a real threat to the national security and to constitutional democracy and freedom.

3. We have credible, first hand sources who insist that ET spacecraft have been targeted by human covert space weapons and on at least two occasions have been destroyed. If true, the risks to world peace and security are real and imminent, and the continuation of these covert activities constitute the gravest dangers to national and world security. Hostile actions taken by human covert assets against ET assets constitute a grave and immediate threat to the national security. A relatively small, covert entity, acting without consultation with the United Nations, the Congress, the President of the United States or the public is engaging in actions on behalf of all humans which endanger the Earth and world peace. Unless controlled, these actions could precipitate interplanetary conflict and a disaster for the world generally and the United States specifically. This covert management must be terminated and control of this issue returned to constitutional authority and to the public domain.

4. The concentration of the technological advances related to the reverse-engineering of ET technology into the hands of a small covert operation constitutes a threat to the national security, to world security and to the future of the Earth. These ET technologies, which have been the object of covert research and development for over 45 years, are potentially of great benefit to humanity if used wisely for peaceful purposes, but are of immense danger when concentrated into a small covert operation which is unresponsive to the pubic or the legal and constitutional chain of command. The threat this poses to the US and world security is great, and the longer this situation continues, the greater the concentration of advanced technological power in the hands of a relative few. The secret control of such powerful technolo-

gies is inherently a threat to freedom, democracy and to our nation and the world. Its utilization for covert agendas outside constitutional control represents a grave danger to our country and must be restrained and reversed.

5. Importantly, secrecy and covert operatives per se constitute a real threat to the national security, since national security in a constitutional democracy can only be legitimately related to freedom and democratic government. Only in very rare and well-justified circumstances can extreme secrecy and covert operations exist, since by nature freedom and democracy cannot co-exist with unrestrained secrecy and secret power. The profound implications of the detection of ET civilizations cannot be allowed to be the exclusive domain of covert operations which are unrelated to public discourse and consultation. To do so is to undermine the US Constitution, democracy and freedom, and this constitutes a serious threat to the national security.

6. Finally, exclusive covert control of this matter has resulted and continues to result in the loss of opportunity for the world to come to terms with the ET presence in a peaceful and mutually beneficial fashion. This means that the people of the world, the United Nations and other international and national institutions are deprived of the opportunity to deal rationally with this issue. National and world security are therefore negatively impacted by the loss of opportunities in the following areas:

- The environment, which is seriously at risk for large scale collapse over the next 100 years, would be profoundly improved if ET technologies could be peacefully deployed. So-called zero point or free energy systems, which are non-polluting, would permit a sustainable technological civilization to exist on Earth and would transform the Earth environmentally and economically. Establishing peaceful and mutually beneficial relations with ET civilizations would eventually permit us to understand and apply such technologies.
- World unity and peace will be enhanced by the global realization that we are not alone in the universe. The acknowledgment of this fact will enhance the awareness that we are really one people living on the shared homeland of Earth, and many of the conflicts currently afflicting the Earth will be seen in a new perspective. This can be achieved without either deifying or demonizing the ET presence, but rather placing it in a fair, scientific and neutral light.

Eventually, world peace and a significant enhancement in the current geopolitical situation may result from the disclosure that we are not alone. An international infrastructure, and institutions capable of dealing peacefully with relations with ET civilizations would, of necessity, evolve, and this in turn would strengthen world unity and cooperation.

- World culture, ideas, science and many other diverse areas may benefit through the development of peaceful relations with other worlds. While this process may take decades, if not centuries, its delay only puts off the time when the people of the Earth will be united not only globally, but with other planetary civilizations as well.

In summary, it is imperative to the national security that the President and Congress undertake measures to terminate the secret, covert management of the UFO/ETI subject. Failure to place this matter in open, public discourse and control constitutes the gravest failure of democracy and government in the history of the world. That we do this is the test of our faith in democracy and our faith in the people. As the 21st Century approaches, we must roll up the cancerous excesses of secrecy which are the legacy of the cold war and unfurl a new era wherein democracy is reaffirmed and a lasting world peace is given a chance.

6

ETI Technology And World Security

1992

The advanced technology which UFOs represent creates several security concerns which explain not only the secretive behavior of the world's governments but the elusive behavior of the UFOs as well. Aside from the broader social, cultural and religious impact which contact with an advanced ET civilization would entail, the technological aspects of such a contact involves matters of security and stability of far-reaching importance. While at first glance such technological advances would appear to be beneficial—even ideal—it will be shown that these technologies if introduced suddenly or prematurely would further destabilize an already precarious world security, and potentially threaten the embryonic ETI/human relationship.

Many proponents of advanced technology argue that the ultra-advanced energy and propulsion systems used by UFOs could revolutionize human technology and create a near utopian society with a limitless source of nonpolluting energy. Various theories regarding UFO propulsion and energy systems would point to an elegant "hyperdimensional" physics which provides vast amounts of energy and an extraordinary means of transportation. It is argued that the acquisition of such technology would revolutionize human transportation, energy production, manufacturing, etc. and eliminate the need for polluting combustion engines and hydrocarbon consumption. The real and theoretical benefits of such a technology are extensive and too numerous to elucidate here.

The problem with this scenario is that it assumes, rather naively, that this technology would be used—first and foremost—if not exclusively, for peaceful purposes. While this is a wonderful idea, the unfortunate fact is that every new technology introduced in the past 100 years has had its first and most extensive use in military applications. In an ideal world, ET technology would be used for progressive peaceful purposes, but this is not yet the case since the world is yet torn by competing interests and militarism. Once the Pandora's box of ETI technology is opened, what—or who—could prevent its application in weapons of mass destruction? It seems clear that the technology behind UFOs—if put to destructive and uncontrolled military purposes—would make H-bombs look like tinker toys by comparison, and would beset an already disunified and fractious world with yet a new wave of wildly escalating and destabilizing arms races and power struggles. It would, in short, be disastrous.

World security—not to mention US national security—would not be served by the introduction and application of ETI technology at this time. On the contrary, until world unity and a just and effective world government are established, world security and stability would be greatly jeopardized by this. Along with social and cultural concerns, this Pandora's box issue of ETI technology has been the motivating force behind government secrecy and the so-called government cover-up of UFO events. While I do *not* agree with all of the methods and policies apparently used by this project, the general thrust of securing this information until the world is less factious and hostile is not only understandable, but imperative. From this perspective, the extraordinary US cover-up of the 1957 Roswell and Plains of San Augustin UFO crashes is very understandable. To acknowledge this event would be to not only acknowledge the existence of ET people and craft (which I think *should* be done), but would, unfortunately, also set into motion a worldwide call for extensive open research into ETI technology—which is preeminently dangerous and must *not* be done. The free and "academic" exchange of such research would certainly unleash a feeding frenzy by both governments and private interests to be first in elaborating this ETI technology. In such a scenario, we have no assurance that this technology would fall first, or exclusively, into a benevolent ruler's hands. To argue even that this technology would remain under United States control should the United States be the first to develop and deploy it is naive and irrational, for how long did it take H-bomb fusion technology to escape United States' control, once fully developed? It is obvious that this technology, once developed *and applied* would result in a world security debacle that would dwarf the Cold War era of madness in scope, complexity and severity. Moreover, I suspect that once fully described, this technology will be both elegantly simple *and* highly reproducible, making its containment much more difficult than, say, nuclear technology. The proliferation of this technology, coupled with the world's predilection towards applying new technology to military ends, would greatly threaten world security and could well lead to the demise of human civilization as we know it.

Related to this, there is an implicit risk in developing this technology by the secret agencies of the US government, since no individual and no government can assure complete secrecy indefinitely. At a minimum our government, and others, must refrain from the development and *application* of this technology, *even if the principles behind it are elaborated.* It would be fair to say that any research and development project utilizing this technology—if ill-timed or premature—would prove to be disastrous in the long run and would ultimately explode ruinously in the hands of those who hold it. While the possessor of this technology would be able to dominate the Earth temporarily, it would be short-lived.

All this is not to say that the systematic ridicule, debunking and harassment of individuals by the US government and others is either wise or justified. The worldwide UFO phenomenon is hardly a secret. For example, over 20 million Americans claim to have seen a UFO. Beyond this, a not inconsequential number of individuals have had direct contact with the EBEs piloting these craft. While the actual craft and technology must be protected from an ill-timed disclosure or application, this does not mean that the entire phenomenon should be covered up indefinitely. In short, our government and others must continue to strictly secure technological aspects of this phenomenon, but cease the debunking and harassment of individuals and groups investigating ETI generally since it is morally reprehensible to do so, and such actions only serve to further erode public trust and confidence in government generally. The majority of educated individuals accept the idea the UFOs are real and represent ET vehicles, and little is gained by this policy of total secrecy, silence and debunking. A wiser course would be to immediately stop harassment and intervention. Then, gradually cease the denials and cover-up of sightings and gradually begin open disclosure and cooperation with civilian groups, institutions and individuals. Failure to do this not only diminishes the government's credibility, but also creates a situation wherein a singularly undeniable ETI event could be revealed to a relatively unprepared world. While maintaining the strictest security for technology-related matters, it is time for a more open policy towards UFOs/ETI generally, and it is in the long-term best interests of both the US and the world to do so.

This policy will work so long as we do not aspire to unilaterally acquire, develop or apply ETI technology. Unfortunately, if a number of rumors are true, our government in the US may already be attempting to reverse-engineer this technology from captured craft. We can only hope that this research is restricted to theoretical physics, general principles and the basic sciences, and is not geared towards the significant application of this technology at this time....

Beyond all this, it is unlikely that the ET life forms responsible for this technology would permit its deployment prior to the establishing of an international peace and the world transition to non-aggression since to do so would also threaten ETI security. The full acquisition of this technology would permit humans to reach ETI home bases or planets, and given human tendencies towards war-making and exploitation, I doubt very seriously that this would be at all permitted.

As director of a private project developing protocols for bilateral communication with ETI, I am frequently asked the theoretical question of what we would do if we were offered the full knowledge behind ET technology. Our firm position at this time is that we do not want it, nor would we accept it, unless it clearly has no possible destructive potential. CSETI has determined that this policy is the only safe one to pursue and has formally integrated it into our principles. To those yearning for the peaceful applications of this technology, the admonition "the road to hell is paved with good intentions" is apt here. While we share the desire to see the world free from pollution, energy shortages, poverty and hunger, this technology is a double-edged sword that requires skill and wisdom for its handling. But significant work must first be done on the issues of world collective security and non-aggression before such skill and wisdom is possessed by the world.

7

Abductions: Not All That Glitters Is Gold

5 November 1996

Since the late 1970s, there has been an unprecedented focus in the UFO subculture and pop media on the subject of so-called "alien abductions." A constant stream of books, videos, movies, lectures and the like have served to keep this subject in the forefront of our awareness. Across America, numerous cities have self-styled "abduction support groups," and an increasing number of therapists have begun to counsel and advise alleged victims of alien abductions.

But we have found that there is something much stranger going on than "alien abductions," and the truth about this matter is far more bizarre than the idea of ETs taking women aboard UFOs to create babies which incubate in space.

Before exploring the really bizarre—and scary—things going on with this phenomenon, let us first state what is obvious to all but the true believers and hard-core abduction aficionados: Not all that glitters is gold, and we are dealing with a multiplicity of phenomena, not a single phenomenon, as conventional wisdom now holds.

Let no one conclude, please, that what follows is a denial of the possibility that some, rare direct human-ET contact has occurred. It is likely that it has, but these cases are like pure gold nuggets, which have deliberately and through human folly been hidden under a mountain of fool's gold. It may superficially look the same, and glitter in the same way—but the difference is vast.

Here we step into a mixture of great mystery, deliberate covert deception, unbridled human foolishness and fear-mongering, all blended together into a belief system which, if challenged, yields the challenger attacks from a myriad of sources. I am aware at the outset that the sharing of the perspectives which follow will induce in many a reactionary response to "shoot the messenger." But I beg for your patience, and just a bit of open-minded inquiry, lest we forever lose those few gold nuggets among the growing mountains of fool's gold.

To begin to get ones mind around this matter, one must be knowledgeable in and a student of:

- the human mind, spirit and full potential of human experience, both conventional and unconventional;
- the UFO subject in general;
- the capabilities of esoteric and exotic covert human technologies, especially those employed by deep cover projects dealing with the UFO/ETI subject and which are using reverse-engineered ET technologies in mind control and psychological warfare agendas;
- an expanded cosmology which takes into account terrestrial and ET capabilities and experiences, whether they be physical, mental, non-local/spiritual etc.

In looking at the raw data and reports of alleged human-ET contact, I would estimate that relatively few cases are what they appear to be. The other cases are a combination of the following:

Misidentification of other unusual experiences, which, due to the dominant pop culture enthrallment with all things alien, get labeled an "abduction." These include so-called (and mislabeled) paranormal experiences related to lucid dreams, out of body experiences, near death experiences, "astral body" encounters with other non-human (but equally non-ET) entities, and similar related phenomena. The need for an expanded cosmological view of potential human experience should be obvious: It is all to easy to mis-label an experience if you do not know what the possibilities are. (See "Extraterrestrials And The New Cosmology" on page 64.)

This is akin to a doctor having only one diagnosis for chest pain—a heart attack. Such a physician, lacking what is called an adequate "differential diagnosis" would mis-diagnose all chest pain as a heart attack, when it could be that the person was experiencing a collapsed lung, a lung infection, a rupturing aorta, various stomach ailments which present as chest pain and so forth.

In this case, however, many researchers have "abduction colored glasses on," and hence see most of these other unconventional experiences as abductions. Lacking an adequate "differential diagnosis" which includes the numerous other types of possible experiences, all such experiences get labeled abductions, and the experiencer, an "abductee." Those looking into such experiences owe it to the experiencers, and to the field of knowledge, to be better informed regarding an expanded differential diagnosis. Otherwise, we will continue to have a majority of mis-diagnosed cases.

Confabulation, wannabees, false memory syndrome and mental illness are also part of the mixture of cases. We have learned of one celebrated abduction case where the person lied about prior serious mental illness, and another where the "abductee" who claimed to have been impregnated by ETs later admitted to having had an affair which resulted in the pregnancy. Now, this is not the sort of thing which proponents of the UFO and abduction field want talked about. But covering up these types of errors only compounds the superstition, ignorance and disinformation which already abounds in this area of study.

Hallucinogenic drug use has been noted to exist among some self-styled "abductees" as well as researchers. Certainly, an already murky picture is made dimmer by the intervening use of psychoactive drugs.

Most importantly, there is the significant segment of those diverse, misidentified contact events which are of decidedly covert human origins. This is the area which will be most bizarre to the reader, and most disturbing, and the majority of the remainder of this piece will concern itself with this problem. Abductions, and the "abduction syndrome" as it is commonly referred to, is largely a creation of covert human disinformation projects. Both the technologies employed, and the agendas motivating their use, are genuinely troubling. Most will not want to hear what follows, but we feel the time has come for the truth to come out, so that those who will listen can stop being manipulated with false information.

(For more background on the nature of covert human operations dealing with the UFO/ET matter, see "Unacknowledged" on page 285.)

To understand the disinformation capabilities of current and recent covert projects dealing with the UFO/ETI subject, it is necessary to look historically at events, beginning in the 1940s (and perhaps before). The acquisition of advanced ET hardware by the mid-1940s (Roswell, NM, 1947; Kingman, AZ, 1948 etc.) led to very deep covert research and development projects related to reverse-engineering ET technologies. While most researchers in the field have focused on energy generation (zero-point) and propulsion systems used by ET vehicles to "transfer" through interstellar space, the area of advanced ET communications has been largely ignored. But not by covert human R&D projects.

If it is obviously true that ET spacecraft are not using jet fuel and internal combustion engines to travel through interstellar space, it should be equally true that they are not using AT&T microwave, radio wave or related electromagnetic waves to communicate. Why? Because these EM waves, which travel at the speed of light (186,000 miles per second) are too slow to effectively communicate in real time across interstellar distances. Even at the speed of light, it takes 100 Earth years for a radio wave to travel only 100 light-years in distance. This means that a two way conversation with one's home planet would take 200 years, and this for only the initial exchange: "Hello, mission control, this is Alpha 1, how are you today?" "This is mission control, we are fine; how are you Alpha 1?" Unless a species lived thousands of years as biological life forms, a routine conversation could not be completed before the death of all parties!

Therefore, the communication systems used by advanced ET life forms are employing advanced non-local technologies NOT dependent on the linear speed of light. They utilize technologies based on laws of physics not even elaborated by human scientists in the conventional, non-covert world. And these are technologies which directly interface with mind and thought.

This explains why so many individuals have seen an ET craft and then projected spontaneously a thought for it to come back, or move one way or another—and lo and behold it does. Just as a hologram or TV would look like supernatural magic to someone 200 years ago, these technological capabilities look and sound like magic to us in the latter 20th century. (And from this the reader can see why so many "paranormal" experiences can be erroneously reported as UFO experiences, and vice versa.)

Now, a well-funded covert enterprise reverse-engineering ET technologies will look at all systems, not just ones related to propulsion and basic energy generation. Thus, as a consequence of this research, the covert entity dealing with this matter has elaborated the communications technologies of these life forms, and unfortunately have put them to some very nasty uses.

Once the ET communications technologies were discerned, a decision was made to see how such technologies could be put to use, especially for disinformation purposes. Because above all things, the project dealing covertly with the UFO/ET issue has desired continued secrecy, and a continuation of their exclusive knowledge and control of this subject.

The problem is, the UFOs continue to be seen all over the world, so this matter, in order to be secret, must be hidden in plain sight. And so it is.

One of the principles of good, effective disinformation is that you psychologically manipulate the environment so that people will not know what they are looking at, even if they see it. Another is that the creation of very similar, hoaxed decoy cases—if strategically executed and played out—will hide the real phenomenon, or at least draw peoples" attention away from the real events. And yet another is that if all else fails, and the secrecy is ended, people will be so confused about the real versus the Memorex, that they will be easily manipulated to the covert project's agenda.

All of this is at play in the UFO field, and the cornerstone of this disinformation effort is the so-called "abduction phenomenon."

Consider this for just a moment: There is a top-secret Canadian document, written by Wilbur Smith (see "Wilbur Smith Document" on page 441), which states that, in 1950, the UFO matter was the most secret project in the US, surpassing even the secrecy surrounding the development of the hydrogen bomb! In 1996, the secret is even bigger, and the resources used to maintain the secrecy many orders of magnitude greater than that of 1950. Moreover, the technological resources available to this covert project involve reverse-engineered ET technology, in the form of operational craft, non-linear communications capabilities, and biological "cloned" entities. It is not hard from this to see that extraordinary resources have been used to maintain the secrecy of this subject.

Everyone in counter-intelligence knows that really good disinformation contains some elements of the truth, thereby making the false information or events more believable to the targeted recipients. In the area of alleged UFO "abductions," by simulating false, but believable, alien encounters, a number of objectives are accomplished:

Actual ET events are lost amid the mounting cases of hoaxed, simulated cases. As mentioned earlier, the real gold nuggets get buried under a mountain of fool's gold—and very few researchers know that they should be doing assays....

By overwhelming the "sound" of actual ET events with the "noise" of simulated ones of an increasingly implausible nature, the civilian research community is not only thrown off track by pursuing false cases, it is increasingly discredited. The wilder and more absurd the scenarios are which are fed to victims of human covert abductions, the more the general scientific and media communities view the entire field as so much nonsense. In this way, human initiated covert abductions not only serve as decoys in the UFO civilian research community, but serve to avert serious inquiry from the "mainstream" scientific and media communities. It is a master stroke of disinformation, which the civilian community has swallowed hook, line and sinker.

The use of reverse-engineered ET communications technology for disinformation purposes via abductions and the like also allows for the testing of such systems to evaluate their efficacy and reliability. For those who believe that the testing of such "non-lethal" weapons on the civilian population by covert operations is unthinkable, remember the covert testing of radioactive substances on innocent civilians during the Cold War. In 1993, the Department Of Energy (formerly Atomic Energy Commission) and its leader, Hazel O'Leary, released documents disclosing the fact that innocent civilians had been deliberately contaminated with plutonium and other toxic radioactive substances to simply see what the effect would be. It was reported that plutonium was actually put on the oatmeal of children in an orphanage to see what effect it would have! The same sociopathic excesses of those secret plutonium testing projects are being replayed in spades in the civilian sector with simulated ET abductions of innocent humans, so-called cattle mutilations (also largely of covert human origin) and related covert projects. We may not want to believe this, because it seems just too horrible. But the longer we live in denial, the more we will be led down the primrose path of deception and the manipulation of our minds and emotions.

Most disturbing are the apparent underlying motives and agendas driving these covert human projects dealing with abductions and the like. Aside from the deflective, decoy value described above, the content of the hoaxed human initiated abduction experience is decidedly negative, xenophobic, fear-inducing and anger-inducing. To what end? Could it be that both the "abductees" and the millions who learn of their horrifying experiences through books, videos, TV specials and movies are being prepared to hate the "alien presence" and thereby accept, somewhere down the road, the sacrifices needed to engage in interplanetary war? And who would benefit from such a "star wars" scenario? The military-industrial complex. The very same interests about whom we were warned by no less a figure than five-star general and conservative Republican president Ike Eisenhower. After all, the classic uses of psychological warfare were (and are) related to preparing a civilian population to hate the enemy, and to be so animated in that direction that any sacrifice would be made to fight them. Could it be that we are now being so manipulated, so that we will collectively accept the costs of building the capability for interplanetary war—a capability which would extract trillions of dollars from the world economy?

Actually, it appears to be even worse than this.

We have learned, by investigating the ties, proclivities and beliefs of a number of people connected to abduction programs, that there is a clear eschatological bent to their endeavors. This means that part of the agenda is serving the bizarre, religious purpose of resurrecting Satan in the form of an ET, and fanning the flames of a future "holy war" against them, to coincide with the end of the world. I know this sounds bizarre and unbelievable (it was very difficult to accept when it first came to my attention) but it is one of the very deep, dark and frightening sub-texts of the entire ET issue. For those awaiting the end of the world with the changing of the millennium, what better vehicle than to frame the "final conflict" between humanity and evil invaders from outer space? More than a few people in the UFO subculture, who present themselves as impartial scientists and/or benefactors, hold to this paradigm. And deliberate actions are being taken to fulfill it.

On one occasion, I had the opportunity to meet with a foreign head of state, who has an interest in this subject. Over the course of an hour-and-a-half to two-hour meeting, I learned, to my horror, that this leader was doing everything he could to see that the world knew about the evil, sinister and manipulative agenda of the "aliens" by advancing the world's knowledge of abductions! Worse, I was categorically informed that every set-back in human history, every international conflict, and the very basis of the non-fulfillment of human potential, since Adam and Eve, was the result of the nefarious manipulations of the "aliens"! After mostly listening politely for an hour and a half, I let this leader know that this was not at all our assessment of the situation.

Later I learned of this person's ties to fringe religious groups, and also a network of similar leaders and benefactors of abduction "research" which has ties to bizarre end-of-the-world religious groups, who demonize the ET presence to fit the current religious paradigm. And the anchor for all of this is the abduction "phenomenon."

If the reader is not concerned by now, check your pulse.

Now, it is not clear if these bizarre beliefs are fundamental to the covert programs, or simply an intended out-growth of them. That is, it is likely that these leaders and benefactors have been manipulated into this assessment by covert projects dealing with abductions and mutilations, and they have created a way to fit the "reality" of abductions into their religious belief systems, as it pertains to the "end times." Such persons may themselves be victims of manipulation, and they are responding to the "content" of the "abduction syndrome" in a predictable way, given their religious beliefs.

Nevertheless, the deception, hoax and manipulation which all of this represents is effective, because most humans are, alas, easily deceived and especially vulnerable to manipulations of their fears of "invasion." Since cave man and tribal times, to the war in Bosnia of the 1990s, one of the basic fears of peoples around the world has been that of invasion, and (no coincidence) the abduction of women and children by the invaders. It is such a basic fear, that it is easily manipulated. We would suggest that this primal fear of abduction, rooted in the ancient collective history and consciousness of humanity, has been used to skillfully manipulate and inflame the fears of ET life forms.

We have, collectively, been all too willing to take this bait.

Even the lexicon developed in the UFO subculture—the "abduction by aliens"—is inherently xenophobic and draws sweeping conclusions about the ET presence, which are unwarranted by the objective facts. And we have learned that when others, who have done their homework on covert capabilities in this regard, have attempted to point this possibility out to the UFO community, they have been shouted down and ultimately black-balled from events. The true-believers in the abduction scenario do not want to consider that there are covert capabilities (and have been for decades) which can simulate an "alien abduction," totally using reverse-engineered ET technologies—including the use of "implants," which are of purely human origins.

How do we know about these capabilities? Research, investigation, interviewing knowledgeable people who have had involvement with these technologies, and personal experience. Over a 3-4 year period, we have interviewed individuals with top-secret clearances in areas related to electronic mind control and related technologies. What we have learned is best summarized by a statement from Officer W-1: "Technologies exist, which are ready, off-the-shelf capable, and which can fit in a panel truck or on an antennae in a city, which can totally induce an experience. If it is desired, a targeted person—or group of people—can be made to have a conversation with their personal God, and they will believe it is real, and they will pass a lie detector that it is real, because for them it is real..."

We have identified people who recall, despite chemical "deprogramming" over a three-day period, being in special para-military units and being "abductors." That is, these individuals were used to "abduct" civilians, in an elaborate and technologically exotic hoax. These humans were the abductors, not the ETs. But the technology, reverse-engineered from the ETs, is so good, that unless one knew to look for a hoax this good, one would be forever deceived.

And yes, these projects have had the capability for decades to place "implants" into humans (and animals) for the purpose of not only tracking and reconnaissance, but for inducing specific experiences.

Worse yet, these capabilities have been used to "abduct," intimidate and deceive world leaders on this subject, and to specifically get them to maintain the secret status of these programs.

Specifically, the abduction of a certain past MAJOR world leader was orchestrated by covert forces attempting to end a planned disclosure on this subject by this leader, the US President, the head of the USSR and others. A first hand witness, who is friends with this world leader and is himself a head of state, has related the details of this abduction to me personally. It was an effective, if horrible attempt to frighten these world leaders into ending their plans to disclose the UFO information to the world at the end of the cold war. Both this world leader, and the head of state and friend who related this to me, did not know that this event was done by covert human forces. They thought it was an actual alien abduction!

And the message offered to this world leader, by these hoaxed aliens? "Cease your plans to disclose our presence to the world, or we can and will abduct every world leader involved..." How convenient. Notwithstanding the fact that in this same time frame ET craft were being seen in a massive wave in Belgium, and one would soon begin in the volcanic zone of Mexico and around Mexico City, we are to believe that the ETs would abduct a world leader to hide their presence!

This, I am told, "blew up like an atomic bomb in the White House," and all plans to effect a disclosure on this subject were ended, forthwith and forever.

Recently, I have learned of a group of researchers who have independently identified a covert operative who was involved in "abducting" a woman in California and who was, not coincidental, in the security detail for the world leader the night of the "alien abduction." It does not take a rocket scientist to see what the agenda is here, and how all of us have been manipulated into a belief in the "abduction syndrome," and our leaders intimidated into inaction.

I realize that this information is harder to accept than (even) the idea that we are being visited by ET life forms. But that is the point. These secret projects are so bizarre and sociopathic, that they are their own best cover. Who would believe it? And by manipulating the images and ideas in the public domain o this subject, we are led to either disgust and rejection of the entire phenomenon, or to anger and hate towards the visitors. How convenient...

It is time for the civilian research community to get serious about this matter. We must do our homework, and ask the hard questions. We must become knowledgeable regarding what the true covert human capabilities are, and how they figure into human induced abductions. We must be more restrained and cautious and avoid sweeping, paranoiac pronouncements regarding so called "alien agendas," since the events upon which we base such assumptions may be of a very human origin.

From what we have learned from first hand witnesses to covert capabilities, covert reverse-engineering projects, and covert human abductions, we need to take another very hard look at the entire "alien abduction" syndrome, as it is currently described. I believe that the entire data base on this matter has to be taken apart and rebuilt, using a more inclusive cosmology, which includes not only ET/Human interactions, but also, other experiences as described earlier, and, most importantly, covert human capabilities and disinformation programs.

Not all that glitters is gold, and discerning this fact, by our leaders and the public, may determine whether we are manipulated into a future of inter-planetary conflict, or, instead, choose a future of rational and peaceful engagement.

For the sake of the Earth, and the generations which follow us, I hope we are wise enough to choose peace.

8

E-Mail from Dr. Helmut Lammer

Austrian Space Agency

February 1999

Dear Steven,

I will send you today a copy of the MILAB (Military Abductions) manuscript for review.

You will see that some prominent abduction researchers will get into trouble for ignoring MILABs in the future! Or it they try to ridicule this important aspect!!!

So far CSETI is the only organization who has information about covert involvement etc., in alien abductions. Prof. Jacob hypothesis about alien hybrids who interrogate abductees at military bases is ridiculous.

Look - only Hopkins, Jacob and Mack are responsible for pushing the alien abduction phenomenon over the globe! And I know that they have also MILAB cases in their files, but they ignore them!! I will not speculate why, by there are two possibilities.

First: they have a dogmatic alien abduction world view and ignore all cases which do not fit this world view.

Or:

Second: They are working with the covert agenda!

I am certain, that Hopkins, Jacob and Alexander, et al. will attack our research, but the abductees who are people who have experienced such encounters would defend us!

and we will get more and more reports.

It is a problem that the covert agenda behind this is very powerful. I was interviewed for a documentary on alien abductions in London last year, from a British documentary firm which produced a film for the US based Discovery Channel. They interviewed also Hopkins, Jacob, etc. in the USA and then they interviewed me in London concerning military evidence! The interview went well and everything was OK. After two months I got a call from the producer who informed me that they were informed from the Discovery Channel people that Discovery Channel will only pay their documentary if they censure my interview, since they do not want the military topic in the documentary!!!

You see how it works. The ordinary people will get the opinions of Jacob, et al. everything points to an ET threat,...but they are not told the whole story!!!! This is mass mind control via the TV!!!

You know what I mean.

I had similar experiences in Germany, where I was interviewed on implants and the interview was censured shortly before it was broadcast on TV.

That means that the usual film staff, the lower level journalists, find this topic interesting, frightening, important, etc. but the higher ups have orders to censure such revealing talks.... I know that the media are controlled, but what is interesting for me is, that MILABS, mind control and implants must be a very sensitive topic!

It could be very dangerous for he so-called free world if we let these people hide this development from the mass public!!!

Best Regards,

Helmut

9

The Case For Non-hostility

1992

Actions Do Not Equal Motives

On a beautiful fall day in 1990, an 11-year old boy was gliding with abandon down a rural North Carolina road. The exhilaration of the moment quickly turned to horror when a car sped over the crest of the hill and smashed directly into the child, crushing his chest and abdomen, but miraculously sparing any serious injuries to his head. Paramedics were rushed to the scene and quickly transported the child to an Emergency Department trauma room. There, the child entered a foreign world of stainless steel, white walls and strange overhead equipment. What followed next was destined to frighten the still-alert child perhaps more than the accident itself: His blood pressure was falling and the staff had only minutes to establish intravenous lifelines and decompress a life-threatening chest injury which is often rapidly fatal. There was no time for general anesthesia, and in order to survive, the hapless victim had to endure emergency procedures while awake. Despite the calm assurances and explanations that the staff meant only well, the child was understandably terrified as needles probed him and a chest tube was put through his chest wall into the chest cavity. The child protested violently, scared and quite convinced that the staff really meant him only harm, pain and further suffering. To the child, they were demons bent on tormenting him; their actions seemed incomprehensible, harsh and even tortuous. But, of course, his perceptions of their actions were the direct opposite of their true intentions, since the staff had only his ultimate welfare and survival in mind. From this child's level of understanding and awareness, their actions—and therefore the medical staff as people—were evil and malevolent. But in truth, in their hearts and minds, they were motivated only by compassion, the sanctity and preservation of life, the alleviation of suffering, the healing of trauma and disease. This story illustrates a point about many commonly-held assumptions regarding the motives and ultimate intentions of the extra-terrestrial beings presently visiting Earth. That is, we must avoid the assumption of negative motives based on the reported actions of ETI. Our perception of an action must not be confused with the actual motives of the beings performing the actions since it is quite possible that frightening or negatively perceived actions are derived from genuinely good motives. Unfortunately, the UFO/ETI literature is filled with the "conventional wisdom" that many aspects of the phenomenon represent sinister actions driven by equally sinister motives.

There is a facile tendency to conclude, either directly or by inference, that many reported actions are indicative of "malintent." A careful reading of many, if not most, 1980s books on UFOs and "abductions" reveals an alarming tendency to jump to sinister conclusions. Even the language used to describe these events is emotionally charged and shows a propensity towards assumed ETI hostility and malevolence. Reports of actions are taken as evidence of hostility or evil motives without a careful analysis of the possible neutral or positive motives which may account for the events. As will be shown, such conclusions are both unwarranted and fraught with danger, since they color our thinking and emotions with unjustified fear, paranoia and negativity, and in turn will negatively affect the future ETI/human relationship. We must be careful that our assumption of false hostility does not create a future of actual hostility.

The reasons for reaching these negative conclusions are probably multiple. Some events, on their face, appear disturbing to human sensibilities. And like the child in the car accident, lend themselves to quick assumptions of hostility. The entire topic of technologically advanced ETs visiting Earth may play to innate human insecurities and fears of domination or loss of control. The tendency of humans to think in linear and dualistic terms of black/white, good/ bad, etc. certainly contributes. A psychological tendency to dwell on or be attracted to spectacularly negative things or events such as monsters, wars, murder stories, ghost stories and the like may provide an impetus to reaching conclusions of ETI hostility (more people go to see a movie like "Friday the 13th" than, say, "Gandhi"). And, unfortunately, sensationalized concepts of vile aliens invading hapless humans sells books, movies and television programs.

To be specific, let us take the most disturbing and sensational reports of ETI involvement with human reproductive events. The story of a female being taken aboard a craft and subjected to abdominal or vaginal needle probes to remove ova has been extensively studied in the past decade. While we do not definitely know this, let us assume that the ETI are taking ova (and sperm) and are preserving them, or are using them to develop test-tube babies, or even ETI/human hybrids. As disturbing as such events may sound, could there be *ultimate intentions* which are non-hostile?

What if the ETI, alarmed by wild nuclear proliferation and/or massive ecosystem damage, perceive a high probability of a human or geological cataclysm in the near future? Could they be motivated by a desire to safeguard and preserve human and other Earth life in the event of a worse-case scenario? If the hundreds of reports of ETI paranormal mental abilities are to be accepted, perhaps they have *seen* a probable future of massive Earth changes, and these actions are viewed by them as a well-intentioned rescue attempt. While human ethics might be offended by this, perhaps Zechariah Sitchin's assertion that ETI genetically intervened several hundred thousand years ago to establish modern homo sapiens is true, and they are now attempting to further advance the human race. While such concepts may shock and offend many humans, they are not motives of hostility or malevolence per se, especially from the ETI perspective. Indeed, if ETI view us as a race of beings whose chief activities are warfare, violence and environmental destruction, and who are on the verge of self-annihilation, such motives may be understood as benevolent and altruistic!

The point here is that there are actually a number of explanations for even the most disturbing reports of ETI actions which involve non-hostile intentions. It is entirely possible—if not probable—that ETI actions which many humans view as hostile are actually neutral or benevolent, and would be seen as such by humans if the "big picture" were appreciated. What follows below is a brief listing of possible ETI motivations which are either neutral or positive:

Non-Hostile ETI Motivations

Human-Perceived Positive / ETI Perceived Positive:

- Protective surveillance
- Emergency intervention or "rescue" (in the event of man-made or natural cataclysm)

- Human war limitation and control (nuclear)
- Documentation and preservation of ecosystems
- Eventual ETI-human knowledge and technology transfer (pending world peace, human non-aggression)
- Eventual Earth incorporation into inter-planetary union
- Inter-cultural exchange and communication, long-term plan

Human-Perceived Neutral / ETI-Perceived Positive

- Observation
- Basic Research
- Sample and data collection

Human-Perceived Variable (may be positive, neutral and/or negative) / ETI-Perceived Positive:

- Limitation of nuclear contamination of space
- Limitation or containment of space exploration pending human evolution to world peace, unity and non-aggression
- Protection of non-Earth civilizations from human aggression
- Human genetic research, preservation and experimentation
    a. to ensure continuance of human species
    b. to develop advanced ETI/human hybrid
    c. basic research
- ETI security considerations (e.g., safe-guarding of ETI technology, protection of intelligence data base, etc., pending human evolution to non-violence.

On balance, UFO/ETI reports provide no overall evidence of ETI hostility. Some disturbing reports exist, but so too do reports of peaceful intentions, kindness, healing, benevolence, and so forth. No conclusions regarding ETI intentions can be reached by simply viewing isolated case reports. The polarizing tendency to declare ETI as either sinister intruders or perfect god-like saviors is unwise at best, and probably dangerous to the long-term health of the ETI-human relationship. This does NOT mean, however, that we must view this phenomenon in a "motive vacuum," and I feel that a strong case for assumed non-hostility can, and indeed must, be made. This assumption of non-hostility means that in our research, analysis and ETI interactions, we assume non-hostility until clearly proven otherwise. It does not mean that we regard ETI as necessarily godlike saviors, but it clearly avoids the premature characterization of ETI actions and motives as hostile or sinister. Such a moderate positivity and optimism is essential for the emerging ETI/human relationship to develop with the least chance of conflict.

The Case for Non-Hostility, The Case Against Hostility

Perhaps as much or more is revealed about ETI intentions by what has not occurred as by what has. UFOs have not attacked humans or fired weaponry unless first threatened or attacked. ETI have not invaded or destroyed any part of Earth, nor have they shown any intention to do so in the future. Notwithstanding superior technology and maneuverability, they have not attempted any domination or aggressive actions over the past decades, if not centuries, of sightings. Such long-term restraint belies any ultimately hostile intentions. The assumption of hostility is illogical when the entire phenomenon is viewed over time. If ETI have been observing, and to some extent interacting, with Earth for centuries, why delay a hostile occupation? The rather marked increase in UFO/ETI activities coinciding with the dawn of the human nuclear age in the mid-1940s would indicate a genuine concern for human hostile capabilities. This would indicate that ETI is: a) concerned for the long-term welfare and survival of humans; or b) concerned about the potential for human nuclear aggression being exported off-Earth to ET civilizations, or both. Neither of these concerns is indicative of hostility towards humans, but rather a concern for human hostility. Certain militarists may find such interest in our nuclear capabilities disconcerting, but on balance this does not warrant a conclusion of ETI hostility. On the contrary, it supports the view that ETI motives are non-hostile in nature.

If the work of Zechariah Sitchin, Richard Hoagland (monuments on Mars) and others is to be believed, ETI involvement and observation with humans is an ancient, not recent, phenomenon. If aggression, domination and the like were actually motivating ETI, why wait until: a) humans possess weapons of mass destruction, capable of inflicting damage on even ETI craft and personnel; and b) the Earth has been significantly damaged and overrun by billions of humans? Certainly, the Earth would have been an easier—and more pleasant—catch even 200 years ago. On balance, the "hostile aliens" theory, while sensational and making great science fiction reading, is illogical and is not supported by the facts of this phenomenon when analyzed comprehensively.

The Evolutionary Selection of Non-Aggression in Intelligent Beings

A more fundamental and essential basis for assuming non-hostility is a theory of the Evolutionary Selection of Non-Aggression in Intelligent Beings. Briefly put, this theory holds that an intelligent species cannot evolve past a certain technological level without concomitant and essential development of non-aggression. That is, malevolent aggression is an attribute which ensures the self-destruction of a species if retained past a certain point in technological and cultural evolution. It stands to reason that any intelligent species such as humans, who operate from a paradigm of malevolent aggression will first turn that aggression on themselves, thus resulting in their "mutually assured destruction" if retained much past the point of developing nuclear technology. Such aggression would perforce severely incapacitate or destroy intelligent species, thus limiting their ability to persist long enough to develop technologies capable of interplanetary or interstellar flight. It is, therefore, unlikely that a species would evolve to possess space travel capabilities while maintaining unchecked aggressive and malevolent tendencies. It is more likely that at some point in the evolution of a technological society (perhaps at the advent of nuclear technology), a species is required to transcend their own aggressiveness in order to survive. There is, then, a self-limiting dynamic which protects other planetary systems from aggressive species since the establishment of non-aggression is a requirement for significant and long-term technological development. The evolution of the consciousness of non-aggression is an absolute prerequisite for the long-term survival of a technologically advanced civilization.

It is doubtful then, that any species—including humans—who fail to embrace peace and non-aggression will survive their own technology, much less make it to another planet or star system. The inner development of consciousness eventually overtakes technology, simply because it must in order for the species to survive or further evolve. The establishment of non-aggression or non-hostility in a species does not mean, however, that such a species would have values, beliefs and behaviors perfectly matched to those of the late 20th century Earth! On the contrary, since aggression, fighting, war-making and the like are pervasive activities of 20th century man, such values and beliefs may be quite opposite! But we must not confuse varying values and behaviors with hostility towards humans per se. That values and behaviors vary between species who have evolved on different planets is to be expected; however, it must not be cited as proof of ET hostility, nor allowed to become the foci of significant conflict. For this is the same disastrous and well-traveled path which humans have gone down for centuries.

Beyond these considerations, the unfortunate and prevalent assumption of ETI hostility is fraught with the high potential for danger and loss. If we assume UFOs/ETI to be hostile, then our thoughts, actions and plans will reflect this. The important possibilities for peaceful communication and exchange will be poisoned with fear, aggression and suspicion. Instead of viewing ETI as an opportunity for peaceful communication, we will view them as yet another target of human aggression and xenophobic reactionary behavior. Instead of viewing their energy and technological advancements as potential sources of peaceful progress on Earth, we will become obsessed (as perhaps our government has) with capturing their technology to be reverse-engineered into human military applications. We run the very real risk of creating our own negative reality, all based on premature assumptions of net ETI hostility.

It is far safer to take the high road and assume non-hostility, and behave accordingly, until ETI intentions are well-proven to be otherwise. We have much to gain, and strategically and realistically little to lose, by such a stance. We must be careful not to squander so golden an opportunity for communication, exchange and progress as is presently presenting itself for mankind. To assume non-hostility means that our thoughts, attitudes and actions will be peaceful, scientific and receptive without the polluting overlay of fear and paranoia. It will avoid the creation of unnecessary and avoidable conflict and will actually facilitate communication and exchange. It does not mean that we go to the other extreme and regard ETI as god-like saviors, only that we regard them as essentially non-hostile and behave accordingly. It means that we will not jump to sinister conclusions every time a UFO/ETI related event occurs which we either do not fully understand, or which offends current sensibilities. Most importantly, it means we will reach out with peaceful intentions ourselves and in so doing maximize our potential for exchange and communication—an exchange which will be peaceful and beneficial to all involved. It is most likely that we have "nothing to fear but fear itself," so let us let go of our fear, and let us step out of the old paradigm of aggression and disunity. Let us create a new reality, and a new way of seeing—one which embraces peace, calmness and unity. Let us give ETI the benefit of the doubt and assume non-hostility, until clearly proven otherwise. The old and disastrous ways of suspicion, militancy and aggression must give way to openness, peace and trust, for we cannot afford to repeat the mistakes of past generations as we begin so grand a journey. Too much is at stake, and we may possess only one chance to create a world—and a universe—guided by virtue.

10

A Harvest Of Fear

1992

The pursuit of truth requires the ability to see beyond the appearance of things to the meaning and substance behind the forms. In no field of study and research is this more essential than that of UFOlogy, a field beset by mystery, partial information, misinformation and deliberate disinformation. And, alas, in no field is there so great a deficiency of this very quality.

Take, for example, the present climate where every rumor, fantasy and observation is given a spin to fit into the preconceived framework of "alien" sinister designs and manipulations. From abductions, to animal "mutilations" to secret goings-on at U.S. military bases, all are described in the "sinister aliens" mold. Their pervasive, if unspoken, status quo is to place all such events, real or imaginary, in the same dark and rather frightening shadows. To depart from this conventional wisdom, this unofficial party line, is to incur the derision of those self-appointed experts who, after all, know best.

It would appear that the UFO hysteria pendulum has swung full cycle: If the 1950s were the era of the gorgeous Venusians, space gods and saviors from the galactic federation, the past decade has brought us to the age of sinister "aliens" snatching mother and child alike from their bedrooms, harvesting cattle, cats, dogs and even fetuses for obviously nefarious purposes, and the collaboration of military fascists and "aliens" in a plan to dominate the Earth! For the most part, those who claim to be objective UFO "abduction" researchers, as well as UFO journalists and authors, have been swept up in this hysteria, this harvest of fear.

Even those who sincerely intend to "just describe the facts" are affected by the dominant milieu of fear, negativity and hysteria. Words such as victim, abducted, alien, mutilation, rape, sinister, disturbing, alarming, deception, controlling, manipulative, evil, and so on are accepted as automatic members of a UFO lexicon at once mandatory and unquestioned. There is an abundance of automatic interpretations and a real lack of deep analysis, which leaves us with nearly unquestioned—and unchallenged—conclusions, which are uniformly negative. Rather than objectively collecting facts, analyzing trends and making intelligent plans for future research and UFO-human interactions, there exists an increasingly powerful machine of hysteria bringing forth a harvest of fear. And facts which do not fit into this fear and negativity paradigm are either ignored or deliberately debunked as "alien" screen memories and deception.

The real victim in all of this, of course, Truth.

Truth is hard to discern amid the din of hysteria and the clouds of fear currently holding sway over the UFO community. Events are prone to misinterpretation and even censure in this environment, and those facts which do survive intact are nonetheless presented with a patina of fear and paranoia. The danger in all of this is that we may perpetuate a trend which, while initially false, may create its own reality—and its own future conflicts. We must give serious thought and much reflection to this matter, for to do otherwise may result in serious and potentially catastrophic consequences for not only humanity as a whole, but for individual observers of the UFO phenomenon as well. Indeed, we do create our own reality, and we must contemplate deeply what reality may be.

Beyond these other sweeping if not abstract concerns, there is the more immediate and ethical question of what all of this hysteria is doing to the numerous innocent percipients of the UFO phenomenon. Aside from the fact that the trust is being continuously if not unintentionally distorted, those individuals who have had close interactions (a.k.a. "abductees" and "contactees") with UFOs and their occupants are being forced, at times cruelly, to deny any positive or edifying aspects of their encounters, and are left to dwell only on the frightening and negative aspects of the experience. Is this common? Exceedingly so! We have interviewed several individuals who have stated that so-called "abduction researchers" not only enforced a certain negative and fear-engendering interpretation to their experiences, but go further and actually "throw out" any aspects of the experience which do not fit this preconceived "fear paradigm." That is, positive, loving, healing and edifying experiences with ET beings are either ignored or deemed screen memories which only constitute a further sinister deception by the ETs. Objectivity, open-mindedness—and the truth—are cast away so that these experiences may be fit into a framework of preconceived (if unstated) negative conclusions. On the one hand, these researchers will go to great lengths to establish the credibility and veracity of their subjects, only to turn around and ignore or actively debunk those aspects of the experience which do not fit the researchers' own paradigm.

If we are to pick and choose among the facts of these cases, could we not just as well content that the negative experiences are the "screen memories" triggered by the individual's own internal fears and insecurities while the edifying and spiritual memories are the "true" ones? If we are to pick and choose among the facts, why not just take the happy alternative? Indeed, one alternative is just as dishonest and dangerous as the other, and both should be avoided. It is imperative that we accept—and report—all the facts, and then analyze their meaning in a calm and *non*-hysterical manner. With the information and experiences we collectively posses thus far, we can neither proclaim these ET beings to be sinister Darth Vader space conquerors, nor can we assert that they are perfect space gods. Our polarization on this question is one of the chief manifestations of a collective hysteria which is at once pervasive and unproductive. And the greatest task facing us is the elimination of this hysteria and the transcendence of our own fear.

11

UFOS, Humanity And The Full Spectrum Of Reality

1992

For more than a decade, a debate has been raging among UFO investigators and theorists regarding the true nature of UFOs. Typically, this debate is divided between those who regard UFOs as "nuts and bolts" spacecraft (usually of ET origin) and those who feel that UFOs defy purely physical descriptions and are actually an "interdimensional" phenomenon. On the side of the "nuts and bolts" argument are the well-documented electromagnetic effects, landing traces, radar evidence and retrieval of actual crashed spacecraft and their occupants, among others. Proponents of the "interdimensional" theory cite a number of extraordinary aspects of the phenomenon, including rapid appearance-disappearance (materialization/dematerialization?) of craft, associated levitation, telepathy, telekinesis and other related events. Both sides of this debate hold that there is compelling evidence supporting one viewpoint or the other, and at times significant rancor has accompanied these debates.

Could it be that *both* are correct?

The reconciliation of these two views is possible by employing a comprehensive paradigm of reality which does not fragment "physical" from "other dimensional" but which instead replaces the either/or argument with and/and. That the predominant western bias for dualism, separatism and reductionism has been applied to UFOlogy, as well as other areas of study, does not mean that such a perspective in any way reflects reality. We are accustomed to speaking of mind-body, material-spiritual, physical-nonphysical as though a real separation exists, when in actuality such distinctions are convenient, though linear, mental constructs. The discussion of "other dimensions" assumes that indeed there are other dimensions which are somehow separate from this dimension, whatever this dimension is.

In fact, what is this "dimension"? It seems certain that we will be confounded in our attempts at understanding the UFO phenomenon so long as we lack a comprehensive understanding of the phenomenon of humans. For if UFOs are more than just "nuts and bolts," then just as certainly humans are more than mere flesh and blood. Conversely, if humans are more than mere flesh and blood, then it is just as certain that UFOs and their occupants are more than flesh and blood flying around in metal craft of some sort. The truth is found in transcending the old "either/or" arguments and seeing that the manifestations of the UFO phenomenon can be viewed in an integrated way which includes both the nuts and bolts physical as well as the "other dimensional" aspects. Such a unified theory or perspective requires a holistic paradigm as well as a comprehensive understanding of what it means to be *human*, since many of the obscure aspects of the UFO phenomenon are illuminated by the apprehension of the reality of man.

Just as the full spectrum of light involves both seen and unseen elements, so also the full spectrum of reality involves aspects which are seen and unseen. This spectrum is, in fact, a continuum, or an integrated reality, and the distinction of seen and unseen is an artificial contrivance wholly dependent on the perception of the individual. That x-ray radiation went undetected by humans for thousands of years does not mean that it did not exist as part of the electromagnetic spectrum until its "discovery"! Similarly, the spectrum of reality is comprised of aspects which are both seen and "unseen," at least from one level of perception or consciousness. That there are aspects to reality which are not as commonly perceived as others does not in any way compromise the integration of reality itself. For purposes of analysis and verbalization, it is convenient to divide reality into variously described components, but in so doing we must be careful not to confuse these artificial conventions with reality itself. Conventional means of knowing, of analysis and communication have innate limitations which unfortunately become determinants of what we hold reality to be. But the full spectrum of reality transcends these conventions and is whole, complete and uninterrupted; it is present in its entirety here and now, no matter how fragmented and partial our perception of it may be. Our predisposition to compartmentalize mind/body, material/spiritual, physical/transcendent is convenient yet false; it is at once an over-simplification and a complex confusion of reality.

One of the great challenges, and thus blessings, of the UFO phenomenon is the coexistence of dramatic and often seemingly opposing manifestations of UFOs. I believe that these perplexing aspects of the phenomenon hold the greatest lessons to be learned not only about UFOs but about reality itself. The coexistence of advanced material technology with advanced "mind technology" indicates that we are dealing with beings who have explored and integrated the full spectrum of reality more fully than human civilization has. Put another way, UFOs represent not so much beings from another dimension as they do beings (and craft) which operate in a broader aspect of the spectrum of reality. That is, the full spectrum of reality includes not only the material and physical laws as currently conceived by humans, but also physical laws and "laws of consciousness or mind" not yet fully understood or utilized by most humans. In this way, we may view UFOs and their occupants as examples of beings who are utilizing a somewhat more expanded spectrum than we humans have yet mastered; but the difference is a matter of *degree* and not of fundamental reality. For this, we should have no problem integrating the clear evidence of the physical reality of UFOs such as landing traces, radar detection and the like with more extraordinary evidence such as telepathy, levitation and rapid materialization. Given the pace of human development in the last 100 years, we should not be too surprised if ET beings 1,000–500,000—or one million—years more advanced than us should have explored and placed into practical application aspects of the full spectrum of reality beyond our current mastery. Indeed, we should be astonished if this were not the case!

All of this would be less astonishing if we would but look to the extraordinary capacities which we know humans possess. The "science of consciousness," while yet embryonic as a field of formal study, has documented those aspects of the spectrum of reality pertaining to mind or consciousness. Both ancient and modern writings testify to the existence of human mental capacities which approximate the most extraordinary reports from UFO encounters. Telepathy, precognition, thought projection and even levitation are all aspects of the human experience which have been documented throughout the ages. Recent research into telepathy, thought projection and precognition would indicate that these experiences are not so uncommon as conventional wisdom would have us believe. If humans possess physical bodies and physical craft and yet are able to manifest extraordinary mental capabilities, why should we be perplexed if somewhat more advanced beings from elsewhere in the universe have physical bodies and physical craft and are able to utilize consciousness as we would matter? As physics and other sciences evolve, we find that the once-clear line between mind and matter becomes rather tenuous, if not obliterated altogether. We are reaching the point where further advances in the physical sciences will require concomitant advances in the realm of consciousness or mind. At that point, we will find that the interface between mind and matter, physical and transcendent, is in reality a matter of perception and dependent on the level of consciousness of the perceiver. Our perplexity over the UFO phenomenon is in part due to a lack of insight into what it means to be human, of the dynamics of mind and consciousness, and a strange addiction to the neat and hypnotic separation between mind and matter, science and religion, objective and subjective. Such fragmentation is a monster of our own devising, and can be conquered only by evolving to a way of perceiving which is inclusive, holistic and unified. In this we find the greatest challenge and the greatest lesson in the UFO phenomenon. May we not fail in this endeavor.

In its greatest sense, the full spectrum of reality is another way of saying "God," and therefore is infinite and all-inclusive. While each generation of scientists and philosophers regard their current knowledge as the apex of all learning, just as surely the next generation will surpass it. We will not exhaust the full spectrum of reality in this generation, not in the next. But the path of exploration will remain open only to the extent that we hold our minds open to an ever-expanding reality. For just as soon as we think we know it all, or say "aha! That's it!", we limit our progress and throw a roadblock onto the path of knowledge.

Those scientists who hold that UFOs could not possibly be ET spacecraft simply because humans have not yet unraveled the laws of physics allowing them to get from "there" to "here" fail to understand that *most* of even physical reality and its laws have yet to be comprehended by humans. And those UFOlogists who dismiss evidence of extraordinary mental capacities of ETs (or, for that matter, humans) fail to appreciate the reality of man, of consciousness and mind, and have blinded themselves to a very large and significant aspect of the spectrum of reality. Such foibles are, in fact, a modern-day reenactment of "the sun revolves around the Earth" episode of a bygone era. We must remember that a mere 200 years ago, lasers performing surgery and holograms at amusement parks would have been considered magic, other-worldly, even witchcraft! Therefore, we should not be dismayed that others are able to traverse interstellar (or should we say *intrastellar*) space, or that they might manipulate matter and gravity even as we would alter atoms and genes. We should be similarly open to the probability that they might use a thought as adeptly as we would use a telephone or alter matter by mind as easily as psychiatrists alter mind by matter. Ultimately, then, the limiting factor in our comprehension of reality in general and the UFO phenomenon in particular is the openness, breadth, and depth of our own consciousness. The old ways of thinking will fail us here, for we are bumping up against the limits of what linear reality and linear thinking will allow. Like never before, our progress is dependent on the evolution of our own consciousness, and our consciousness is dependent on what our will allows.

And so we should have no difficulty accepting that structured material craft occupied by physical beings are able to demonstrate both physical and so-called interdimensional characteristics. For we are also interdimensional beings, and are not limited to the physical plane alone, and our differences are more a matter of degree than anything essential. It is most likely that both humans and other conscious beings potentially have open to them the full spectrum of reality, and the differences observed are due to the extent to which this potential is realized. We should not be dismayed that one group appreciates this spectrum more fully than another; on the contrary, such a realization is cause for celebration, not alarm. Our task is to be open to the full spectrum of reality, in all of its manifestations, and to grow in our appreciation of it. If we do this, our progress will be unlimited.

As we contemplate the various aspects of UFO evidence, we would be well served to keep in mind the full spectrum of reality, all that is known and all that its potentially unknown. While most humans yet hold to linear processes and dualistic ways of perceiving reality, it seems clear that ET beings responsible for UFO events do not. The unified, full spectrum of reality which includes, in an elegantly integrated whole, the total range of physical and transcendent, mind and matter, is open to exploration by humans as well as other beings in the universe. We are potentially as interdimensional as they; our only limitations are those which we place upon ourselves. Perhaps then the ultimate meaning of the UFO phenomenon is that it serves to move us towards the next quantum jump in human evolution, towards the realization of the full unified spectrum of reality.

12

Extraterrestrials And The New Cosmology

1995

The universe is teeming with intelligent life.

In fact, the universe itself is intelligent and alive.

The seen and the unseen, the apparent and the transcendent, the physical and the realm of spirit, all are part of a universe, alive, awake and intelligent. The multiplicity of life in the universe, while diverse, is essentially a singularity; beyond division, it exists in the unitize state, a marvelous, conscious Oneness.

From one level of consciousness, there is neither inner nor outer, neither this nor that, neither physical nor spiritual. All that there is exists in its true nature as pure, undifferentiated, eternal Mind.

And yet from the awareness of that which is relative, we find inner and outer, mind and body, good and evil, oneness and separation. And this also is real, from the awareness of that which is relative, for would you pluck out your eye as easily as you trim your nails? Truth is often born from the contemplation of these paradoxes; both perspectives are true, but are dependent on the level of awareness of the observer. As we ponder the universe and a new cosmology which accounts for the existence of advanced non-human life forms, the lesson of the paradox will visit us over and over again. But if we look intently with the eye of oneness, perhaps the cosmos will offer up a few of its mysteries.

Cosmological Confusion. This term best describes what happens when 20th century humans are confronted with the existence of advanced ET life forms. For not only are these beings not human, they possess technologies which are inherently mystifying to us. Any civilization which is several thousand (and perhaps several million) years more advanced than ours will by definition manifest in ways which are bewildering to us. It is unlikely that a people capable of interstellar travel will be using microwave signals for communication, or fossil or nuclear fuels for propulsion. Indeed, the very laws of the universe currently held high by modern Earth scientists are likely to be mere distant shadows of the ones grasped and applied by civilizations capable of interstellar travel.

The technological and cultural manifestations of star-faring civilizations are likely to appear magical to most humans, even as a hologram or a laser would appear magical to someone on Earth 200 years ago. A large measure of scientific and cosmological humility and patience will be needed for us to begin to understand these civilizations, their technology, and most importantly, the lessons about the nature of reality which may be learned from them.

Moreover, the co-existence of a non-linear, non-local and transcendental universe with the so-called "physical universe" must not only be factored into our understanding of cosmology in general, but of the manifestations of advanced ET people in particular. For as we shall see, both humans and ET life forms are not merely physical, quantifiable entities, but they, and we, exist in realms which are not bound by the physical universe.

That is, we and other biological life forms which are of an ET origin, possess both mind and body; we both manifest a reality which is both physical and spiritual, linear and non-local, fixed in time and space yet simultaneously transcendent. And what happens when science and technology find the point of communication between the hard physical and the unitive state of mind? The manifestations of such a technology would truly be confounding to both the modern physicist and the modern philosopher or theologian. For such a quantum leap in the understanding of the universe would bring into close relation the separately held realms of science and spirituality, mind and matter, body and spirit.

Now add to this perplexing situation the existence of non-physical intelligent beings who, while not possessing a physical biological body, are nevertheless intelligent, sentient, and to a certain extent, capable of interacting with biological humans and biological ETs. The tendency in the popular culture is to dismiss such beings as being figments of ones imagination (or of a primitive belief system) or to lump all such beings, be they human, ET or purely non-biological into a veritable smorgasbord of undifferentiated "entities." It is obvious that the risk of profound cosmological confusion rises exponentially as the multiplicity of intelligent life forms is contemplated. A new cosmology is needed if we are to understand the universe around us, and the lenses of the old Cartesian paradigm must be cast off and a new, more encompassing paradigm adopted.

Perhaps the greatest challenge of the detection of advanced, interstellar civilizations is to formulate a new cosmology, viewed through a new paradigm which is adequate to the task of understanding the universe around us.

In the civilian UFO community, there is much confusion over the nature of the objects and life forms which are moving about in our time/space reality. On the one hand, we find indisputable physical manifestations, such as crashed spacecraft, radar returns, verified photographs and videotape, and metal samples from landing events. Not to mention "flesh and blood" biological ET life forms. And yet on the other hand we find multiple accounts of non-linear manifestations of these same objects and beings: Telepathic communications, lucid dreams, mind-matter interactions, remote viewing, bi-location, levitation and others. No objective student of the ET phenomenon can ignore these manifestations; they are numerous and widespread. Our bewilderment and confusion is no excuse for dismissing this aspect of the phenomenon out of hand, and yet our acceptance of these manifestations really requires that we re-think our entire understanding of "reality." And humans, not liking change, are reluctant to confront evidence which requires a total reevaluation of our cosmological understanding.

This cosmological confusion has advanced so far that you have various camps arguing about phenomena, some of which are manifestations of advanced ET civilizations, and some of which are manifestations of non-biological "spiritual beings," which have the ability to manifest in some ways similar to ETs. That is, some of the advanced technologies and capabilities of ET civilizations, especially those interfacing with mind and thought, can appear in ways very similar to so called 'astral" or spirit beings. In fact, the manifestations can be so similar as to lead many to say that the originating beings are one and the same. Not true. Not all that glitters is gold, and similarity of manifestation does not equate to sameness of origin.

Now add to all of this the fact that certain adept humans can manifest abilities which are extremely similar to both ET and 'astral" beings. Remember the list of unusual manifestations of ET technology mentioned above? Telepathy, precognition, levitation, telekinesis, bi-location, mind matter and mind body interactions.... These are all abilities which, from time to time (and more often than many would think!) appear in the human world.

Finally, let us add one more factor into all of this: Covert military and paramilitary human groups which have developed both technologies and innate mental abilities approximating those of both the ET civilizations and the non-biological spirit beings.

The universe is a big, and complex place. But it need not be overly difficult to understand, and its comprehension is aided by first utilizing a few simple principles and concepts. This task recalls the ancient Sufi saying "Knowledge is a single point, but the foolish have multiplied it!"

Core Principles Of The New Cosmology

- Linear, relative reality and non-local, non-linear reality both simultaneously exist as Reality; their perception and understanding is wholly dependent on the level of consciousness of the observer. Even physical matter has an aspect of its nature which is non-local, transcendent and conscious.
- Conscious, intelligent biological life forms, whether on Earth or from some other planet, have physical realities as well as spiritual realities; all have the potential to manifest physically and spiritually in a multitude of ways. Pure mind, or unbounded consciousness, is innate to all such life forms and is the ultimate highest denominator which all life shares; it is essentially non-local, and is not bound by the constraints of time or space, but can manifest in time-space reality.
- Beings which do not have biological bodies (so-called astral or spirit beings) are also conscious, intelligent entities, and as such can interact with other conscious life forms, both biological and otherwise. On rare occasion they can even effect a physical manifestation. Once again, the highest common denominator linking these beings with other life forms and biological beings is that of unbounded consciousness, or non-local mind.
- The universe consists of both linear and non-linear, or transcendent, aspects which, while seeming paradoxical, simultaneously exist at every point in time/space and non-time/space. From this point of view, every point in time and space exists in every other point in time and space, through the quality of non-locality.

- The concept of God, or of a Universal, All-Knowing Being, is enhanced and not diminished by the recognition of the vast multiplicity of life in the universe. The glory of God is magnified by the recognition of the infinite diversity and limitless scope of life in the cosmos.

So how does intelligent life in the universe actually manifest? While keeping the above basic concepts in mind, let us now review the diversity of life and how they may present to our various inner and outer senses:

Categories Of Intelligent Life Forms

Biological: Types

Humans—Intelligent, higher life form existing initially in a biological body and native to Earth.

ET Life Forms—Intelligent, higher life forms existing initially in a biological body and native to various planets other than Earth.

Planetary Life Forms: Non-anthropomorphic intelligent beings identified with an entire planetary body; for example, the Earth as Gaia, an intelligent, awake being that is the entire planet Earth, as a living organism. Other planetary bodies, as well as solar and galactic bodies are thought to be individual conscious organisms.

Other biological life forms: On Earth, organisms such as dolphins and cetaceans which are thought to be highly intelligent and yet non-human; theoretically, other planets may possess corollaries to these as non-anthropomorphic intelligent biological life forms.

Biological: Manifestations/presentations

(This listing describes how biological intelligent life forms may present or be perceived by both inner and outer senses.)

Physically, that is in physical bodily form, with or without spacecraft

Technologically, that is via radio, TV, and also advanced systems involving technological interface with mind/thought (advanced ET technology)

Mentally, via telepathic, lucid dream or other direct mind interface

Astral body projection, that is the presentation of a human, ET or other biological life form in its subtle, non-biological component; this may be perceived by another

biological life form in either waking state or while asleep in a dream state

Causal or Thought Body presentation; that is the perception of another biological life form in its most subtle individual aspect, the thought essence "body," which may be projected or conveyed without either biological or astral body components

Pure Mind/One Mind; the ultimate state of oneness; any conscious life form may be experienced or perceived as pure, unbounded mind; by definition, every conscious life form is essentially non-local, pure mind and may be so perceived

Types Of Experiences And Abilities Of Biological Life Forms

Physical Senses—Sight, Hearing, Smell, Touch, Taste

Physical Capabilities—Movement/Motion, others with and without technological augmentation

Mental Abilities, Traditional—Thought, ideation, creativity, visualization, memory, sensory perception and recognition, others.

Non-local Mental Abilities (Non-traditional)—These involve recognition and utilization of non-local aspects of both mind and matter:

- Telepathy—the ability to send and/or receive thought from one intelligent being to another
- Precognition—Since the subtle, non-local aspect of mind is not bound or limited by time or space, any intelligent higher life form capable of being aware of awareness can access via non-local mind probable events of the future; note that any such precognition is less than 100% certain because events in the "present" affected by free will may alter the probability of future events.

- "Postcognition"—(See precognition above) The ability to perceive via non-local mind distant past events not personally experienced by the perceiver; this ability permits the perceiver to see events dating back in time indefinitely, since nonlocal mind can access past as well as future points in the time/space linear continuum.
- Remote Viewing (or Remote Sensing)—Here defined as the ability to see via non-local, unbounded mind distant events in space, either in real time or in the past or future (see Precognition and Postcognition above). In real time, the remote viewer can perceive distant places in potentially great detail through the faculty of non-local mind.
- Dream State Abilities—While in the dream state, a higher intelligent life form may experience Precognition (precognitive dreams), Postcognition (postcognitive dreams) Remote Viewing and Lucid Dreaming (defined as when the dreamer is conscious, awake and self-aware in the dream and may affect the events of the dream).
- Celestial Perception—Perception involving both physical biological senses and higher conscious sensing which enables a being to perceive aspects of both physical and non-physical realities in their most subtle and refined aspects; the perception of "auras" is one simple example of this
- Intuitive Knowing—The ability to know detailed and reliable information and insights via non-local mind and so-called inner knowing, without the aid of conventional outward means of knowing. For example, a life form may perceive a plant and intuitively know its specific medicinal utility.
- Non-traditional Healing Abilities—a life form may demonstrate healing of self or another life form by way of non-physical and non-technological means, either remotely, or in person. These abilities and modalities are diverse and may include mind/body interactions, subtle astral body/bodyinteractions and others.
- Levitation (non-technological)—The annihilation of gravitational influences via subtle mind interactions with either a body or other material objects. This is possible because both mind and matter has subtle, non-local aspects which can interface with each other and effect phenomena such as levitation.

- Telekinesis—The ability to move an object through observable space by effecting an interface between subtle, non-local mind and a comparable aspect of an object. For example, a life form may mentally lift a chair and move it across the room without any traditional physical or technological assistance.
- Teleportation—The ability to move, or manifest, an object a substantial distance via non-local mind and the non-local aspect of matter, which negates the linear aspect of space. For example, a life form may teleport a jewel from one continent to another using this ability.
- Transmutation (non-technological)—The ability to convert one material object to a different element or object using the subtle interface of mind and non-local matter. Note that this may also be achieved technologically
- Bi-location—The ability to manifest a body, or object, in two or more points in the time/space continuum. For example, a life form may appear simultaneously in two or more places at the same point in time. A related" bi-timing" ability is the ability to appear in the same space in more than one point in time (so-called time travel)
- Materialization/Dematerialization (non-technological)—The ability of a life-form to make manifest or unmanifest a material object by using the mind/matter interface. Note that this may also be achieved technologically.
- Out of body experiences/Astral Projection—The ability to project at will the subtle astral, or light body, to a point in time or space outside the biological body.
- Near Death Experiences—The experience of the transient separation of the subtle or astral body from the physical biological body due to bodily illness or injury. The experience may involve the perception of the so-called 'next world" in a brief experience of the non-material, subtle aspect of the cosmos (usually astral but advanced perceptions may involve the causal or pure thought realm).
- And Many Others......

Note that all of the above abilities are innately possible in both human and ET life forms. Whether or not they are actually manifesting in a culture is dependent on that culture's degree of evolution and the focus of the culture. The significant point here is that by virtue of being conscious, awake and intelligent, such life forms, be they human or otherwise, can potentially develop and experience all of the above capabilities.

It is also important to remember that each of these abilities can be achieved through material technological augmentation of innate mental abilities, or may be totally achieved by technological advances alone. Many advanced ET technologies appear to be "magical" to us because they utilize aspects of both mind and matter which are currently beyond a quantifiable understanding by current human science. Ironically, for this reason certain so-called primitive peoples who have remained in touch with the mysteries of non-local mind and matter may comprehend ET technologies better than western scientists.

Non-biological Intelligent Life Forms

Adding to the complexity of the universe is the existence of realms, dimensions, aspects (call it what you will) of the cosmos which are entirely non-linear and non-material, as we currently define it. This "part" of the cosmos is actually more vast and complex than even the physical material universe, and no cosmology can be complete without at least an initial attempt to assess its basic characteristics and manifestations. Because this aspect of the cosmos can interact with the physical one (and with both humans and ets who live in biological bodies), it is important for us to consider it and account for how it may resemble and differ from the diverse manifestations and abilities of humans, ets and other biological life forms mentioned above.

Types Of Non-biological Intelligent Life Forms

Astral or light beings

- of Earth origin, that is deceased previously biological humans
- of non-Earth origin, either deceased ET biological life forms, or those originating in the astral or causal realms

Causal or Thought Beings (those existing primarily as "thought bodies"

- of Earth origin (that is deceased biological humans)
- of non-Earth origin (that is those who were previously biological ets, or which originated from the causal or astral realms)

Note that these non-biological beings, whether previously human, ET, or originating from a non-biological source can appear to biological life forms in a myriad of ways, including in waking state, dreams, meditative states, etc. Depending on the culture, degree of evolution and degree of acceptance of non-material beings, these entities may be known by a number of terms and be seen to fulfill various roles. A partial listing would include:

- Ghosts or spirits
- Spirit Guides or Angels
- Archangels
- Ascended Enlightened Beings (Avatars, Prophets such as Christ, Krishna others)
- Planetary Nature Spirits (known as Devas in Vedic tradition)
- Animal Spirits
- and others too numerous to list

Types Of Experiences And Abilities Of Non- Biological Life-Forms

Essentially, all of the experiences and abilities, and perhaps others, listed under Biological Life Forms pertain to these non-biological life forms, except that they interface less frequently with the world of matter since they primarily exist in non-material realms. However, they can and do interact with the material aspect of the cosmos from time to time, as evidenced by various anomalous events such as materializations and poltergeist activity. Certainly there are numerous accounts of interactions with the human mind and spirit, and also with ET minds and spirits.

When analyzing the multitude of experiences which humans can have, it is important to have a cosmological understanding which is broad enough to comprehend the diversity of the cosmos. Otherwise, we will be unable to discern the distinction between an anomalous manifestation of an ET technology and an unusual manifestation from the astral or causal cosmos.

Apples, Oranges And Stardust

The foregoing in no way is an exhaustive treatment of the question of a comprehensive cosmology; such a task would comprise one if not several books. But as an overview it brings us to a very important question about our main focus here, the ET presence. The universe, being filled with both biological and non-biological intelligent species, presents a special challenge to anyone attempting to understand the ET peoples currently visiting Earth. And this is because there are areas of phenomena that overlap between quite different types of beings.

For example, a non-biological astral being may appear to manifest in ways very similar to some advanced ET life forms. However, the ET life forms may be using a very advanced technology which superficially (or even essentially) looks like a non-biological entity. Would a hologram projection of a person not be interpreted by a person living in the 17th century as a ghost? And what of live satellite TV video conferencing? For that matter, what of the simple flashlight? Absolute magic!

For this reason, and others, a cosmological crisis has dominated the ET/UFO question for several decades. Mind you, this has been helped along by deliberate disinformation and psychological warfare programs of certain covert groups (more on this later). The result has been a mixing of apples, oranges and stardust, and calling them all one thing.

This perhaps is a predictable and natural result of a tumultuous world encountering new and perplexing phenomena. We are reminded of the movie *The Gods Must Be Crazy*, where a small plane flies over a remote and primitive area of Africa and one of the occupants drops a Coke bottle out of the window. This item becomes an item of great mystery, conflict, and supernatural meaning and power to the indigenous people who find it. While the movie is a comedy, it contains an important and relevant message here: Are we now behaving like the finders of the Coke bottle?

For example, many observers of the ET phenomenon will conclude that the ET spacecraft are actually not at all physical/material in nature because they can at times appear to be there and then suddenly "disappear". Magical? Interdimensional? Or could the ET technology simply allow the craft to go from hovering to several thousand miles per hour (or even beyond light speed) in one instantaneous quantum acceleration? The neural pathways of the human eye are incapable of tracking an acceleration of this magnitude, and so the object appears to simply "disappear".

In fact, there are three main factors contributing to this cosmological confusion. First, as mentioned, there is the innate nature of advanced ET technology, which is so far advanced from anything we can even imagine that it appears "supernatural" rather than just super technology. There are laws of the universe which we have not even begun to ask questions about in our scientific community on Earth, and which are not only understood, but have been applied in advanced technologies by ET civilizations. For this reason (as well as good old fashioned scientific arrogance) even rigorous scientists are inclined to dismiss certain aspects of the ET phenomenon out of hand, or regard it as "not real," supernatural, superstitious etc.

Take the development of consciousness assisted technology (CAT). This is when mind, thought or consciousness interfaces with machine or matter to assist the machine in its tasks, or to bypass direct physical input. For example, rather than touching sequentially a number of buttons on a computer to enter data or give a command, one might simply think the command to the computer, which has been pre-programmed to recognize and accept your "thought signature," and then carry out the command. There are a number of witnesses who have seen ET life forms doing exactly this: an ET is standing at a console on board a spacecraft, and without touching manually the console, is able to give it instructions mentally, which result in various mechanical actions by the craft. Impossible? Magical? Nonsense?

Be careful! A very human scientist at UNLV in Las Vegas named Dean Radin is working on a so-called "psychic switch," which is precisely what is described above. Major corporations are interested in the outcome of his work which would enable workers to turn on and interact with computers simply by "thinking to it." If human scientists are already contemplating and attempting to design practical applications of mind-machine interfaces, how far along this path might advanced ET civilizations be?

The flip side of consciousness assisted technology is technology assisted consciousness (or TAC). TAC is the use of specialized machines to assist in the function of mind, thought or consciousness. A basic example is the Monroe Institute Hemisync tones, which are designed to assist in developing the mind's ability to achieve deep states of relaxation, expansion and eventually other powers and abilities. (The hemisync tones interact with the brain wave function is such a way as to facilitate synchronizing the two hemispheres of the brain.) A more advanced (though to modern scientists bizarre) application of this principle is the ability of ET life forms to use certain technologies to communicate with each other and with humans telepathically. There are literally hundreds of cases where a human has had an ET craft overhead or nearby, and has received clear messages mentally which are identified as coming from the occupants of the craft. It would be easy to just dismiss such cases as nonsense, except that they persist and are found world wide from diverse and credible people.

In the case of ET civilizations, the ability to communicate at speeds exceeding that of light becomes an essential technology of any star-faring species. And to quote an old song by the Moody Blues, "Thinking is the best way to travel." Why? Because it is instantaneous. And in the case of precognition, one can actually receive a thought before it is sent (remember that pure mind is not linear; it is not bound by either space or time). So it really should come as no surprise to us that star-faring peoples would have developed reliable means of communicating with "thought stuff" rather than with radio waves. After all, if you are 100 light years from your home planet (a fairly short distance cosmologically speaking), it would take 200 years at the speed of light to say "Hello home base, how are you today?" and for them to respond "Fine thank you, how are you?"

Nor is this a one way capability as it manifests here on Earth. There are numerous cases where a witness to an ET craft will think a thought such as "Oh, I wish that thing would come back this way so that I can get a better look!", and suddenly the craft changes direction and comes right over to the person. The high accuracy of such exchanges would indicate that these craft and their occupants have technology which accurately interfaces with both their thoughts and the thoughts of others, if needed. For us, it may seem bizarre and magical; to the ET life forms, it may be no more extraordinary than a human in New York talking to a friend in London on the telephone.

Nor is communication the only way in which ET technology may be utilizing the principle of TAC. Technology assisted teleportation, telekinesis and even higher states of consciousness and remote viewing may be the result of advanced ET technologies. Once the nexus between mind and matter and mind and space/time is clearly understood the potential applications are almost limitless, and boggle the imagination.

The reason the question of advanced ET technology is important to this discussion of cosmological confusion must be obvious by now. Very advanced technologies of ET civilizations may appear similar or identical to other so-called paranormal phenomena. ET technology interfacing with mind is easily confused with a person interacting with a spirit guide, or even the delusions of a schizophrenic. To discern one from the other requires insight, knowledge, patience and above all, experience.

For example, a few years ago I interviewed a woman who had an anomalous experience which an abduction researcher told her was a "classic ET abduction experience." On closer examination, however, it turned out that this person had an out of body experience with a subsequent interaction with a "spirit being" or astral being. However, while being hypnotized by the enthusiastic UFO researcher, this woman subconsciously filled in quite a few details so that the experience would look like "a classic abduction." This type of "filling in" details while under hypnosis, especially to please a hypnotist who has a strong bias towards retrieving alleged memories of ET abductions, is quite common. Is it real or is it memorex? When dealing with the human mind, great care must be taken, or we will confuse those aspects of the new cosmology which have clear areas of overlap. In the case of this particular woman, she felt all along that her experience was something unusual, but not ET, but the abduction researcher, not being knowledgeable about the nature of out of body experiences, tried to fit a round peg in a square hole.

This case brings us to the second factor contributing to cosmological confusion: The overlap of non-biological intelligent life forms, humans and ets.

A spirit being or astral being may appear to a person, or to even several people, almost as a hologram; this may occur in waking state, dream state or in meditation. Now, if someone who accepts the reality of UFOs (but is not accepting of the existence of other non-material realms) hears of an experience where a person awakens in his room to a being standing at the end of the bed, the UFOlogist may jump to the false conclusion that this person was being visited by an ET.

But wait. A more holistic cosmology as outlined above would allow us to consider that this person had a visit by a spirit guide or angel; or by another living biological human who projected his or her astral body into the bedroom; or by a deceased grandparent; *or* by a technological or mental projection of an ET into the room. Or simply, that the person had a hypnogogic hallucination.

The point is this: If you do not know about or accept the diversity of possibilities, you are very likely to misinterpret the phenomenon. If only one or two options are allowed for as even possibilities, then all unusual occurrences will be categorized, often wrongly, as only those options. This is akin to a doctor knowing only one possible diagnosis for abdominal pain: Appendicitis. But what if the pain is from a gallbladder attack, an ulcer, pancreatitis, etc.? Obviously, a great deal of the time the doctor will make the wrong diagnosis.

Similarly, many people experience a myriad of unusual phenomena (*plural*) but they will be considered as only one possible phenomenon (*singular*). The result is the mixing of apples, oranges and stardust. Adopting and understanding a truly holistic cosmology will greatly assist us in avoiding this confusion. But even then, because there are areas of profound overlap, where one phenomenon will mimic the other, tremendous care and repeated mature experience is required before clear discernment is possible.

Otherwise, how will we differentiate an experience with a spirit being from an advanced mind-matter interaction effected by ET technology? Or for that matter, from human technology and experiences?

A number of observers have concluded that the UFO phenomenon is actually interdimensional in nature. I agree. But this statement is meaningless unless we acknowledge the fact that humans are interdimensional, that ets are interdimensional, and for that matter the paper you are reading this on is interdimensional. The error arises when the statement is made that UFOs are interdimensional but *not* ET, as if the two were somehow mutually exclusive. They are not. From the fundamental level of non-local reality, both mind and matter are non-linear, conscious and unbounded by space or time. So even the rocks beneath your feet are interdimensional and multi-dimensional. Because there is an aspect of the rock which is conscious, non-local and multidimensional, a human (or ET) mind can interface with it and levitate it across a field. The nexus of non-local, unbounded mind and non-local unbounded matter is the non-place place "where" all of these interactions occur.

Now, in the case of ET people, their development and technology permit certain feats which appear magical to us—and we label it "other," interdimensional, etc. But in reality, we have much in common with these ET cultures. For human history is filled with examples of people on this planet performing" miraculous feats" which appear supernatural. But one person's miracle is another's every day event. That ET spacecraft seem to move from one 'dimension" to another, or that their occupants perform what seem like interdimensional feats does not mean that their nature or reality is really different from ours. We are as interdimensional as they are, but we have not developed certain abilities and technologies to the degree they have. But our fundamental nature is the same.

And this brings us to the third factor contributing to cosmological confusion—human covert programs designed to confuse, mislead and deceive society on the ET question. It is relevant here, simply because so many alleged ET events are not what they appear to be.

It must be remembered that covert human attempts to back-engineer ET technology have been going on for over 45 years, and more than a little headway has been made. Additionally, certain covert cells in the military and intelligence agencies have been working on electronic and psychic techniques which are highly invasive, very specific and operationally effective. In short, let the observer beware, since these technologies are much farther along than most could imagine, and the real capability exists to deliberately mimic ET technology and events for the purpose of disinformation.

Take for example the so-called (and badly misnamed) abduction scenario (See "Abductions: Not All That Glitters Is Gold" on page 36.) We have been briefed by trusted members of the military who have Top Secret Clearance with special access into areas of "Non-lethal Defense" and related fields who have confirmed to us that psycho-electronic technologies exist which are mimicking ET encounters. One such military source stated to us that "We have off-the-shelf technology which, if we should want to, we can target an individual or group of individuals and remotely make them have a personal conversation with their personal God. And they would believe it was real. And they would pass a lie detector test that it was real. Because for them it was real."

This is a wake-up call. The simple approach of taking all anomalous experiences on face value is not only unscientific, it is immensely dangerous. Technologies do exist which can induce personal and collective experiences which appear to be ET or UFO related, but which are really quite human. Like the plutonium experiments on humans in the 40s, 50s and 60s, and the germ warfare tests on civilian populations, these "experiments" are real, "black budget" activities which have been developed and perfected over the past 30-40 years. Electronic and implant technologies, all human, exist which can induce a very convincing "abduction event." The clustering of abduction experiences around military installations, and the presence of unmarked black, electronic filled helicopters near so-called abductee homes is no coincidence.

The public has been misled, and the civilian UFO research community has been quite victimized by these special projects, which are designed to deceive, mislead and above all disinform the public on the ET subject. The "Body Snatchers" fix on the ET presence is driven by a complex plan to convince the public that there is "...an alien threat which we must all unite against and fight..."

Do not be deceived. The future of life on Earth, and of our emerging relationship with other ET civilizations may depend on our eyes being open.

Again, while other chapters will deal with these issues in greater detail, the relevance of covert human activities to cosmological confusion must not be underestimated. For human awareness on the subject of ets has been manipulated, played like a harp, by those who would hide the real gold under a mountain of fool's gold. And events which look, feel and sound like ET ones may in fact be part of a deception of very human origins. And if we do not at least consider the role of covert disinformation programs in our list of cosmological options, then we will be doomed to misidentify and misinterpret many of these events.

Nor is the human factor which adds to cosmological confusion limited by covert activities. There is the usual array of misperceptions, hallucinations, delusions, wannabees, false memory syndromes, hoaxes, scientific arrogance and general human egotism. All of these contribute to a collective cosmological indigestion which is in dire need of a cure. And acknowledging the problem is the first step to healing.

ET civilizations. Humans. Non-biological life forms. The cosmos is a complex, diverse and fascinating place. Or Non-place? Ultimately, education, and above all experience, will guide us on this journey. For if we are to set sail over this vast ocean, we are in need of a rudder, a compass and a few journeys along the near shoreline first.

We must join together to gather our knowledge and experience, and with courage and resolve set sail first along the shoreline, then farther from shore and then into the vast and limitless ocean of inner and outer space. For we are not at the end of time, or of history, but rather we stand on the threshold of unbounded possibilities, a time when all that we may dream together will come to pass.

13

The Crossing Point

5 November 1998

Experience and observation combined with insight often yield a new breakthrough into truth and the nature of reality.

Science (and the pursuit of truth in general) is a coordinated blending of empirical observation with knowledge, intellect, insight and often inspiration. And just as it is true that no problem can be solved from the level of consciousness which created it, so too insights into reality and the great scientific developments seldom arise from the current milieu alone but rather are born from something beyond the current status quo. It is frequently resisted, even vilified, when first brought forward—and the current high priests of science are little changed from the Vatican hierarchy who condemned Galileo.

In dealing with the question of ET life, this is true in spades. Because the reality which we are pursuing is intrinsically non-human, non-earthly and therefore outside the tidy box of current scientific understanding. By definition, any advanced non-human life form capable of interstellar travel will possess technologies which will look like magic to us. And if we view this quest through late twentieth century anthropocentric eyes alone we are guaranteed to miss 99.9% of the truth. Because the new truth always hovers just outside the current view finder and even the lens of this view finder is lamentably defective.

As we scan the heavens for intelligent life with our much vaunted billion channel BETA system at Harvard have we paused to consider that our instruments may be akin to smoke ring detectors looking for us? That is, if our ancestors tried to detect our civilization by looking for smoke signals rising from the forests they would be rather disappointed. For we have forsaken the smoke signals for TV and radio signals—but they would lack the instruments to detect these exotic things called electromagnetic signals.

Do we really imagine that ET life forms—who have evolved on different planets around distant suns—would really be using twentieth century human technologies? Could it be that—between the era of smoke signals and *something else*—the era of radio waves may be a very brief instant in time...a virtual fad, a fleeting ephemera?

CSETI has spent literally thousands of hours with thousands of people out under the stars observing phenomena which can only be described as extraordinary. And while we have some few interesting pictures and videotapes of craft appearing and disappearing from view, what has been really interesting could not have been videotaped or photographed—indeed the best of it perhaps could not have been measured at all.

This is because the really good stuff, if you will, has occurred just barely in what may be termed conventional reality. Much has happened on both sides of the crossing point of light—but the most interesting has been on the *other* side.

UFOs of ET origin simply are not using our current technologies—and if we try to detect and understand them purely from within the tidy box of current scientific knowledge, we are going to be sorely disappointed. Indeed, we will miss 99.9% of the data, and the discovery will be hidden by the fog in our own vision.

What will be presented in this paper will win us few friends. It will be protested as nonsense and it will raise many more questions than find answers. It will greatly disturb the status quo and upset the hidebound. It will be used as evidence that we have gone round the bend, as it were, and that the entire ET matter is just so much hogwash, and so on and so forth. It has been ever thus....

Nevertheless, while I have personally been extremely reluctant to put on paper what follows for reasons which will be obvious, it is equally true that this information is the crux of the mystery, and quite possibly the real lesson which the ET phenomenon has to teach us. It is all about going to the next step—in knowledge, in science, in truth and in personal experience.

The observations and hypothesis which follow will bring together the conventional empirical data of UFO reports with the more bizarre "high strangeness" experiences of many close encounters. Once a unified theory is understood which bridges matter and mind, machine and consciousness, the physical sciences with the emerging sciences of awareness and thought then and only then will the disparate and seemingly contradictory ET phenomena make some sense. We are stepping off into a terrain which is our future—and a hidden current reality, though it is largely unappreciated. Upon reading these pages one may be confused as to whether this information is science or spirituality or both or neither or....Choose your label as you need it and as it makes you comfortable. Truth is always beyond labels anyway.

There is no question that there are ET life forms which have found this planet and have been observed for decades near or on the Earth. Some think they have been around for hundreds of years, even millennia, and still others think they have been here for millions of years. What is certain is that they are here now. The evidence for this is overwhelming and will not be recounted here.

But consider these questions: How did they get here? How does one travel through vast interstellar distances and get someplace within a biological life form's natural life time? And how does one communicate through such vast distances in real time?

Consider: If an ET life form is from a star system 1000 light years away (that is the distance a beam of light travels in 1000 years while moving at a speed of 186,000 miles per second) it would take 1000 years for such a life form to get to Earth traveling at the speed of light! And another 1000 years to get home again. That is, traveling at the speed of light, it would take at least 2000 years to make a round trip journey. This is the time which has elapsed since the birth of Christ and it is very unlikely that one life form would live long enough to get here, never mind back home. And 1000 light years distance is in our relatively nearby galactic neighborhood.

Now lets consider communications. Using radio, microwave, TV or any other electromagnetic signal currently en vogue now on the Earth, it would take this ET 1000 years (at the speed of light which is how fast EM signals like radio waves travel) to communicate back home once he arrived here. And another 1000 years for the ET's home planet to answer back. Another 2000 years!

Obviously, any star-faring civilization, perforce, will have developed technologies which operate outside of the current twentieth century Earth gadgets in use today. Way outside, in fact. So far outside that an entire ET craft could (probably has) hovered right above the SETI radio survey project and they never "saw" it. Why? We were looking with the wrong instruments. We are trying to detect civilizations which are not human with strictly 20th century current technologies. But is there another way?

By definition, as you can see from the above analysis of the time delay in "speed of light" travel and communications systems, any ET civilization capable of getting here from interstellar space will be using technologies which bypass linear time/space as we know it. That is, they must drop out of linear time space reality and actuate communication and travel using technologies—and spectra of reality—way outside of the electromagnetic spectrum currently being used by Harvard and SETI to detect them.

Just as x-rays, gamma rays, UV radiation, infrared radiation, radio waves and the like existed *before* we had instruments to accurately measure them so too do spectra of reality utilized by advanced ETs. *That is, ETs are using aspects of the physical universe which are beyond current non-covert scientific instruments to adequately measure.*

Remember, we did not invent gamma rays just because we finally developed scientific instruments to detect them. Gamma rays existed for eons before we 'discovered' them. They existed, but since they were outside of the visible spectrum seen by the human eye, they were not perceived.

Similarly, the ETs are here, but usually exist in spectra of energy outside of current civilian instruments to measure them. Occasionally they pop through/into our measurable reality and end up being seen, photographed, land and even crash (or get shot down). They then will leave traces on a radar scope, or create a significant field flux in certain energy spectra, such as microwave, ultrasound and the like. But then they are gone. To....where? To...what? To...when?

Indeed, this is the real challenge. After 35 years of observing these objects at various times, I am convinced that through frequency shifts and very high energy physics, these objects and the life forms within them move between linear space time and other spectra of physical energy and physical reality outside of current detection capabilities. Some have called this inter-dimensional or multi-dimensional shifting, verbiage only useful once defined clearly. But once understood and experienced, you find that it is other dimensional in the same way gamma rays would have been supernatural to cavemen: in reality, all of these 'dimensions' are not so 'other' after all, but are part and parcel of this reality and folded away within it.

Unfortunately, some researchers have concluded that the UFOs are not ET but are rather inter-dimensional instead. It is quite clear to us from our own direct research that they are *both*.

That is, the nature of the ET reality is very much like our own—only they are using a bit of a wider spectrum of reality for travel, communication and related tasks. This wider spectrum crosses over into phenomena which some have termed inter-dimensional and the like, but in reality it is all present within this reality, only it is finer, more subtle and currently immeasurable by our scientific instruments in the civilian arena. (Covert programs do have such capabilities.)

To bring this discussion into focus and tangible reality, consider this account from a CSETI military witness.

One evening I got a phone call from a gentleman who had worked in the Air Force and also with Kelly Johnson at Lockheed Skunkworks. He had called ostensibly to offer to be one of the CSETI military witnesses to UFO events—but his larger purpose was to get my feedback on an experience which he had in the early to mid 1960s. At that time he was studying a tradition which helped people to have so-called out of body or astral projection experiences. This is when the subtle or astral body leaves the physical body and flies off somewhere. One day, his teacher told him that he was ready to have such an experience fairly soon, and that evening he indeed had his first OBE (out of body experience). But what happened really surprised him. After many disclaimers on his part to the effect that he was an altogether sane and rational person, and apologizing in advance for going into something so strange and bizarre, he related the following:

As soon as he left his physical body, he shot up through the ceiling of his house, into the space above—and then slammed into the side of an ET spacecraft hovering somewhere high in our atmosphere. As he did so, he literally rocked the spacecraft (remember this is in his astral body) and popped into the craft, whereupon he saw some ETs at a console who looked over at him, saw him, and had an expression as if to say, "My God, why don't you watch where you are going!"

I have no doubt that this man is telling me the absolute truth about what he experienced. I have no doubt whatsoever that he had an OBE, went out into the space above his house uncontrollably, and slammed into an actual ET craft—*which was hovering in an energy form closely akin to whatever energy form we are in when we have an OBE or a very lucid dream.*

He rocked the spacecraft with his astral body and the ETs inside saw him (and he saw them). Now consider: what form of energy was this military man in and what form were the ETs in? If the ETs were the same as an angel or a ghost or the like, why would they be in a technologically advanced spacecraft operating a computer console? Angels do not need computers....

Now, this man—who was very timid about relating this story to me because he thought that I would consider him a crack pot of some type—was surprised when I explained that this is a very common experience and went further to explain the nature of ET technologies as they function beyond the crossing point of light. That is, the spectrum or aspect of physical energy which ET craft and people are capable of shifting in and out of approximates what the mystics and ancient traditions would call the astral field or plane. That we cannot adequately detect and measure this component of reality is no reason to dismiss empirical observation and experience. After all, empirical observation and experience is the mother of all science. Remember Newton observing the apple falling from the tree.

But what is the connection between this so-called astral or etheric aspect and ET technologies? And why are they related at all?

To understand this we have to ask the question "What is beyond the crossing point of light?" That is, what is beyond the light barrier—what do you experience when you exceed the speed or vibration of light and electrons and even subatomic particles? What exists when you traverse that barrier and go beyond the speed of light and the frequency and energy of matter?

By definition any ET civilization which is here has interstellar travel and communications capabilities. This means that they operate on the *other* side of the light/matter barrier as easily as we use radio signals and fly on jets. This is their reality and world. This is their cell phone and automobile. This is their existence technologically, theoretically and every-day practically. But it sure looks like magic to us.

Consider this: When you traverse the veil of light, what do you find? What is beyond the crossing point of light? How do the physics work? What is space and time like? At that level, can we measure a thought and call it a thoughtron? Can mind and machine become integrated and operate seamlessly? What is life like there? What is experience like? How would we know that reality?

To begin to address these issues, however briefly, we must elucidate a cosmology which can accommodate the observed facts and experiences from both sides of the crossing point of light/matter. Here, I must digress into my own understanding of reality, inwardly and outwardly, and will ask for your patience in advance. This discussion will take us into areas which make many uncomfortable, especially those with scientific backgrounds or very conventional religious backgrounds. What I share here is admittedly from my own experience and background and so I ask your forbearance in considering the ideas and terminology which follows.

First, let me state my bias: That God exists and is omnipresent in every way imaginable. Now, this is quite counter to my up-bringing and training since I was raised a very devout atheist by parents who did not believe anything existed which could not be measured in a test tube. Nevertheless, my experience has shown otherwise and at any rate God exists whether we acknowledge Him or not...

Therefore, the cosmology which I present below factors into the equation the universal component of mind, which some may call the impersonal aspect of God. The Great Mind, the Universal Mind, the Pre-existent Mind, the Absolute.

As I have come to understand this cosmos, the basis of all existence—every atom, every star, every molecule and every person—is a *non-local essence which is present at every point in time and space and yet is bound by no point in space or time or matter.* This essence is awake, intelligent and knowing. It is conscious. It is mind. It is the awakeness of awareness, the undifferentiated pure intelligence and mind of the universe. It is present in every blade of grass and pervades the vacuum of space and the farthest reaches of the universe—and yet it cannot be divided or localized to one point in space or time or matter. That is, it is a unitive state, present always, but indivisible, and its effect is to create a oneness without the possibility of division. Its effect also, once recognized, is to make everything non-local, that is every point in space and time is a window, an entry point to every other point in space and time. The permeating, integrating aspect of this intelligent essence is such that all that exists is always connected and actually accessible through this non-local, integrated aspect of existence.

The structure of existence is that this non-local, conscious and intelligent component of existence is unchangeable and is unaffected by relativity or changes in space, time, matter and so forth. And yet paradoxically it is very present in every grain of sand and every galaxy - only in a form which is always one, indivisible and whole.

Through its organizing and integrating aspects, non-locality exists at the very local level, whether one considers the microscopic or macroscopic level of existence. That is, the cosmos is integrated in such a fashion that there is absolute integration at every level—and so the mystics were right when they said that one could behold the cosmos in a drop of water.

From this pre-existent, absolute field of intelligence and consciousness emerges all else. Again, paradoxically, the unified field of consciousness and intelligence, while indivisible, is present at every level, no matter how small or large. The Absolute remains the Absolute—and yet it is present in every quark—*but not bound or limited or divided by the quark.*

For this wonderful Nothingness (which is the fullness of absolute awareness) to give rise to the expressed cosmos, with all of its stars and galaxies and atoms and peoples, a creative process exists which is at once simple and elegantly complex. That is, from the plane of the Absolute—that pervasive, ever-present and indivisible state- creation comes forth and is maintained by what has been termed the Creator aspect of God. The critical elements of this process are will, the sound component of thought, then the visual component of thought and then the structural aspect of the astral world and then the matrix of the material world, expanding and encompassing the entirety of the universe.

The Creator aspect of the Absolute, through the operation of His Will, creates the cosmos from very subtle to very material as follows:

• The sound component of pure idea-forms/thought give rise to the aspect (you may think dimension if you must) of the universal which is the sound quality of the idea/thought for each and every created thing—whether an ant or a galaxy. Evolution and change occurs around and through the blue-print of this initial idea form of creation. The entirety of the cosmos exists as and through this sound component of thought. The essence of non-local, omnipresent mind/intelligence is present at this and every stage which follows. In some traditions, this idea/sound component or form of the entire universe and everything within it is called the 'causal or causative world'. In Biblical and other traditions I believe this is what is meant by the Word of God, 'In the beginning there was the Word...'.

• The sound/idea component of thought then gives rise to a less abstract but still very fine and subtle aspect which some have called 'astral' but which I prefer to regard as the conscious-intelligent visual

(CIV). This aspect, which has within it the blueprint causal or idea/ thought/ sound of the causal world, is more defined and is 'seen' or visible as expressed thought-related forms. It is vast and beautiful and many lucid dreams involve interactions with that realm or aspect. The military man who had the out of body experience had an astral or CIV body interaction with an ET craft, which was phase shifted primarily into this energy form or aspect (more on this later).

• Absolute, undifferentiated Mind, together with the causal idea/ sound/thought form and the CIV or astral form create a matrix which supports or gives rise to the so-called material universe. The blue-print, if you will, of ideas/thought/sound and subtle CIV form actually supports and helps create the more gross or expressed material universe. But the material universe has within it the unitive, indivisible Absolute mind, as well as the causal and CIV aspects. Indeed, each and every aspect of the expressed material universe which science can study and measure with current instruments has associated with it all of these finer aspects or spectra of energy. It is incorrect to regard, therefore, these aspects as purely distant 'other dimensions' since the warp and woof of the material cosmos is conscious, thought form based and has an astral or CIV matrix within it (or associated with it).

This rather brief and simple overview admittedly leaves out a number of details, best left to another treatment. However, it should be noted that at each level described above there are many gradations and expressions of detail. That is, the causal and CIV aspects have within them a multitude of differentiations, expressions and laws of function much like the material cosmos has fine sub-atomic particles and vast swirling galaxies and clusters of galaxies. Indeed, the details and laws affecting these vast realms dwarf those of the material cosmos and it is too obtuse a matter to elucidate in this paper.

The human being (and this would include other non-homo-sapiens higher intelligent life forms, i.e. ETs) has every aspect (or dimension) folded within him. Human consciousness, or spirit, is always connected, however unknowingly by the individual, to the Absolute conscious being. In fact, as mentioned earlier, consciousness or pure mind in its essential aspect is simply that whereby we are awake—or that whereby we are. It is a unitive state and is not divisible. It is always essentially one with the Absolute, but we are trained to see only multiplicity and separation. Thus individuation overwhelms the unitive state—and we think we are separate. It is a perceptual defect which the practices of all religions, in the form of rituals, prayer and meditation, attempt to correct.

An ancient Sufi tradition attributed to Ali states "Thinkest thyself a puny form when within thee the universe is folded?" This rhetorical question serves as a reminder of the holographic nature of mind and the human being's potential place in the universe: Through the experience of the non-local, omnipresent aspect of mind or consciousness, every aspect of the universe can be directly accessed and experienced. This is because the non-local aspect of consciousness is essential to awareness itself. It is always 'there' and need only be experienced.

This aspect or nature of mind is why people occasionally have spontaneous experiences of non-locality: They will have a dream and the next day, or the next year, the events perceived in the dream will unfold precisely as seen. How can this happen?

The nature of mind is that it is unitive, indivisible and present at every point in time and space—but bound or limited by no aspect of space or time. This means that both distant points in space and time can be accessed through this faculty. Human history is filled with such accounts, and while they are generally dismissed as curiosities by modern day science, in fact they hold the key to understanding the next great leap in scientific exploration: The study of consciousness and non-local reality.

In the lucid dream, the individual experiences increasing non-locality as the so-called astral or CIV aspect of the person awakens or perceives a distant point in space and/or time. This is less mysterious once we understand that mind or consciousness is always existing in its basic nature as a unitive state which transcends the limits of both time and space. Through it, any point in space and time can be accessed, at first one at a time. This should not be confused with the prerogatives and powers of God however. God, the Absolute universal mind, knows all things at all times and at all places, all at once, all of the time. But the individual person, through the faculties described above and by the very nature of the unitive state of mind which is essential to his basic awareness, can experience precognition, inspiration, intuition, remote viewing and the like.

Dr. Robert Jahn at Princeton University has studied another aspect of this non-locality of consciousness as it pertains to mechanical systems. The reader should study the results of these experiments which demonstrate that mind and thought, directed for example at a random number generator, can affect the outcome of the device. This can be accomplished because there is a nexus or link between awareness and matter: the warp and woof of matter is woven in with consciousness and in fact is simply mind-stuff expressed at a different frequency. Thus, an individual can affect his body, another person's health through prayer and visualization or even mechanical systems via thought and consciousness.

Dr. Larry Dossey and others have collected many interesting scientific studies which demonstrate this non-local nature of mind or of reality. The reader should study these for a fuller understanding. History is filled with accounts of such enigmas: the person in prayer who spontaneously levitates, the adept who can materialize or dematerialize objects or teleport objects across the room etc. While easy to dismiss as anecdotal or superstitious tales, the history of humanity as well as recent scientific experiments clearly establish that consciousness is non-local, can operate outside of time and space as we define it and can clearly affect distant inanimate objects or machines.

This is easily understood once the basic cosmology is appreciated: Consciousness is never divided, is present everywhere, is never limited by space or time and yet paradoxically is present at every point in space and time—in every atom and throughout every galaxy. Thus, the interface between consciousness and matter is essential, not contrived or difficult. Actuating events, then, becomes a matter of working in this nexus.

In previous papers I have discussed some of the unusual technological manifestations of ETs in recent times. Many of these aspects of ET activity get left out of reports or get suppressed even by main stream UFO organizations and researchers because they are so far out of the 'box' of conventional scientific norms. But it is precisely these unusual manifestations of ET technology which should interest us the most: They are the ones which will open the door to new understandings of the universe which make our current scientific knowledge look like kindergarten musings.

Back to the main problem: How are ET craft and personnel traversing the vastness of interstellar space and time? Well, it turns out that the rigidity of that vastness of space becomes quite flexible and can be largely bypassed once you frequency shift to the other side of the light barrier. In one quantum movement, the ET craft and all its occupants phase shift to a finer aspect of the cosmology outlined above, and exist then in an aspect or dimension which is more non-local than the material universe known to modern science. That is, the observed phenomenon of these objects which often seem to disappear and then reappear instantly at a considerable distance is due to the fact that they can phase shift in and out of the fixed time/space material aspect to one which is inherently more non-local. (Yes, non-locality is relatively relative.)

From what I have observed, this is done through very high energy physics and electronics which literally phase shift, in one quantum leap, the material ET craft and all its occupants into an aspect of the cosmology which closely approximates what was described above as astral or CIV. This is done through a complex interaction between powerful rotating electromagnetic fields and the gravitational field and mass inertia. When the craft is on this side of the crossing point of light, it is seen like any other material, manufactured object, but it can maneuver in ways which appear to negate mass inertia and gravity. Once it phase shifts onto the other side of the crossing point of light/ matter, it seems to disappear. But it has not. It is in that place beyond our SETI Beta radio wave survey—the place where our military contact bumped into them in his astral body!

While in that form or energy spectrum (or dimension) the craft can hover, or move within the material universe at many, many multiples of the speed of light. The velocity is non-relativistic, at least as measured on this side of the light barrier. However, 1000 light years will not be traversed instantly because there is an element of 'drag' as it moves in this aspect through the material cosmos. Put another way, there is a component of the object which adheres to the underbelly of the material cosmos and there is a coefficient of cosmic drag which prevents the transport from being instantaneous across vast interstellar distances. Operating, then, in a sort of 'junction' between aspects (or dimensions) the ET craft can phase between either. Actually, it can also be partially in both.

The spacecraft then can be hovering outside the SETI Institute—and remain undetected by them unless it pops into the material aspect fully and then only if the people in the building bother to look outside, see the device- and honestly report it.

Similarly, ET communications systems are ones which interface with mind, thought and computerized telemetry. For decades, people have reported having what has been dismissed as telepathic experiences with UFOs. As soon as such accounts are admitted to, the scientific community howls and tosses out the entire case. Alas, they have tossed out the baby and the bath water. As Dr. Jahn and Dr. Dossey and others have demonstrated, mind and thought can interface with and affect material—even technological—systems. What is obvious from 35 years of experience with this phenomenon is that ET communication protocols are not using AT&T microwave systems to communicate in real time through interstellar distances. This cannot be done. They are using computerized systems which are advanced enough to interact directly with thought and consciousness, and by so doing access non-local spectra of energy, thus bypassing linear time and space.

Literally thousands of people have had interactions with these objects which have a thought/matter or telepathic component to them. I feel that we dismiss such accounts at our peril, as we may be slamming the door on the next great science: the science of consciousness and its interface with material and technological systems.

Do not confuse these systems with current human experiments with brain wave activity and links to computers: those are still using electromagnetic energy which only travels at the speed of light. The ET systems referred to here operate on the other side of the crossing point of light and, while technologically facilitated, interface with thought and mind directly. Through such a system, information can be instantly transmitted through millions of light years of space since the non-local aspect of mind, thought and energy are being utilized. The communication systems do not have real time delays due to the coefficient of cosmic drag mentioned above.

Essentially, there are spectra of energy which are sub-electromagnetic and sub-material—but which are nevertheless very real and very physical. The use of the term meta-physical in relation to this area is very incorrect and time-restricted: A hologram or a flashlight would be metaphysical or supernatural to a human 500 years ago! This is a key point, that the energy and spectra of energy referred to here are naturally occurring aspects of the creation. They are all around us and within us. It is not "other." It is not supernatural. It is not metaphysical. It has simply not be studied and understood adequately by modern science—and it has been by advanced ET civilizations which are interstellar competent.

There are numerous accounts, dating back for decades, of very ordinary humans seeing one of these ET craft and directly interacting with it *by thought alone*. That is, the person may think 'Oh, I wish it would move to the right' and the craft will move to the right, or as it starts to leave he may think, 'I wish it would turn around and come back' whereupon it immediately stops, turns and comes over. A few such accounts may be dismissed as coincidence. But there are so many of them that empirically one must reach the assessment that these objects have telemetry capabilities which can interface with directed thought.

As I have written elsewhere, this class of ET technologies may be viewed generally as consciousness assisted technologies (CAT) and technology assisted consciousness (TAC). That is, their technologies utilize that nexus referred to above where mind/conscious thought interface technologically and reproducibly with matter, machine, communication devices etc. CAT is when the individual (or group) consciousness and thought assists or interfaces with a receptive device. TAC is when a device augments, projects or assists an individual or group's consciousness or thought.

For example, CSETI has located a former Bell Labs/Lucent Technologies scientist who, more than 35 years ago, while working on a covert research project, was given an ET communication device by a general. This scientist was asked to study and reverse engineer the device—that is, take it apart and figure out how it worked. Here is his story.

Upon receiving the device, which was a round object about the size of a grapefruit, dark and textured on the surface, it began to 'speak' to him directly in his awareness with thought. He was startled by this—especially when the device mentally told him that the people who had asked him to study the object had malice in their hearts and that the scientist should destroy the device!

After struggling with what to do about this conundrum, the scientist 'accidentally' over-heated the device in an experiment and it was destroyed (at least materially). But after it was destroyed, he heard one last thought which said 'Thank you...'.

I know that this sounds very strange. But the strangest things are true, and this account is one of those very strange but true accounts. We may wish to run at light away speed from such information—and go back to our radio signals. But the future is here and if we do not meet it wisely others—like the general who originally provided the device—will hijack the future to places where we do not want to go.

Over the past 8 years, CSETI has gone all over the world pursuing this phenomenon and observing its manifestations. Others are better at photography, landing traces and the like. There are dozens of day light photographs of these devices. There is radar evidence. There are over 4000 landing traces documented by Ted Phillips. Dr. Richard Haines has hundreds of pilot accounts of these objects.

Our purpose has been to interact with these ETs on *their* level. To consider what their reality is and to go there. It is an experiment and an experience. It has been mind-blowing for all concerned.

Over these 8 years we have had experiences and seen phenomena which involve every aspect of what has been described qualitatively in this paper. A brief listing of this phenomena follows:

• RV x 2. (See CSETI training materials) Our experiment, the CE-5 Initiative, involves numerous protocols, some obvious and practical, some very experimental and immensely controversial. One of the controversial protocols involves group access to non-local consciousness followed by remotely viewing (through consciousness) ET craft or persons which may be at a great distance or which may be nearby and phase—shifted beyond the visible spectrum of human sight. Once an object or person is 'locked on' and viewed, the process is reversed and the object or person is directed to the CSETI research site via CIV / visual thought component vectoring. That is, the ET object/person is shown clearly our coordinates and location via the CIV component discussed earlier. The CSETI research experiment in this protocol attempts to RV (remote view via consciousness) the ET object, connect to its CAT telemetry system and vector or guide the object to our exact location. Essentially, we are doing in a dynamic, applied setting what Dr. Jahn is doing at the Princeton PEAR lab experimentally: Connecting clearly directed conscious- visual thought to ET communications devices and attempt to do so with adequate precision so that they see us and we see them, and a trajectory is established for contact.

I am quite aware how ridiculous this may seem to some. But this is an experiment which not infrequently results in a object popping in over head—or more. While using lights, lasers and radio signals to vector and confirm contact, the core of the protocol does involve CAT (and often in response from the ETs TAC—see below).

Key to RV x 2 are the following components:

1. Human access to the non-local component of consciousness

2. Remote viewing of ET objects or persons with accuracy

3. Connecting to ET CAT communication systems while in the CIV mode of awareness

4. Clearly vectoring (guiding) the ET object into the research site area through sequential and coherent visual thought which shows the site from deep space down to the specific details of the site.

5. RV'ing the response if any from the ETs prior to appearance (interactive RV mode)

The entire protocol is done with the clear intent to establish peaceful contact and relations with these life forms.

During RV x 2 often more than one person will 'lock on' to the same object or life form and receive the same information regarding its location and/or time and place of appearance. This information is regarded as unconfirmed unless an actual event seen by the group confirms it.

As a result, during these experiments around the world, we have had the following general types of experiences which demonstrate the technologies referred to earlier:

• Sudden appearance of large structured craft (discs, triangles etc.) which 'pop in' and then vanish in seconds and even a fraction of a second, but which is witnessed by multiple people

• Longer term appearance of objects, up to many minutes, which then disappear (phase shift out of visible/material perception)

• Intelligent probes consisting of ball shaped objects, of various colors, which come over and even within the group and which are not only intelligently controlled, but are themselves conscious and intelligent (advance AI—artificial intelligence). Usually these are translucent to slightly opaque red, blue, green or golden spheres ranging in size from 6 inches to 1-2 feet. They interact consciously with the individual or group and then vanish. They are most likely demonstrations of TAC where the consciousness and thought (even personality) of an ET on board a craft is technologically assisted and projected in a controlled fashion into the group.

• Anomalous beeping or high pitched tones which have an omnidirectional component, as if heard from all directions at once. Often these occur after projecting over radio waves the CSETI beeping tones which are routinely transmitted from the site.

• Anomalous electromagnetic effects (EM) on equipment, cars etc. Often, equipment will fail with a close approach of an ET craft, as happened in Mexico in 1993 when an 800 foot diameter silent triangle approached the group and all camera and other electronic equipment failed. Other manifestations include setting off radar detectors, laser detectors, car electronics dimming down or browning out, electrostatic energy on peoples' skin or clothing. On multiple occasions my compass has rotated counter-clockwise around the dial as a counter-clockwise rotating craft has approached. During one CIV/Material interface case (see below) the compass changed magnetic north to almost due south (off 160°) and remained that way for nearly 3 months. It now works perfectly fine (until the next very close encounter!)

• Fast-walker interactions. Frequently, after RV x 2, the group will experience multiple objects which initially appear to be satellites—but which interact with directed thoughts or signals. For example, a high flying object will, as soon as a thought command is given, stop or change directions abruptly. Satellites do not back up, make right hand turns or descend suddenly and get brighter while interacting with people on the ground. These types of events have been witnessed by dozens of people during multiple CSETI research events.

• CIV/Material interface phenomena. This is a broad category of phenomena when ET objects are just on the other side of the crossing point of light and matter—and begin to "bleed through" to this aspect or dimension. Frequently the team will observe sudden strobe-like light discharges all around us. These are not retinal firings from the eye since multiple people see them at the same instance. Subsequently, the form of an ET craft or even individual will appear faintly and then will form -as if some type of shimmering electronic hologram. These have appeared within the group itself or within a few feet from the group. During such very close encounters there are often multiple phenomena occurring: RV'ing of objects along with visual perception of scintillating craft or people, AI probes coming into the group and anomalous sounds being experienced. Not infrequently, participants will report being touched by someone, but when they look only a faint shimmering glow is seen. During prolonged events of this type, an unusual time/space dilation or contraction will occur: time seems to stand still—or proceed very quickly and the space around the group becomes more defined. These types of encounters have had durations of over 2 hours or may be very fleeting. In England in 1998, near Alton Barnes, after first seeing a very large circular craft on separate nights which would pop in and disappear in seconds, the group had the same object descend around them in a scintillating, sparkling form complete with discreet areas of ET life forms seen shimmering, spaced between each person in the group! The temperature of the setting raised at least 10-15° Fahrenheit. All participants saw the object and the life forms. None of them were fully "hard" material, but rather remained only partly in this dimension.

In 1997, while in England on a training expedition, my trusted colleague Shari Adamiak and I were upstairs in a room in the manor house which we had leased. The remainder of the team, about 6 people, were out on the manor grounds. Suddenly, I saw a blue white light or object fly through the closed window and into the room. It hovered over by the fireplace and then expanded to become a shimmering ET about 3 feet tall, as if a subtle electronic hologram had appeared. It was conscious and sentient. It was just barely material and visible, but clearly so. This was an AI projection of the consciousness and CIV/astral form of an ET which had been projected into the room. What the other team members saw from outside (they were not initially aware that we were in that room and did not learn of our experience until the following morning) was a blue white object swooping down from the sky and flying into the window of the room where we were located. They all saw this object, but were unaware of the further experiences which Shari and I had with the person. This is another good example of TAC.

• Lucid dream state interaction with ET craft and / or persons. Because the ET technological reality allows them to move seamlessly between the CIV dimension and this material one, and since their communications systems *prefer* CIV transmission modes, frequently individuals (and sometimes more than one individual) will have a detailed interaction during the dream state. Remember that the CIV/astral component and technologies which interface with that energy spectrum allow for easy interface with the dream state since the lucid dream state is the activation of the CIV/astral body or component of an individual. ETs can interface as easily with that aspect as we pick up a phone and call New York. It is my opinion that the most common way in which ETs have interacted with individual humans is in lucid dreams and not material contact (bodily contact). While material contact has occurred, it is risky and unnecessary once these more subtle technologies are mastered and understood. Once it is appreciated that the CIV/astral spectrum is the preferred field through which ETs must pass for interstellar communication and travel—and that it is the same spectrum activated or used in a lucid dream—it is easy to see why so many people report this type of experience. The RV x 2 protocol described above is a conscious activation of expanded awareness and CIV component to deliberately interface with ET technologies and individuals.

• ET craft transfer through solid matter. On more that one occasion we have observed solid appearing ET objects or craft (daytime sightings with the sun shining off the metal surface) pass directly into a mountain without crashing. This is accomplished by a frequency shift in the material of the craft so that it can mesh or pass through matter of traditional density without actually affecting either. That is, a frequency phase shift allows one solid object to pass through another without interacting. Remember that most of what we call 'solid matter' is not solid at all—it is mostly space (or something—hint: see the cosmology outlined above). This phenomenon has been reported for decades and has caused some to dismiss such accounts as 'ghost-like' or poltergeist. Actually, it is only another expression of ET technologies operating on a more profound or subtle level of existence which can alter the frequency of matter (they can also alter time/space relationships as well through similar means). I should also point out that covert military sources known by me personally have testified to the fact that at least by 1953 human secret projects were materializing and dematerializing objects and transferring them across defined spaces. If we were doing this covertly by 1953, one can only imagine what advance interstellar ET technologies can achieve.

This list could go on much further but what is described above should give the reader a sense of how unusual manifestations of ET technology may be. From the above, it is easy to understand why ET events can be confused with phenomena which originate from the CIV/astral or causal level, that is are not ET but have components of the same manifestations. No wonder the literature is filled with confusing accounts of ETs, angels, ghosts and strange phenomena of all stripes, all lumped in together. Of course, modern man would look like something supernatural to people a few hundred years ago: imagine showing up at a church meeting in Salem Massachusetts in 1692 with a cell phone, a hologram, a satellite TV and a Range Rover. You would be burned at the stake as a witch forthwith!

Still, it is important to keep in mind that the cosmos contains many levels of existence. There are CIV/astral and causal worlds and beings which are not ET. And yet there are ETs which some or much of the time interface with and utilize aspects of the physical cosmos which are in those subtle realms. (See "Extraterrestrials And The New Cosmology" on page 64.)

It should also be remembered that not all ETs may be so advanced. Given the billions of galaxies each with billions of stars, it is likely that some ETs are the equivalent of human cave men while others may be at our level of evolution and yet others are millions of years more advanced than we are today. For those at the SETI Institute, may you find those ETs which are at our level and which are primarily still using linear radio wave technologies. Odds are, there are some out there.

But know this: ETs far advanced beyond radio signals and internal combustion engines do exist. They are here. They may be all around us. Let us open our minds and our eyes to the extraordinary opportunity that hovers right in front of us. For most of what *is* exists beyond the veil—through the crossing point of light. And it awaits our exploration.

14

Nonlocal Mind/ Unbounded Consciousness

March, 1994

Associated Experiences, Abilities and Levels of Consciousness

Levels of Consciousness:

I. Pure Unbounded Consciousness/ Pure Nonlocal Mind, experience in its fullness—smadhi, "the beatific state," etc.

II Cosmic Consciousness" = Pure Unbounded Consciousness while yet awake, or even in sleep and with dreams, the first "higher state of consciousness"

III "God Consciousness" as with Cosmic Consciousness, but perception is broadened to include "celestial perception," perception of finest aspects of relative creation

IV. Unity Consciousness—as in God Consciousness above, but perception extends to the realization of Unbounded Mind in / through/as every aspect of relative existence.

(And it goes on from there....)

Experiences Along the Journey which naturally develop and which appear at various points for each individual:

- Telepathy
- Precognition
- Lucid Dreams
- Precognitive Dreams
- Remote Viewing (while awake or in dream state)[1]
- Telekinesis
- Teleportation

- Transmutation
- Healing Abilities (remote and in-person)
- Celestial Perception (of fine aspects of reality, "angels," etc.)
- Levitation (of self or objects)
- Out of Body Experiences
- Materialization/Dematerialization
- Bi-Location
- and other TNTC (too numerous to count)

Every higher, intelligent life form is potentially capable of having all of the above experiences; this includes human and other higher life forms which have evolved on other planets. the only prerequisite is to be able to be aware of awareness itself. If you can be aware of awareness, then you can be aware of awareness in its non-local, unbounded form. It is likely that the state of consciousness, in all of its aspects and manifestations, will be the great focus of study and science in the coming centuries. consciousness is the integrating thread, the highest common denominator, and real foundation of interplanetary unity.

Categories of Unconventional Experiences

In order to understand unconventional or anomalous experiences, and to avoid confusion and the mixing of apples and star dust, it is useful to have a working cosmology. Here we must see that people describe many types of phenomena, not just one phenomenon, and yet maintain a deeper realization of the deeper, essential until of reality. Note in particular the categories where overlap potential exists, and where, therefore, discernment is especially needed.

Interaction with/perceptions of:

Biological ET Life Forms (ETLF) ("People" from other planets)

Remote Viewing Experiences:

- of ETLF or
- of non-biological entities (see below) or

1. Remote Viewing: The ability to "see" via non-local mind, events, places, people regardless of space or time; by accessing non-local mind, you can "see" any place in any point in time (past, present, or future). By definition, non-local mind is not bound by time or space Once this is understood, anyone becomes proficient at accessing the aspect of one's consciousness which is non—local, then the extraordinary slowly becomes routine, and all things are possible.

- of other human elsewhere located on Earth

Non-biological Entities/Beings

- "Astral" or Light Beings
- 1. of Earth origin ("deceased" previously biological humans)
- 2. of non-Earth origin
  - a. "deceased" ETLF
  - b. astral or causal realm originations
- Personal "spirit guides" or angels
- "Ascended Enlightened Beings, "Masters and "Avatars"
- Earth or nature devas/spirits (plant, animal mineral, other
- Other planetary nature spirits/ devas, as above
- Other (probably too numerous to count)

OBE's (Out of Body Experiences) with any of the above, including ETLF

NDE's (near death experiences) with any of the above, including ETLF

Intra-psychic/psychological experiences: Drug-induced hallucination, Delusions, Psychosis, Confabulation/ "Wannabees"/ Fantasy prone personalities/ Hoaxes, false memory syndrome,

Post-Traumatic Stress Syndrome, and others

CSETI studies ETLF in all of their aspects or manifestations, but we do not deny the existence or reality of other beings.

Part II

The Evidence and the CE-5 Initiative

In this section an overview of the evidence is presented, followed by a description of the CSETI CE-5 Initiative, which began in 1990.

I owe a great debt of gratitude to my late trusted assistant Shari Adamiak who spent some of her last days on Earth compiling the case evidence and writing the clear summaries presented here. Thank you Shari. Thank you.

The reader must know that the evidence here presented is just the tiniest tip of the iceberg—there are over 4000 landing trace cases where these UFOs have left physical evidence; over 3500 military and civilian aircraft pilot cases, many with radar confirmation; there are over 500,000 cases in the UFOCAT computer system; and there are hundreds of photographs and videos of these objects, many in broad daylight which have been authenticated by scientists as real, and not hoaxes. As the late Dr. J. Allen Hynek said, it is really an embarrassment of riches, and what we present here is only a glimmer of the vast amounts of evidence which exists on this subject.

I recommend the reader obtain the following books for a further treatment of the evidence: *Above Top Secret* by Timothy Good; *Unconventional Flying Objects*, by Paul Hill, *CE-5* By Dr. Richard Haines; *Night Siege* by Dr. J. Allen Hynek and Philip Imbrogno; *The Day After Roswell*, By Col. Philip Corso.

The Close Encounters of the Fifth Kind Initiative (CE-5 Initiative) is really a prototype hybrid project which has both scientific research and diplomatic, inter-species relations components.

That is, in the CE-5 Initiative we have endeavored to combine real—time field research on the UFO / ET question with a clear intent to establish inter-active communication and peaceful relations with these visitors from beyond.

We can only say that this experiment has been a prototype of what the world should have been doing since the 1940s: A conscious, open effort to study the ET presence in a setting which is peaceful and which has as its over-arching goal the establishment of peaceful, sustainable relations with all such life forms visiting this planet.

Alas, we have never been funded to properly carry out such an ambitious undertaking: These efforts have been at the expense of each person involved. People like Shari Adamiak and dozens of others who have taken time away from work and family to respond to the ET presence throughout the world. Such progress has been made only by the huge sacrifice of such people—a sincere and humble attempt to do what the giants of world government have failed to do: Extend the hand of peace and recognition to these visitors from other worlds.

At the end of this section you will find the draft of a grant to professionally do what so far has been only an ad hoc voluntary effort. We estimate that this undertaking—which envisions multiple rapid response and diplomatic teams deployed throughout the world to respond to ET events—will cost around $10 million over a three-year period. A small price for the beginning of inter-planetary peace and diplomatic relations in a theater heretofore relegated to the black world of covert military operations—or the back page of the tabloids. We invite your help and participation.

It is time that the people of the world show by their example how the governments of the world should respond to the ET presence. Not down the barrel of a laser weapon but by extending the hand of peace and understanding. If we do not do this, who will? The time has come for universal peace, but it will arrive only when we *show* that we are ready to receive it.

15

Quotations On UFOs And Extraterrestrial Intelligence

Section I: The Scientists

Note: Please see "Sources" on page 116 for sources of quotations.

Carl Sagan, Ph.D.

Late Professor of Astronomy and Space Sciences, Cornell University

"It now seems quite clear that Earth is not the only inhabited planet. There is evidence that the bulk of the stars in the sky have planetary systems. Recent research concerning the origin of life on Earth suggests that the physical and chemical processes leading to the origin of life occur rapidly in the early history of the majority of planets within our Milky Way galaxy—perhaps as many as a million—are inhabited by technical civilizations in advance of our own. Interstellar space flight is far beyond our present technical capabilities, but there seems to be no fundamental physical objections to preclude, from our own vantage point, the possibility of its development by other civilizations."[1]

Margaret Mead, Ph.D.

Anthropologist, author

"There *are* unidentified flying objects. That is, there are a hard core of cases—perhaps 20 to 30 percent in different studies—for which there is no explanation... We can only imagine what purpose lies behind the activities of these quiet, harmlessly cruising objects that time and again approach the Earth. The most likely explanation, it seems to me, is that they are simply watching what we are up to..."[2]

J. Allen Hynek, Ph.D.

Former Chairman, Department of Astronomy, Northwestern University; Scientific Consultant, Air Force Project Blue Book (1947 - 1969)

> "Each wave of sightings adds to the accumulation of reports which defy analysis by present methods... An investigative process in depth is necessary here if, after twenty years of confusion, we want some answers."
>
> "When the long awaited solution to the UFO problem comes, I believe that it will prove to be not merely the next small step in the march of science but a mighty and totally unexpected quantum jump."[3]

Frank B. Salisbury, Ph.D.

Professor, Plant Physiology, Utah State University

> "I must admit that any favorable mention of the flying saucers by a scientist amounts to extreme heresy and places the one making the statement in danger of excommunication by the scientific theocracy. Nevertheless, in recent years I have investigated the story of the unidentified flying object (UFO), and I am no longer able to dismiss the idea lightly."[4]

James E. McDonald, Ph.D.

Senior Physicist, Institute of Atmospheric Physics, University of Arizona

> "The type of UFO reports that are most intriguing are close-range sightings of machinelike objects of unconventional nature and unconventional performance characteristics, seen at low altitudes, and sometimes even on the ground. The general public is entirely unaware of the large number of such reports that are coming from credible witnesses... When one starts searching for such cases, their number are quite astonishing."[5]

American Institute of Aeronautics and Astronautics UFO Subcommittee (1967)

> "From a scientific and engineering standpoint, it is unacceptable to simply ignore substantial numbers of unexplained obser-

vations...the only promising approach is a continuing moderate-level effort with emphasis on improved data collection and objective means...*involving available remote sensing capabilities* and certain software changes."[6] [emphasis added]

and regarding *The Condon Report* (Project Blue Book), 1986:

"The opposite conclusion could have been drawn from *The Condon Report*'s content; namely, that a phenomenon with such a high ratio of unexplained cases (about 30 percent) should arouse sufficient scientific curiosity to continue its study."[6]

Peter A. Sturrock, Ph.D.

Professor, Space Science and Astrophysics, and deputy director of the Center for Space Sciences and Astrophysics, Stanford University

"The definitive resolution of the UFO enigma will not come about unless and until the problem is subjected to open and extensive scientific study by the normal procedures of established science and administrators in universities."[7]

"Although...the scientific community has tended to minimize the significance of the UFO phenomenon, certain individual scientists have argued that the phenomenon is both real and significant... To a scientist, the main source of hard information (other than his own experiments [and] observations) is provided by the scientific journals. With rare exceptions, scientific journals do not publish reports of UFO observations. The decision not to publish is made by the editor acting on the advice of reviewers. This process is self-reinforcing; the apparent lack of data confirms the view that there is nothing to the UFO phenomenon, and this view works against the presentation of relevant data..."[7]

Helmut Lammer, Ph.D.

Physicist, Space Research Institute, Department for Extraterrestrial Physics, Austria

[Writing about the formations in the Cydonia region of Mars]

"It is the author's belief that the Viking data are not of sufficient resolution to permit the identification of possible mechanisms of the origin for these objects, although some results to date suggest that they may not be natural. Clearly these mysterious objects deserve further scrutiny by the forthcoming Mars missions. If one of these missions finds that the face on Mars, the pyramids and the other strange structures are indeed artificial, then the "unlikely" Prior Colonization or Previous Technical Civilization hypotheses would provide a possible answer." 8

Professor Hermann Oberth *(1894-1989)*

German rocket expert and a founding father of the space age.

"It is my thesis that flying saucers are real and that they are space ships from another solar system. I think that they possibly are manned by intelligent observers who are members of a race that may have been investigating our Earth for centuries. I think that they possibly have been sent out to conduct systematic, long-range investigations, first of men, animals, vegetation, and more recently of atomic centers, armaments and centers of armament production."[9]

Dr. Carl Justav Jung

"A purely psychological explanation is ruled out...the discs show signs of intelligent guidance, by quasi-human pilots...the authorities in possession of important information should not hesitate to enlighten the public as soon and as completely as possible."[10]

Section II: The Government Speaks—

Political, Military And Intelligence Figures

President Harry S. Truman

"I can assure you that flying saucers, given that they exist, are not constructed by any power on Earth."[11]

President Dwight D. Eisenhower

"Beware the military-industrial complex."[12]

President Gerald Ford

"...I have taken a special interest in these [UFO] accounts because many of the latest reported sightings have been in my home state of Michigan... Because I think there may be substance to some of these reports and because I believe the American people are entitled to a more thorough explanation than has been given them by the Air Force to date, I am proposing that either the Science and Astronautics Committee or the Armed Services Committee of the House, schedule hearings on the subject of UFOs and invite testimony from both the executive branch of the Government and some of the persons who claim to have seen UFOs... In the firm belief that the American public deserves a better explanation than that thus far given by the Air Force, I strongly recommend that there be a committee investigation of the UFO phenomena. I think we owe it to the people to establish credibility regarding UFOs and to produce the greatest possible enlightenment on this subject."[13]

President Jimmy Carter

"If I become President, I'll make every piece of information this country has about UFO sightings available to the public, and the scientists. I am convinced that UFOs exist because I've seen one..."[14]

President Ronald Reagan

"...when you stop to think that we're all God's children, wherever we may live in the world, I couldn't help but say to [Gorbachev], just think how easy his task and mine might be in these meetings that we held if suddenly there was a threat to this world from some other species from another planet outside in the universe..."[15]

"Perhaps we need some outside, universal threat to make us recognize this common bond. I occasionally think how quickly our differences worldwide would vanish if we were facing an alien threat from outside this world."[15]

J. Edgar Hoover

"I would do it [study UFOs], but before agreeing to do it, we must insist upon full access to discs recovered. For instance in the L.A. case, the Army grabbed it and would not let us have it for cursory examination."[16]

General Nathan D. Twining

"a.The phenomena reported is something real and not visionary or fictitious.

b.There are objects probably approximating the shape of a disc, of such appreciable size as to appear to be as large as a man-made aircraft.

c.There is a possibility that some of the incidents may be caused by natural phenomena, such as meteors.

d.The reported operating characteristics such as extreme rates of climb, maneuverability (particularly in roll), and action which must be considered evasive when sighted or contacted by friendly aircraft and radar, lend belief to the possibility that some of the objects are controlled either manually, automatically, or remotely."[17]

General Walter Bedell Smith

CIA Director, 1950–1953

"The Central Intelligence Agency has reviewed the current situation concerning unidentified flying objects which have created extensive speculation in the press and have been the subject of concern to government organizations... Since 1947, approximately 2,000 official reports of sightings have been received, and, of these, about 20% are as yet unexplained. It is my view that this situation has possible implications for our national security which transcend the interests of a single service. A broader, coordinated effort should be initiated to develop a firm scientific understanding of the several phenomena which apparently are involved in these reports..."[18]

H. Marshall Chadwell

Assistant Director, Scientific Intelligence, CIA

"Since 1947, ATIC has received approximately 1500 *official* reports of sightings plus an enormous volume of letters, phone calls, and press reports. During July 1952 alone, *official* reports totaled 250. Of the 1500 reports, Air Force carries 20 percent as *unexplained* and of those received from January through July 1952 it carries 28 percent *unexplained.*[19] [emphasis in original]

Captain Edward J. Ruppelt

Former head [1951-1953], U.S. Air Force Project Blue Book

"This report has been difficult to write because it involves something that doesn't officially exist. It is well known that ever since the first flying saucer was reported in June 1947 the Air Force has officially said that there is no proof that such a thing as an interplanetary spaceship exists. But what is not well known is that this conclusion is far from being unanimous among the military and their scientific advisors because of the one word, *proof*; so the UFO investigations continue."[20] [emphasis in original]

Admiral Roscoe Hillenkoetter

First Director, CIA, 1947-1950

"It is time for the truth to be brought out... Behind the scenes, high-ranking Air Force officers are soberly concerned about the UFOs. But through official secrecy and ridicule, many citizens are led to believe the unknown flying objects are nonsense... I urge immediate Congressional action to reduce the dangers from secrecy about Unidentified Flying Objects..."[21]

Major General E. B. LeBailly

Director of Information, office of the Secretary of the Air Force

"...many of the reports that cannot be explained have come from intelligent and technically well qualified individuals whose integrity cannot be doubted. In addition, the reports received officially by the Air Force include only a fraction of the spectacular reports which are publicized by many private UFO organizations."[22]

Congressman William Stanton

Pennsylvania

"The Air Force failed in its responsibility in thoroughly investigating this incident [April 17, 1966 sighting, Pennsylvania]...

> Once people entrusted with the public welfare no longer think people can handle the truth, then the people, in turn, will no longer trust the government."[23]

Wilbert Smith

Department of Transport—Canada, senior radio engineer, head of Project Magnet

> "The matter is the most highly classified subject in the United States Government, rating higher even than the H-bomb. Flying saucers exist. Their modus operandi is unknown but concentrated effort is being made by a small group headed by Doctor Vannevar Bush. The entire matter is considered by the United States authorities to be of tremendous significance."[24]

Lord Hill-Norton,

Admiral of the Fleet, Great Britain (Five Star)

> "I have frequently been asked why I am so keenly interested in UFOs; people seem to think it odd that someone who has been so closely involved with Defense for many years should be so simple. I am interested for several reasons. First, I have the sort of inquiring mind that likes to have things satisfactorily explained, and the one aspect of this whole matter which is starkly clear to me is that UFOS have *not* been explained, to *my* satisfaction. Indeed, so far as I am concerned the U stands more for un*explained* than un*identified.* Second, there is a very wide range of other unexplained phenomena which may or may not be related to UFOs but which have come to my notice in the UFO connection. Third, I am convinced that there is an official cover-up of the investigations which governments have made into UFOs, certainly in the United States... The evidence that there are objects which have been seen in our atmosphere, and even on terra firma, that cannot be accounted for either as man-made objects or as any physical force or effect known to our scientists seems to me to be overwhelming."[25] [emphasis in original]

Major-General Wilfred de Brouwer

Deputy Chief, Royal Belgian Air Force

"In any case, the Air Force has arrived to the conclusion that a certain number of anomalous phenomena have been produced within Belgian airspace... Until now, not a single trace of aggressiveness has been signalled; military or civilian air traffic has not been perturbed or threatened. We can therefore advance that the presumed activities to date constitute a concrete menace... The day will undoubtedly come when the phenomenon will be observed with technological means of detection and collection that won't leave a single doubt about its origin..."[26]

Section III: The Astronauts

Gordon Cooper, *Astronaut*

"I believe that these extraterrestrial vehicles and their crews are visiting this planet from other planets, which are a little more technically advanced than we are on Earth. I feel that we need to have a top level, coordinated program to scientifically collect and analyze data from all over the Earth concerning any type of encounter, and to determine how best to interfere with these visitors in a friendly fashion.

We may first have to show them that we have learned how to resolve our problems by peaceful means rather than warfare, before we are accepted as fully qualified universal team members. Their acceptance will have tremendous possibilities of advancing our world in all areas."[27]

Edgar Mitchell, *Astronaut, Apollo 14, walked on the moon.*

"We all know that UFOs are real. All we need to ask is where do they come from."

Space Shuttle Discovery, *March 1, 1989 - 03/14/89 ES*

"Uh Houston, this is Discovery. We still have the alien spacecraft under (observance)"?? (note last word difficult to make out on tape.)[28]

The previous statement was recorded by Baltimore resident Donald Ratsch from a HAM radio rebroadcast between the space shuttle Discovery and Houston ground control. The HAM broadcast was direct from the shuttle without going through the delayed filter used on the official NASA public fee. The

NASA select audio channel did not contain this one way broadcast from the shuttle to ground control. The HAM station making the rebroadcast was WA3NAN Goddard Amateur Radio Club in Greenbelt, MD, transmitting on 147.450 MHZ. Preliminary analysis shows that the voice could be either Michael Coats (Commander) or John E. Blaha pilot). The recording was sent for further expert voice analysis the results of which are unknown at this time to the author.

Sources

Section I - The Scientists

1. Sagan, Carl: "Unidentified Flying Objects", *The Encyclopedia Americana*, 1963.
2. Mead, Margaret: "UFOs—Visitors from Outer Space?", *Redbook*, Vol. 143, September 1974.
3. Hynek, J. Allen: From interview in *The Chicago Sun Times*, August 28, 1966;
   The UFO Experience: A Scientific Inquiry, Regnery Co., 1972.
4. Salisbury, Frank B.: Fuller, John G., *Incident at Exeter*, Putnam, 1966 (quoting a paper presented at the U.S. Air Force Academy in Colorado in May 1964.)
5. McDonald, James E.: "Symposium on Unidentified Flying Objects", *Hearings before the Committee on Science and Astronautics, U.S. House of Representatives*, July 1968.
6. American Institute of Aeronautics and Astronautics, UFO Subcommittee (1967), *The Encyclopedia of UFOs*, 1980.
7. Sturrock, Peter A.: "An Analysis of the Condon Report on the Colorado UFO Project", *Journal of Scientific Exploration*, Vol. 1, No. 1, 1987.
8. Lammer, Helmut: "Atmospheric Mass Loss on Mars and the Consequences for the Cydonian Hypothesis and Early Martian Life Forms", *Journal of Scientific Exploration*, Vol. 10, No. 3, 1996.
9. Oberth, Hermann: "Flying Saucers Come From a Distant World", *The American Weekly*, October 24, 1954.
10. Jung, Carl: *Flying Saucers: A Modern Myth of Things Seen in the Sky* (R.F.C. Hull translation), 1959.

Section II - The Government

11. Truman, Harry: White House press conference, April 4, 1950.

12. Eisenhower, Dwight: Last speech as President, January 1961.
13. Ford, Gerald: Letter to L. Mendel Rivers, Chairman of the Armed Services Committee, March 28, 1966.
14. Carter, Jimmy: *The National Enquirer*, June 8, 1976; confirmed by White House media liaison Jim Purks, in a letter April 20, 1979.
15. Reagan, Ronald: 1) White House transcript of speech at Fallston High School, December 4, 1985; 2) Speech to the United Nations General Assembly, September 21, 1987.)
16. Hoover, J. Edgar: Letter to Clyde Tolson, July 15, 1947.
17. Twining, Nathan: Letter to Commanding General of the Army, September 23, 1947.
18. Smith, Walter: Memorandum to National Security Council, 1952.
19. Chadwell, H. Marshall: Memorándum to Director of Central Intelligence, 1952.
20. Ruppelt, Edward: *The Report on Unidentified Flying Objects*, Ruppelt, Doubleday, New York, 1956.
21. Hillenkoetter, Roscoe: *Aliens from Space*, Maj. Donald E. Keyhoe, 1975.
22. LeBailly, E.B.: "Unidentified Flying Objects" (No. 55); hearing by Committee on Armed Services, House of Representatives, April 5, 1966.
23. Stanton, William: Quoted in *Ravenna Record-Courier*, Pennsylvania, April 1966, cited in *Mysteries of the Skies*, Lore and Deneault, Prentice-Hall, 1968.
24. Smith, Wilbert: Memorandum on Geo-Magnetics, November 21, 1950.
25. Hill-Norton: Foreword (© 1988) to *Above Top Secret*, Timothy Good, William-Morrow, New York, 1988.
26. DeBrouwer, Wilfred: *UFO Wave Over Belgium—An Extraordinary Dossier* (original title in French), SOBEPS, 1991.

Section II - The Astronauts

27. Address to a U.N. panel discussion of UFOs and ETS in new York, 1985, chaired by then U.N. Sec. General Kurt Waldheim.
28. From Astronaut Sightings by Harvey S. Stewart HUFON Report March/April 1996.

16

1942–1945: The Present Era Of UFO Sightings Begins

Some of the earliest case histories come from military officers in the early 1940s. In 1942, a photographer had set up on a busy street in China. With his large camera, he hoped to take photographs of visitors which they would purchase as a souvenir. Suddenly, his attention was drawn to the sky, along with many others on the street. There, hovering silently was a large, dark disc-shaped object. The quick-thinking photographer focused his camera on the disc and obtained an excellent, clear photo of it. A military officer serving in the Chinese campaign prior to World War II was present on the street as well. He bought the photograph and apparently tucked it into a scrapbook of photographs he collected while stationed in China.. It went unnoticed for years until a Japanese gentleman discovered the old album containing the 1942 photograph.[1]

In August of 1942, U.S. Marine Sergeant Stephen Brickner was stationed in the Solomon Islands. He witnessed the appearance of multiple unconventional, although loud, flying objects. Sgt. Brickner wrote an account describing over 150 "wobbling" objects flying in a formation of straight lines of ten to twelve craft each.[2]

Foo Fighters: During World War II in the European and Pacific theaters, and in India, pilots and crew members began reporting unexplained glowing balls flying in formation beside their military aircraft. Beginning in 1943, pilots flying over the Indian Ocean, Germany and elsewhere reported similar events, stating that the "balls of fire" raced across the sky at fantastic speeds. While it was suspected that the Nazis were flying some sort of mis-

---

1. "UFO Sightings: Photographic Evidence, Vol. #1", video, © 1996 AFS/Dialogue Productions, producer, ThomasTulien. Photograph owned by Wendelle Stevens, obtained from Paul Dong.
2. Good, Timothy, *Above Top Secret*, William Morrow and Company, 1988, p. 18

siles, rockets or flying bombs, intelligence efforts eventually surmised that the Nazis were also being tagged by these odd balls of light. Reportedly, an American pilot paraphrased a comic strip title from the day and stated "Where there's foo, there's fire."[3] The term "Foo Fighters" was coined and stuck.

American Air Force pilots and intelligence officers flying over Germany, and particularly the Rhine Valley, radioed to the American radar center instances of seeing dozens of red or orange lights, flares or possible Nazi night fighters, "kraut fighters" or "kraut balls". The radar center, however, reported to the pilots that the radar screen showed the military plane to be alone in its airspace. Rather than being an isolated incident, the balls of light reappeared with increasing frequency throughout 1943 and 1944.[4] Indeed, in 1944, two P-47 pilots each observed a "Foo Fighter" in broad daylight. Flying near Neustadt, Germany, one pilot reported observing "a gold-colored ball with a metallic finish." The second pilot, also flying near Neustadt, described "a phosphorescent golden sphere" with a diameter of three to five feet.

In May of 1945, American soldier Lynn R. Momo described "a fireball of rather startling nature" over Ohrdorf, Germany:

"It was brighter than any star, or even the Planet Venus. It passed completely from horizon to horizon in about two seconds. The path was through the zenith, so that whatever its altitude, its speed must have been enormous."

Momo went on to state that the object was soundless and had a "rising and sinking" or bobbing motion as it traversed from horizon to horizon. Momo said it reminded him of the reflection from a mirror that, when held in the hand, causes the reflected light to bounce erratically with the slightest movement."A similar device was employed in World War II to project images of religious scenes on the clouds to frighten superstitious enemy soldiers. It was quite successful until they caught on," Momo reported.[5]

The late American journalist Frank Edwards cited a report by Major E.R.T. Holmes from England which summarized sightings by B-17 bomber pilots of the 384th Group during a bombing run on the Schweinfurt, Germany industrial complex on October 14, 1943.

3. Lore and Deneault, *Mysteries of the Skies: UFOs in Perspective*, Prentice-Hall, Inc. 1968, p. 116.
4. *UFO Encounters*, Golden Press, 1978.
5. *Mysteries of the Skies*, pp. 119-120.

Major Holmes stated in his report that the discs caused no damage to the bombers. The official military report was signed as follows:

"Major E.R.T. Holmes, FLO, 1st Bombardment Squadron, to the Minister of Information 15, War Office, Whitehall, London, under date of October 24, 1943. (Mission No. 115 in the British records)"[6]

Frank Edwards and others believed that an investigation into this phenomenon was initiated in Britain, although it was flatly denied by the British military. Further, no evidence for its existence, other than a few documents such as the Holmes report mentioned above, has been uncovered. The alleged report was known as the Massey Report, apparently named for a Lieutenant General Massey. But Air Marshal Sir Victor Goddard, the first Deputy Director of Air Intelligence to the Air Ministry in Britain, stated that there was no General Massey in the records of the British Army. However, a Hugh *Massy* was listed in the 1945 *Who's Who*. Lieutenant General Hugh R. S. Massy was appointed eventually to the office of Deputy Chief of the Imperial General Staff. Was this Massy, who retired in 1942, the general who investigated the Foo Fighters? As with the nature and origin of these enigmatic flying objects, the report and its namesake remain a mystery to the present day.[7]

---

6. Edwards, Frank, *Flying Saucers--Here and Now!*, Lyle Stuart, New York, 1967, p.77.
7. *Above Top Secret*, p.28

17

1947–1964 New Mexico Crash Retrieval and Landing Cases

According to an article in the April 1, 1966 issue of *Life* magazine, between June 1947 and early 1966, 10,147 UFO sightings had been reported.[1] The term "flying saucers" itself sprang from private pilot Kenneth Arnold's experience on June 24, 1947 near Mount Rainier, Washington. He saw a formation of nine rapidly moving disc-shaped objects while flying in a small plane. In the wild publicity and wave of sightings that followed during the summer of 1947, the term "flying saucers" was coined by the popular press.

The Roswell Incident

On July 2, 1947, an object crashed into a remote field on rancher William "Mac" Brazel's land. Mr. Brazel reported hearing a loud explosion during a severe thunderstorm. The next morning, he discovered debris scattered over an area which may have spanned fifty acres. Mr. Brazel notified the local sheriff's office who in turn called the Army. The case created a stir when the 509th Bomb Group at the Army Air Force Base at Roswell Field, New Mexico, officially released to the press the astounding story that a flying saucer had crashed near Roswell. The Public Information Officer at the base who released the story to the press was First Lieutenant Walter Haut, who still lives in Roswell. The Roswell Daily Record ran the story on the front page in bold headlines: "RAAF Captures Flying Saucer on Ranch in Roswell Region." Two days later, the Army recanted, issuing a second press release claiming that only a weather balloon had crashed.

Major Jesse Marcel, a staff intelligence officer at Roswell Field, was assigned to the recovery operation. To bolster the 'validity' of the second press release, a press conference was held in Fort Worth,

1. "The Week of the Flying Saucers," Bill Wise, *Life* magazine, April 1, 1966, © 1966 Time Inc.

Texas, where the debris was first taken, and a photograph of Major Marcel kneeling to examine remnants of a torn, silvery weather balloon was released. This balloon was eventually declared by the Air Force to be a "Mogul balloon"—balloons which carried top secret acoustical apparatus designed to 'listen' for evidence of Soviet nuclear bomb testing. The Mogul was actually designed so that a string of much larger balloons kept it airborne It bore little resemblance to a sole weather balloon. However, a major military retrieval effort resulted from this alleged 'crash' of a balloon. Teams of Army personnel combed the site for days, clearing it not only of the wreckage (and, reportedly, the bodies of ET life forms) but of every shred or scrap. The recovered debris was flown under deep cover first to Carswell Air Force Base in Fort Worth, Texas and ultimately to Wright Field (now Wright-Patterson Air Force Base) in Ohio. It is difficult to imagine any sort of balloon configuration spreading debris over a fifty-acre area, or requiring a top secret operation to retrieve the pieces.

During the early phase of the retrieval operation, Major Marcel showed some pieces of the debris to his family, admonishing them never to discuss it. The late Major Marcel's son, Col. Jesse Marcel, Jr., M.D., is a witness who is part of CSETI's Project Starlight Coalition. Dr. Marcel clearly remembers his father calling the family around the kitchen table that night. Dr. Marcel, then twelve years old, was shown items from the crash site, particularly small beams of lightweight material, lavender to purple in color, with hieroglyphic-like markings along its length. Dr. Marcel had a model made to his specifications from his vivid recollections as a 12-year old boy when he held and examined the material.

Another CSETI Project Starlight witness who was on President Eisenhower's staff recounts being shown two sections of the small I-beams and a piece of foil-like material when he was in cryptography training in a basement office in the Pentagon in 1960-61. He was told that the material "came from the crash of a UFO"; he was not told from where and was not allowed to handle the material. He recalls being told that the metal foil could not be pierced, cut or burned. Our witness also clearly recalls hieroglyphic markings along the length of one of the small beams.[2]

2. CSETI transcripts of Project Starlight closed witness meetings; June 1995 and April 1997.

Roswell dwelled in the realm of rumor until 1978 when the late Major Jesse Marcel appeared on an NBC radio program and talked about the official debris retrieval at the crash site near Roswell. Major Marcel stated the following in an interview by nuclear physicist and UFO researcher Stanton Friedman:

> ...that afternoon, we loaded everything into a B-29 on orders from Colonel Blanchard and flew it all to Ft. Worth. I was scheduled to fly it all the way to Wright Field in Ohio, but when we got to Carswell at Ft. Worth, the general nixed it. He took control at this point, and ordered me not to talk to the press under any circumstances. I was pulled off the flight and *someone else was assigned to fly the stuff up to Wright Field...*" [emphasis in original][3]

Why Roswell? Quite simply, because the 509th was the *only* military facility in the country, and most likely in the world, holding nuclear warheads.

Other Crash Sites

Whether the Roswell crash actually occurred near Roswell, or at another location in New Mexico, particularly Magdalena or Socorro (the Plains of San Agustin), Corona, or Aztec, remains in dispute, and whether there was only one or more than one crash of a possible ET spacecraft in New Mexico has yet to be proven. In 1997, some of the best-known investigators of the Roswell crash reversed their opinions and claimed they no longer believed an ET spacecraft crashed in Roswell but rather it was either a balloon-tethered device or a highly classified atomic-powered military prototype craft. However, witness testimony as outlined above, as well as statements given to CSETI by other former military witnesses, confirm that there were *several* crashes in the southwestern United States in the late 1940s and 1950s. These witnesses and evidence uncovered over the years by several UFO researchers point to crashes of ET space craft at these sites, along with Roswell: in or near Aztec, New Mexico; Kingman, Arizona; the Great Sand Dunes of Colorado, inside the Mexican border near Laredo, Texas; and Paradise Valley (near what is now Carefree), Arizona. There is also a report by researchers Tommy Blann and Leonard Stringfield of a crash in Northern New Mexico in 1962. This pair of

3. Berlitz and Moore, *The Roswell Incident*, Granada, London 1980.

researchers also reported on a UFO on the ground at Wright-Patterson Air Force Base the same year, 1962, under heavy guard in a hangar.[4]

Regardless of the precise location of any of the possible crashes, there is a significant body of evidence, including documents obtained from the U.S. government through the Freedom of Information Act ("FOIA") which clearly indicate that secret retrieval operations occurred. It stretches the credulity to imagine that such closely-guarded operations would be necessary for a weather balloon, if we are to believe the second press release out of Roswell in July of 1947.

But an effort to obtain those documents spearheaded by Rep. Steven Schiff (R-NM) culminated in a disappointing dead end. Rep. Schiff sent requests through the GAO (Government Accounting Office) for any and all documentation regarding the crash of an airborne object in New Mexico in 1947. The GAO representatives performed a search and were unable to provide Rep. Schiff with any documentation.

However, other requests through the CIA and FOIA produced a memorandum dated March 22, 1950, to the Director of the FBI stating that three flying saucers had been recovered in New Mexico (see "Director of FBI—Information re Flying Saucers —22 March 1950" on page 509). Two memoranda from October and November of 1947 which state that a study was underway at Wright Field of flying saucers recently sighted over the United States, and that *models were being constructed to be tested in a wind tunnel.*

The New Mexico crash investigations have yielded persistent stories of ET biological entities ("EBEs") who perished in or shortly after the crashes and whose bodies have been shuttled from one secret military base to another since the late 1940s. When we add into the equation the testimony of multiple living witnesses, or whose close family members confessed on their death beds, that small nonhuman life forms were found at the crash sites, one or more of which may have been still alive at the time they were found, we have at minimum cases which cry for thorough scientific investigation with all of the documents released for review.

4. Stringfield, Leonard H., UFO Status Reports II and III, 1982.

The Socorro Landing Case—1964

A police sergeant in Socorro, New Mexico—Lonnie Zamora—reported the sighting of a UFO on the ground—complete with landing traces and small humanoid life forms. The incident occurred on April 24, 1964 and was the subject of official investigations by the Air Force, the FBI, and private investigations by other researchers, among them Dr. J. Allen Hynek. This incident is the first reported in the official Air Force UFO records involving landing traces and the sighting of humanoid life forms.[5]

During daylight hours while on duty that day, Sgt. Zamora was in hot pursuit of a black Chevrolet which he first saw speeding past the Socorro courthouse. He pursued the vehicle north along US Highway 85 outside of town. He was suddenly distracted by what he thought was the roar of an explosion. Seeing blue-orange flames, he gave up the car chase for this greater emergency and headed towards a dynamite shack he knew to be in the area. Driving was difficult on the steep gravel and dirt road. He approached the area where he'd seen the flames, reached the crest and slowly drove westward. A shiny object came into sight about 150-200 yards off the road Zamora initially thought he was looking at a car overturned into a gully. He saw two small humanoid occupants, reportedly dressed in white overalls.

At about 4:45 P.M., Sgt. Zamora radioed to headquarters and reported a possible automobile crash, stating his intent to be outside of his patrol car investigating. Zamora stated that he drove up the road to a vantage point where he could see into the gully. Zamora reported:

"As I approached the scene, I thought it was an overturned car—on end, sort of. As I finally got a look at it, it was a shiny-type object. The object was like aluminum—it was whitish against a moss background, but no chrome. Seemed like a football shape like this. I saw two pair of overalls."[6]

Zamora went on to relate that one of the people turned and noticed his car, seemingly startled. Zamora was approaching closer with the intent of offering help when quickly a loud roaring began. It started at a low frequency, rising to a high and very loud frequency, accompanied by a flame. Sgt. Zamora hurried back to his patrol car, hitting his leg on the fender and knocking off his glasses. The roaring

---

5. Emenegger, Robert, *UFO's Past, Present & Future*, Ballentine, New York, 1974.
6. Ibid., p. 64.

object rose into the air and moved away from him. Zamora was quite frightened. He flung his arm across his face but turned to look at the object. "I heard a whine, then total silence," Zamora reported. He quickly radioed back to police headquarters, almost hysterical. A fellow officer, Sgt. Chavez, soon arrived at the scene. He stated:

"When I arrived, Zamora was sweating and white...very pale. I went down to where the object had been. I noticed the brush was burning in several places. I could see the tracks on the ground. The object had left four perpendicular impressions in the ground. I noticed smouldering bushes, but they felt cold to the touch. I knew Lonnie had seen something--the proof was right there. Before I arrived, he had made a sketch of an insignia he saw on the side of the object. I secured the area and called the local military authorities."[7]

Soon the area was swarming with spectators, reporters, an FBI agent and several others. Astrophysicist Dr. J. Allen Hynek flew in to investigate immediately. He in fact returned for two more visits to the site and interviews with local residents and Zamora, in whom he expressed belief. The FBI chief investigator on the case, Captain Hector Quintanilla, stated that soil and vegetation samples were obtained and tested at Wright-Patterson, measurements were taken and a thorough investigation was conducted. Yet the case was lost in red tape and no official determination was ever made. Several secret military test vehicles were mentioned by the press as possible explanations, all of which remained inconclusive. Sgt. Zamora was subjected to ridicule and finger-pointing which led him to leave the law enforcement profession and avoid discussion of the incident.

The sheer number of reports from credible civilian, law enforcement and military witnesses from New Mexico cry for a serious scientific investigation and a release of all evidence and material collected therein.

---

7. *Ibid.*, p. 65.

18

Military Aircraft Encounter—1951

On February 9, 1951, United States Navy Flight 125 departed from Keflavik, Iceland en route to the Naval Air Station in Argentina, Newfoundland. The co-pilot was U.S. Naval Reserve Lieutenant Graham E. Bethune, a CSETI Project Starlight witness who served 26 years on active duty. Lt. Bethune, who was stationed in Maryland at the time, was one of three officers suggested to fly to Keflavik for a classified meeting between Lockheed and the Icelandic government. The Icelanders had asked for American troops to protect them, stating they had been seeing unidentified craft off the coasts of Iceland. Lt. Bethune assumed they were observing classified, experimental craft. However, his opinion changed while on board Navy Flight 125.

Just after midnight, at 0055 on February 10, 1951, Lt. Bethune and his crew had an encounter with an unknown object. The following report is in Lt. Bethune's own words:

> I was the pilot from Iceland to Newfoundland. 240 miles out I saw something on the water 40 miles away. Moonset had occurred an hour previous. Nothing was scheduled to be in that area. I called it to the attention of my navigator and co-pilot. It looked like a city in the distance. There was a pattern to the lights on the water—an odd pattern. I thought it was a classified rescue mission. 20 miles out, the lights went out. A yellow halo appeared on the water. It flew towards us, some 20 miles, at approximately 1,000 miles per hour. It stopped 200 ft. below us. I observed a faint dome shape to it. I had a knowing that it was intelligently controlled—it came over to look at us. The object stayed about five miles away, at about a 45° angle. It flew with us, looking at us. I estimated its size at 300 feet in diameter. My plane had no guns. The on-board magnetic compass did

> spin. We had 31 passengers on board, including a Navy commander, a psychiatrist. I went back and spoke to the psychiatrist and asked him if he had observed anything unusual. The commander said he saw what we saw. The psychiatrist said, "Yes, it was a flying saucer and I didn't look at it because such things don't exist."
>
> I told my crew not to report it. But it was picked up on Gander radar. We were interrogated in Iceland. It was obvious from the questions and demeanor of the US Navy men who debriefed us that they'd seen things out there before. A report on this event was kept at Wright-Patterson AFB. I found it in 1991, in the archives. I have the report, along with letters from NICAP, Keyhoe's report to congress, and photos of the plane I was in. All five pilots described it, the UFO, the same—its size; the aura around it. A lieutenant who was on duty the night we were interrogated was told they tracked it by radar in excess of 1,800 m.p.h. No radar report was included in the 17-page report—it was missing from the report when I finally found the report in 1991. Radar was confirmed at the time. I estimated the speed of the object at 1,000 m.p.h. The other pilots estimated 1,000–1,500 m.p.h. The fastest fighter we had at time could go 500 m.p.h. There were no jets at the time—in February 1951.
>
> This object was not a shooting star. It was always between the plane and the water. We had extensive recognition training then. We didn't have the instrumentation assists that we have today. We navigated by stars. We had about a 54th of a second to identify something while we were flying in a moving plane. We are the ones who gave the information to the astrophysicists since we were the ones up there. We had many sightings but this is the one that we have documentation for. [1]

Upon landing in Argentia, Newfoundland, Lt. Bethune and his crew were interrogated by Naval officers about the incident. In Lt. Bethune's official, confidential report filed at the Fleet Logistic Air Wing, Atlantic/Continental, Air Transport Squadron One, U.S. Naval Air Station, Patuxent River, Maryland, dated February 10,

1. Taped transcript from closed Project Starlight witnesses' meeting, April 9, 1997, Washington, D.C.

1951, he gave additional details: The object was first seen when the aircraft was at least 250 miles off the coast of Iceland. Bethune and the co-pilot kept the object under observance for four to five minutes before calling it to the attention of the rest of the crew. When the object lifted and rushed towards them at an estimated 1,000 miles per hour, Lt. Bethune's first feeling was that the Navy plane would collide with the UFO in mid-air. When it approached the plane, its shape was clearly discernible to be that of a disc, at least 300 feet in diameter. Its color changed from yellow to reddish-orange. When it reversed course and flew away from the aircraft to vanish over the horizon, its speed tripled

The other members of the Flight 125 crew submitted written reports as well. Lt. Fred W. Kingdon, serving as second Plane Commander, stated, "I was an eye witness to an unusual sighting of an unidentified object." Lt. Kingdon was in the right-hand seat (co-pilot) while Lt. Bethune was in the left-hand seat. When the UFO rose from the surface of the water and sped towards the plane, Lt. Kingdon described it as "very large and was circular with a glowing yellow-orange ring around its outer edge." Although the object was very close, it was difficult to determine its exact speed and configuration since it was observed over water at night. "However, the speed was tremendous and the size was at least 200 to 300 feet in diameter. The object was close enough to me to see and observe it clearly," Kingdon reported.

Plane Commander LTJG A. L. Jones was in the cabin of the plane when one of the navigators came aft and pointed to the object. He stated:

> "I watched it for a minute and went forward to the cockpit to get a better view. Upon reaching the cockpit, I took the plane off of the autopilot and turned to a true heading of 290° in pursuit of the object. The object left on a heading of about 290° true and went over the horizon in a very short time. I would guess the speed to be well over 1500 miles per hour, and the diameter to be at least 300 feet. My first view of it resembled a huge fiery orange disc on its edge...When it went over the horizon, it seemed to go from a vertical position to a horizontal position, with only the trailing edge showing in a half-moon effect"[2]

2. Memorandum Report of A. L. Jones, LTJG, U.S. Navy, 10 February 1951.

The plane's navigator, Lt. Noel J. P. Koger, remarked in his report:

> "Lieutenant Kingdon pointed out an orange colored object about 060° relative, or 290° true, saying it appeared like a small village or a ship. Due to our position, I was certain it wasn't a village. I had been looking at the object about thirty seconds, which it appeared to me was another demonstration of the 'northern lights' phenomenon...when the object suddenly started getting much brighter, taking on shape and coming in our direction at a great rate of speed... The best view I had of the object showed it to be a circular, bright orange-red disc, which was approaching us at a very great, undeterminable speed."[3]

The Air Intelligence Information Report prepared for this encounter summarizes the observances of the crew members, stating that Lt. Bethune was the first to see the object. The report states that all five crew members were experienced North Atlantic fliers and that all five observers agreed on the facts as stated.

For additional details, please see the official government documents regarding this incident, which CSETI obtained through a FOIA request.

3. Memorandum Report of Noel J. P. Koger, Lt. U.S. Navy, 10 February 1951.

19

The Summer of 1952: UFOs over Washington, D.C.

One of the most frequent rhetorical questions posed about UFOs is: if they are real, why don't they just land on the White House lawn? Actually, they came pretty close to doing just that on two consecutive weekends in July of 1952.

The summer of 1952 was one of the most prolific for reported sightings of UFOs. There had been a significant number of reports flowing in all along the Eastern seaboard and from the Midwestern states for weeks. Intelligence officers grew increasingly more uneasy over the sharp rise in sightings. Of special concern was that many of these statements were coming from civilians. Prior to that fateful summer, most sightings had come from military personnel and had been kept from the public. But now the citizens themselves, including commercial airline pilots had become sources of information:

- July 10, 1962: A National Airlines plane over Quantico, Virginia observed a light at 2,000 feet which the crew stated was too slow to be a big meteor and too fast to be a lighted balloon.
- July 12, 1952: Former Air Force jet pilot Jack Green in Delphi, Indiana was one of many who witnessed a blue-white saucer-shaped object high in the sky.
- July 13, 1952: Thousands of people in Indianapolis witness a huge oval speed over the city at 5,000 feet, frightening many. An Eastern Air Lines captain, an Air Force pilot, and a private pilot all saw a controlled craft initially flying much higher which descended to about 5,000 feet and flew over the city of Indianapolis. This was the first low-range sighting witnessed by thousands of people, at least in the era of UFO sightings that began in the 40s. Just prior to its appearance over Indiana, possibly the same object—certainly one bearing the same descrip-

tion—was seen on Air Force radar at Kirksville, Missouri. It was estimated to be flying at 1,700 m.p.h. and to be the size of a B-36 bomber.

- July 13, 1962: A commercial pilot and crew, flying at 11,000 feet sixty miles southwest of Washington, spotted a light below them. The light rose to the same altitude as the plane, hovered to the left of the plane for several minutes, then rose rapidly when the pilot turned on the plane's landing lights.
- July 14, 1952: A PanAm flight headed south to Miami from New York reported observing glowing orange UFOs near Newport News, Virginia. (*Note:* The first formation consisted of six discs were seen; two more were seen soon after the first formation flew off.) As the formation approached the plane, the lead disc turned on its edge. The others instantly did the same. All the discs flipped to horizontal, changed direction and sped off.
- July 17, 1952: An American Airlines flight near Denver received a radio transmission warning of a craft ahead. Captain Paul Carpenter and crew observed four saucers in formation flying at an estimated 3,000 m.p.h.

From the ground:

- July 16, 1952: Langley Air Force Base was the scene for a sighting of two large amber lights. One of the two observers was a well-respected civilian scientist from Langley. The lights made a 180° degree turn, returned to where they were first spotted, jockeyed with each other, were joined by a third light, started climbing and when doing so, were joined by several other lights—all flying in formation. It is estimated that the entire event lasted three minutes.

UFOs Buzz the White House

At ll:40 pm on July 19, 1952, dual radar stations at Washington National Airport picked up seven objects east and south of Andrews Air Force Base. Andrews also picked up the targets on their radar. Conventional aircraft were quickly ruled out as the cause; these targets would fly at 100–130 m.p.h., suddenly accelerate to extremely high speeds and leave the area. One object was clocked at 7,200 miles per hour. Reportedly, the objects appeared in every sector of the radar scopes, including flying through restricted air space over the White House and Capitol building. The objects returned several times throughout the night and were also seen by airline pilots (at midnight and 2:00 A.M.), air traffic control tower operators, and jet fighter pilots who were dispatched from Andrews.

Edward Ruppelt wrote:

> "But the clincher came in the wee hours of the morning, when an ARTC traffic controller called the control tower at Andrews AFB and told the tower operators that ARTC had a target just south of their tower, directly over the Andrews Radio range station. The tower operators looked and there was a 'huge fiery-orange sphere' hovering in the sky directly over their range station."[1]

Apparently, Air Force Intelligence was not informed about the events until they, along with everyone else in the area, read the newspaper headlines the next morning: **Interceptors Chase Flying Saucers Over Washington, D.C**. Even a major at the Pentagon stated to Project Blue Book investigator Edward Ruppelt that all he knew about the events was what he'd read in the newspaper. A full investigation ensued immediately under the supervision of said major—Dewey Fournet. The air traffic controllers at Washington National told intelligence officers that the targets they observed were caused by radar waves bouncing off a hard, solid object— these were not temperature inversions. The Air Force radar operator at Andrews and the two veteran airline pilots concurred.

Second Washington Flap

Serendipitously, the second wave of sightings over Washington occurred seven days later, nearly to the hour. Those seven intervening days had been far from quiet; UFO reports were flowing into Wright Field in Dayton, Ohio at the rate of thirty to forty per day—triple the previous numbers. Edward Ruppelt claims that "many were as good, if not better, than the Washington incident." The most outstandingly unexplained of those reports included amber-red lights observed over the Guided Missile Long-Range Proving Ground at Patrick Air Force Base, Florida; a rapidly moving large, round, silver spinning object in Uvalde, Texas; and military jets unsuccessfully chasing UFOs over Los Alamos, New Mexico; Massachusetts (two events), and New Jersey.

---

1. *The Report on Unidentified Flying Saucers*, Ruppelt, Edward J., Doubleday & Company, New York, 1956.

A stunning prelude was the forerunner to the second wave over Washington. In the early evening of July 26, a saucer-shaped vehicle flashing red light winked in over the Naval Air Station in Key West, Florida, reportedly seen by hundreds. The events then speed up the Eastern Seaboard, focusing again on the nation's capitol. There, beginning around 9:00 P.M., Washington area radar operators were once more picking up 'bogies' similar to the previous weekend's mayhem. Within an hour, four or five UFOs at once were a continuous presence on the radar screens. Military jets were dispatched and commercial airlines were rerouted. According to Ruppelt, the press who had gathered at the control tower at Washington National were asked to leave. He wrote:

> "When I later found out that the press had been dismissed on the grounds that the procedures used in an intercept were classified, I knew that this was absurd because any ham radio operator worth his salt could build equipment and listen in on any intercept. The real reason for the press dismissal, I learned, was not that a few people in the radar room were positive that this night would be the big night in UFO history—the night when a pilot would close in on and get a good look at a UFO—and they didn't want the press to be in on it."[2]

However, the ET UFO pilots had other ideas. As soon as the F-94 jets were airborne, around midnight, the UFOs all vanished from the radar scopes. The pilots could make no visual contact despite good visibility and weather. However, it was later learned that Langley AFB and civilians in the area had visuals on colored, rotating lights in the sky. But—surprise!—as soon as the military jets left the area, the UFOs popped back up on the Washington radar screens once more. One F-94 pilot who did see a light and was vectored to it by air traffic control reported that it went out as soon as he got near, "like somebody turning off a light bulb." Brief radar lock-ons were obtained by the pilot.[3]

The UFOs continued to play games with the F-94s, staying put while they approached, then speeding away or vanishing. The UFOs played "catch me if you can" until the jets had nearly depleted their fuel, which coincided with the approaching sunrise. Once it got light, the UFOs had gone for good. Once more, the radar operators con-

2. *Ibid.*, p. 164.
3. *Flying Saucers from Outer Space*, Keyhoe, Major Donald E., Henry Holt and Company, New York, 1953.

firmed that they believed the targets were caused by solid, metallic, moving objects and were not due to any weather aberrations. And, once more, newspaper headlines were devoted to the UFOs. In the Pentagon, it was mass confusion, bolstered by the fact that new UFO reports were flowing in which verified visual sightings in the same areas where the radar targets had been located. This did little to support the Pentagon's working hypothesis that freakish weather conditions had caused the radar bogies. And, prior to the Washington flap, very few reports indicated both radar and visual lock-on.

By now, there was tremendous pressure to tell the public *something*. Rather lame excuses by the military did nothing to stem the tide of outcry flowing into the Pentagon, additionally fueled by more significant sighting reports coming in from coast to coast and by the creeping suspicion that the Russians were perhaps involved. According to researcher Donald Keyhoe, Director of Air Force Intelligence, Major General John A. Samford grappled with several *false* explanations which the Pentagon hoped would dowse the escalating agitation of John and Jane Q. Public. Calmly and glibly explaining the saucers away as various quirky natural phenomena, while admitting that "twenty percent" of the cases remained unsolved, the General went on to state that no pattern had remotely been revealed that indicated any threat or menace to the United States. The spin to debunk the existence of ET spacecraft and visitors was printed by newspapers all over the country. According to Donald Keyhoe, just as the presses were rolling out this yarn, the Air Force had jets chasing saucers over the Midwestern states. Keyhoe stated, "[O]ne case, if it had been made public that night, would have ruined the inversion answer and wrecked the debunking plan. But I didn't learn this until weeks later."[4] Yet, the denial—and ridicule—of all UFO cases continues to the present day.

Within CSETI's Project Starlight Coalition is a living military—Air Force—witness to the overflights of our nation's Capitol. And CSETI's Best Available Evidence briefing video, for educational, noncommercial purposes, contains a color photograph of a formation of UFOs flying low directly over the White House.

---

4. *Ibid.*, p.88

20

Air Command Base Overflights

While 1975 is considered the "banner year" for unidentified flying objects appearing over Strategic Air Command bases, significant incidents occurred much earlier.

A Project Starlight witness supplied the following report to CSETI:

> I am 49 years old, a college graduate, a disabled vet, and served in the United States Air Force from 1964 to 1974. In 1967, I had two direct observations of foreign technology and heard of at least two related incidents.
>
> The first direct observation of ETV ("ET vehicle") occurred November 1967 en route to a Minuteman I site for repairs at 2200 hours in North Dakota (Minot AFB). There were three staff in our vehicle, two Ballistic Missile Analysts, myself and my assistant, an armed security policeman. The guard made a comment to the effect that it was "awfully quiet out here." I decided to check the four channels on our radio when we heard, "I am going to shoot at it, sir. It's about 300 feet above the site!"
>
> We immediately went into a duress condition which calls for all personnel to respond to the assistance of the crew under duress. The entire episode took maybe 2-3 minutes. We were able to hear the Launch Control Combat Crew Commander ordering the two security guards at a nearby site to NOT shoot at the ETV. We headed in the direction of the site and observed a large, bright object with blinking red/green/blue lights at about 10-12 miles. The object began to rise as radio transmissions were flying back and forth. It rose and accelerated straight up at extremely high speed and disappeared as F-102's and/or F-106 interceptors flew overhead.

The two security guards were guarding the site (sites are unmanned) due to security systems failure and were awaiting a maintenance team to repair. This could take up to 3-4 days depending if it was a weekend. At the height of the incident, up to six other security police were at or near the site in three vehicles (strike teams) in response to the duress codes.

One of the guards (the one that was gong to shoot at the ETV) went on a maintenance trip later that week with my crew and after prodding from me for 30-40 minutes gave me details of their ordeal and their debriefing. The two guards were debriefed by Dr. J. Allen Hynek and other staff not from Minot AFB. Dr. Hynek made the comment "this craft has been observed before." According to the guard, he and his team member were ordered by a USAF colonel to not discuss what had happened or they would be sent to Viet Nam immediately. They were both scared to death.

The second incident occurred several weeks later when, while light snow was falling and a low ceiling was observed by me shortly before nightfall, a guard made a comment about the "strange moon" in the sky.

Directly overhead of where we were repairing a Minuteman site was a moon-sized object, same color as the moon BELOW the cloud cover. I immediately called the Launch Control Facility (LFC) 8-10 miles away to report the "Moon". The security staff said they had the object under observation and had reported it to the Wing Security Control (WSC) at Minot Air Force Base.

As I watched the object and talked to the LCF, the object slowly retreated through the clouds and disappeared. I have info on several other incidents— two credible—at Minot AFB, North Dakota and others at Duluth AFB, Minnesota.[1]

The 1970s

Malmstrom Air Force Base, Montana

The Senior Director of the 24th NORAD Region, Col. Terrence C. James, submitted a written report of multiple overflights of Malm-

1. Private correspondence to Steven M. Greer, M.D. and author, February 1997.

strom AFB on multiple dates in November 1975, from which we quote:

- 7 Nov 75 (1035Z)[2] - Received a call from the 341st Strategic Air Command Post (SAC CP), saying that the following missile locations reported seeing a large red to orange to yellow object: M-1, L-3, LIMA and L-6. The general object location would be 10 miles south of Moore, Montana, and 20 miles east of Buffalo, Montana. Commander and Deputy for Operations (DO) informed.
- 7 Nov 75 (1203Z) - SAC advised that the LCF at Harlowton, Montana, observed an object which emitted a light which illuminated the site driveway.
- 7 Nov 75 (1319Z) - SAC advised K-1 says very bright object to their east is now southeast of them and they are looking at it with 10x50 binoculars. Object seems to have lights (several) on it, but no distinct pattern. The orange/ gold object overhead also has small lights on it. SAC also advises female civilian reports having seen an object bearing south from her position six miles west of Lewistown.
- 7 Nov 75 (1327Z) - L-1 reports that the object to their northeast *seems to be issuing a black object from it, tubular in shape. In all of this time, surveillance has not been able to detect any sort of track except for known traffic.* (emphasis added)
- 7 Nov 75 (1355Z) - K-1 and L-1 report that as the sun rises, so do the objects they have visual.
- 7 Nov 75 (1429Z) - From SAC CP: As the sun rose, the UFOs disappeared. Commander and DO notified.
- 8 Nov 75 (0635Z) - A security camper team at K-4 reported UFO with white lights, one red light 50 yards behind white light. Personnel at K-1 seeing same object.
- 8 Nov 75 (0753Z) - J330 unknown 0753. Stationary/seven knots/ 12,000. One (varies seven objects). None, no possibility, EKLB 3746, two F-106, GTF, SCR 0754. NCOC notified.

  [Note that fighter jets were scrambled to intercept - ed.]
- 8 Nov 75 (0820Z) - Lost radar contact, fighters broken off at 0825, looking in area of J331 (another height finder contact).

---

2. Refers to time of sighting in Zulu (military) time.

- [Note that fighters did have radar contact with the UFOs.]
- 8 Nov 75 (0905Z) - From SAC CP: L-sites had fighters and objects; fighters did not get down to objects.
  [Note: L-sites are Minuteman ICBM missile launch sites.]
- 8 Nov 75 (0915Z) - From SAC CP: From four different points: Observed objects and fighters; when fighters arrived in the area, the lights went out; when fighters departed, the lights came back on; to NCOC.
- 8 Nov 75 (0953Z) - From SAC CP: L-5 reported object increased in speed - high velocity, raised in altitude and now cannot tell the object from the stars. To NCOC.
- 8 Nov 75 (0305Z) - SAC CP called and advised SAC crews at Sites L-1, L-6 and M-1 observing UFO. Object yellowish bright round light 20 miles north of Harlowton, 2 to 4,000 feet.
- 9 Nov 75 (0320Z) - SAC CP reports UFO 20 miles southeast of Lewiston, orange white disc object. 24th NORAD Region surveillance checking area. Surveillance unable to get height check.
- 9 Nov 75 (0320Z) - FAA Watch Supervisor reported he had five air carriers vicinity of UFO, United Flight 157 reported seeing meteor, "arc welder's blue" in color. SAC CP advised, sites still report seeing object stationary.
- 9 Nov 75 (0348Z) - SAC CP confirms L-1, sees object, a mobile security team has been directed to get closer and report.
- 9 Nov 75 (0629Z) - SAC CP advises UFO sighting reported around 0305Z. Cancelled the flight security team from Site L-1, checked area and all secure, no more sightings.
- 10 Nov 75 (0125Z) - Received a call from SAC CP. Report UFO sighting from site K-1 around Harlowton area. Surveillance checking area with height finder.
- 10 Nov 75 (0153Z) - Surveillance report unable to locate track that would correlate with UFO sighted by K-1.
- 10 Nov 75 (1125Z) - UFO sighting reported by Minot Air Force Station, a bright star-like object in the west, moving east, *about the size of a car*. First seen approximately 1015Z. Approximately 1120Z, the object passed over the radar station, 1,000 feet to 2,000 feet high, *no noise heard*. Three people from the site or local area saw the object. NCOC notified. [emphasis added]

- 12 Nov 75 (0230Z) - UFO reported from K-1. They say the object is over Big Snowy Mountain with a red light on it at high altitude. Attempting to get radar on it from Opheim. Opheim searching from 120° to 140°.
- 12 Nov 75 (0248Z) - Second UFO in same area reported. *Appeared to be sending a beam of light to the ground intermittently*. At 0250Z object disappeared. [emphasis added]
- 12 Nov 75 (0251Z) - Reported that both objects have disappeared. Never had any joy (contact) on radar.
  Note: After a week's time, another incident was reported.
- 19 Nov 75 (13272Z) - SAC command post report UFO observed by FSC & a cook, observed object travelling NE between M-8 and M-1 at a fast rate of speed. Object bright white light seen 45 to 50 sec following terrain 200 ft. off ground. The light was two to three times brighter than landing light on a jet.

Extracts from a NORAD Command Director's Log from the fall of 1975 chronicles a long list of sightings at a number of other SAC and Air Force bases:

- 29 Oct 75 - An 'unknown helicopter' landed in the munitions storage area at Loring Air Force Base in Maine two nights in a row. There is mention of an unconfirmed report of Canadian air bases being overflown by a 'helicopter.' Loring AFB turned in another report of a 'probable helicopter overflight' on November 1 as well.
- 31 Oct 75 - Wurtsmith Air Force Base (Michigan) reported a 'helicopter' hovering over a SAC weapons storage area. A tanker plane had visual lock-on and radar 'skin paint' and was able to track the object over Lake Huron.
- 8 Nov 75 - This entry details the first of the 'unknowns' flying above Malstrom AFB and vicinity in Montana, stating that pilots had visual and radar lock-ons. The UFOs eluded the fighter jets by turning off their lights when the jets were bearing towards them, then turning them back on when the F-106's left.
- 10 Nov 75 - A bright, silent object the size of an automobile buzzed Minot Air Force Base in North Dakota.

- 12–25 Nov 75 - Civilians call in reports from Minnesota, Virginia, Ontario and Mendicino County, California of many diverse types of UFOs, including cigar-shaped craft, diamond-shaped objects, cup in a bowl-shaped, rotating lights, balls of light, ovals with blinking lights, and fireballs.

New Mexico

The National Military Command Center in Washington, D.C. issued a report dated 21 January 1976 with information from the Air Force Operations Center regarding an incident over Cannon Air Force Base in New Mexico (see "National Military Command Center—21 January 1976" on page 463):

> "Two UFOS are reported near the flight line at Cannon AFB, New Mexico. Security Police observing them reported the UFOs to be 25 yards in diameter, gold or silver in color with blue light on top, hole in the middle and red light on bottom. Air Force is checking with radar. Additionally, checking weather inversion data."

Maryland

The National Military Command Center issued another report, dated 30 July 1976, detailing several reports of UFOs around Fort Ritchie, Maryland, in the wee hours of July 30th. After civilians called in sightings reports, two separate military police patrols described observing three reddish, oblong cylinders hovering very low (100-200 feet) over an ammunitions storage site. Independently, an Army police sergeant reported seeing a UFO over the same site while he was driving to work approximately 50 minutes after the report by the two patrols. Interestingly, the final paragraph of this report attempted to explain away the sightings as moisture-saturated temperature inversions.

Taken as a whole, the myriad of reports detailed here make an irrefutable case for United States military involvement in reporting UFOs. It is apparent from these reports, which are certainly not all-inclusive, that the U.S. military did indeed have an interest in UFOs and certainly investigated sightings well after the conclusion of Project Blue Book in 1969, which supposedly closed the door on the military's interest in the subject of ETs and their space craft.

21

Military Chase Over Iran—1976

The distinction for the best government documentation of a UFO event falls to the remarkable events that occurred in and above Tehran, Iran in September of 1976. The official U.S. government documents in Section IV were distributed at the time of its writing by the Defense Attaché at the United States Embassy in Tehran to the Defense Intelligence Agency, the White House, the CIA, the National Security Agency, the Joint Chiefs of Staff, the Secretary of the Air Force, the Secretary of Defense, and the Secretary of State.

At half-past midnight on September 19, 1976, the Imperial Iranian Air Force received telephone calls from residents in the Shemiran area of Tehran. The citizens reported "strange objects in the sky," some calling them bird-like and others referring to them as lighted helicopters. The command post knew there were no airborne helicopters at the time and told the citizens they were seeing stars in the sky. The command post checked with Memrabad Tower. Then, looking for himself, observed a large, bright star-like object. At 1:30 a.m., an F-4 jet was scrambled from Shahrokhi Air Force Base and sent up to investigate.

F-4s are Scrambled

The pilot reported that the object was so bright, it was easily visible from 70 miles away, which would place it approximately 40 miles north of Tehran. The IIAF pilot pursued the unusual craft. At 25 nautical miles from the unknown object, the pilot suddenly lost all UHF and intercom communications and instrumentation. When the pilot turned back towards Shahrokhi AFB, away from the UFO, he just as suddenly regained communication capabilities. Due to the strangeness of the unfolding events, a second F-4 was dispatched. The back seat pilot obtained radar lock-on with the UFO at 27 nautical miles distance. When the F-4 got within 25 miles of the object, the UFO increased its speed and moved away, pacing itself to maintain a sustained 25-mile distance from the jet.

Colored Lights Observed on the UFO

Written by Col. Frank B. McKenzie, United States Air Force, the report states that the F-4 pilots compared the size of the object on radar to a 707 tanker, stating that a visual size estimate was difficult due to the extreme brilliance of the UFO. However, the pilots were able to describe flashing, rectangular strobe lights in blue, green, red and orange. The sequence of the strobing lights was so rapid that all four colors could be seen at once, according to the report.

Objects Within Objects

The incident grew even more strange as it continued. As the F-4 pursued the UFO south of Tehran, a second object ejected from the primary target. It was brilliantly lit and was estimated to be one-half to one-third the size of the moon. The second object zoomed towards the F-4. At this point, the F-4 pilot attempted to fire an AIM-9 missile at the UFO. Instantly, his weapons control panel lost all power, and communication capabilities were down once more. The pilot made an extreme evasive negative G dive to escape the UFO. As he did so, the UFO trailed the F-4 at an estimated distance of three to four nautical miles. As the pilot turned the jet, the secondary object appeared on the inside of his turn. It then returned to the primary UFO, rejoining perfectly with it. Almost immediately thereafter, another object ejected out the opposite side of the primary UFO. It fell towards the ground at a tremendous rate of speed. By now, the F-4's communications and weapons systems were once again functioning normally.

The UFO Lands

The F-4 crew watched the nose-diving UFO in anticipation of seeing a huge crash and explosion. Much to their astonishment, the UFO appeared to come to rest gently on the ground with no impact whatsoever. Moreover, it cast an extremely bright light extending over a two to three kilometer range (well over one mile).

More Radio Interference

The Iranian F-4 began to descend, while the crew continued to observe the landed UFO and mark its location. It took several attempts before they could land the fighter jet. Each time they passed through a certain magnetic bearing, the aircraft lost communications and the on-board instrumentation fluctuated dramatically. Moreover, a civilian aircraft in the vicinity also reported communication failure but reported no visual contact with the UFO. During the F-4's final approach into Shahrokhi, the IIAF crew observed another object - this one cylindrical with bright steady lights on either end and a flashing light in the center. The control tower reported no other known air traffic in the area. The tower was able to get a visual lock-on when the pilots told them in which area to look as the cylinder-like UFO passed over the F-4.

Follow-up Investigation

The following day, the F-4 crew was taken by helicopter to the area where they had tracked the landed UFO. The spot turned out to be a dry lake bed. Instrumentation aboard the helicopter registered a strong beeping signal over and around the lake bed. The strongest signal came from the area of a small house. The helicopter landed and the residents were questioned by military personnel about events of the previous night. The family members said they heard a loud noise and saw a very bright light, similar to lightning. Further investigation was apparently done to determine possible radiation residue. We have found no documentation of the results of the radiation testing and other post-event investigation.

See "Iran Sightings—19 September 1976" on page 485 and "Department of Defense—Iran Sightings—19 September 1976" on page 488.

22

RAF/USAF Bentwaters - Woodbridge—December 1980

One of the most important close encounters ever reported by the military, with documentation obtained through the Freedom of Information Act, is the multiple-witness events which occurred at a joint British/American NATO air base in England. The release to American researchers of the memorandum detailing the eye witness account of Lt. Col. Charles E. Halt (later promoted to Colonel), deputy commander of the base, gave tremendous credence to the investigative reports done at the time of the incident.

RAF/USAF Woodbridge is located eight miles east of Ipswich, Suffolk in England, and is one-half of the twin bases whose other half is the RAF Bentwaters NATO Air Base. All of the main buildings and quarters were at Bentwaters, although Woodbridge had its own runway. During World War II, the twin bases served as a maintenance unit for front line forces in Germany. Hercules transports and huge helicopters were based here. It was entirely a US base, manned almost exclusively with US personnel, with only a token Brit in residence who was given the rank of squadron leader.[1] The large and dense Rendlesham Forest surrounds the bases.

The Close Encounters

Over two nights on the Christmas holiday weekend in 1980, astonishing close encounters occurred on the twin air bases of Bentwaters and Woodbridge. Preceded by a visit outside the forest to a nearby residence, a UFO landed in the forest on the Bentwaters Air Force Base around 2:30 A.M. on December 26, 1980. It was witnessed first by two soldiers on patrol. The men first thought they were seeing a beam from a lighthouse and then guessed it could be

1. Randles, Jenny, *Out of the Blue*, Global, 1991, Berkley Books, New York, 1993.

"light-alls"—large, portable bright lights which effectively turned night to day to provide visibility for nighttime maneuvers. As they watched, the hovering light descended below treetop level. The soldiers thought perhaps a plane had just crashed on the Bentwaters runway. The men radioed to headquarters. Three relief guards were sent out, and this first pair missed the rest of the encounter. Two of the relief guards went by jeep and then by foot through the forest in pursuit of the UFO. The men described it as somewhat triangular in shape and possessed blue, white and red lights around the perimeter of the bright white body of the craft. When the soldiers came within sight of the UFO, it was hovering just above the ground, or resting on landing gear on the ground. It lifted up and drifted slowly when one of the soldiers got very near, then shot straight up at a dizzying speed while casting a bright light onto the forest, causing cattle to panic. The two soldiers were dazed by the event. A search party found them almost an hour later, still disoriented. British police were called in; airport radar controllers were contacted. Heathrow reported a target on radar that disappeared in the Bentwaters vicinity, and reports of bright lights in the sky had come in at various times from all around southern England. It was confirmed that no air traffic was above Rendlesham at the time of the incident.

Additional encounters ensued the following night. Several military personnel saw UFOs perform maneuvers that no known human-engineered devices could carry out, including changing shape and size.

Near midnight on the 26th, a four-man team set out to investigate the area in Rendlesham Forest where the UFO had come to rest the night before. Soon they observed a highly unusual curtain of light with mist or fog below it. As the soldiers got closer, they could see a structured object, described to be of indeterminate shape but with yellow, red and blue lights on it. The multi-colored object backed away while a high level of static electricity saturated the atmosphere, causing hair to stand on end. The soldiers radioed to Lt. Col. Halt, the deputy commander at Bentwaters, who told them to stay put, that he would bring reinforcements and join them.

Lt. Col. Halt and approximately thirty soldiers arrived who began to erect light-alls, which initially failed to function. Halt dictated notes into a portable tape recorder, registering radiation readings that increased in the area where the UFO had landed the previous night and left three imprints in a triangular shape in the soil, and detectable heat signatures on the surrounding trees which were visible through a starlight scope.

Shortly before 2:00 A.M., a single yellow-red light on the ground was seen by Col. Halt and the soldiers which caused the animals on the adjacent farm to become agitated. Suddenly, the lighted object rose and glided in the air towards them, issuing from itself a stream of multi-colored lights. Other military men saw the light merge into the foggy essence on the ground and implode within it. There was a tremendous flash of light and the fog transformed into a solid, domed disc with a fluorescent glow to it, rimmed with blue light. The area of blue light on the craft showered out sparkling colored bits which fell onto the ground. Allegedly, photographs were taken of this object by two separate military men. The craft lifted and began to produce more spectacular light displays around its rim. It hovered and bobbled in the air in front of the soldiers. As the UFO moved away, up to five separate lighted objects were observed.

The men watched the objects move out over Woodbridge and towards the sea where they put on a lengthy display, sometimes appearing as half-moons and sometimes as full circles, always sparkling with colored light. However, the encounter was to become close once more. One of the UFOs raced above the forest toward them, sending down beams of light. Two soldiers on a separate detail reported an amorphous structure of light weaving through the trees that sent light beams straight through tree trunks then seemed to explode above them like a dying star. The night's incredible events had spanned more than four hours.[2]

Civilian Witnesses

The first eye witness was a resident on the other side of Rendlesham Forest in Sudbourne named Gordon Levett. Levett was outside preparing to put his dog away for the night. A huge mushroom-shaped bright object drifted in from the sea and hovered silently in the sky above Levett and his large guard dog, who began trembling and remained shaken by the event throughout the following day. During an interview with British UFO researcher Jenny Randles, Levett recalled:

> "My attention was drawn to the sky by some unknown means. I do not know what made me look up. But I saw a shape over the

---

2. Details in this narrative taken from Out of the Blue by Jenny Randles, and NBC-TV television program Unsolved Mysteries, first air date, September 18, 1991.

> coast which was headed towards me. My dog saw it too and his attention became fixed upon it...The thing glowed with a strange phosphorescence as it dropped down to a very low height and hovered...I would say that its size was similar to the roof of my house...The object moved away across the woods towards RAF Woodbridge...The next day my dog was still upset. It refused to come out of its kennel and was trembling and cowering. This was most unusual behaviour."[3]

The second night's events were witnessed independently by other non-military citizens who had sightings off the premises of the base. Arthur Smekle saw a mass of lights in the sky above Rendlesham Forest about 11:00 P.M. while driving home through the forest. He mentioned it when he got home but was reminded that since he was adjacent to the air base, it was probably just an aircraft. The Webb family all saw a huge white mass of lights in the sky at 2:30 A.M. (now 27 December) while driving home to Martlesham. They stopped the car by the side of the road and watched it hover silently, then shoot off through the sky at extreme speed. Several farmers in the area also were interviewed or submitted reports to the British investigators. One of the farmers had even called into the base and reported bright lights in the sky just before the UFO came into the Bentwaters compound.

Forest Ranger James Brownlea found physical traces of the landing in the forest the following month. While the official government memo by Col. Halt was not released for another two and one-half years, Brownlea's January 1981 report describing finding a hole in the tree canopy, scorched trees and unusual marks on the ground coincide with what Lt. Halt officially reported to the British Ministry of Defense and the United States Air Force.[4]

Col. Halt's report details the events of the second night's encounters as follows:

> Later in the night a red sun-like light was seen through the trees. It moved about and pulsed. At one point it appeared to throw off glowing particles and then break into five separate white objects and then disappeared. Immediately thereafter, three star-like objects were noticed in the sky, two objects to

3. Ibid., p. 73.
4. Ibid., p. 75.

> the north and one to the south, all of which were about 10° off the horizon. The objects moved rapidly in sharp angular movements and displayed red, green and blue lights. The objects to the north appeared to be elliptical through an 8–12 power lens. They then turned to full circles. The objects in the north remained in the sky for an hour or more. The object to the south was visible for two or three hours and beamed down a stream of light from time to time. Numerous individuals, including the undersigned, witnessed the activities in paragraphs 2 and 3.[5]

As of the writing of this book in 1997, Col. Halt is a still-living military commander who witnessed one of the most remarkable, documented UFO encounters in military history.

5. Official Department of the Air Force memorandum by Lt. Col. Charles I. Halt, 13 January 1981.

23

The Japan Air Lines Incident

On November 17, 1986, Captain Kenju Terauchi was at the helm of a B-747 cargo jet. The two-person crew consisted of a flight officer and a flight engineer. Captain Terauchi was a 29-year veteran pilot in 1986. Flight 1628 was en route to Tokyo via Rekyjavik, Iceland and Anchorage, Alaska. At approximately 6:00 P.M. in the evening, the aircraft was passing over the Canadian/Alaskan border and the crew was making preparations to land at Anchorage. At 6:19 P.M. Alaska Standard Time, Capt. Terauchi radioed a traffic information request to the Anchorage Air Route Traffic Control Center. Air Traffic Control Specialist Carl Henley checked his radar and told the captain there was no traffic in his vicinity. Capt. Terauchi responded that lighted traffic was in close proximity at 12 o'clock at the same altitude as Flight 1628, following or shadowing his aircraft. Terauchi declined a request by Specialist Henley to check higher and lower altitude traffic, stating later that the object was level with the plane. Henley checked with Elmendorf Air Force Base radar and learned they had a primary target in the same position Terauchi reported. During some of the frequent radio exchanges between Henley and Flight 1628, Henley did find primary returns in the same areas JL1628 reported traffic. Terauchi requested and obtained permission to make turns and deviations. The captain reported to Henley that the object stayed right with the 747.

At one point, Terauchi asked for and obtained permission to make a 360° turn to the right to fly parallel to the object, at which time it was not visible. When Terauchi returned to his original course, the object was there, as if it had been waiting for them, the Captain later said in his statement for the FAA. Specialist Henley also vectored a United Airlines aircraft and a military C-130 within range to have a look. Each pilot reported no contact, although Terauchi had also lost visual sight of the UFO by then.

During the course of the event, Henley observed three types of tentative radar targets. When Henley asked Terauchi to describe the object, he stated that he could not identify any markings nor state what kind of aircraft it might be. Under clear, cloudless conditions, Terauchi stated that he saw white and yellow strobing lights on the unidentified craft. The 747's on-board color radar was employed throughout the course of the sighting to determine the distance from the plane to the object as five to seven nautical miles.

Capt. Terauchi and his crew were interviewed and debriefed by Jack Wright of the FAA upon landing at Anchorage. During the debriefing, Capt. Terauchi stated that this was the first time anything like this had happened to him. Explaining the incident, Terauchi said that just after passing the Canadian/Alaskan border, flying at 35,000 feet, an object, at times larger than the B-747, with four or five lights in a line, appeared approximately five to seven nautical miles in front of the aircraft. At times, more than one UFO was visible. The sighting lasted nearly an hour—55 minutes per the FAA report.

Although the Captain and his crew were a bit shaken, the FAA determined them to be professional and rational.

According to Timothy Good's account in his book *Above Top Secret*, Captain Terauchi reported that he was unable to explain the event in conventional terms and said that the object may have been ET in origin since they moved and stopped so quickly. The Captain remarked that they were carrying French wine to Japan, stating "maybe they wanted to drink it."[1]

See "FAA Report and Supporting Documents—Carl E. Henley" on page 475.

1. Good, Timothy, *Above Top Secret*, William Morrow, New York, 1988, p. 432.

24

The United Kingdom Wave Of The 1990s

Triangular Craft And More

Flying triangles - huge, silent, low- and slow-flying, yet capable of acceleration at extremely high speeds. We began to learn of these objects during the massive Belgium wave beginning in 1990. CSETI activated its first investigative team to do real-time research in March of 1992 (see *UFOs over Belgium*, by Steven M. Greer M.D.). Over 2,000 sightings were registered in Belgium, many of them by law enforcement and military personnel. Indeed, the triangle had been tracked on both civilian and military radar through maneuvers and exhibiting speeds far in excess of that which any conventional or experimental aircraft could be capable.

In 1992, UFO activity increased dramatically in Scotland. Settled in the towns and valleys between Edinborough and Glasgow, reports started coming in with regularity. One particular town, Bonnybridge, seemed to be the focal point of the flap. A close-knit community of about 5,500 people, young and old alike have reported numerous sightings of various craft, including the triangles. Bonnybridge Councillor Bill Buchanan stated in August of 1996, "to my knowledge, 3,000 people have seen something unusual in our skies during the past few years....And there may be many more who have been afraid to come forward."[1]

In the early years of the wave, most sightings involved balls of light, often spinning and maneuvering among themselves, or black discs. In the mid-1990's, sightings of triangular craft were often reported. Skysearch Scotland, an investigative group led by the Malcolm family in Falkirk, began amassing not only reports but videotape footage of what appeared to be lights in triangular formation, balls of light, and black triangular-shaped hovering craft. Wit-

1. Daily Mail, (London) *Weekend* section, August 3, 1996.

nesses reported seeing these objects dive into the sea or emerge from it. Several Bonnybridge area residents recounted Close Encounters of the Fifth Kind, or human-interactive experiences. A young gentleman from Armadale told of an 35-40 foot bar-shaped object that came rapidly down from the sky during a lightning storm. It flew low over the hedge rows and passed directly over the man's car, then came to a halt in a field. The witness reported, "it just sat there, hovering silently, about 15 feet off the ground. I got out of the car and pointed my halogen lamp at it to get a better look. Immediately, the bulb blew. Then my headlights went out. I tried the car ignition, but it wouldn't start. Suddenly, the thing lept up and reversed at incredible speed over the top of the car."[2] The witness called the police on his cell phone, but it was an hour later than when the sighting occurred. The gentleman cannot account for the missing hour. After his vehicle was towed back to town, the electrical system functioned perfectly once more.

Starting in 1994, a spate of sightings of huge triangular craft began to come in from England. Most reports came from the Midlands and to the north. However, several reports were received from the southwest of England. Each incident had remarkable similarities. Eye witnesses reported the triangular craft to be dark or black, blending in with the night sky. The craft often had a light at each apex of the triangle, and a different type of light in the center. The huge objects flew at a low altitude and a low speed. They were either totally silent or emitted a slight humming noise.

In the summer of 1996, a family was coming home to Glastonbury in southwestern England about dusk on a Sunday evening. Suddenly, the driver— the father—noticed a dark, silent shape pacing the car. The entire family observed a huge triangular craft at low altitude above them. After observing it for a bit, the object was seen to simply vanish.[3] In October and November of 1996, significant waves of sightings of black triangles occurred in the United Kingdom, including a hot spot in the Cardigan Bay area of West Wales where numerous sightings were reported within these two months.

Two articles in *The Sunday Times* (London) in August of 1996 report that the triangular craft has been identified as an experimental craft unveiled by the U.S. Air Force and NASA in August 1996. The articles speculate that because of a near collision with a 747 commer-

---

2. *Ibid.*
3. Personal correspondence, CSETI.

cial jet in 1995, the government had come clean. Rumors have surfaced since 1995 of an experimental triangular craft sighted in California and Nevada which was called "The Flying Dorito," no doubt not its official name. According to *The Sunday Times*, the "waverider" craft was proposed in the 1950s by British scientist Terrence Nonweiler. The account goes on to give specifications of the craft—capable of speeds in excess of 3,000 m.p.h.; "surfs" on the air; low speed flight and ability to float or hover near ground level (termed "LoFlyte"). The article further cites avionics experts who claim the triangle cannot be traced by radar and that a computer "flies" the craft because human pilots are unable to perform all of its complex maneuvers.[4]

While a significant percentage of triangular craft sightings since August 1996, particularly in the United States, may possibly be attributed to this experimental "LoFlyte" craft, it certainly does not account for them all. All of these events predate the release of any such experimental aircraft: The important and impressive wave in Belgium beginning in 1991; the sighting of a huge triangular craft dipping down from the clouds observed by the CSETI investigative team in Belgium in March 1992; the triangular craft encountered at close range by a CSETI team in Mexico in February 1993; and the statement made to the press in 1995 by Admiral of the Fleet Lord Hill-Norton, commenting on the impressive wave in Belgium and the many reported sightings from the United Kingdom, that perhaps the Ministry of Defense was withholding information from the public on ET spacecraft.

The mystery of the gigantic triangular craft is far from solved. Sightings continue to be reported around the world to the present day.

4. *The Sunday Times*, London, August 11, 1996, as reported by Greg Little, Alternate Perceptions magazine, Issue #36, Fall 1996.

25

The Mexico Wave—From 1991

The solar eclipse in 1991 was total in Mexico City. Many people were outdoors observing and videotaping. Much to their surprise, what they captured on tape in addition to the eclipse began an unprecedented wave of UFO sightings that has continued unabated from 1991 to the time of this writing in 1997.

On the day of the eclipse, seventeen people in four cities videotaped what appears to be the same object: a silver disk whose chunky shape earned it the moniker of the "hockey puck". One tape was shot by a television network executive, another by a priest; indeed, by people from all walks of life in cities spread out across the vast Mexican landscape. The tapes began arriving in the mail of Jaime Moussan, the host of "60 Minutos," the Mexican version of our "60 Minutes" in the USA. Sr. Moussan launched a thorough, in-depth investigation of the phenomenon. He had as guests on his show many of the people who had taken the videotapes. His investigation included extensive computer analyses. The results revealed that the same type of UFO, or OVNI, as it is called in Mexico, was captured by all the tapes, and each one appeared to disturb the air behind it. These features were noted in each one of the videotapes taken on that July day. Further investigation ruled out stars, planets or balloons as possible explanations. As time went on, tapes continued to be taken and sent to investigators, including Sr. Moussan. Many UFOs were filmed near jets taking off or landing at the Mexico City airport. There was often a visual lock-on with the UFO by pilots or air traffic controllers; however, the objects did not appear on radar. There were several reports from pilots of instruments suddenly malfunctioning momentarily when the UFO was nearby. There was concern about safety for the aircraft. Thankfully, none experienced any danger at all. This fact has followed through in all of CSETI's research: there is no factual evidence that the ETs have hostile motives towards humankind.

An interesting correlation to the Mexico wave of 1991 came from 4,000 miles away on the same date. What appears to be the identical object was videotaped from Mt. Unsen, Japan. Indeed, when the videos from the four cities in Mexico are split-screened with the object shot in Japan, it is impossible to discern any differences. Those who would claim the entire Mexican wave on the solar eclipse is an elaborate hoax would be hard pressed to explain an identical, simultaneous sighting on the other side of the globe. Moreover, Sr. Moussan has received over 3,000 videos since 1991 of the "hockey puck" UFO as well as huge triangular craft.

CSETI's Rapid Mobilization Investigative Team encountered such a craft at close range in early February 1993. After having followed the Mexican wave through the work of Lee and Britt Elders, CSETI decided to investigate the flap by sending a five-person team to the volcano zone of Mexico. Concurrent with the ongoing wave in Mexico City, another flap began in the volcano zone southeast of Mexico City, in the state of Puebla. There, the world's fourth largest volcano, Mt. Popocatapetl ("Popo" for short), known as the Sleeping Warrior, and its counterpart, Mt. Izzachuatl, the Sleeping Lady, became the site of nightly movement of UFOs. The Warrior is sleeping no more; Popo has awakened and as of late 1997, several major eruptions of toxic gas and ash have occurred over the remote countryside south of the volcano, and over parts of Mexico City, which is 60 aerial miles from the northern slopes of Popo.

Since 1993, CSETI has taken teams to Mexico five times, each resulting in multiple sightings of UFOs, both day and night. We met an oral surgeon in Atlixco who had videotaped the same type of large, silent triangular craft our team encountered on our first trip. Dr. Rosas is a well-respected citizen of his town, active in the community. A radio station in Atlixco acts as a clearinghouse for UFO reports, Atlixco's chief of police has seen the UFOs and an officer has photographed a craft. Over 90% of the citizens of Atlixco have seen the anomalous airborne objects.

In the tiny village of Atlimeyaya at the base of Popo, where the road literally ends, the mayor of the town, who is also the most prominent local businessman, has had several sightings himself. Daylight photographs and at least one video have been taken of UFOs hovering over the steeple of the village church. Citizens ranging from grandmothers who still speak only Aztec to small children report encounters with ET lifeforms on the ground. To a person, these folks have no knowledge of the UFO literature or subculture. The message given to each by the ETs concurs with CSETI's assessment of the constant ET presence here: the volcano will erupt; the ETs will temper the geologic action for as long as they can. The ETs tell the citizens not to worry, they will be back for them.

Here, in these dusty villages and countryside, the *paisanos* live a simple life. They work the land, use every resource available, honor their families and friends, and respect other life. They have the knowledge of living upon the Earth and sustaining themselves from it. Perhaps they are recognized as having the skills for survival and may be taken aboard craft during the times of greatest upheaval, then returned to do the restoration when it is once again viable.

CSETI allowed a crew from the CBS network program "48 Hours" to accompany us on an investigative trip to remote central Mexico in 1994. It was disruptive to be followed constantly by a TV crew. But the cameraman and his assistant were fascinated with the objects they were filming during CSETI's field work each night. Even the on-air correspondent exclaimed during a particularly close-range sighting, "no skeptic can call that an airplane!" The camera crew even petitioned the New York office for permission to stay on with us after the perfunctory 48 hours had elapsed. In fact, they returned to our research area in central Mexico late one night when we had traveled to five different field sites before settling on one. We soon realized the film crew was attempting to locate us, and we "vectored" them in to our location with our powerful halogen lights. The crew continued to film anomalous events. At one point, the chief cameraman told us he expected they could qualify for an Emmy nomination with the footage of UFOs they had shot.

All went well until one of the final nights when humans attempted to fool us by blinking large lights down from a rocky ridge behind us. CSETI's protocols call for us to investigate anything anomalous that occurs, and we'll determine what it is as we go along. Our motto is act now while the event is occurring; figure it out later. The camera crew of course diligently filmed the entire event. At some point in post-production, someone up the line decided to put a "spin" on the CSETI story. The events on the rocky ridge, and one of our sightings, were subjected to ridicule and the viewing public was misinformed about the events that occurred. However, some viewers were more intelligent than expected. CSETI heard from several people involved in avionics who had seen the show. To a person, they told us that when the footage that "48 Hours" was attempting to explain away as a conventional aircraft aired, they knew immediately it was an effort to discredit our work. These aviation experts told us that the craft shown on television was certainly not any kind of known conventional plane. It became clear to them that the show was simply attempting to spin it off as prosaic when indeed it was not. As a correlation, the program refused to honor their written agreement with us to provide CSETI will a copy of all raw footage shot in the field.

Conversely, CSETI allowed a British television crew from Carlton U.K. Productions to accompany us on a journey to Metepec, Mexico in 1997—the Metepec near Mexico City, not the Metepec by Mt. Popo. During our field work, which was being filmed, the crew obtained footage of a highly unusual airborne object. The program will air in the United Kingdom and in the U SA, several months apart. When it first aired in England, the UFO footage was treated with all due respect and presented as a true unknown.

We are often asked why the wave has continued for so many years in Mexico, and why the rest of the world hears so little about it. We feel there are several reasons: the world's fourth largest volcano is moving towards a major eruption. If it violently erupts, the most populated metropolis in the world will be devastated. The population of Mexico City and the countryside on the far side of the volcano is home to over 40,000 million people. It appears that the ETs are monitoring the volcanic activity, tempering it as long as possible so that people have warning and there will be more survivors. It is obvious that the ETs wish to be seen in Mexico; they appeared in broad daylight, beginning at a time when everyone's eyes were turned to the sky. They continue to appear over Mexico City, showing themselves to commercial jet liners and citizens from all walks of life. The press in Mexico reports on these events factually, with no attempts to discredit or ridicule. Law enforcement, government and the military take a laissez-faire attitude towards these visitors and their craft, resulting in a broader general acceptance of the phenomenon than could occur in the United States at the present time. Still, word of these amazing events rarely reaches major media beyond the boundaries of Mexico. It is the task of intrepid investigators to continue to bring the evidence and the facts to the rest of the world. This is something which potentially affects us all. It is a harbinger for future events and what the ETs may reveal of themselves should there be a disaster that will reverberate around the world.

26

The Incident In Varginha—January 1996

Extraterrestrial Life Forms Captured in Brazil?

Facts supplied by Vitorio Pacaccini, Belo Horizonte, Brazil

On January 20, 1996, military forces captured two apparent ET creatures—still alive—in Brazil. The captures occurred in neighboring areas of the city of Varginha, located in the state of Minas Gerais in central Brazil. The event is to be considered one of the most significant ever registered in Brazil, and perhaps in the entire world. Military authorities are keeping secret the details of the operation, but information has leaked to the UFO community due to the investigative work of Professor Vitorio Pacaccini and Ubirajara Rodrigues. Both men live nearby and are considered serious and dedicated researchers. They have devoted over 3,000 hours of investigation to this case.

On the afternoon of January 20, about 3:30 A.M. local time, three young girls named Liliana, Falquira and Katia were walking outside of town. It was a Saturday and the girls were returning home from their jobs. Crossing an empty area, their attention was attracted by a very weird creature just a few meters away. The ET was kneeling and looked as if it were hurt and suffering pain. No UFO was seen at that time. The girls observed the creature for a few minutes then ran away, afraid that what they had just encountered might be the devil.

The three girls were extensively interrogated by the above-mentioned researchers, leaving no doubt whatsoever about what had happened. Very simple kids, they described the creature as being of a dark color with a small body of four to five feet in height. It had no hair at all, had a large brown head and small neck. The face was described as possessing two eyes—large and red—with no pupils visible. There was a slit in place of a mouth, a very small nose and, interestingly, three protuberances right on the top of its forehead. The girls described the protuberances as horns, thus causing them to fear they had just encountered a devil.

Following the leads, researchers Pacaccini and Rodrigues started making enquiries everywhere around the town of Varginha to see if anybody else had seen the same creature. They found several people who observed the military operations as well as the creature in the same location and, perhaps, other creatures in different locations. While conducting the investigation, both men discovered that different witnesses had seen army trucks and other military vehicles and personnel that very morning, just a few blocks from where the girls had their encounter.

While trying to find out what the military were doing, Pacaccini and Rodrigues came to meet a few soldiers and sergeants. One of the soldiers decided to talk secretly about the military mission and gave a confidential taped interview. The military man confirmed that at about 9:00 A.M. on January 20, the Fire Department of Varginha was called by the military to capture a strange 'animal' in the Jardim Andere district. Among the firemen who responded were Sergeant Palhares, Soldier Nivaldo, Corporal Rubens and Soldier Santos, under the command of Major Maciel who was reportedly present as well. Arriving at the scene, the firemen saw that this was no strange animal at all and realized the finding should be reported to the Army Sergeant School Command—Escola de Sargentos das Armas (ESA) in neighboring Tres Coracoes, about ten miles from Varginha. Before there could possibly be time for the Sergeant School to respond, an army truck appeared on the scene. The firemen understood that the high staff of ESA also had been informed about the incident.

The creature was captured using nets and other equipment normally used to capture wild animals. The still-living creature was placed in a one meter square wooden box, which was covered with a resistant fabric and the whole affair was placed atop the army truck. The creature was curled up in the box and wrapped in net. The witnesses stated that it was emitting a buzzing sound similar to a bee. The vehicle headed to the ESA. All personnel involved were ordered by Lieutenant Colonel Wanderley to refrain from talking about the incident with anyone else, telling the men it was a secret operation. Interestingly, Lt. Col. Wanderley's expertise was in atomic-biological-chemical warfare. Perhaps this is why he was put in charge of the operation even though there was a general in command of the ESA at the time.

Policeman Marco Chereze was involved with the capture of one of the creatures. He touched the life form without protection. He died two weeks later with a general infection. The family showed Sr. Pacaccini the last blood exam, which showed that his blood contained 8% of an unknown toxic substance. According to Sr. Pacaccini, the Varginha police department has gone to great lengths to attempt to prove that Sr. Chereze was not even working on January 20, 1996. However, the Chereze family confirms that he was indeed on duty that night, that he came home briefly to change clothes and inform them that he could not come back for dinner because he would be working late on a mission.

After the first soldier gave the taped interview to Pacaccini and Rodrigues, a few other military people came forward to speak about the incident, under the condition that their identities would be kept secret. All those who came forward gave confidential taped interviews. All confirmed that a second creature, probably the one seen by the three girls in the afternoon was captured the same night by personnel from the army, fire department and police secret service. Through the investigative efforts of Pacaccini and Rodrigues, many of the details of the recovery operation are now known.

The second creature, identical to the first, was taken alive to the regional hospital in Varginha. After spending a few hours at the regional hospital, the creature was transferred to the better equipped Humanitas Hospital. Two days later, on the afternoon of January 22, the creature—now dead—was the subject of a huge and well-disguised operation to remove it to the AS.

A few nurses and other personnel from the regional hospital confirmed some facts, although they were suppressed for some time after the incident. All individuals at Humanitas Hospital who had contact with the creature were admonished to not discuss it with anyone, not even their relatives, and to specifically avoid the press and UFO researchers.

Interviews with some of the military men involved in the removal operation who gave confidential interviews reported that three army trucks were used, each with a two-man team. They speculated that three trucks were used to remove one possibly ET body so that none of the trucks would know who was indeed transporting the body of the creature. The Brazilian investigators have since determined these facts. The driving teams, although kept outside the hospital itself, observed details of the operation. Military personnel from Brazil's S-2—the army internal intelligence section—were in charge of getting the corpse from the interior of the hospital, placing it lying down in a wooden box and then loading it into one of the trucks.

All three trucks went back to ESA. The next morning at 4:00 A.M., the trucks headed to another military facility located in Campinas in the state of Sao Paulo, a 200-mile drive. There, the corpse was transferred to the University of Campinas, one of Brazil's best institutions. The body was autopsied by Dr. Fortunato Badan Palhares, who gained worldwide acclaim as one of the best forensic doctors alive when he conducted the autopsy of the famous German Nazi Mengle, whose body was found in Brazil. However, Dr. Palhares has publicly denied having taken part in the autopsy of the creature found in January of 1996.

One year after the Varginha incident, another witness came forward—Joao Bosco Manoel. He called Sr. Pacaccini. He and Sr. Rodrigues met with him and heard his story. He was an independent witness to the capture of the first creature. At approximately 10:45 A.M. on January 20, Sr. Bosco was in the area selling fish door-to-door when his attention was diverted by a fire truck and firemen, but no evidence of a fire. He hid and watched the goings on. He observed six firemen hurriedly emerging from the bushes, followed by four firemen wearing big gloves and between them were carrying the creature wrapped in a net. The life form was put into the truck and the men drove away. Sr. Bosco noticed an extremely acrid, ammonia-like smell permeating the open air. Sr. Bosco spoke at a press conference and made his story public, stating that he could identify at least two of the firemen. This caused something of an uproar due to the official denial surrounding the story. Sr. Bosco was intimidated and threatened following his press conference, and Sr. Pacaccini spent a great deal of time meeting with him following threatening incidents. Sr. Bosco eventually moved out of the state of Minas Gerais.

The Brazilian media has widely reported on the incident and the majority of the population understands that the case is real and that the military and civil authorities are keeping the facts absolutely quiet. Researchers Pacaccini and Rodrigues have determined that the policemen involved in the captures have since been transferred and promoted. Since the incident, the region where Varginha is located, in the southern part of the state of Minas Gerais, is experiencing one of the largest waves of UFO sightings ever registered, including reports of huge UFOs observed at close range and reported contacts with inhabitants.

27

The Arizona Sightings—March 1997

On March 13, 1997, flying objects traveled across a large portion of southern Arizona. Seen by thousands, videotaped by many, evoking comment from the military and government, the most significant UFO event in a decade occupied a prominent place in the press and gained worldwide attention.

The National UFO Reporting Center in Seattle, Washington, received its first call at 8:16 P.M. on March 13. A retired police officer from Paulden, Arizona, sixty miles north of Phoenix, called in to report observing five red lights in a cluster headed south. In less than two minutes, another report came in from Prescott, fifteen miles south of Paulden. It all broke loose after that, with multiple calls coming in from Wickenburg to Tempe. The Center's director, Peter Davenport, who describes himself as usually skeptical about the reports received at the Center, stated:

"The incident over Arizona was the most dramatic I've seen...what we have here is the real thing. *They* are here.[1] [emphasis in original]

As the airborne objects came over the flight paths leading to the Phoenix Sky Harbor Airport, more than one commercial pilot radioed to the control tower asking for an identification of the lights. The air traffic controllers had no answers. They could visually see the objects, yet nothing unaccounted for appeared on their radar screens.

Investigation subsequent to March 13 revealed that callers jammed police department phone lines, as well as television and radio station phones. Luke Air Force Base near Phoenix was also besieged with calls of sighting reports as the objects traveled south over the greater Phoenix metropolitan area. The objects' speed over greater Phoenix was estimated by many observers as a leisurely

1. *USA Today* newspaper, article by Richard Price, June 18, 1997.

30 m.p.h. This certainly suggests that the objects indeed wanted to be seen and videotaped.

A variety of UFOs were reported: triangles, lights in a straight line, orbs in a V-shaped or delta formation, an actual solid triangular-shaped object. Many witnesses stated that the lights seemed to glow from within—they were very bright but did not shine or cast light. Most observers who saw them at closer range stated the lights were white with orange to red edges and centers. Some witnesses could discern a dim, dark shape behind the light formation that distorted or blotted out the stars as it slowly passed. CSETI's director and research director spoke with a retired Air Force pilot on the evening of March 14 who saw the lights clearly from his home. He resides in Carefree, which is north of Phoenix and has much less light pollution than within the city. He described the lights as silent, slow moving and maintaining a formation. He stated that this was unlike anything he had witnessed in the skies during his entire career as a military pilot.

Regardless of the type of formation seen, all observers agreed that the lights or objects were slow moving, very large and totally silent. The size of the object was estimated as being from 900 feet to more than a mile in length. Computer analysis of witness's videotapes done by Village Labs in Tempe marked the length as 6,000 feet—well over a mile long. Jim Dilettoso, a partner of Village Labs, was asked by a CSETI senior member in July of 1997 whether after having done analyses of the best videotapes made on March 13, he considered the objects to be of terrestrial origin. Mr. Dilettoso stated emphatically, "no."

Is it a coincidence that on March 13, 1997, a CSETI team had arrived in Phoenix and convened at Village Labs to put together CSETI's best available evidence video for use at CSETI's Project Starlight congressional briefings scheduled in Washington, D.C. for the following month? The CSETI team was culling video clips and photographs from hundreds of sightings around the world to compile the best UFO photographic and film evidence into a video briefing. Mr. Dilettoso had graciously granted CSETI the use of the state-of-the-art facilities and personnel at Village Labs in order to create the video chronicle. Moreover, Jim Dilettoso stated on ABC Television's *World News Tonight* in June 1997: "Perhaps they [the ETs] were listening to the conversations and decided to come down and put on a show for everyone."

Interestingly, in July 1997, a video taken of several orbs of light in broad daylight on March 13 came to the attention of Phoenix researchers. Shot near the Estrella Mountains, where the objects hovered about 9:00 P.M. on the night of March 13, the video correlates with the observation of another independent witness. A professional cameraman who lives in Phoenix related to CSETI's research director that he was driving on Highway 10 about 1:45 P.M. on March 13 when his attention was attracted to a very unusual group of bright white balls of light *moving* at low altitude in front of the Estrella Mountains. The eyewitness stated that he was able to get four or five glances at the objects while driving before they vanished. The cameraman revisited the same area a few days later with camera in tow and videotaped from the side of the freeway the vicinity where he had seen the lights. Showing his tape to CSETI's research director, he stated that he wanted to ascertain whether any street lights or ground lights could be responsible for the orbs. After careful review of his video footage, the witness determined to his own satisfaction that no pole lights were in a correlating location or altitude to explain what he observed on the afternoon of March 13.

Richard Price of *USA Today* in an article appearing in the June 18, 1997 issue, interviewed witness Bill Greiner, who stated he would never be the same after the sighting. Mr. Greiner turned from a skeptic to someone who saw what he describes as "astonishing and a little frightening." Mr. Greiner, a cement truck driver, was hauling a load of cement down a mountain north of Phoenix when he saw two white, orange and red UFOs. He described them as having spinning tops. Greiner observed one of the orbs break away and fly over Luke Air Force Base. He stated that three F-16 fighter jets went in pursuit of the UFO. As the jets approached, the UFO shot straight up and quickly vanished. In Mr. Greiner's words: "It was crazy. I know those pilots saw it. Hell, I'll take a lie detector test on national TV if that guy from the base does the same thing...I wish the government would just admit it. It's like having 50,000 people in a stadium watch a football game and then having someone tell us we weren't there."

The analyses of the amateur video tapes undertaken at Village Labs by Jim Dilettoso and his partner Michael Tanner reveal that four different formations or objects traveled from north to south on the evening of March 13, 1997. The transit across the region lasted 106 minutes. The lights were uniform, did not vary in brightness or intensity across the span of each light, and did not glow. They were determined *not* to be aircraft lights, holograms, lasers or military flares. Comparison with the lights on the Phoenix skyline seen in the videos shows the UFOs to be markedly unique.

The residents of southern Arizona were intrigued, curious and expected an explanation from the civilian and military authorities. While several reports from various military personnel stated that the lights were flares being used during National Guard war game maneuvers, Mr. Dilettoso stated that investigation revealed the National Guard could not, would not and did not cause the lights that were seen by thousands of Arizonans on March 13, 1997. While jets from Luke Air Force Base were in the Phoenix skies on that night, a spokesman from the base assured the press that the jets' lights could not account for the sightings.

Reacting to the groundswell coming from the local citizenry, Phoenix Councilwoman Frances Barwood raised a question at a city council meeting as to whether anyone was conducting an official investigation. Instantly, the public seized upon her comment and made her their "official" contact to the government. Although Councilwoman Barwood said she did not see the objects herself, many of her constituents did. When the public and the media learned of her raising the question of an investigation, hundreds of calls were received from the curious citizens who now had a public servant upon whom to focus.

But the city council, the mayor's office, the governor's office and US Senator John McCain were unable to effect any official action. Senator McCain referred it to the US Air Force, who announced in June 1997 that it would do nothing to investigate the incidents, referring it back to the local jurisdictions. And, of course, this would be the Air Force's position since they have officially been out of the UFO investigation business since the closure of Project Blue Book in 1969.

The search for additional clues into this momentous day in March 1997 continues to intrigue researchers, analysts, the media and thousands of residents of Arizona and beyond.

28

CE-5: A Proposal For An Important New Research Category

1992

Introduction

With the exception of archaeology and anthropology, every viable area of scientific inquiry requires real-time research and observation. While difficult, this is none the less true for UFOlogy than any other field of inquiry, and requires the development of prospective direct research protocols. This research approach requires extensive field observation, particularly in areas of UFO "waves" so that UFOlogists may directly observe and interact with the phenomenon in situ. This paper will present a new research category, called a Close Encounter of the Fifth Kind (or CE-5 for short), and propose ways in which this category of close encounters may be used to evolve direct, real-time research for UFOlogists.

Background and Rationale

First proposed by Dr. J. Allen Hynek, Close Encounters were initially divided into those of the First, Second and Third kind. A Close Encounter of the First Kind, or CE-1, is described as the observation of a UFO within 500 feet. A Close Encounter of the Second Kind, or CE-2, is one where some form of trace evidence is obtained, such as in a landing case or radar case. A Close Encounter of the Third Kind, or CE-3, denotes the observation of a humanoid, generally but not necessarily in the vicinity of or within a UFO. In more recent years, the category of a Close Encounter of the Fourth Kind, or CE-4, has generally been accepted as an interaction where a human is taken on board a UFO, presumably in the presence of humanoids.

A thorough review of the UFO literature has yielded several dozen cases, however, where a new and important research category is evident. This research category, called a Close Encounter of the

Fifth Kind, or CE-5, is characterized by human-initiated and/or voluntary human interactive encounters. That is, encounters with UFOs or their occupants are initiated or furthered by voluntary, direct and willful means by human observers. For example (see specific cases cited below), there are multiple cases where individuals are by chance in the area of a UFO sighting, and they flash a car light or flashlight, which directly results in the UFO moving or signaling back to them in an intelligible fashion. Such interactive episodes have occurred as a result of intentionally directed light, sound (such as voices) and, remarkably, thought. CE-5s which occur secondarily, as in the example cited above where an individual was by chance in the area of a UFO sighting and then initiated contact, is called a Second Degree CE-5. Significantly, a First Degree CE-5 is distinguished by intentional human actions which attract a UFO to an area in an interactive fashion (see below for specific cases).

It should be noted that a CE-5 may initially involve or result in a CE-1, CE-2, CE-3 or even CE-4. That is, an intentional and interactive human action may result in, or occur during, a sighting within 500 feet, a landing with trace effects, the observation of a humanoid and/or an on-board experience. In this regard, while relatively few close encounters of the first, second, third or fourth kind involve CE-5s, every CE-5 involves a CE-1, 2, 3 or 4.

Specific Case Reports

Second Degree CE-5s

1. Father William Melchior Gill at the Boianai Mission in Papua, New Guinea, along with 38 other people witnessed over a three-hour period on June 26, 1959, a disc-like brilliantly lit object with four humanoids on the deck-like structure. Twenty-five people signed the case report from this sighting. Then on the following night, June 27, 1959 at 6:02 p.m., Father Gill and others observed a large "mother ship" with four humanoids on the out-side "deck" with two other UFOs in the distance. Then Father Gill initiated waving at the humanoids, and to everyone's astonishment one of the humanoids immediately did likewise in response. Following this, all four humanoids began to wave at the human observers. A Mission boy was sent to get a flashlight, and this was used to signal in Morse, dashed, towards the UFO. This elicited a response wherein the humanoids were seen waving and "making motions like a pen-

dulum, in a sideways direction." At this point, the UFO advanced towards the group for about 30 seconds, and after 2-3 more minutes the humanoids went below deck. However, the UFO stayed in the area of the Mission for at least another hour. Incidentally, this report was later researched and confirmed by Dr. J. Allen Hynek. He regarded it as a true and inexplicable UFO event. (This encounter is reported in various journals and books, including "The World's Greatest UFO Mysteries," N. Blundell and R. Boar, 1983, Octopus Books (pp 11-14).

2. On July 27, 1967, Gary Storey of Newton, New Hampshire observed a flashing disc-shaped UFO through his home telescope. Mr. Storey's brother-in-law then impulsively flashed a flashlight at the UFO three times, whereupon the UFO went into reverse and flashed back at the men three times. The two men, both former radar operators, began to flash repeatedly to the UFO. Each time, it would respond in the exact sequence sent by the men. This exchange was repeated at least a dozen times, then the UFO flashed all of its lights and disappeared behind the tree line. (Ibid., pp 9-10)
3. In March of 1981, near Tacuarembo, Uruguay, Police Chief Miguel Costa, along with his wife and another couple, were driving in the early morning darkness when they saw a huge UFO. Mr. Costa stopped his car and on impulse flashed his car headlights at the UFO. Immediately, the UFO stopped and then zigzagged in response. Mr. Costa began driving again, and he was followed by the UFO. Again, he stopped the car and flashed his headlights at the object, which in turn stopped and wavered in reply. The humans continued to drive and the UFO followed them for approximately 30 miles, at which time it descended to about 50-100 yards and was joined by another UFO. At this point the craft could bee seen as a disc-shaped object with a dome on top. The UFOs then hovered over them for 90 minutes. (Ibid., pp 139-141)
4. On March 29, 1978 at 9:30 P.M. outside of Indianapolis, Indiana, a caravan of trucks was traveling on Interstate 70 when suddenly several of the trucks were engulfed in a bright blue light. This caused complete silence inside the trucks, the engines sputtered and the CB radios on which the truckers had been talking failed. This lasted a few seconds, then the light disappeared. Then the rear driver shouted on his CB radio, "hey, UFO, if you have your ears

on, I want to go with you!" Suddenly, the blue light returned and again surrounded all the trucks for about 15 seconds, resulting in the same EM effects as before. This event was witnessed by several other drivers along the interstate highway. (from *Uninvited Guests* by Richard Hall, p. 53)

5. On October 23, 1980, five men saw a boomerang-shaped craft approach a smokestack of the huge copper smelter in Morencia, Arizona. This UFO shone a brilliant light into each of the two smokestacks and then rapidly accelerated towards the town of Sanford. Then, Joe Nevarez stated verbally that he wished the UFO would come back so that he could get a better look at it. Immediately, the UFO performed an instant reversal and returned to the slag dump area of the smelter. It then accelerated out of sight to the north. (from *MUFON UFO Journal*, No. 270, October 1990, p. 22)
6. In 1990, the television program *Unsolved Mysteries* carried a story about the multiple CE-5 experiences of Dorothy Isaat, beginning on November 9, 1974, outside Vancouver, British Columbia, Canada. On this date, she saw a large UFO in the sky and wished to communicate with it. She mentally said, "whatever I do, please imitate back to me." As she moved her flashlight three times in a certain direction, the UFO would respond by moving to the left, right, up or down. Then she mentally asked it to come closer, and it did. These events have been ongoing for a number of years and have been accompanied by photographs taken by Ms. Isaat.
7. Multiple CE-5s are reported in the 1987 book *Night Siege* by the late Dr. J. Allen Hynek and Philip J. Imbrogno, which documents the extensive UFO wave in the Hudson Valley, New York area. One example: On New Year's Eve 1982 near Kent, New York, Edwin Hansen was driving home when he saw a huge boomerang-shaped UFO with a brilliant searchlight on the ground. Mr. Hansen thought to himself, "I wish it would come closer so I can get a better look at it." As soon as he had that thought, the UFO began to descend and head straight for his car. He stated that the huge object came very close and, as his anxiety increased, some sort of communication occurred between him and the UFO. He states: "I felt thoughts that weren't my own, but a kind of a voice telling me not to be afraid..." (*Night Siege*, pp 7-8)

8. Also from *Night Siege*, pages 8-10: On February 16, 1983, Monique O'Driscoll and her 17-year old daughter saw a large UFO near Kent, New York. Several minutes later, as the UFO began to leave the area of observation, the witness said to herself, "Oh, please don't go, I want to look at you some more." The witness states: "At that split second, it stopped, made a complete turn, and then it was facing toward me. Then it started moving toward me, very slowly..."
9. On March 17, 1983, Dennis Sant near Brewster, New York saw a large triangular UFO over Interstate 84, with many cars and trucks stopped to watch it. The witness states: "I remember saying to myself, 'I wish I could get a better look at it.' And as I was thinking that, it made a 360° turn, as if rotating on a wheel, stopped, and started to float in my direction. It continued to approach me, and I just stood there transfixed. It stopped forty feet from me and was hovering twenty feet above a telephone pole in front of my house..." Multiple witnesses observed this CE-5. (*Night Siege*, pp. 17-20)

First Degree CE-5s

1. Author Preston E. Dennett writes in an article entitled "Calling All UFOs" that multiple CE-5s have occurred in conjunction with very bright outdoor light and laser shows, such as those performed for grand openings, movie premiers and outdoor rock concerts. On May 19, 1983, Arni Wyler and Rick Liebert observed three large UFOs near the La Brea Tar Pits in Southern California during an outdoor light show using special effects with multiple brilliant lights. The UFOs came closer and seemed to be investigating the source of all the unusual bright lights activity. Mr. Liebert states that he has seen this sort of response from UFOs whenever he has set up the lights in regular patterns.
2. Again, Mr. Liebert states that in 1978, in San Diego, California, he was preparing for a laser light show atop a downtown office building. While tuning the 22-watt green argon spectrophysics laser through an opening in the building's roof, a large V-shaped UFO with ten lights on its underside passed less than 100 feet above ten witnesses on the roof. The UFO was large enough to fill up the entire sky as it passed at about 25 knots over the witnesses. Mr. Lie-

bert and others are convinced that it was the attention-getting power of the laser which attracted the UFO to the building.

3. In October of 1973, a college student was hiking at sunset up a remote mountain outside of Boone, North Carolina, when he had a close encounter first with a craft and then with a humanoid outside the craft. This individual reports a period of missing time and an extensive interactive experience. Following this experience, the witness was able to contact the occupants of the UFO telepathically, and using a specific series of thought projections, was able to precipitate numerous UFO sightings in the area, which were reported in the press at the time. The student became apprehensive about these events and stopped the experiment some months later. In 1977, on December 27th, this individual again initiated contact via thought projection as before, to see if any results could still be obtained. The individual, who was born in Charlotte, North Carolina, projected the information of who he was as well as a mental "map" of where he was born and where he was now living. After falling asleep, he and his housemate were awakened by a large, disc-shaped UFO hovering over the house emitting a brilliant blue-white light. The witness felt a definite conscious presence from the craft, which after a few moments accelerated and flew off towards Grandfather Mountain. The individual was astonished to hear on the news and read in the Charlotte papers that a UFO had been seen that night over Charlotte, North Carolina, in the area where he was born. It was seen by multiple witnesses, including the Charlotte police helicopter pilot. The police helicopter, Snoopy II, pursued the UFO over Charlotte, coming within 200 feet of the craft and observed a definite metallic skin. The Charlotte Douglas Airport recorded these events, and the UFO was seen on Air Traffic Control Radar. (from CSETI case reports)

Research Implications and Applications

The above cases, which represent only a small fraction of cases which we found, indicate that CE-5s are an integral part of the UFO phenomenon. From analyzing these and many other reports we have concluded that there are three main components of these interactive episodes which can be integrated into UFO research: light, sound and, remarkably, thought. The Center for the Study of Extraterrestrial Intelligence (CSETI) has developed research protocols that are incorporated into a CE-5 Initiative involving various select Working Groups around the world. These Working Groups are utilizing the protocols, both in de novo settings (i.e., where no known UFO wave is occurring) and in selected, high-quality wave areas. A subgroup of the Working Group is the Rapid Mobilization Investigative Team (RMIT) which is comprised of individuals capable and willing to respond to significant UFO activity around the world so that on-site research and protocol applications can be pursued in a timely fashion.

The philosophical basis and rationale for the CE-5 Initiative is elaborated in other CSETI position papers. Briefly put, it states that UFOs are real, that they are under intelligent control, that the beings controlling these craft are capable of interacting with humans in a peaceful and non-hostile manner, and that real-time research requires the human-empowering step of getting out there with this phenomenon and engaging with it in a mutually non-threatening way. Contrary to conventional wisdom, the barriers to such research and to the development of a carefully open relationship between these beings and humans, are not based on logistics, technology or economics, but rather in human will, vision and motivation. We recognize that it is a visionary, if not radical, step to engage in such a project, but the time has come to put our time, energy and resources into real-time research out there where the UFO phenomenon is actually occurring.

Practically speaking, this research initiative involves utilizing powerful lights, lasers, sound technology, and what is termed sequenced coherent thought projection to engage UFOs and/or their occupants in an interactive episode, however simple. The Working Groups, consisting of 5-15 well-trained and motivated researchers, are carefully selecting secured CE-5 sites for this research, some of which are in documented UFO wave areas. We are dedicated to maintaining a flexible and open mind about how this research will evolve and which protocols will be most efficacious. While unafraid of failure, from early results we are confident of steady, if initially modest, success.

Free of fear, with peaceful intentions and with an open mind, we are preparing to meet this phenomenon face to face. For those of us who know that this phenomenon is real, that UFOs are real, it is time to test our convictions and interact with it in a voluntary, conscious way. Who knows, perhaps much of the involuntary interactions of the past is a result of the paucity of voluntary, peaceful civilian efforts. Our limitations are really self-imposed; let us empower ourselves to remove our limitations and create our own reality. For the time may be short, and there is no greater loss than that of a missed Destiny....

The Next Generation of UFO Research

The modern era of UFO sightings and research began in 1947. In that time, thousands of cases of aerial sightings, landings, crash retrievals, humanoid encounters and on-craft visitation have occurred. The virtually all-volunteer group of civilian UFO investigators have done a remarkable job of documenting these events and further obtaining official government papers which substantiate the reality of the UFO phenomenon.

This hard work, dedication and personal sacrifice merits our full attention and respect since it is these efforts alone which have prevented this extraordinary phenomenon from vanishing from public view.

The question presented here, however, is this: Have we reached the 'critical mass' of information, sighting patterns and well-documented details to draw some important general conclusions and begin a new era of UFO/ETI research? The answer to these questions is a firm yes.

Conclusions

First. Some, though by no means all, UFO reports represent encounters with structured craft with measurable physical characteristics, indicating that we are dealing with ET Spacecraft (ETS) belonging to intelligent beings of an ET civilization.

Second. These ETS display energy and flight characteristics indicating applied physics which transcend our current understanding of the natural universe. These may involve applied unified field physics, "hyperdimensional" physics and/or "other dimensional" physics.

Third. The Extraterrestrial Intelligence (ETI) behind these craft do not at this time desire open and fully "official" contact with human civilizations. However, an analysis of the data from the past half-century indicates that a plan is in place which allows for gradually deeper and more widespread contact and communication, perhaps so that humans may become accustomed to the idea that there is, in fact, other intelligent life in the universe.

Fourth. Crash retrieval and numerous world-wide humanoid reports indicate that these ET spacecraft belong to more than one ET civilization, which may be working in concert on various research and observation missions to Earth.

Fifth. Persistent worldwide reports of telepathic communication and other so-called paranormal experiences associated with ETI indicate mental capabilities which may parallel the physical and technological development of these beings. The "science of consciousness," which has only recently received serious research by humans, appears to be well advanced in these beings.

Sixth. Certain agencies of the world's major governments are quite concerned with this phenomenon and obviously know more (and are doing more) than they are officially willing to acknowledge.

Seventh. While some aspects of ETI behavior, research and reconnaissance have been disturbing to some human observers, no data exists to indicate that ETI are motivated by net hostile intentions. It is our conclusion that, while ETI behavior does not always coincide with human values and expectations, the motives and ultimate intentions of the ETI currently visiting Earth are non-hostile. However, ETI appear to be wary of and have an aversion to the human propensity towards violence and war-making, and certain elusive or enigmatic aspects of their behavior may relate to this concern, as well as their own security considerations surrounding their advanced technology and planet of origin. This is: they do not want a divided and war-prone civilization to acquire their technology at this time since this would greatly endanger both ETI and human civilizations.

Eighth. Research from the monuments on Mars, Zechariah Sitchin and elsewhere indicate that ETI contact with Earth is probably an ancient, as opposed to purely recent, phenomenon.

Ninth. A limited though definite interest in peaceful bilateral contact with humans is evident in many case reports and should be the focus of the next major thrust in active UFO research.

Certainly, there are a number of additional conclusions which can be stated about this phenomenon, such as ETI interest in human nuclear facilities, technology, reproduction and so forth. But with all of the above nine preliminary conclusions, all of which are supported by both civilian and government UFO evidence, we can begin to formulate a new line of study and research—one which may bring us to new horizons in the ETI-human relationship.

Prospective Active Research Vs. Retrospective Passive Research

Virtually all non-governmental UFO research in the past has been, by definition, retrospective and passive. That is, there have been investigations and research into sightings, crash retrievals, abductions and so forth which have already occurred. The accuracy and completeness of data obtained by investigating past events are necessarily limited by the passage of time, loss of data, variable memory retention, etc. While such passive, retrospective research is valuable and must continue, its limitations would be compensated by initiating active, prospective research. This type of research involves "real-time" monitoring of UFO/ETI events as they occur and provides an accuracy and dynamism previously not possible. More importantly, active prospective research would allow for ETI/human interaction and "dialogue" and the furthering of the ETI/Human relationship. Prospective research means having observers or researchers present at a time a UFO event is occurring, and providing them with training and protocols to engage the UFO/ETI in dynamic exchange and communication—a close encounter of the fifth kind.

Close Encounters Of The Fifth Kind

Contrary to popular beliefs, not all UFO/human encounters have been human passive in nature. There are many accounts in the UFO literature which describe a chance sighting of an ETS or humanoid whereupon the human initiates some action or contact which results in an ETS or humanoid response. (See Part I of this section for an explanation of CE-5 and some case histories.) The distinguishing aspect of a CE-5 is that a human actively initiates or actively participates in a bilateral ETI/human interaction, no matter how simple. (Note that a CE-5 may precipitate or initially involve a close encounter of the first, second, third or fourth kind.)

CE-5s are further divided into first and second degree CE-5s. A first degree CE-5 is when the actual sighting or encounter is caused by some intentional human action. For example, researchers might place a bank of specially arranged lights in an area of an ongoing UFO wave which then precipitates a close encounter with either a craft or humanoid. A second degree CE-5 is when the ETS is already in the area, but human-initiated actions result in a response from the craft or humanoids. For example, a chance encounter is furthered when the human flashes his/her car lights at the ETS, which then comes closer or shows some other responsive action. A review of the UFO literature to date reveals that both first and second degree CE-5s have occurred in the past (see Part I), and we believe that humans should explore the potential for such interactive events in the context of active prospective UFO research.

Of course, the opposition to prospective, active research is based on the assumption that close encounters a) are not under human control or influence, and b) close encounters or UFO sightings cannot be precipitated, anticipated or predicted. But is this correct? A review of thousands of case reports has led CSETI to conclude that neither of these assumptions are true. While it is true that humans do not ultimately control ETS sightings, evidence exists that humans can and do influence ETS appearances and/or behavior. The well-documented responses of ETS to human actions—be they friendly, communicative or otherwise—are some examples of human influence on ETS behavior. Human military, space-related and nuclear activities are known to influence not only ETS behavior but have actually precipitated sightings, albeit unintentionally. Moreover, the propensity of ETS to appear in so-called "waves" or "flaps," frequently in a well-defined geographic area, provides us with potential opportunities for basic bilateral communication and real-time active research—a CE-5 Initiative. Such a CE-5 Initiative or research project utilizes waves, trained individuals who are willing to volunteer, and other active means to facilitate prospective research that is both interactive and, eventually, reproducible.

We feel that active, prospective research is feasible and should be seriously considered by UFO researchers. Our initial program is a cooperative, low-budget, primarily volunteer effort, utilizing trained observers at "wave" locations, individuals who have had repeat encounters, and active experiments designed to precipitate events. We have concluded that the obstacles to successful CE-5 Initiatives are not so much based in logistical, economic, personnel or technological problems as they are rooted in the question of human will, imagination, motivation and motives, and what can best be termed "spirit." That is, the rate-limiting factor in this experiment has been and will continue to be human consciousness itself.

The Imperative Of Consciousness

When we speak of interacting with ETI, we are, after all, talking about reaching out to advanced conscious intelligent beings, and not the mere observation of some natural phenomenon or biological process. For this reason, careful consideration must be given to not only our view of ETI's intentions but, more importantly, to our own intentions and attitudes. The human tendency—well evidenced by both military and civilian reactions to ETS—for xenophobic, violent and even paranoid reactions to the new or unknown must be addressed and rectified. The human predisposition to view anything which we do not understand or control as intrinsically hostile and threatening must be overcome. The blind quest for personal gain, profiteering and an inclination towards viewing ETS/ETI in a predominately 'acquisition' framework needs to be altered. If we are motivated by a desire to 'outsmart' ETI and acquire their technology and energy source, then our efforts will fail. If we approach ETI with greed, fear, assumed hostility and suspicion, then we shall expend our efforts in vain.

There is no doubt that we are dealing with beings who are capable of reading, by both telepathic and conventional means, our true intentions and motivations, and who can sense the "spirit of our endeavor." Success requires that the spirit of our endeavor be one of scientific openness, the search for truth, altruism, selflessness, harmlessness and non-covetousness. A desire for the peaceful furtherance of the ETI-human relationship is paramount. For these reasons, "purity of motive" on the part of human researchers and investigators is a primary requisite, while specific skills, expertise, and technology are important but secondary considerations. The breadth and clarity of our consciousness is imperative and transcends all other considerations. Our obsession with technology and outward things tends to obscure the Big Picture of the ETI/human relationship, and all that it entails. While competence and knowledge cannot be slighted, we must insist on the primary importance of consciousness. In this regard, it is likely that a novice possessed of noble intentions and equipped with only a flashlight would meet (has met?) with greater success than a governmental agency motivated by lesser intentions, even though it has advanced technology, personnel and billions of dollars at its disposal. Indeed, an aboriginal with only a bonfire may go further in the establishment of communication and the discovery of truth!

Of almost equal importance is the question of how we view ETI intentions and motives. If the tabloids, sensationalist books and rumor mills are to be believed, ETI are all either guru-like space gods or Darth Vader space conquerors! Our tendency to polarize on either side of this issue is both premature and unwarranted—and it is dangerous. It is unlikely that they are either perfect gods or evil empire operatives, yet these views of their motives have influenced and will continue to influence our attitudes and actions unless consciously addressed. A review of the cases to date would indicate that while some actions are enigmatic and even disturbing to some human sensibilities, no evidence of net hostile intentions exists. Here, we must differentiate between our perceptions of actions and actual intentions or motives, since these are two separate considerations. (For a more thorough treatment of this topic, See "The Case For Non-hostility" on page 48.) A seemingly disturbing action may occur for a net neutral or even benevolent purpose. Certainly, as an Emergency and Trauma doctor, not a day goes by where a child or impaired adult victim of trauma could view my efforts to help him as painful and therefore motivated by a desire to do harm, even though my motives are just the opposite. That a frightened child perceives my actions as hurtful or malevolent is a function of the child's level of awareness and knowledge, and in no way reflects my true intentions. Could not an analogous process be occurring with some ETI events which conventional wisdom has deemed hostile and therefore as evidence of malevolent intentions?

Certainly for CE-5 Initiative research it is important to give ETI the benefit of the doubt, and until proven otherwise, assume non-hostility. An assumption of ETI hostility will poison the atmosphere of future bilateral contact and prevent the development of an ETI-human relationship free of conflict. This is one time in human history where fortitude, trust and self-discipline are essential prerequisites to further progress. The assumption of non-hostility does not equal either blind naivete or an assumption that ETI are perfect god-like saviors. But it does mean holding an open, non-suspicious and positive attitude towards ET beings. To do otherwise is to create a reality based in conflict and hostility, a thorny path already well traveled by the human race.

Beyond the consciousness of actual researchers or those who have had close encounters is the importance of the background consciousness of humanity as a whole. The type and quality of any further ETI-human interactions—and therefore the specific results of any CE-5 Initiative efforts—will be in part dependent on and limited by the level of evolution in human society. We should not be surprised if an ET civilization prefers to limit the degree of open contact with humans given the present preoccupation with militarism, conflict and violence. As human society makes the necessary transition to world peace and cooperation, I believe we will see a concomitant increase in ETI openness and bilateral communication. In this sense, the success of the CE-5 Initiative is directly dependent on the peace and unification of the human race. World peace and world unity and cooperation then are important determinants of future ETI-human events. The depth and quality of the CE-5 Initiative may prove to be modest, but these will increase as human society evolves towards peace and unity.

The CE-5 Initiative: Some Preliminary Concepts And Protocols

How then might we go forward? A few general scenarios and basic protocols have evolved which have proven to be productive. Important to all of these is the "imperative of consciousness" mentioned above, and a dedication to an integrated multi-disciplinary approach which utilizes both technology and consciousness. For it may be that a thought is as effective as a laser in facilitating a CE-5 event!

Communication Techniques To Be Considered:

1. Simple light or laser signals or codes;
2. Telepathic contact and projection;
3. Ground-based visuals, such as crop circle-like (or other) symbols placed on the ground to be visible from the sky;
4. Auditory and/or non-auditory sound waves;
5. Direct speech/language (assume ETI translation capabilities)

Possible Programs and Protocols:

1. The Rapid Mobilization Investigative Team (RMIT) of initially volunteer investigators who will rapidly respond to areas of major confirmed UFO waves. For example, the dispatch of 5-10 people to the Belgian wave of 1989 who were trained in employing various CE-5 communications approaches (see above) may have yielded a true breakthrough in ETI communications. These teams would work

with local investigators and authorities in coordinating locations and specific activities. We believe that a core of 50-100 trained, dedicated people could supply a wave site with a presence of 5-10 observers.

2. The British Crop Circle Investigating Team is similar to the above team but would provide rotating members throughout the "circle season" to not only monitor circle formation, but to further employ communications techniques as mentioned above to "answer back" to the circle-makers. In this way, it is hoped that a crop circle "dialogue" of sorts would be developed.
3. Individually Based ETI Research is a program which would draw on volunteers who have had repeat close encounters or contact with ETS or ETI. Such individuals would voluntarily cooperate with a research network and use various communication protocols to facilitate ETI-human contact and exchange.
4. The Telepathic Extraterrestrial Outreach Network (TETON) would be based on the telepathic capacities of both humans and ETI and would utilize protocols designed to precipitate ETI-human events, which in turn could be monitored by collateral field investigators. For example, a group of trained TETON researchers could employ thought projection to request an ETS sighting or landing at a previously designated and secured site at a specific time. We have reason to believe that such an endeavor would be successful if properly conducted and if driven by the right motives and understanding. A safe and secure venue would certainly be essential.

Certainly, other programs could be suggested and we are open to any other ideas which might further the CE-5 Initiative. These are only initial ideas and concepts, and we welcome serious input from other analysts and researchers.

Postnote: Since this article was written in 1992, the CE-5 Initiative and RMIT have had progressively successful encounters. See research reports and later articles from CSETI. —Ed.

Developing Appropriate Collective Self-esteem

For any of this to go forward, it is essential that we address the question of how humans view themselves, and how the human race is viewed, by humans, as a whole. How many times do we read in the UFO literature the word "superior" in reference to the ET beings currently visiting Earth? And how often have we heard theologians and others indicate that we humans are the only beings that matter in this universe so grand! Both of these extreme views—that of innate human uniqueness and divine superiority—are dangerous distortions of the collective appropriate self-esteem needed for a healthy ETI-human long-term relationship.

On the question of ETI superiority, we must make a distinction between possessing more advanced technology or even more developed intellectual abilities, and actual superiority as beings. Were the Europeans who possessed greater technology superior as people to the Native Americans which they found here? Certainly not! And is an MIT scientist with an IQ of 160 superior as a person to a wood craftsman with an IQ of 100? No! To state that a race or people possess more advanced technology or social systems is not to say that they are superior beings. On the other hand, it is equally true that if their values and attributes vary from 20th century human values and attributes then they are not inferior beings either. We must be careful not to repeat the old mistake which humans have made with each other: confusing sameness with equality. Both between two individuals and between two peoples from two different planets we will find variation, difference and strengths and weaknesses; this does not mean that one is superior or inferior to the other, only that they are *different*. Our equality as beings is founded in the fact that both humans and ET beings are conscious, intelligent, sentient creatures. Conscious intelligence is both our point of equality and our point of unity; it is the basis for the relationship itself. If we look to our point of unity; we will discover delight. While we must avoid the arrogance and chauvinism which has characterized human relationships, we must also avoid a sense of inferiority or worthlessness based simply on greater ETI technology or even intelligence. For there is more to the life of a conscious, intelligent being than IQ and material advancement. While exhibiting genuine humility where warranted, we must maintain the appropriate sense of collective self-esteem born out of the realization that to be human is to be conscious, awake, intelligent and self-aware, just as every other being in the universe is conscious, awake, intelligent and self-aware. Beyond this, it is entirely likely that humans may have as much to offer to the development and enlightenment of ETI as the other way around. If we are to gallop our steed into this arena, then mutual respect and self-respect are required, not puffed up arrogance or cowering inferiority. The strict materialist model of looking only to things and differences, or endless reductionism and fragmentation, will assure only confusion, consternation and loss. We must be wise and perceptive of the whole while yet discerning the distinctions. Our vision must be clear, for it alone can be the foundation of our success. We must learn to see with the eye of oneness, for in a universe so diverse we shall be lost without it. To be human is wonderful: it is to be conscious, intelligent, loving and aware. And what is wonderful about being human is what is wonderful about being any intelligent being in the universe; this, let us share.

The CE-5 Principles

Definition: CE-5 is a term describing a fifth category of close encounters with Extraterrestrial Intelligence (ETI), characterized by mutual, bilateral communication rather than unilateral contact. CE types 1-4 are essentially passive, reactive and ETI initiated; CE-5 is distinguished from these by conscious, voluntary and proactive human-initiated or cooperative contacts with ETI. Evidence exists indicating that CE-5s have successfully occurred in the past, and the inevitable maturing of the human/ETI relationship requires greater research and outreach efforts into this possibility. While ultimate control of such contact and exchange will (and probably should) remain with the technologically more advanced intelligent life forms (i.e., ETI), this does not lessen the importance of conscientious, voluntary human initiatives, contact and follow-up to conventional CE type 1-4.

Core Principles And Premises Of The CE-5 Initiative:

1. ETI and ET transports (UFOs) have been and currently are in contact with human society.
2. ETI has a net peaceful, benign and probably protective motive for the relationship with humanity at this time.
3. The CE-5 Initiative is proactive, bilaterally communicative and multi-disciplinary in nature and is not primarily motivated towards the current acquisition of ETI technology,

except as mutually permitted by the ETI-human relationship.

4. ETI's enigmatic and elusive behavior may be understood as human-protective when viewed from their perspective; a war-torn, aggressive, nuclear armed and disunified Earth civilization must not receive further potentially harmful technologies until a lasting world peace and unity is achieved, and international human goals become peaceful, cooperative and unified in nature. Such a transformation will then indicate the readiness for a fuller contact and exchange between humans and ETI. We must respect and accept ETI's control and wisdom in this regard.
5. Notwithstanding the protective limits mentioned above, ETI is apparently desirous of an expanded contact with humans, and is open to voluntary, human-initiated contact and exchange. There is strong evidence to suggest that ETI has been systematically introducing themselves to human civilization for the past 45 years or longer, and that such contact has steadily deepened and intensified over this period.
6. CE-5 communication based in the paradigm of love, unity, non-violence, cooperation and shared interest has been and will continue to be most effective.
7. In addition to point number 4 above, we may expect a certain limited nature to ETI contact so that the disruptive potential of such contact will be minimized. Certainly, a massive influx of ETI culture, technology, etc. would prove harmful to long-term human evolution if said influx was sudden or ill-timed. Though the exact limits of such contact are not known, we are probably destined to experience an expansion of these limits as human civilization evolves and grows in peace and unity, or at times of significant worldwide crisis.
8. All CE-5 Initiative contact will be for the benefit of all humanity (as well as ETI) and will not redound to the benefit of only one nation or culture. This is essential.
9. All CE-5 Initiative contact will be free of hostile intent, and will be free of the presence of any and all weaponry, defensive or offensive.

10. All CE-5 Initiative contacts will be shared with all CE-5 associates to the extent possible. The CE-5 Initiative will cooperate with all other UFO/ETI research organizations so long as such groups are credible and have non-harmful and peaceful procedures and intentions.
11. Both humans and ETI have physical and mental/spiritual aspects to their reality. Contact and communication will proceed on all levels of our shared reality.
12. The CE-5 Initiative affirms that humans and ETI are conscious beings and are essentially more alike than dissimilar. Regardless of how different we may externally or physically appear, the reality of humans as conscious and intelligent beings establishes the common basis for communication, deeper and bilateral contact, and mutual self-respect.
13. Our embryonic efforts now will have ramifications throughout the next millennium and should therefore be undertaken with all due deliberation, vision and integrity. Our goals, methodology and conduct are oriented towards a broad-based, long-term endeavor.
14. The primary model for communication and exchange, as well as internal communication within the CE-5 Initiative, is that of consultation and respect for the views of others.
15. The most important characteristics required of CE-5 Initiative participants are honesty, open-mindedness, intuitive ability, good communication skills and trustworthiness. Technical skills and academic credentials are certainly valued, but the above qualities are primary. CE-3 and CE-4 contactees are especially encouraged to participate as research associates. Participant confidentiality will be assured if requested. In addition, CE-5 Initiative Core Groups will ideally have participants expert or competent in:
    a. Medicine/Physiology
    b. Physics, Theoretical & Applied
    c. Psychology/Counseling
    d. Higher mental/spiritual functions (e.g., meditation, telepathy)
    e. Communications and Electronics

f. Public Relations
g. Research/Documentation, including video, audio and print
h. Astronomy and Astrophysics
j. Sociology and Anthropology

16. CE-5 Initiative Core Groups will work with ongoing research efforts to maximize our collective knowledge and data base. Current and ongoing CE-1 through 4 site/locales or individuals will especially be integrated into CE-5 strategic planning.
17. CE-5 Initiative projects, training and results will be shared through conferences, symposia and publications.
18. The activities of the CE-5 Initiative will maintain high standards of conduct and professionalism, while preserving an atmosphere of open-mindedness and creative "brainstorming." Anyone found to be spreading misinformation or falsified cases intentionally will be prohibited from participating in any of the activities of the CE-5 Initiative.
19. We hold that carefully planned Close Encounters of the Fifth Kind will unlock new frontiers in the relationship between ETI and humanity. All sincere researchers and theorists are welcome to join in this profound endeavor on behalf of mankind's growth and evolution.

29

Brief Summary Of Some CSETI Research Results

Mexico, January 30, 1993

On January 30, 1993, the RMIT was activated and sent to the volcanic zone outside of Mexico City, Mexico. Just before 12:30 A.M., local time, on January 31, 1993, while engaging in CSETI protocols to vector ET spacecraft into the site, the entire team was briefly engulfed in a beam of amber light, which originated in the northwest sky. No conventional source for this beam was found. Later, on February 1, 1993, the team was able to vector into the site a large triangular craft, measuring 300-800 feet in diameter (one to three football fields). This craft responded to the team's signals, circled the area, and descended with its leading edge fully illuminated in what appeared to be a landing attempt. This triangular craft was approximately 300 feet in elevation and under 5000 feet from the research site. It had a brilliant light at each corner of the triangle, and a red pulsating light in the center. It was accompanied by a small red-orange probe or scout craft. As the craft left the areas, it repeatedly returned signals from the team, and then dipped below a ridge and was not seen again that night. This contact lasted about ten minutes. On February 2, 1993, the same type craft returned, this time under 200 feet, and again signaled in an interactive manner with the team. During the last 24 hours the team was in Mexico, it encountered during daylight hours brilliant, shiny metallic discs which hovered or flew near the team members. Four such discs on four separate occasions were encountered by the team on February 3 and 4, 1993.

England July 27, 1992

At approximately 12:20 A.M. on July 27, 1992, on an 1800 acre farm near Alton Barnes, Wiltshire, England, the CSETI RMIT was successful in vectoring into the site a large, brilliantly lit, disc-shaped, domed craft, measuring 80-150 feet in diameter. This craft was silent, and less than 400 yards away, and came to within 10-30 feet of the ground. It was, in fact, in the same wheat field in which the RMIT was located. This craft signaled repeatedly to the group of four researchers, and a small amber object at one point detached from the object and went up into the clouds. While at close proximity, this craft caused magnetic disturbances to the compass so that the needle rotated counterclockwise 360 degrees around the compass dial. This near-landing event concluded with the craft receding into the mist and out of visible range after 10-15 minutes of signaling with the team.

Belgium February 5, 1992

Having learned of a significant UFO wave in Belgium, the CSETI RMIT, consisting of four people, departed for Brussels on February 5, 1992. On the night of February 9-10, the team conducted research under unfavorable weather conditions near the town of Eupan, Belgium. At 12:30 A.M. on the 10th the team saw at low elevation four objects approximately 300 feet away, brightly lit, which vanished suddenly after about five minutes of observation. The team returned the next morning to the site, and no explanation for the objects was found.

On the night of February 10, 1992, the team proceeded to a high ridge near Henri-Chapelle, and at 12:45 A.M. on the 11th successfully vectored into the site a large triangular, silent craft which dipped below the low cloud cover to reveal a brilliantly lit apex of the triangle. The light on this part of the craft was about the size of a full moon. A few minutes later the team heard a low vibratory rumbling directly above them, which seemed to be turned on and off in rapid succession twice. This vibration was above the team in the clouds and was stationary.

Florida March 14, 1992

On March 14, 1992, at 8:24 P.M., CST, on a beach near Pensacola, Florida, over 40 people present for a CSETI research team training exercise, were able to vector into the area four silent, hovering craft, which signaled repeatedly to the group, and changed formation in response to the group's light signaling. This event was observed from six locations, and videotapes and photographic evidence were obtained. These objects were under intelligent control and moved towards the group while exchanging light signaling with the team. This event lasted for 10-15 minutes.

30

UFOs Over Belgium—February 1992

Introduction

On February 5, 1992, members of the Center for the Study of Extraterrestrial Intelligence (CSETI) executive committee departed for Europe to investigate the current wave of UFO sightings in Belgium. The purpose of this trip was to conduct first-hand research of this extraordinary UFO wave, to interview principle witnesses, to meet with the primary investigators at SOBEPS (Belgium's principal UFO research organization), and to conduct on-site CE-5 Initiative research. All of these goals were met with success, and we left Belgium convinced that this UFO wave was one of the most significant and well-documented ones in UFO history.

Here, I wish to personally thank the many gracious and helpful people at SOBEPS, without whose assistance none of these goals could have been met. At SOBEPS: Patrick Ferryn, Lucien Clerebaut, Dr. Leon Brenig and Professor Auguste Meessen, as well as many others gave of their time and were of immense help to our efforts. The integrity, kindness and professional quality of the people at SOBEPS serves as an inspiring example to UFO researchers everywhere. A special thanks also to Mr. Nicoll, the gendarme who, along with his fellow police officer, first saw these large triangular UFOs near Eupan, Belgium on November 29, 1989. Mr. Nicoll generously spent an entire afternoon sharing his experiences and observations with us, escorted us to all the sites where his observations were made, and showed us every kindness and courtesy.

On Saturday, February 8, 1992, we met with SOBEPS investigators at their headquarters in Brussels. Here, we were able to interview witnesses, receive an excellent overview and briefing from Patrick Ferryn, and make a presentation regarding the CSETI CE-5

Initiative protocols. To our great satisfaction, we learned that Dr. Brenig and others were organizing research observations teams to engage in real-time research, and the day we arrived were making plans to place these teams in areas around the country to achieve direct scientific observation and to actively engage these spacecraft using light signals, sound and Coherent Thought Sequencing. These suggestions were enthusiastically received, and it is hoped that we will soon be hearing of Close Encounters of the Fifth Kind in Belgium.

Summary Findings From Interviews and Briefings

Below follows a brief summary of the salient features of the current UFO wave in Belgium, and of our interviews with various UFO witnesses and investigators.

The current wave began on November 29, 1989 at 5:24 P.M. when police officer Nicoll and his fellow officer were on patrol near Eupan in eastern Belgium. There they saw at close range a large, triangular-shaped aircraft with three bright lights, one at each corner and a large red-orange pulsating light in the center of the craft. This object, and another like it, were observed for approximately three hours as it glided over various areas near Eupan. To adequately describe this case would require at least a long chapter in a book; in lieu of that, we must be content with the following summary:

- The UFO was seen at close range, was a structured craft over 100 feet and possibly over 200 feet in length, and was completely silent.
- There were multiple other police and civilian witnesses to the UFO.
- The UFO glided over the land, following the contour of the land in a constant fashion and emitted a laser-like red light parallel to the land which would stop at limited distances (!) in space as if measuring something on or under the ground. The UFO would stop and go, as it appeared to be measuring "something."
- The UFO hovered at close range over a field and emitted a brilliant blue-white light many times brighter than a helicopter search light.
- The craft was initially moving away from Eupan, but when the officers started to pursue it, it changed directions; the officers were armed and it may be that the UFO took this initial evasive action because of the presence of weapons.

- The officers then followed this UFO at a distance through the countryside near Eupan until they arrived at a small chapel along a dirt road. Here, they observed the UFO hover over the Gileppe Dam then descend below the ridge, apparently to hover directly over the water.
- At this point, the two officers saw a large second UFO rise directly from a ravine very near to their location. It was huge, within 300 feet, brightly lit—and a lit dome could be seen on top of the triangular craft. Again, no sound was heard. The UFO then departed towards Henri-Chapelle where other police officers saw the craft.
- Mr. Nicoll felt no fear, but was amazed and dumbfounded by the experience. He insists that it was a real, structured physical aircraft, completely silent even at close range, and unlike any known human aircraft. Mr. Nicoll is highly credible, sincere, and he and the other witnesses are unimpeachable.
- Mr. Nicoll personally took us to each of these sites and we can attest that from his description, this triangular craft was large and at close range.

Mr. Nicoll related that he felt this craft was on some sort of technical mission relating to the measurement of the land or subterranean features of the area. We later learned that this area has many old, presently inactive volcanic sites, geological fault lines and old hot springs sites, and that the region is occasionally rocked by earthquakes. We also learned that there are nearby nuclear weapons bases as well as a nuclear power plant in not-so-distant Tihange (more on this later).

Other general findings:

- Belgium, which has ten million people but is only one-third the size of Indiana, has had over 3,500 UFO sightings since November 1989; remember, some of these 3,500 cases have had hundreds of witnesses and a large number of these cases are multiple witness cases by highly credible people.
- Most cases involve a large, triangular-shaped craft, but other craft have been seen as well, including rectangular platforms, disc-shaped craft and others.
- There have been no humanoid sightings, nor have there been any close interactions (so-called "abductions") by humanoids.
- The Belgian Air Force is cooperating with civilian researchers and has given them technical and logistical assistance, including the

use of magnifying infrared night scopes, Air Force observation towers and joint airborne research efforts. Neither their Air Force nor NATO can explain these craft as terrestrial in origin. It should be noted that NATO, with its large US military influence, has been less cooperative and forthcoming concerning these events, even though at least one NATO nuclear air base has been overflown at low altitude by one of these UFOs.

- There is at least one clear picture of this UFO which has been shown to be authentic and which conforms with the description of the UFO given by police and military personnel. There are video tapes of the UFO which are of lesser quality.
- There have been more than one multiple radar/visual confirmation of this UFO. On the night of March 30-31, 1990, the UFO was tracked on four separate Belgian NATO radar stations as well as an F-16 on-board radar. (The F-16 was scrambled to pursue the UFO which was also seen visually from the ground by multiple witnesses.) In addition, other radar/ visual sightings have occurred, one in December 1991 when a commercial pilot, ground control radar and ground-based witnesses all saw the UFO at low altitude. The radar tape of the March 1990 event has been analyzed by Prof. Meessen and is considered hard evidence of an extraordinary craft with non-terrestrial performance characteristics.
- There have been several Close Encounters of the Fifth Kind in Belgium. Notably, in one case several Belgian military members saw a large, triangular UFO at close range. The UFO was moving away from the group when one of the men decided to try flashing a flashlight towards the craft. At this point, the craft stopped, came closer and signaled back to the man in the same sequence as that sent by the man. This interactive exchange, initiated by the human observer, continued for about 30 minutes and constitutes a significant CE-5 with multiple witnesses.
- Although there have been a few daylight sightings, as well as sightings at all hours of the night, most of the sightings occurred between 5 P.M. and 9 P.M., often in full view of dozens if not hundreds of people.
- Sightings have occurred throughout Belgium but are concentrated along a river valley which extends from Eupan in the east of Belgium to Liege, Tihange and Mons.

- Contrary to what a number of armchair speculators in the US and elsewhere have claimed, there is no evidence that these sightings are due to secret US aircraft, nor did we meet any military, civilian scientists or first-hand observers who felt this. Moreover, given the secret handling of state-of-the-art aircraft in the US, it is not plausible that the US military would fly such secret and experimental weapons over densely populated areas in the early evening hours when many people would be out to observe them. We spoke to no scientists or observers who felt that these craft were of a terrestrial origin.
- There are several cases where apparent transluminal /telepathic capacities are demonstrated. We interviewed a young man at length who had an extraordinary experience while driving home in the early evening hours in 1991. At some distance from his home he observed a UFO which was only several hundred feet in altitude. The UFO was ahead of where this man was going, and he was amazed when the UFO turned in advance of his actions. That is, before he would turn his car onto a new road to go home, the UFO would turn first, as if leading him to his house. He felt that the UFO was able to "read his mind" in advance of each turn, and the UFO continued to lead him home, turning precisely at each intersection. Finally, he arrived home to find the UFO hovering at a very low altitude (50-100 feet) above his house. He called to his wife, who came out of the house and also saw the craft. While the man was unafraid, his wife became very frightened, and at this point the UFO left the area. An almost identical case was reported by a veterinarian who was driving to her home not far from the Tihange nuclear power plant. Again, the UFO anticipated her every turn precisely, and was hovering over her house upon her arrival. The UFO was observed by her husband and son at the house. It is not known whether such events, which have been reported elsewhere around the world, indicate the presence of Technology Assisted Consciousness on board the craft, innate mental capabilities of the occupants, or both.
- These UFOs have been observed near nuclear military installations and nuclear power plants. Of particular interest are the remarkable sightings near the Tihange nuclear facility involving numerous UFOs seen throughout one evening. There were multiple sightings in the area for at least two years, but one evening virtually the

entire town was awakened to loud booms coming from these slow-moving craft as several of them roamed the area and converged on the nuclear reactor. Witnesses stated that these UFOs appeared to be making loud booming noises to intentionally draw people out of their houses to see the large triangular objects. This particular incident lasted several hours and was witnessed by hundreds of people at close range (100s of feet).

Summary of CE-5 Initiative Research

As mentioned earlier, one of the purposes of the trip was to engage in real-time research in the area of peak UFO activity while using CE-5 Initiative research techniques. With this in mind, after completing our initial investigations with SOBEPS in Brussels, we headed for Eupan. Here, we were briefed by Mr. Nicoll, shown the areas around Eupan where these objects have been seen, and with the assistance of Mr. Nicoll secured a strategic field for our night research program. There we were joined by two SOBEPS members who brought with them the Air Force magnifying infrared night scope.

At about 8:30 P.M. on Sunday, 2/9/92, we gathered in the prearranged field and, braving cold, rain, wind and seemingly endless mud, began our research and observations. Using high-powered search lights, specific UFO related auditory tones (played from our cars' stereo system via cassette tape), and Coherent Thought Sequencing, we began our CE-5 Initiative research. Observations were hampered by the weather which was certainly less than ideal, with intermittent driving rain with periods of relative clearing and only scattered low clouds. Then, at approximately 8:50 P.M. Belgian time, we noticed towards the southeast several bright white lights hovering above a ridge on the other side of Eupan. This ridge was traversed by a road which led into Eupan and had been the location of a number of UFO sightings in the past. At this point, the weather had cleared somewhat. With our infrared scope, I was able to clearly see first one and then up to eight UFOs hovering above the ridge. These lights were several miles away and no distinct craft were seen. However, their movement defied any prosaic explanation. At times, these lights would move in a circular fashion, reverse their direction and appear to merge with one another. After 5-10 minutes of these observations, one of the UFOs signaled back to us in the same sequence which we had used to signal to them. These observations continued for about 30 minutes, at which time the weather became unfavorable for further observations. Later, while the area was still rather foggy, we saw lower lights which moved in a repeating fashion; these turned out to be only distant cars traversing the ridge road to Eupan. Earlier, however, the UFO lights were seen while it was clear and they were well above the ridge and moving in a distinctly anomalous manner.

From there we proceeded to the area on the dirt road where Mr. Nicoll and his partner had observed the UFO rising from the ravine at close range. There we continued our CE-5 techniques. A rather strange event occurred there which we cannot adequately explain: While we were looking over the area near the ravine, we saw four lights of some sort. These were bright white and located just over the area of trees on the other side of the ravine, but clearly in the field and no more than 300 feet away. While we had not seen any light poles or wires in that area during our inspection earlier in the day, we assumed that we had simply not observed them. Than at approximately 12:30 A.M., all of the lights disappeared, as if a switch had been thrown and all of the lights turned off at once. We were momentarily amazed at this, but then tentatively concluded that these lights were on a timer of some sort and went off automatically at that hour of the morning. To confirm this theory, we returned to the same site the next morning, but were astonished to find that no such lights existed and that the field in question was devoid of any lights, poles or wires. Later we learned from Dr. Brenig that others have observed blue-white and red lights in association with these UFOs. At the time of our observation of these lights, it was very overcast with a low cloud ceiling and no observation above a few hundred feet was possible. The next night we returned to this area with Dr. Brenig, but saw no lights in the area where they were seen the previous night.

On the night of February 10, 1992, we proceeded with Dr. Brenig to a high ridge near the town of Henri-Chapelle, about ten miles from Eupan. There we continued our observations and CE-5 research, and shared information and ideas with Dr. Brenig. About 10 P.M., we observed a convoy of military/ official vehicles carrying a white canister on the back of a flat-bed truck. This truck was escorted by several other vehicles with flashing yellow warning lights. It was obvious that the cargo in question was a hazardous material of some sort which required a high degree of security. The road over which this material was being transported was rather deserted at that hour of the night. Dr. Brenig left around 11 P.M. to return to Brussels, where he had an early class to teach at the university. We remained at this site for several more hours, and around 12:30–1:00 A.M. observed another, even longer convoy of vehicles moving in the opposite direction on the same road, again carrying a canister under tight security. This convoy appeared to be between 0.25–0.5 mile in length and at this hour the road was virtually deserted of any other traffic. While observing this event, we noticed through a break in the clouds a bright, large yellow-white light appear which moved slowly and was larger than the full moon. It should be noted that we could see the moon through thin clouds in the opposite direction from this other light. This light was in the clouds in the area of the transport convoy, and was soon obscured by rapidly moving clouds. A few minutes later, after the convoy had moved out of sight, we heard—and felt—a deep vibratory rumble directly over our car which lasted 10-30 seconds. This vibration was coming from the clouds directly overhead (the ceiling of clouds was very low from our position on the ridge). It was unlike anything any of us had ever heard; it certainly was not the distant rumble of thunder or jets, nor was it a sonic boom. Each of us felt that this sound was emanating from an immense and powerful object directly overhead in the clouds—like a million transformers humming almost to a roar or boom. It should be noted that this sound did not appear to be coming from a moving object, and that a second episode of vibratory rumbling occurred shortly after the first one. We all felt that it was associated with the mysterious light previously observed, and that it emitted this sound once overhead to let us know that it was there because it could not safely descend below the very low cloud cover. Indeed, it appeared to be a sound which was intentionally turned on, then off, then on again. It reminded us of the case relayed by Dr. Brenig of the multiple UFOs over the nuclear power plant at Tihange. Could there be a connection between the high security convoy, the light, the vibratory rumble/roar and the events which occurred over Tihange? We have reason to think so.

Conclusions, Correlations and Reflections

- The Belgian UFO wave continued through the early 1990s and is one of the most important UFO events in history. It involves multiple credible witnesses, police and military confirmation, radar evidence, CE-5s, photographic evidence, and government cooperation with civilian research efforts.

- The main body of these reports indicate the presence of ET spacecraft over Belgium. No conventional, prosaic or secret "stealth" aircraft can account for the facts of this UFO wave.
- The events occurring in Belgium provide an excellent real-time laboratory for studying the UFO phenomenon and performing CE-5 Initiative research. The probability of having close range interactive experiences with these spacecraft and perhaps their occupants is deemed high.
- Why Belgium? Belgium is NATO headquarters; it has numerous nuclear facilities and bases; some of these facilities may be in areas of possible future geologic activity; Belgium is quickly becoming the economic capital of the new unified European Community; Belgium is strategically located; its people are gracious and unusually open-minded; the people of Belgium have reacted to this phenomenon intelligently, with governmental honesty and in a non-hysterical and non-hostile manner.
- Why did this UFO wave occur at this point in time? Perhaps the fall of the Berlin Wall in the Fall of 1989—when the current wave began—holds the key to this question. The collapse of the Eastern Bloc and the Warsaw Pact, the dissolution of the Soviet empire and the unification of Europe are all temporally related to this wave. While generally positive developments, all of these events have a high potential for geopolitical instability in the short term, and would understandably attract the attention of any ET group observing this planet. Also of note —NASA has confirmed the existence of a much larger than expected ozone hole in the atmosphere over this part of the world. This may be both a spatial and temporal determinant of this wave, as well as the nearby crop circle phenomenon in southern England (see below).

What are these spacecraft doing in the Belgian area? These spacecraft appear to be involved with three major areas of activity in Belgium:

1) Technical geological surveillance. Many of the best and most thorough reports indicate that these objects are doing some type of measurement of the Belgian terrain/geology. This activity has been observed in areas of geological faults, dormant volcanoes and dormant hot springs. As mentioned before, these areas are near various nuclear facilities.

2) Observation/tracking of nuclear materials and facilities. Over-flight of NATO nuclear facilities, the multiple sightings in and around the Tihange nuclear facility, our own observations on February 10, 1992, and other cases lend support to this idea.
3) Social reaction experimentation. Like the large UFO wave in the early and mid-1980s in the Hudson Valley, New York area, the Belgium wave also involved low-level sightings in highly populated areas during the early evening hours when large numbers of people are outside and in a position to observe these UFOs. Many people we talked with had the distinct impression that the occupants of these UFOs were intentionally allowing large numbers of people to see them. This may serve several interrelated functions: to observe human social, governmental, military and individual reaction to their presence; the educate and condition large numbers of people and governments around the world to their presence. (By doing this in Belgium, which is NATO headquarters and the center of Europe, large numbers of people and various governments are systematically exposed to them in a gradual yet undeniable way.)

We believe they are also possibly awaiting an affirmative response from the non-military sector of society.

- Reports from credible observers of psi or telepathic capabilities in association with these UFOs would indicate that transluminal research techniques should be incorporated into observation teams' protocols. That we cannot fully explain such events must not serve as grounds for rejecting valid empirical evidence.
- Further correlations. At the risk of incurring the wrath of UFO researchers and debunkers alike, I must state that we believe there may be a connection between the crop circles of England and the Belgian UFO wave. Consider: While crop circles have been reported for centuries (as have UFOs), the time period of the UFO wave in Belgium—1989–1992+—corresponds temporally with the growth in both the number and complexity of crop circles in southern England. Spatially, the correlation is obvious to anyone who looks at a map of Europe since these two remarkable events are separated by only 200-300 aerial miles. These events in Belgium are due east of the southern England crop circles. Both events have been occurring just north of the 50th Parallel North and in the vicinity of the alarmingly large ozone hole over Europe (which we found incredibly polluted by US standards!). The two seem-

> ingly unrelated events both involve strong evidence witnessed by thousands of people locally and millions of people worldwide via the media. They are both temporally and spatially related. And both the crop circles and the Belgian UFO wave provide strong evidence for the interaction with Planet Earth by an intelligence at once enigmatic and real. But perhaps what is most extraordinary about both "waves" is that they could be occurring in such close proximity to one another and yet be regarded as separate and unrelated events! It is as if 3,500 sightings of had occurred in eastern North Carolina while at the same time hundreds of complex pictograms appeared in western North Carolina—and all the while human observers and researchers assumed the events to be unrelated. Indeed, they may be, but we assume this blindly at great risk, and I for one would encourage a hard look at these correlations in the chance that we may uncover something most profound.

In closing, I wish to add that these investigations have shown us the great value of—and need for—close international cooperation and the exchange of ideas and information. It is our hope at CSETI that we may facilitate this sharing process and thereby bring us closer to the comprehensive understanding which we all seek.

31

CE-5 Near Gulf Breeze, Florida—March 1992

Introduction

On March 14, 1992 at 8:24 P.M. EST on a beach near Gulf Breeze, Florida, an event with profound and historic implications occurred: a confirmed, close-range, multi-witness, human-initiated and interactive encounter took place between a Center for the Study of Extraterrestrial Intelligence (CSETI) training group and five ET Spacecraft (ETS) for over ten minutes. This event was observed from at least six locations in the Gulf Breeze area and resulted in at least five videotapes from two locations, a photograph, and two on-site audio recordings. This special report documents this historic event and discusses its implications for humanity's relationship with ET peoples.

Background

CSETI is a non-profit scientific research and educational organization which, among other programs, conducts real-time on-site UFO research via the CE-5 Initiative. The CE-5 Initiative involves trained Working Groups who use specific protocols which are designed to engage UFOs and their occupants in an interactive, cooperative exchange. A Close Encounter of the Fifth Kind, or CE-5, is a close encounter which is initiated by humans or which involves voluntary human interaction with ETI/UFOs. (See, "Close Encounters of the Fifth Kind: A Proposal for an Important New Research Category," also in this volume.) The CE-5 Initiative is a scientific and diplomatic program which endeavors to establish a cooperative, peaceful and sustainable relationship between humans and *any* and *all* ET "peoples" which may visit Earth. CE-5 Initiative protocols are used to "vector" UFOs into an area and then engage them in a peaceful, cooperative exchange using lights, sounds and other modalities. Working Group members are selected according to their ability to engage in this research in an open-minded and non-prejudicial manner which is free from premature and fear-based negative conclusions regarding the intentions of these visitors to our planet. The integrity of this diplomatic perspective is fundamental to the success of the CE-5 Initiative since it is probable that these visitors are capable of assessing the attitudes, motives and intentions of the Working Group members.

CSETI is developing advanced protocols to be used in the event of a high level CE-5 landing of an ETS, including the activation of a Boarding Party to go on-board the craft, should that opportunity arise. Recent events indicate that the activation of these protocols may occur in the reasonably near future.

The Gulf Breeze CE-5—Prelude

Dr. Greer, Director of CSETI, was invited to the Gulf Breeze-Pensacola area March 13, 1992 to present information regarding the CSETI program. With the assistance of Vicki Lyons and other members of the Gulf Breeze Research Team, a local skywatch group operating for about 1.5 years, a lecture and CSETI training workshop was arranged for March 13 and 14, respectively.

On March 13, while flying en route to Gulf Breeze, Dr. Greer subjectively received information indicating that a sighting of the Gulf Breeze UFO would occur at midnight on the 13th. This information was conveyed to several members of the Gulf Breeze Research Team, who replied that the UFO usually appears between 7 and 10 P.M. and not as late as midnight. However, following the lecture on the 13th, Dr. Greer and approximately ten other people went out to the Gulf Breeze side of the Pensacola Bay Bridge to observe the sky and use some of the CSETI protocols. By 11:50 P.M., all but five people had left the area. Those remaining: Art and Mary Hufford, Jeanne Reed, Ann Russell and Steven Greer. At approximately 11:59 and 45 seconds, a UFO appeared at close range in the direction of Gulf Breeze and in the direction, from the group's location, of Santa Rosa Island. The UFO appeared as a bright deep glowing cherry orange-red object which throbbed in a pulsatile fashion. This sighting lasted only about one minute, but prior to the UFO "winking out" Dr. Greer was able to observe it for a few seconds through binoculars. The object was quite close (less than one mile) and through the binoculars, a definite round and solid super-structure was observable above and attached to the light/energy source. As soon as this was observed, and just as Art Hufford was about to take a picture of the UFO through a high-powered telephoto lens, the object "winked out" and was not seen again that night. The congruency of the time (the atypical and precise hour of midnight) and place (over Gulf Breeze directly above the site of the evening lecture) is significant and presaged events of even greater magnitude on the following night—March 14th. It is likely that the sighting on March 13th was itself a First Degree CE-5.

On March 14th in Gulf Breeze, Florida, a day long CSETI training workshop was held with approximately 40 people in attendance. During this workshop, the CSETI CE-5 Initiative protocols were presented and training in the use of high-powered lights, the CSETI tones and Coherent Thought Sequencing (CTS) occurred. It is significant that sometime *after* the CSETI beeping tones (which were recorded directly from an ETS) were played, several workshop participants heard from their part of the room those same tones emanating from an unknown source and location. These beeping tones were objectively heard by at least three people, yet the tape player was off and no conventional source for the sounds could be located. It should be noted that this same phenomenon has occurred in other areas before and after a CSETI program, and outdoors during field work, where people have clearly and objectively heard the tones though no source could be located.

The workshop ended at approximately 5:00 P.M. Following a dinner break, we proceeded to a prearranged site on Santa Rosa Island, arriving there at about 7:30 P.M. The site is directly off the road which connects Gulf Breeze with Navarro Beach and is along a deserted stretch of beach with the Gulf of Mexico on one side and Santa Rosa Sound on the other. A parking area directly off the main road was the location of the CE-5 Initiative experiment.

Another group of observers were located at South Shoreline Park in Gulf Breeze. There were 39 participants at the primary site on Santa Rosa Island, including a large number of people from the Gulf Breeze Research Team, and Dr. Greer. Following a period of on-site Coherent Thought Sequencing, the group began using the CSETI tones and high-powered 500,000 and one million candle power lights. The sense of unity, peace and excitement in the group was very high, and the atmosphere was filled with confidence that a significant event was about to unfold.

The night was cool and clear with a stiff wind blowing off the Gulf. The stars were bright and a partial moon was shining. From time to time, a motorist would pull into the parking area to see what the group was doing, but would then move on. Following the Coherent Thought Sequencing, Dr. Greer and several others sensed a definite consciousness "lock on" between the group and several ETS. Dr. Greer specifically mentioned to Vicki Lyons and several others that he felt several—4 or 5—craft were en route or already in the area. This impression was also confirmed by several members of the group who had similarly remotely viewed this fact. It should also be noted that it was remotely viewed that these occupants were as positive and excited about this event as the group was, and that a link up was viewed between these five spacecraft and a central command structure. The lights were used in a coherent fashion, creating a display which from the air would have conveyed signs of intelligent activity at the site. Large triangular formations were "painted" in the sky with lights, and light signaling occurred in conjunction with the CSETI beeping tones.

About 20-30 minutes of this activity, at 8:24 P.M. CST, a squadron of five UFOs were seen in the WNW at 26° above the horizon. (Initially four UFOs were seen but a fifth UFO was confirmed to be hovering below on the horizon and was seen from several locations in the Gulf Breeze area.) After a brief period of excitement (and pandemonium!), the group came together and effectively engaged in Coherent Thought Sequencing and coherent light work. Initially, as the craft came into view, they appeared with a bright circle of white light. As they hovered, this quickly evolved into a pulsating cherry red-orange energy/light source. The appearance of five of the craft at once was unprecedented in the history of the Gulf Breeze UFO wave and at no time in the past had more than two been seen by a group of observers. Preliminary triangulation figures place the UFO at *under* one mile initially and as they approached the group, moved within an estimated 2000-3000 feet.

Immediately after regaining a group focus, Dr. Greer began signaling to the UFOs with a 500,000-candle-power light in intelligent sequences. To everyone's astonishment, when he flashed three times to the UFOs, the lead craft flashed back three times. Then after two flashes, it returned a signal of two flashes, then five and so on. There was clear and definite congruence of the human-initiated signaling and the return signals of the craft — a sort of "photon dialogue." After several minutes of this activity the UFOs "winked out" but remained in the area. At this point, Dr. Greer began "drawing" a large equilateral triangle in the northwest sky with the light. Then three of the UFOs visibly returned and formed, in clear response, an equilateral triangle.

At this point, the "light conversation" continued with a series of flashes, again with direct response from the craft. At the same time, the group was continuing Coherent Thought Sequencing and directing the craft's occupants to approach and, if possible, land on the beach behind us. Information concerning the peaceful intentions and motivations of the Working Group were similarly conveyed.

At this point, the formation began to move directly towards the group on the beach. Dr. Greer then took the light and flashed it in a continuous strobe-like manner, directing the formation of craft to the beach location. As he did this, the lead craft rapidly responded to the signaling and began flashing in a similar strobe-like manner, and moved directly toward the group and into the zenith of the sky. It then flashed a bright ring of white light and "winked out," as did the other craft. The team sensed that these UFOs remained in the area without their lights on for some time after this, but no further signaling occurred.

Words cannot describe the excitement, joy and unity present in the group during and after this historic encounter. A number of people, who had seen this UFO on other occasions, stated that this was the most important event of their lives. All present realized that they had not only witnessed, but had participated in and co-created an event of great significance—a turning point in the history of our embryonic relationship with ET peoples. Our human team had invited these ET people to interact with us as a group, and they responded in a clear and unequivocal way. We had made the quantum leap from passive observers to active, cooperative participants -- and this transition was enthusiastically received. The implications of this are profound and far-reaching and will be discussed later.

Documentation

This First Degree CE-5 lasted approximately 10-12 minutes. The first few minutes were not videotaped or otherwise recorded because the confirmed lock-on between our Working Group and the spacecraft was desired prior to electronic recording. (It has been observed that these craft will often evade electronic recording of their presence.) We have a total of five videotapes of this event, two of which are of high quality and clearly show four of the five UFOs. These videos clearly show the formation of an equilateral triangle and signaling by the craft. There are also two audio tapes of the event and one photograph of three of the UFOs in formation.

Observers were present in two locations—Santa Rosa Island and South Shoreline Park in Gulf Breeze. The primary CE-5 site was on Santa Rosa Island where 39 people witnessed the event. (See Appendix I.) Additionally, these five UFOs were observed from at least six locations in the area and a number of reports have been received throughout the region. A headline in *The Islander*, a Gulf Breeze newspaper, reported the event also. The presence of over 50 credible witnesses, including two former Air Force pilots, five video tapes, two audio tapes and a photograph establishes these events as a real and unequivocal CE-5.

Aftermath

Following this extraordinary event the Working Group, sensing that these UFOs were still in the area, made emergency contingency plans for a high level CE-5 involving a landing and possible boarding. While the site was far from ideal for this (a main road ran directly adjacent to the site), we could not rule out a beach landing later in the evening once traffic decreased. Keep in mind that this was the inaugural meeting for this Working Group and that many people present were virtual strangers to one another, having only met each other earlier the same day. People present were from North Carolina, Texas, Alabama, Louisiana and Florida. Nevertheless, high level CE-5 protocols were discussed, and an initial Boarding Party of four people was selected. The discussion of this phase of the research caused palpable apprehension among some of the people present. Several people became overwhelmed with the prospect of a landing and left the area immediately. This underscores the fact that preparation is essential and that Working Group members must honestly assess their own readiness to participate in research of this type. It should also be noted that a marked increase in apprehension occurred among some participants as the UFOs moved directly toward the group. This increase in anxiety among some participants may have resulted in the termination of the CE-5.

It should be noted that following this CE-5, a number of helicopters and jet aircraft were seen in the area, but it is not known for certain whether this was an official response to the squadron of UFOs or normal activity for that hour (around 9 P.M.) on a Saturday night. Additionally, two vehicles were seen in the area after this event. They moved back and forth, from east to west of our location. One of these vehicles, a pick-up truck with one male inside, remained close to our location until nearly 5 A.M. when the last members of the team left. It is thought that no further interactions occurred due to this security breach.

Post-Event High Strangeness

Two married members of the Working Group present at the primary site and who are know as very level-headed "nuts and bolts," practical UFOlogists, had an extraordinary experience upon their return home that night. Earlier in the day they had been playing with their grandchild. They have a toy UFO which is battery operated and which, no matter what they did, would not work that day. However, upon returning to their home after the CE-5 event, they were astonished to enter their home and find this same toy vigorously flashing and whirling on the shelf where they had left it. Amazingly, the switch was in the "off" position, yet the toy was warm from running so furiously. The couple interpreted this high strangeness event as meaning, "Yes, you're on the right track."

Another participant was at home the next morning when suddenly the glass windows in her living room started vibrating and a sky quake was heard. Her remote control for the television was vibrating and became hot to the touch. Amazingly, a music box, high upon a shelf, which had not been touched for many months began to make a repetitive ding-ding-ding sound reminiscent of the CSETI beeping tones!

Additionally, other members of the Working Group heard the CSETI beeping tones at various times throughout the next week. They were emanating from an unidentified source, but were objectively heard by at least three people.

It is felt that all of these post CE-5 high strangeness events were ETly caused and serve as affirmations and confirmations of the CSETI CE-5 Initiative.

Implications and Reflections

The March 14th Gulf Breeze CE-5 has profound implications to the future of UFO research and ETI-human relations. This event verifies the efficacy of the CE-5 Initiative protocols and establishes the important fact that humans can interact as a group with these ET people. These Gulf Breeze UFOs are clearly under intelligent control and will respond to and interact with an appropriately motivated, peaceful and unified group.

Transluminal sciences involving mind/consciousness are efficacious and have far-reaching applications in this scientific, diplomatic initiative. Assuming human Working Group preparedness and appropriate CE-5 site selection, we are certain that a landing and full meeting with these ET people is assured and relatively imminent. In only a few more minutes, a full landing could have occurred at Gulf Breeze had the site and the group been prepared for such an event.

We have started down a path which will culminate in a full meeting and on-board experience between our research team and these ET people. We are already engaged in the early phase of a continuing open relationship which has extraordinary implications for Earth and all of humanity.

CSETI is now preparing formal advanced protocols to be activated in the event of a high level CE-5 involving a landing and on-board opportunity. As a diplomatic project, we are acutely aware that these actions are done on behalf of humanity as a whole, and that everything we do now has deep ramifications for the future of the Earth's relationship to other peoples in the universe. The continued success of the CE-5 Initiative rests upon the altruism, unity and peaceful motivations of the Working Group members. Our methods and intentions must be beyond reproach, for the opportunity for success is high and the responsibility is great. By beginning a human initiated and diplomatic program we have begun a new and important volume in human history. We have made the critical transition from passive observer to active participant, and we have thereby signaled our readiness to advance into an open and mutually beneficial interplanetary relationship. We have now established that, given the right approach, we can invite these visitors to relate openly to us—and they will.

As the Earth and her people make the inevitable transition from warring tribes to a true world civilization at peace, the capacity for higher level CE-5s will increase exponentially. That we are soon to witness this transformation of the Earth into the organic unity of one homeland, there can be no doubt. That we will, in the relatively near future be called upon to establish a peaceful and sustainable relationship with other planetary peoples, we can be assured. That we are now only in the first day of first grade is cause for hope and not despair, for what is significant is that we have indeed entered the schoolhouse. And, if we stay on course we shall rapidly progress to fulfillment of our potential.

As we progress in this endeavor, we must maintain those universal principles of unity, diplomacy and peace which are free from the fear and prejudice of our time. Open mindedness, altruism, and enlightened human interest, peace, mutual benefit and cooperation—these qualities must remain as the foundation of our efforts. We must remind ourselves, and convey to our guests, that while our peoples may vary in both profound and superficial ways, that on the level of conscious intelligence, of universal mind, that there is but one people inhabiting one universe, and we are they.

Appendix I

Witnesses to the March 14, 1992 CE-5 at the primary site on Santa Rosa Island.

1.	Shirley Adams	Florida
2.	Andy Ambercrombie	Texas
3.	Kim Amberg	Florida
4.	Marsha Athey	Florida
5.	Tom Boyle	Florida
6.	Brian Boldman	North Carolina
7.	Glenn Bradley	Florida
8.	Carol Calin	Florida
9.	Pat Crumbley	Louisiana
10.	George Crumbley	Louisiana
11.	Tracie Crumbley	Louisiana
12.	Dirk Dupuy	Florida
13.	Boots Eckert	Florida
14.	Steven Greer	North Carolina
15.	Monica Hubbard	Florida
16.	Mary Hufford	Florida
17.	Art Hufford	Florida
18.	Sue Jones	Alabama
19.	Clopton Jones	Alabama
20.	Marianne Jones	Alabama
21.	Topper Jones	Alabama
22.	Vicki Lyons	Florida

23. Kelly Martin	Florida
24. Carol Meyer	Florida
25. Anne Morrison	Florida
26. Bruce Morrison	Florida
27. Bland Pugh	Florida
28. Gayle Radcliff	Florida
29. Laura Reutter	North Carolina
30. Walter Rule	North Carolina
31. Becky Smith	Florida
32. Donald Ware	Florida
33. Candy Waters	Florida
34. Jeremy Waters	Florida
35. Keith Sanders	Florida
36. Jane Waters	Florida
37. Patti Weatherford	Florida
38. Michael Wetzel	Florida
39. Jane Doe*	anonymity requested

Appendix II

Partial list of witnesses from South Shoreline Park.

1. Wayne Peterson	Louisiana
2. Betty Peterson	Louisiana

And ten others—unnamed

32

CE-5 In Southern England—July 1992

Introduction

For many years we have received reports of extraordinary crop circle formations in the fields of southern England. Over the past decade these have evolved from simple circles and circular shaped arrangements to complex pictograms, often several hundred feet in length. In my discussions with Colin Andrews, who is the chief crop circle researcher in England, we increasingly became convinced that these were under intelligent design and were not of human origin. Time does not allow here to go into the full analysis of these crop circles, but suffice it to say that there is convincing evidence that these crop circles are of extramundane origin. In the detail of the crop circle formations themselves, as well as cell wall changes in the crop stalk and radionucleotide findings in the soil within the crop circles, we have found evidence of a technologically mediated process resulting in these extraordinarily beautiful formations.

The big question has always been: From whence did these crop circles come, who is responsible for them, and what is their purpose? In England and elsewhere, a myriad of theories abound which explain these crop circles as everything from Earth consciousness herself creating shapes to warn mankind of future Earth changes, to intelligent energies such as angels or fairies which are creating these shapes through interacting with our environment. However, this author has noted that over the years there have been substantial credible and close range sightings of UFOs in the area where these crop circles have been appearing. One of the long standing hypothesis surrounding the formation of these crop circles is that they are being directed by an ET civilization for purposes not yet fully elucidated.

It was our assessment at CSETI that these crop circles were most likely of ET origin and given reports from Colin Andrews and others, that there was potential for an interactive aspect to this phenomenon.

A number of crop circle researchers, including Colin Andrews, have related to me episodes where there appears to be clear interaction between humans and the crop circle makers, whoever they may be. With this information at hand, the CSETI leadership discerned that it would be a worthwhile project to take a team of CSETI investigators to southern England to investigate this phenomenon and to determine, if possible, whether or not these crop circles were due to ET intelligences interacting for some purpose with our planet. It is important to note that in this crop phenomenon we have extraordinary evidence of something clearly nonhuman and yet under intelligent control leaving undeniable evidence in the fields of southern England and increasingly, other countries around the world. We theorized that if these were under intelligent control by an ET civilization, they were obviously attempting to get our attention and engage us on some level. Because of this, we felt it appropriate to devise some means of engaging this intelligence and to interact with it, if possible.

At CSETI, we have determined that the most important aspect of any such initiative is in the human motivations which are driving it. It is essential that the purpose of the project itself and its individual members be that of a genuine interest in establishing a sustainable and peaceful relationship, and not centered around any mundane or self-centered objective. In a field beset by commercialism, grandstanding and turf battles, this, of course, is no mean feat. This is a project which includes not only scientific process, but also a diplomatic initiative, and beyond that, a spiritual journey in the as yet uncharted area of inter species communication.

It is important to note that the following report is admittedly an *interpretive* one. The purpose of this report is to record not only the significant events which occurred, but also our interpretation of them, our assessment of the situation, and to convey those conclusions which we feel are warranted at this point. It is important in any field of endeavor to state what one's assessment is, what conclusions, if any, can be drawn, and to interpret to the extent possible the events which have been experienced and seen. What follows is not only an account of the events which occurred, therefore, but it is also an interpretation of those events which is intended to assist us in formulating a comprehensive understanding of this phenomenon.

Before beginning the body of this report, I would like to thank Colin Andrews, who is head of Circle Phenomenon Research, for his assistance in organizing this research effort, for his support, and for his vision. Without his skilled assistance, I am quite certain that this project could not have been realized. In addition, I would like to thank Polly and Tim Carson who graciously allowed us the use of their 1800 acre farm at Alton Barnes for this very important research initiative. They were gracious, loving, and they are extremely special individuals who I believe are at the right place at the right time.

Additionally, I would like to thank the other members of the research team: Shari Adamiak, Ron Russell, Maria Ward, Peter Russell of London, and others who were able to withstand the rigors of this research project, which as you will see, involves staying out until three or four in the morning, night after night, over the period of ten days. I would like to acknowledge here publicly the dedication and sincerity of all those who took part in this effort. The reader should note that this project required a tremendous amount of effort on the part of all participants. Keep in mind, that all those who participated have full time jobs, have families and other obligations, and that they paid for their expenses for this trip out of their own funds. It is truly moving to see the level of dedication, which a number of people have found in pursuing this important endeavor.

Prelude

After some discussion, we determined that July 20th through 30th should be the dates for this initial research project for CSETI in the southern England area. A team of CSETI working group members which include myself, Shari Adamiak, Ron Russell and a Ph. D. psychologist from Cincinnati who does not wish to be named, and others arrived between the 21st and 23rd.

Except for one night, and that is the night of July 26th and early morning of the 27th, we enjoyed fine and clear weather every day that the research continued. This I learned was in stark contrast to several weeks of rainy weather which resulted in a number of crop circle researchers getting stuck in muddy fields and going through other harrowing experiences related to the weather. We felt fortunate as a team blessed with clear and fine weather for such a long duration, particularly since our research requires us to be out in the elements essentially from dusk till the wee hours of the morning, usually until 3 or 4 A.M.

I do not believe that any of us could have foreseen the magnitude of the events which were to follow. In the coming nine days we were to witness events which, without a doubt, rank as some of the most extraordinary, multiply witnessed close encounters in the history of this phenomenon. Within these few days, our team was to successfully achieve contact with ET intelligence on at least three major occasions, and as you will learn, probably on several other occasions. Certainly, I believe it can be stated without exaggeration, that the lives of everyone involved was changed forever by what they saw, what they felt, and what they collectively experienced.

Our research location was on Woodborough Hill at the farm of Polly and Tim Carson in Alton Barnes, in the county of Wiltshire in southern England. It should be noted that no one besides Colin Andrews and myself knew the precise location of this research site. However, the first night we arrived, there were at least 30 people who were not members of the team who appeared at the site. This obviously created some logistical problems which took some creativity in resolving. To use a term favored by Dr. J. Allen Hynek, it did not take long for "high strangeness" to greet us in southern England. The first night we arrived on Woodborough Hill, there were people literally coming up through the fields, through the woods, and from all directions. They were converging on that spot as if expecting something. Therefore, on the night of July 21st there were a number of people that had not been briefed on the project. For this reason, we endeavored to give a brief account for the purpose of describing the project and the processes which were to be used.

One of the initial high strangeness events happened during this briefing. As I was discussing the CSETI protocols and the purpose of the research project, a number of unusual events transpired. I had brought to the site a radar detector (as is used in detecting radar for automobiles in the United States) which was hooked up to a portable battery. I was holding this radar detector while discussing the equipment we were using and the overall research project. Each time that I would get to a key point in the discussion—that is, at each point when a significant aspect of the project was being emphasized—the radar detector would spontaneously go off. At least 40 people present that night saw this occur three separate times. People speculated that there was some sort of monitoring activity going on which signaled each time that the radar detector went off.

To this date, we have not been able to explain how or why the beeping detector was activated. And, at no other time during that evening or subsequent evenings, did this occur.

It is also worth noting that on this first evening (July 21st) we did a brief coherent thought sequencing as sort of an orientation project. During this time, we visualized the double ended crystal which Dorothy and Burl Ives had sent with me. This is the primary shape that we were projecting that evening. It is interesting that the next day we learned that the most complex crop circle of the year to that date had appeared at East Moen and resembled in many respects the configuration and shape of that item. Of course, we cannot prove that this was related, but in many of our minds it was highly suggestive of events to come.

The Progression of Contact

On July 22, 1992, the research team assembled at approximately 9:30 P.M. During the coherent sequencing process, a metallic noise was heard by a number of people on the western side of Woodborough Hill: it appeared to be emanating from behind the group. Later investigation showed that those present in the group had not seen anything associated with this sound. It is interesting that on this night, we tried to reach consensus on a shape to project to the crop circle makers. The intention of this was to arrive at a shape which would be held by the group collectively, which could be painted in the sky with a high powered light, and which could be received by the crop circle makers and result in a confirmed authentic crop formation of the same shape. This, of course, would be a crop circle CE-5. The group discussed several different shapes. It was finally decided upon to utilize a triangular shaped structure. After a number of configurations, it was finally agreed upon that we would make a triangle which consisted of three circles joined by three pathways which would make an equilateral triangle:

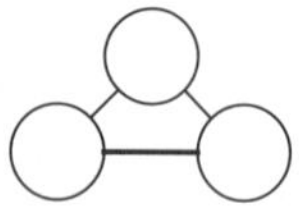

It is interesting to note that a large number of people on top of Woodborough Hill were able to see a scintillating ball of light in a field below our location over in the direction of Milk Hill. It was rather faint, and as darkness was growing, it was difficult to get an exact location of this object. The way that this object scintillated and moved was very reminiscent of the strange disk shaped object which was video taped in broad daylight, both in 1990 and in 1991 in the crop circle field areas. It is also interesting to note as a minor event, that at 1:45 A.M., a brilliant ball of orange amber colored light appeared on the southeastern horizon on the wee hours of July 23, 1992. The light traveled upwards from the horizon to remain stationary for about three to four minutes. There was no sound evident, no smoke trail, or any evidence of any conventional activity. As the light began to disappear, a white darting object was then seen moving rapidly along the edge of a cloud. An explanation for these events has not been reached.

On July 23, 1992 a number of extraordinary events occurred which are worthy of note. As a prelude to the night's activity, Maria Ward and Edward Sherwood were present earlier in the day near the Towsmead Copse, which is located directly below Woodborough Hill at Alton Barnes, when they heard a trilling sound, very much like what has been heard in the area of the crop circles over the past several years. The research team gathered later at about 9:15 P.M. on Woodborough Hill and began to note that Maria and Edward Sherwood arrived late and did not join the group immediately, but stayed in an area on top of Woodborough Hill separate from the group. Over the next few minutes, an extraordinary event occurred, which while lacking objective clarification, may be very significant. Both Maria Ward and Steven Greer experienced a "mental override" which was conveyed as a specific shape over southern England. (An override during coherent thought sequencing is when an image which appears not to be self generated, i.e. imaginary, persists in the mind, and which appears to have some objective reality). Maria Ward again was sitting separately from the main group, and independently, both of us experienced this override. It consisted of the following: An image of a milky colored mushroom-shaped dome over that part of southern England which was an energy field or an energy grid which somehow was related to the formation of these crop circles. Significantly, I described this to the group separately from Maria Ward. Then moments later, she came up and said that she had the most extraordinary mental override, and she too described it as a large opal, milky colored dome over that part of southern England. The exact meaning of this synchronously received image is yet to be determined, but it is certainly worth noting.

A significant event occurred at approximately 12:45 A.M. when a large amber, orange colored ball of light, which was spinning, appeared on the northwestern horizon. It was significantly larger than any object we had seen up to that point, and it remained there for approximately five minutes. One of the individuals working with Colin Andrews, Greg Pressley, was able to video tape this object. Some individuals nearby who had night scope binoculars, saw a military helicopter approach this object. At that point, this object moved away rapidly to the north and dimmed as it did so, and then it was gone.

Almost simultaneously, a red object appeared traveling above the northern edge of Woodborough Hill, and this object was noted to split into two parts before disappearing. This object displayed no aircraft lights and made absolutely no sound. People on top of Woodborough Hill also saw a white object that moved rapidly from the N.W. towards the zenith of the sky. It was described as a silver white object, and I personally saw this as it approached Woodborough Hill at some altitude. This object was seen immediately after the bright amber orange colored object vanished. These objects which were observed that night were definitely not aircraft, nor were they known natural phenomenon such as meteorite or lightening activity. At approximately 3:00 A.M., we concluded the night's research session.

During the day, the research team investigated reports of new crop circles which had appeared, and gathered for debriefing meetings and to plan the next night's activities. On Friday, July 24th, we decided to undertake an expedition through the fields surrounding Milk Hill and Alton Barnes to personally investigate all of the known confirmed authentic crop circles. There were several beautiful crop circles and elaborate formations near Milk Hill, which we investigated and personally entered. We were struck by the beauty, the symmetry, and the subjectively-felt energy within each of these crop circles. The crop circles themselves are of extraordinary design, and there is a gentleness and peace which cannot be objectively measured. The individual wheat stalks themselves are not broken, but are gently curved from the base in a way that cannot be done by mechanical forces.

Interestingly, I took one of these wheat stalks to preserve and carry back to America, and it was perfectly curved, having no broken places in it whatsoever. However, the force of simply holding it and walking to the next field resulted in it breaking in three places, even though I was being particularly careful not to damage the stalk. This was an impromptu experiment which I found personally significant since it showed that these stalks were very fragile and easily broken under even light mechanical forces, and yet these huge crop circles were able to be formed with the stems of these stalks of wheat only slightly curved and with no broken places in them whatsoever. To me, this is one of the most significant findings which establishes that the authentic crop circles are of extramundane origin, and are not formed by crude mechanical forces.

We took time to do coherent thought sequencing and remote viewing inside the center of several of these circles. Both Shari Adamiak and myself independently sensed that the mechanism of action for forming these crop circles was not mechanical, but that they were pulled down in some fashion. We sensed that there was a short-lived augmentation of the gravitational field over the area where the crop circle was to appear, and that it was an interaction between the electromagnetic spectrum and the gravitational field which resulted in the formation of the crop circles. Again, this is only a theory, but it conforms with much of the known evidence, and it was remotely viewed independently by two people while in a crop circle. Certainly there is evidence of rapid heating and electromagnetic energy affecting the cell wall of the crops. In addition, we know that there are radio-nucleotide changes in the area of the crop circle which is not present in the soil samples outside of the crop circles. There does appear to be, therefore, some rapidly applied electromagnetic energy which, given what we know about the UFO propulsion systems involving gravitational fields, could result in the type of mechanism which we jointly visualized. By being in the crop circles, you can sense that there was not a mechanical force that pushed the stalks down, but that there was an energy field which altered the nature of the stalks themselves.

By the night of Friday, July 24, 1992, the research team had decided that it would be necessary for us to move from the top of Woodborough Hill into a field directly below Woodborough Hill where there were two significant crop circle formations. One of these was a large ring. The other was a large circle, and they were adjacent to each other, separated only by a few yards. It is worth noting here, from a logistics point of view, that the research team had multiple people intrude who had not been trained and who were not prearranged members of the team. Obviously, this is disruptive and erosive to any group cohesion and to the overall flow of research activity. It is also interesting to note, here, that word of the research effort had spread throughout the area, and that there were multiple attempts by intruders to enter the farm of

Polly and Tim Carson for the purpose of infiltrating the research team. On more than one occasion, men who were in the employ of the farm's owners were required to circumambulate the farm for security purposes. On one occasion, local police were called to remove a number of intruders who had gotten very close to our research site. Beyond this, there was the usual collection of tabloid reporters and others who, while not understanding the mission, were wanting to be a part of the process. Moreover, because of the use of the high powered lights, a number of people in the area had detected our activity and had determined that they should somehow infiltrate the research group. For this reason and others, we decided to move off of the top of Woodborough Hill and to a more protected site below the summit. There were a number of observers, however, who did remain on top of Woodborough Hill.

After gathering in the crop circles themselves to conduct our research efforts, we noted collectively we were seeing multiple, strobe like, bright white and yellow flashes of light in various directions surrounding our location. These appeared as bright strobe lights as would be emitted by a camera discharging a flash bulb. Then at 10:25 P.M., while we were looking into the zenith of the sky, slightly towards the south and east, there came across the sky a structured spinning spacecraft. You could clearly see, in the dimming blue light of the sky, a spinning structure, with blue-green, red and white lights, that were spinning around its periphery. This object traversed 20 to 30 degrees of arc in the sky, and lasted for only about five to ten seconds. As it moved across the sky, it was also spinning in a counter clockwise rotation.

Please note that this was no distant light in the sky. It was a structured craft with individual lights which were clearly discernible. It was at this point that I was convinced that we had a "lock on" with a structured spacecraft of non-terrestrial origin. I believe that it is the same craft which later visited us on the night of July 26th and the wee hours of the 27th. I must emphasize here, that the sighting of this craft was clear and unobstructed. The individual lights could be determined as well as the metallic structure of the craft itself. It moved very rapidly across the zenith of the sky well in excess of the speed of any known aircraft. Beyond this, it should be noted, that this craft was completely silent as it passed overhead. As an interesting side note to the night of the 24th, I should mention that Ron Russell's cameras would not operate for the time he was in the crop circles. All of us present observed the malfunction, of not one, but both of his cameras, which to this date has not been explained. It is important to note that they worked fine the next day.

Then at 12:05 A.M., on the night of the 24th of July (actually the wee hours of July 25th) the entire group witnessed three separate balls of light moving over the Towsmead Copse. They moved rapidly and were an orange-amber color. There was no sound heard by those who were located in the crop formation. However, Edward Sherwood, who had walked over to that area a few minutes prior to this, did experience a metallic ringing noise as he neared the edge of the Copes. He did not, however, see the anomalous lights. He also reported that his right eye experienced a significant amount of irritation for the next 24 hours, and the next day we noted that his eye was red and inflamed. In addition, his eyelid appeared somewhat swollen. Exactly what these lights were and what the energy form was that resulted in the metallic ringing sound has yet to be determined. None of our instruments, including the tri-field meter or the radar detector, picked up any specific energies.

These events were preceded around 11:20 P.M. by the appearance of an object, amber in color, that was spinning. It emitted a red and bluish color. This was preceded by several lights that flashed through the sky in rapid succession. These were the luminosity of a bright star or planet. At 11:25 P.M., a UFO came over, visible for at least five minutes. It had a strobe on top, though it was most definitely not an airplane as seen through binoculars. There was no sound coming from the object. As soon as the group said, "Let's signal to it", it became illuminated and emitted a much brighter gold and amber light with the strobes still flashing on top of it. Again, no sound was heard, but it made an arc around the field we were in, and it headed off towards the south.

Over the course of the evening, we were to see four UFOs which were all moving towards a specific direction, that is, they appeared to be converging from four different directions towards one location. One originated in the zenith, one originated in the west, one originated in the north, and another in the northeast, and all converged towards the southeast. We noted that the next day, a new significant agriglyph was found in that direction on the other side of the Salisbury Plain at Pepperbox Mill. This may be a coincidence, but we note it here for possible correlations.

Then, on the morning of July 25th or 26th, a farmer, at Roundplay, near Devizes, found in his field, a crop circle of profound importance.

We did not learn of the presence of this crop formation until the morning of the 27th. However, Ralph Neyes, a prominent crop circle researcher in England, states this was most likely formed the night of the 23rd, 24th, or 25th of July. When we asked Ralph Noyes what the shape of this new formation was, he showed me a drawing he had made in his log book where he was keeping a very careful account of all crop circles. I was astonished, as was Shari Adamiak and others who were with me, to see that he had drawn precisely the shape which we had been visualizing and conveying to the crop circle makers. It is not possible to convey the emotion which all of us felt at that moment. Without a doubt, there had appeared a crop circle (felt to be authentic by the Argost team, which had entered it prior to our knowing of its existence) which exactly corresponded to the shape which we had been projecting both with the high-powered lights and through coherent thought sequencing. Since no one outside of our research group knew of the shape which we were projecting, the likelihood that this could be a hoax is thought to be nil. Nor is it likely that this was a mere coincidence, although the debunkers could always point that out as a possibility. It is our assessment that this was a specific crop circle formed in collaboration between the research team and the crop circle "makers". This was not just three circles in a triangle. They were in an equilateral triangle, and they were connected precisely by the bands which we had visualized. Moreover, they had appeared near our research site.

On the morning of the 27th, Shari Adamiak and myself, as well as others, went up to the top of Oliver's Castle and looked down upon the plain below us and saw this astonishing crop circle. It is not an exaggeration to say, that it was as if it had been lifted from our minds and placed in the field in absolutely perfect order. We feel that the significance of this can hardly be overstated: That a group of humans endeavoring to contact the intelligence responsible for the crop circles should be able to project a specific, and heretofore unknown shape, and that within a few miles of the location of their research, a crop formation of precisely that form should appear, indicates that we have reached a significant point of contact. It raises the question of what might be achieved through concerted efforts between properly motivated human research teams and those responsible for the crop circles.

We feel that this crop circle CE-5 experiment clearly establishes: (1) That the crop circles are under intelligent control, and (2) that they can be interacted with by a team of humans. If this amount of dialogue can occur, what other form of communication is possible? What does this indicate to us about the crop circle maker's willingness to communicate and cooperate with humans? These and other questions arise from this extraordinary event.

If there was any question in our minds that these crop circles were the result of ET peoples interacting with our planet, those doubts were greatly reduced by what followed. On the night of July 25th 1992, the group again gathered in the crop circles below Woodborough Hill. Once again, a brightly lit amber orange colored object was observed at about 11:00 P.M., moving from north to south. Once again, no sounds were heard from this object. At 1:10 A.M., in the wee hours of July 26th, while walking in a circle with high powered lights pointing straight up into a cloud bank, we noted that from above the clouds, a bright light was shining down from the sky into the cloud bank, mimicking our light formation. There was no question that this light was shining down from the sky onto the top surface of the cloud bank, and that it was mimicking our light work. Because of the cloud cover which had moved in at this time, we could not see any specific UFO, however, the beam of light shining from the sky down into the clouds was striking and could not be explained. It is also interesting to note that on Saturday, July 25th, the group's activities were interrupted by intruders into the research area. There were unknown individuals who had placed themselves on Adam's Grave, Milk Hill, Nap Hill, and Goldenball Hill. They had acquired their own high powered lights, and were flashing them down onto our group trying to detect our location.

In addition, it should be noted that our colleagues on top of Woodborough Hill were harassed by four individuals with cameras. These individuals took photographs of the people stationed on Woodborough Hill against their will. At this point, the four men who had forcibly taken pictures on top of Woodborough Hill came toward the CSETI group which was located in the crop circle formation at the base of Woodborough Hill. Our colleagues then warned the CSETI group that we were being approached, and at that point the night's activities were curtailed.

The Near-Landing of a Spacecraft

The night of July 26th, and the wee hours of July 27th, proved to be of profound importance. It is on this date, that the CSETI research team had a confirmed, close range lock-on with a structured spacecraft which came towards us in a near landing. The significance of this night's activities can hardly be overstated. Remember, that this is a multiply witnessed event that was human initiated and which included, as you will learn, a near landing of a structured ET spacecraft at close range.

Before recounting that event, however, we should review the circumstances leading up to that experience. On Sunday, July 26th, I had been asked to address a crop circle conference in Glastonbury, England. While there, I met a gentleman named Roy Dutton who had devised a system for predicting the appearance of UFO's given various locations and time frames. Apparently, this gentleman had analyzed reports for over 30 years, and had been able to come up with a periodicity which he had tested to be accurate. We informed him about our research project, and he gave us information relating to the following days appearances in that part of England, stating that there would be significant opportunity for sightings around 10:30 P.M., and then again at 12:30 A.M., and 1:30 A.M. We made note of this, and thought that it would be interesting to see if any actual correlations arose.

After returning from Glastonbury, we had a brief dinner, and then gathered around 10:00 P.M. at the research site in Alton Barnes. There were gathering clouds at that time, although it was not raining. Then at 10:25 P.M., on July 26th, two UFO's appeared in the east. They moved slightly towards us and were completely silent. There were no normal aircraft lights noted on these objects. At one point, they rose above a cloud bank and moved towards the group. While originating out of the east, they silently moved towards the south. It is felt that they were on the order of two to four miles away at this point. (It is interesting that 10:30 P.M. was the time frame that Roy Dutton had mentioned as an opportunity for a sighting).Present during the sighting was again Edward Sherwood, Maria Ward, Chris Mansel, Shari Adamiak, Marcia Morris, and others.

What follows next admittedly sounds like something out of a science fiction movie; however it was observed by everyone present, and will be recounted in order as the events unfolded. From our location in the crop circle, we began to see multiple areas of strobe-like lights that appeared in all directions. At around 11:00 P.M., in the clouds directly above us, there were noted to be brilliant lights spinning in a cartwheel-type fashion, anti-clockwise from above the clouds. This moved over directly above the CSETI group, and then stopped, remaining there for approximately ten minutes before ceasing its activity. Then looking towards the northeast, we saw that the sky was getting considerably darker, and at that point, four elliptical shapes detached themselves from the western edge of the cloud line and traveled rapidly eastwards into the edge of those clouds. These objects appeared to move in circular motion as if joined together around a cartwheel. It is important to note that several people in the group felt electrostatic effects on their skin during this part of the event. I must say that the impression of the object above the clouds, which was spinning with lights in a cartwheel fashion onto the upper surface of the clouds appeared to be rather large. We had an Englishman arrive on site, whose name is not known to me, who did confirm that these same lights were also seen from the direction of Lockeridge. He confirmed that there was no light coming from the ridges or below, and that this cartwheel formation of lights in the clouds was originating from above the clouds. These events, which of course were preceded by the sighting of the four UFO's mentioned earlier, were felt to be very significant.

At this point, it suddenly began to rain, first gently, and then a tremendous downpour. This period of rain immediately followed the cartwheeling effect in the sky and the gathering of very dark clouds from the north. The group then decided to break because of the rather hard downpour. Our cameras and other equipment were getting drenched, and visibility was reduced to only a few feet. Here I must mention something which can only be related again, as a consciousness override. While we were gathering to leave, I personally felt compelled to proceed to an area on the concrete farm road, located on the Carson farm, where there was a small turnout. I had this overriding vision of our remaining at that site pending some further event that evening. From a logical point of view, we should have disbanded, and taken the opportunity for a normal nights sleep! (By now you have gathered that we had been up many nights in a row until three, sometimes four o'clock in the morning, and many of those with us took this as an opportunity to leave and get an early rest.) However, four of us insisted on staying, and we proceeded to the concrete farm road only a few hundred yards from our present location.

At the same time that we were preparing to move from our location in the crop circle field (which was increasingly becoming mired in mud and water) Colin Andrews and others were leaving the top of Woodborough Hill. Apparently as Colin Andrews was pulling away from the barn area where the cars had been parked, members standing outside of his car heard the strange trilling sound, which had been recorded several times in the crop circle area. In addition, Don and Peggy Tuersley, walking down from the top of Woodborough Hill, noticed two lights which were shining in the field alongside where they were walking. These progressed through the field and then repeated after a few moments in the same sequence. (These events were not observed by the CSETI team because we were on the opposite side of Woodborough Hill preparing to depart from the now muddy crop circle.) Four of us remained on the concrete farm road waiting for further events. We were located in two automobiles with two persons in each. Significantly, at this point, it was around midnight and the people who had been attempting to infiltrate the CSETI group, were fortuitously flushed off of Adam's Grave, Milk Hill, and the other areas by the downpour. This may have been a helpful coincidence or a planned effect by the visitors. At any rate, in addition to these individuals being removed from the area due to inclement weather, we also had the misfortune of having our video camera doused by rain, and therefore, rendered inoperable.

After sitting in the cars waiting for the rain to subside for some time, I was startled when suddenly Chris Mansel in the car behind me jumped out and started beating on my window. I rolled the window down, and he exclaimed that there was a spaceship coming right through the field only a few hundred feet from our location! At this point, all of us were astonished to observe a large, disk shaped craft with brilliant lights rotating counter-clockwise along its base. The object rose to a high dome or cone on which sat three other amber lights on the top of this structure. The entire object was no more than thirty feet above the ground, and it was only four hundred yards from our location at the edge of the very field were we were standing! You could see the metallic structure between the rotating lights at the base of the spacecraft and the other three or four amber colored lights at the top of the cone. Again, I must emphasize that this was a close sighting of a structured spacecraft. At one point, we could hear a humming sound which we believed was coming from the object, but this could not be definitely determined. While our video camera was rendered inoperable, luckily, we were able to make real time recordings on the micro-cassette recorder which we kept with us continuously during our research trip. The lights which were at the base of this spacecraft were blue-green, red, amber, and white. Note that the shape of this spacecraft, its movement as well as the counterclockwise rotation of the lights, are identical to the spacecraft which was seen on Friday the 24th, which you will remember passed directly overhead in the zenith of the sky. It is my personal assessment that this was the same spacecraft.

When we first saw this spacecraft, it was at the edge of the wheat field. It then moved through the field behind some trees where we could see it clearly scintillating through the branches of the trees as it moved towards the north. The spacecraft initially appeared in the southwest, although as you will note in a moment, our compass readings at the time of the event were not accurate. The size of the spacecraft which was 400 yards away, was approximately one and a half inches at arm's length. This gives us an estimated size of eighty to one hundred fifty feet in diameter, and I believe that this spacecraft was one hundred feet in diameter. The lights, which were rotating counterclockwise around its base, were contiguous. The blue, white, greenish and red-amber colored lights seemed to blend into each other in an unusual fashion. I have never seen lights like this from a terrestrial origin. These were brilliant, obviously technologically associated lights attached to a structured metallic spacecraft. The craft continued to move towards the north, and then emerged in a notch in the trees and hovered. At this point, it seemed to flip or turn upwards, so that either another side of the spacecraft or the underside of the spacecraft was seen. At this point, it looked exactly like a Christmas tree lit up. Here it is worth quoting from the live tape recording:

> "We are observing a close range spacecraft that is conical shaped. Lord, it looks like a Christmas tree lit up! Chris mentions a Christmas tree lit up—exactly! Mother of Mary, Christ, look! Now it's rotated a bit. It is conical and looks just like a Christmas tree. It is floating down through the trees at this time. Do you hear humming? Yes. When it first approached you could see the lower part. It looked disk shaped. It was rotating, and the lights were going back and forth. This thing is big, quite large, that came across here!"

Now at this point, an amber colored probe detaches from the upper right hand side of the spacecraft and goes off into the mist. Later, we were to learn that Busty Taylor and others gathered on a nearby hilltop, who had remained during this part of the event but whose location was unknown to us, did see an amber colored light moving off from that direction. I must also convey that all members of the group, felt an electrical charge, a tingling, and in my case, I felt it from my toes all the way to the top of my head. We noticed that the magnetic compass (which was a Swedish compass purchased only a month beforehand and which had a lifetime guarantee) would not work properly. Each time that we checked the compass magnetic north had altered its location. At one point, we were checking the compass with a flashlight every two minutes, and each time we checked it, the needle rotated part way around the dial, counterclockwise. Note that the lights moving on the spaceship were also rotating counterclockwise around its base. At this point, we took the high powered lights from the car, and began to signal to the spaceship. We signaled to it, two bright flashes and a pause, and it then flashed back to us in the same sequence. This sequence was repeated again with a similar response from the spaceship. On the tape, you can hear gasps from the people present as the object begins pulsing, flashing back to us in the same sequence. Importantly, had we remained in the previous location (in the crop circle field) we would not have been in a position to have seen the event.

Immediately after this CE-5, which took place over a ten to fifteen minute period, a couple came driving down the farm road who had remained up on Woodborough Hill. Their presence there was unknown to us during the course of the near-landing event. One was named Judy Young, and the other, Peter Davenport, both from England. Just as I had felt compelled to remain on the concrete farm road, they also felt compelled to remain on top of Woodborough Hill sensing that something significant might happen. From their vantage point on Woodborough Hill, they were able to see off in the direction opposite from our location. It was there that they were able to see a huge shaft of light illuminating the field where we had been prior to the rain storm. We were fascinated to hear that they were able to see the light going down into the crop circle area where the CSETI team just had been conducting its research. There is no explanation for their sighting, but we feel that it probably preceded the near-landing, and is therefore highly significant.

Then at approximately 1:30 A.M., another UFO was seen in the southwest. This was a large amber colored object further away than the spacecraft which had come through the field. It was estimated to be one to two miles away. It appeared and then wobbled as it hovered. We then took our high powered lights and signaled to it, two flashes. It then returned the signaling back, two flashes. It moved in our direction slowly and then disappeared below a tree line in the distance. Once again, it is interesting to note, that these sightings occurred at approximately 12:30 and 1:30: A.M., which were windows of opportunity noted by Roy Dutton in his mathematical prediction formula. Also, the compass continued to rotate counter-clockwise. for several minutes after the second spacecraft was seen at 1:30 A.M.

Interesting corroborating evidence for this sighting, in addition to what was seen by Busty Taylor on a nearby hill, and by Judy Young and Peter Davenport on top of Woodborough Hill, comes from Maria Ward.

Maria had separated from the group to take someone home who was not feeling well. As she returned to the farm, she parked the car down by the manor house so that she would not run over the grates (cattle grids) and awaken the people in the farm house. She then began to walk towards our location. At that point, she noticed it was 12:30 A.M., she saw a large, dense, conical shape in the distance, with part of it hidden by a tree line. She could see continuous lights revolving around the base of the object that were blue, white and reddish colored. As it cleared the tree line, she could then see three orange lights above the rotating band of lights. Note that this corresponds precisely with our sighting which was closer to the spaceship. Again, Maria Ward described these lights at the base moving counterclockwise. Shortly after this, she saw a beam of light being directed at the object itself. Presumably this is the beam which we were shining from our location up on the concrete farm road. At this point, she noticed that the spacecraft flashed for a moment back towards the originating light. At this point, she noted the object looked almost triangular with the point facing upwards. Again, note that this correlates very well with our observation of it having the appearance of a Christmas tree. It is also interesting to note that Maria Ward felt a tingling sensation along her back and on her head. At this point, she also noticed that an object broke away from the spacecraft that was orange in color, and moved away in a northerly direction. Once again, this corresponds accurately with what we have observed from our location. She gave an estimate of length of seventy-five feet to one hundred feet, and no more than forty feet above the ground. And again, she noted that it was silent, except for a slight buzzing sound which seemed to be coming from the south of her position.

We have full reports from four people who were present during this event. These include on-site transcripts and drawings. It is significant that this was a multiply witnessed event of a near landing of a structured spacecraft at close range. It was no further than four hundred yards from our location and approximately thirty feet above the ground. There was a clear interactive component to this event with light signaling observed by at least five people. These five people included the four people at the primary site, as well as Maria Ward who was approaching the site from the manor house located on the farm. The significance of this event can hardly be overstated. This event constitutes a close range, close encounter of the 5th kind with a clear interactive component. It appears that the CSETI team was successful in vectoring in a spaceship to its location, and then engaged it in signaling. It is my considered opinion, that had the team been adequately prepared for it, there would have been a full landing, and in all likelihood, an on-board experience.

It is fair to mention here that I feel the rate-limiting aspect of this project, which is attempting to establish a mutual and sustainable relationship between humans and ET peoples, is the readiness of the research team itself. It is clear to all involved with this project, that there is a crescendo of events which has been occurring over the last year and a half, and which we feel certain will culminate in a confirmed landing and probable on board experience by a CSETI boarding party. It is my opinion, that to the extent that we are able to prepare ourselves for this level of close encounter of the 5th kind, to that extent, it can occur. Nevertheless, this experience, in and of itself, stands as a watershed event in the history of human initiated close encounters. For not only were we able to vector this spacecraft in to our location, but it was able to come so incredibly close to our group.

In addition, there has been much discussion surrounding the circumstances of this event. For example, it is noted that this spacecraft came under cover of darkness and at the end of a rain storm. This rain permitted the event to unfold under darkness of night and in private. Had it occurred on a night when it was clear and bright, it doubtlessly would have been observed and interfered with by multiple intruders. This also brings up the question of obtaining photographic evidence. Is it any coincidence, for example, that the camcorder became wet and was unable to be utilized? Why were others who had been present during the previous night's research not present who would have had still-photographic equipment to record the event? Was our inability to obtain photographic evidence: (1) a coincidence (2) a necessary result of being able to clear the area of unwanted and disruptive influences such as those that had infiltrated the site on the previous night, or (3) an intentional event indicating that they did not wish to be photographed at close range? It should be noted that the video camera which we had in our possession was a Canon L1 Pro with an extensor lens and a telephoto lens which would have given us approximately sixty X magnification. Certainly, at only four hundred yards, this camera would have recorded extraordinary detail of the spacecraft.

To be honest, at this point, I have not reached any conclusion as to the meaning of these events except to say that I'm quite certain that it is no coincidence. That this spaceship chose to come on an evening when others would have been out of the area, under the cover of darkness, and after a rainstorm I believe to be deliberately planned. The same spacecraft was seen rotating across the sky on the night of the 24th when it was crystal clear, and yet it made no further close approach. It should be noted that there were many people on Adam's Grave and on other nearby hillsides that would certainly have seen a large spacecraft of that sort coming so close to our group on the 24th.

I also do not think it is a coincidence that I personally received an override to go and stay on the concrete road, and to remain there for some time. This decision was against all logic, and it is interesting that the people who were on top of Woodborough Hill had a similar compelling drive to remain there for another hour or so. All of this might be considered in the category of "high strangeness", and it is crucial that we consider these aspects of the phenomenon.

Postscript

The nights of July 27, 28, and 29 continued to have significant aerial phenomenon. None, however, were so close and so certain as the near landing that occurred in the wee hours of July 27th. The following day, on the 27th, Colin Andrews disclosed to us that several people had heard the trilling sound similar to what had been recorded by the BBC and at White Crow at about 12:20 A.M. This would have been only five minutes prior to the near landing in the field. The next day we met a woman named Una Daywood who stated that, at East Kennet, in England, last year, a spacecraft apparently identical or very similar to what was seen in the wee hours on the 27th, was reported.

Conclusion

Based on the experiences of July 20 through 30, we have formulated the assessment that the crop circles are constructed by an ET civilization and are technologically related. The unequivocal sighting of a large structured spacecraft in the vicinity of the crop circles in the wee hours of July 27th, the collaborative formation of a specific crop circle shape which appeared near Roundplay, England, and the multiple UFO sightings which occurred over this period of nine nights, all speak to the ET origins of this phenomenon. Of equal significance is the fact that there is clear evidence that humans can interact with the phenomenon, and if carefully planned initiatives can be carried out, that significant progress in an open relationship between ET people and humans can be obtained. As the world progresses towards a global civilization and an organic unity, the potential for a sustained and open relationship between humans and ET visitors will increase. It is our assessment that the ET peoples responsible for the crop circle phenomenon are increasingly ready to enter into a period of relative openness. It is our responsibility as humans to similarly prepare ourselves mentally, physically, and spiritually for the next step in our relationship with these visitors. As the old order of the world all around us is collapsing, and as a new order, however embryonic, is evolving, we stand at a point in history of great potentiality. These potentialities include, but are not limited to, the integration of human civilization into an interplanetary civilization: the development of means of communication and travel which will dwarf current human capabilities, and the exploration of a unity in consciousness which transcends both the relative differences amongst ourselves and between various planetary species.

It is imperative that those who wish to join in this visionary, and yet practical, endeavor, continue to prepare themselves and their colleagues for further potential contact. Given a correct setting and an adequately motivated and trained group, it is our assessment that the possibility for a landing and on-board encounter is very high. While the precise timing of this is not known, we can discern that it is a relatively near, as opposed to distant event. It should be pointed out that CSETI's goals of establishing working groups of individuals capable of significant Close Encounters of the 5th Kind, has reached its ten year goal point in one and one half years. At this rate of progress, we can only imagine what events the next five years will bring us.

In addition to these considerations, the events of July 20th through 30th in England, underscore the importance of previous CE-5s, including those which occurred in Gulf Breeze, Wyoming, Colorado, North Carolina, Belgium, and elsewhere. There are those who would have us believe that all of the preceding events just mentioned are coincidence. However from these events we can discern a pattern of increasing contact between CE-5 Initiative Working Groups and those ET visitors who are involved with a project concerning the Earth. In addition to this, we note with some fascination and promise, that individual working group members have been having increasing numbers of sightings of structured craft at close range, and in some cases, in broad daylight. This includes, of course, the sighting in Wichita Falls, Texas, on April 24, 1992 by Ron Russell which resulted in a very good photograph at close range of a structured spacecraft (see Plate 3, page 402), and goes on to include a working group member in California, who was able to see a clearly structured spacecraft pass over the ridge near her home outside of Los Angeles. The meaning of this, it is my opinion, relates to an attempt on the part of the ET people to let us know that, given the right opportunity and adequately trained people, that they are ready to approach more boldly and with greater certainty than ever before. Certainly, as the world passes through this transformative period in its history, the likelihood of such high level Close Encounters of the 5th Kind will steadily increase.

Of greatest importance at this time is the evolution of cohesive unified teams which are competent to fully participate in a high level Close Encounter of the 5th Kind, to include a landing and an on-board (and possibly off-planet) experience. The preparation required for so extraordinary an endeavor involves not only the evolution of the appreciation of non local mind and universal consciousness, but it also involves the development of those skills, communication abilities, and psychological readiness so that the event can unfold in a smooth and productive fashion. To this end CSETI is increasingly dedicated to sponsoring extensive training sessions lasting days, and in the future, hopefully weeks so that people will be adequately prepared.

Let us go forward then, with a clear vision, and with determined hearts into the great future which awaits us. While I believe these efforts will bring results in the immediate future, we must also appreciate that we are laying the foundation for a future interplanetary unity. The hallmarks of this foundation are: The realization of the oneness of intelligent life in the universe through the direct experience of non local or unbounded mind; the maintenance of ideals which are centered around non hostility, peaceful intentions, and mutuality of benefit in the relationship, and the renunciation of unilateral aggressive or exploitative motives At present, we are at once preparing ourselves, and also, I believe, being prepared by these ET visitors for future events, the ramifications of which can already be partly discerned. Central to our success, is the realization that the process that we use transcends any ultimate goals—that if we pay attention to process, if we pay attention to the integrity of the moment, the future will unfold in such a way that nothing on the Earth or in the heavens, can defeat it.

33

Rapid Mobilization Investigative Team Report Monterrey, Mexico—December 1994

December 11–16, 1994

We learned of a major wave of activity in the large metropolis of Monterrey from a tape that was sent to us of a "Hard Copy" television story. We contacted the investigator who had filmed many of the sightings, Sr. Santiago Yturria. Santiago and his friend, television host Diana Perla Chapa, have been involved in the investigation of suspected space craft and ET presence for over 23 years.

Our team for this mission included Dr. Steven Greer, Shari Adamiak of Colorado, Sandra Wright Houghton of New York, and Tom Tuliene of Minnesota. We had the assistance of Lisa Huff, a friend of Tom's who worked in Monterrey.

We had significant activity while in the Monterrey area. For two nights running, we had unusual moving lights, clouds that formed over the face of a mountain, close approaches by ET intelligence and extended displays of dazzling enormous lights under intelligent control, with cogent signalling between our team and the intelligent beings behind the lights.

—Shari Adamiak

Combined Field Dictation and Notes from Steven Greer (SG) and Shari Adamiak (SA)

December 11, 1994 (SA)

Its December 11, 1994 and we're in Monterrey, Mexico on the first night of our RMIT. There are 12 of us on the upper site right now. There are a few more down on the lower site. We're on a hill up near San Pedro, south of Monterey. It's very clear, cold. The moon is between one-quarter and one-half full. We are here with members of the Ovni Club of Nuevo Leone. We arrived in the city after nightfall so have not been able to get a view of our surroundings.

December 11, 1994 (SG)

This dictation is on site in Monterey, Mexico with a local UFO group. We are outside Monterrey on a mountain side. Its approximately 11:35 on December 11th. At approximately 1:00 A.M. we saw an orange object in the North moving quickly and erratically across the sky for about 15–20 seconds.

December 12, 1994 (SA)

It is now about 12:30 P.M. on the 12th. We are getting ready to go to an area of the volcano, Topochico, which has recently heated up and has hot springs around it. It has been dormant for thousands of years. We are waiting for Sr. Yturria, Lisa and the others. We will travel out with Jose, our driver, in our Suburban. This morning Steven had a very clear, lucid experience in real time. He saw a phalanx of craft coming over the mountains directly over the city in daytime, in real-time. There were approximately 5–12 craft that formed a triangular shape. This happened about 8:30 A.M. this morning. At the same time, Sandy, who was sleeping in the downstairs bedroom, had a message in which she felt she was told that they were preparing for a meeting between us. During the night, I also had my usual dreams I have had for the last ten days of basically the same message that Sandy got. They knew we were coming, a way was being prepared, and that we would be encountering one another.

Notes from field work on the night of December 12, 1994 (SA)

The Mexican team took us to an area about 50 miles from Monterrey. We stopped to see some petroglyphs that were remarkable similar to ones Steven and I had seen in New Mexico at Three Rivers in October. One petroglyph was in the shape of a large domed spacecraft. We then journeyed farther along the rough gravel roads to an area where we had an excellent view of the mountain Mesilla—"little table." We noted that it was similar to Devil's Tower in Wyoming. Many sightings have occurred around Mesilla, often appearing as the sun is setting. We ate a picnic supper and observed the mountain. Several flashes of light were seen by numerous members of the team as the sun was setting. We did have a number of anomalous things happen: flashes in the sky, lights on the ground, orange lights on the ground. Nothing came close. It was a very interesting area, obviously very sacred land.

As it got dark, we carried our gear to the top of a small hill. We could see the country side in all directions, hear a river running, and had a clear view of Mesilla. A number of unusual, but not definitive events occurred.

The Mexican team had to leave to make the drive back to Monterrey at about 8:30 P.M. As our Suburban had experienced mechanical difficulty on the trip out when a rock was thrown up from the road and pierced the radiator, we decided to leave at the same time lest we be stranded in this desolate desert location.

December 13, 1994 (SA)

It's December 13 and its 8:30 P.M. We're in the Suburban now and we're driving to our site where we're going to be tonight. As we pulled out of the end of our street, we are seeing below the ridge of the mountain, where Lisa Huff says there is absolutely no electricity— it's called the mountain of the poor people—and we have been observing a light that has brightened up and dimmed completely off approximately four times now over a period of about five minutes. It's NNW of our location now as we're going along the road. So far now it is still out and we haven't seen it again. We think it's significant that it would appear just as we turn out to go to our field site. Lisa first saw it. She just now told us it is exactly the other side of the mountain from where we are going tonight.

It's 8:45 and we're now seeing another ET craft above the mountains. It's a beautiful amber-red-orange color.

We are now at our site by the mountain Las Mitres with the caves in it. Just as we pulled up, Lisa Huff saw a very rapidly moving blue light disappear over the edge of the peak. We're looking out over Topochico, the volcano, which doesn't look anything like a volcano. It's a very low, flat, sloping mountain range, obviously very ancient, but recently has become active. The water on its top has now become hot. We have a bit of a conflicting story on that. Santiago says he thinks the water has always been hot, but Lisa says she is sure that it recently has become much hotter.

We have been seeing some activity, but a lot of it is in the area of the airport, so we think probably most of what we are seeing so far in the East has been air traffic. The time is about 9:30 P.M. The site where we are looks completely out over the city of Monterrey. It's absolutely gorgeous with multi-colored lights, especially with all the Christmas lights everywhere. It's a very large city approximately the size of Denver.

In the NE on the Eastern slope of the volcano we just saw at 9:30 P.M. a fairly large red-amber light. Through the binoculars it was quite red. We flashed to it. After a few moments it completely blinked out.

At about 10:30 P.M., near the end of the CTS (coherent thought sequencing), I had my eyes open and was looking up at the zenith when a very bright white lit object started from the NE and took an upward arc through the sky and went right into the center of Orion. The sighting lasted for 2-3 seconds. It was extremely bright and was at least as bright as the moon.

Its about 10:45 P.M. and on the Las Mitres mountain right behind us the most unusual thing has happened. First, on the left side of the mountain a huge, white, very dense cloud has formed right at the edge of the mountain behind the edge of the ridge. At one point the left hand edge of the cloud became right-angled squared off. Now at 10:50, Tom, Lisa and myself all happened to be looking at the mountain peak when we saw in the area of the large cave an extremely dense white cloud literally materialize out of nothing right before our eyes. It was extremely dense and it formed right over the cave. At one point, it assumed a dome shape. Now it almost looks like a bat and the one on the right has basically dissipated. Through the night vision scope there apparently is some light above the ridge top that is directly above the cloud. It is directly in front of the cave.

Notes on the remainder of the field work this night

Because of the nature of the events of the rest of this night's field work, these notes were not dictated on site. First of all, early that morning, I dreamt that the ETs were showing where to come to meet with them. I related this dream to Steven and Sandy this morning. The terrain was green, with high mountains rising straight up, and the city behind us. I was shown it in the daylight from above, and at night from the ground. In the night scene, there were two stars in a certain configuration above the left-hand edge of the mountain top. When Santiago took us to Las Mitres during the daylight, I remarked that it looked very much like the terrain in my dream. We decided to do our field work at Las Mitres that night as it had been a location of many sightings. It was felt by the Mexican team that spacecraft hid in the cave and concealed their comings and goings with clouds that formed over the mountain face. When we arrived on our site that night, as the stars became visible, I observed that two stars were indeed positioned exactly as they had been in the dream.

At approximately 1:30 A.M. Steven and Tom were down the road a bit conversing. I was lying on the tarp with Sandy. Something compelled me to get up, walk behind the stone wall, and look at the left-hand edge of the mountain. Within a few moments, Steven came up to me and said that my radar had been right on. He had been looking for me to report that he and Tom had just seen a flashing light that seemed to come down the left-hand edge of the mountain. Shortly after this, Steven and I saw another flash in the same area. Steven walked back to speak to the other team members and I stood in the brush facing the mountain. I suddenly felt my body leaning forward, as if pulled by a gentle force. I felt it was a signal to move close to the dense brush, so I moved forward about ten feet. I then became aware that there seemed to be two or three small beings on the ground nearby. I received a thought of concern about Tom's large camera that was mounted on a tripod behind me to the right. I assured them that the camera was not on and that we wouldn't touch it. I felt that the beings were waiting for Steven to return. He did indeed return to where I was and I briefed him on what had occurred. He also could sense a presence on the ground. From a series of dreams I had had for several weeks prior to this mission, I recognized this scenario. In the dreams, a close encounter occurred to Steven and me when the rest of the team was removed from us by some distance. He then instructed the rest of the ream to stay where they were unless he called them forward, and told Tom not to turn on his camera. The beings could never quite be clearly seen. We could sense a lot of discussion occurring about whether or not they could fully manifest in the physical. The small beings seemed very shy and reticent, almost child-like. They were very short and I had the sense that they were rather boxy or squarish in shape. Both Steven and I got the message to remove our glasses, and I was told to remove my hat. I could then feel that there was a balanced flow of energy throughout my being.

At this point, shafts of dim golden light came from the edge of the mountain near the ground, and swept across the bushes in front of us. We learned later that Sandy, Tom and Lisa were able to see this as well. A concentrated area of dim bluish fog appeared to manifest in front of Steven and me. Within the fog we could sense another being. It was male, tall and very human-looking, surrounded by a blue glow. With our glasses off, it was easier to perceive the beings. Again, there was telepathic communication about whether or not they could manifest in the physical. They sent a message that at least one person with us would be very badly frightened if they revealed themselves fully in the physical. Steven and I sent messages that they could take us to where they were if they wished. I received the message that it would frighten our friends just as much to see us disappear in front of their eyes as it would for them to manifest in front of us. However, when we had this thought exchange, we could see a globe of golden -copper light about ten feet in diameter become faintly visible in front of us and to the right. After what seemed like a brief time, the taller being sent a message that they were not going to come fully into the physical but said, "soon again, soon again." Steven then stepped back to speak with the rest of the team.

Upon rejoining the group, I learned that they had perceived the golden light and the blue fog. Sandy reported that an arm of the fog traveled along the ground and wrapped itself softly around her legs. She said that it did not frighten her as it was very gentle. We also learned that Lisa Huff had become very frightened by what she had seen—the lights coming across the ground and the presence she felt. She retreated to the designated "safe area"—the Suburban. She told us later that if anything more had happened, she would have run screaming down the mountain. We knew then that the ETs were correct in the fright they had perceived from one of the people present. The most surprising thing we learned was that when this event ended, it was 3:00 A.M. Steve and I thought it had taken perhaps half an hour.

December 13, 1994 (SG)

We are on site outside Monterrey on the side of the mountain Las Mitres facing towards the low volcano on the edge of the city where a lot of activity is seen. It's approximately 9:20 P.M. We have already seen a couple of unusual objects as we drove in and one bright blue object that I just saw the edge of it.

9:50 and we just saw an object in the NE about 10–20° above the horizon. An amber red color, single light, stationary, was sort of pulsating, several miles distant. After signaling to for awhile, it extinguished without any obvious normal movement. This is certainly an anomalous object but some distance away and no structure could be seen.

We had a cloud—alleged cloud—shaped exactly like a disc with a dome on it form as we were watching the mountain to our South.

Right at the area where the cave is located where they say the craft come in and out. This cloud formed from nothing. It just manifested there and grew right in front of our eyes and another one to our right as we were facing it, which would be West, also formed. We also noticed a starlight-like light in the valley between these two peaks. It is interesting because it is moving in the valley.

At approximately 1:55 I saw a bright, strobe-like white light come on to the SSE, right along the hillside near us. I came over to tell Shari about it at about 2:00am and on the first peak South of us was a distinct bright strobe flash that we both saw simultaneously and later that part of the mountain was covered over by cloud. My sense is that there was an ET presence and craft fairly near by.

December 14-15 (SA)

Its about 1:00 in the morning on December 15th. Steven thinks we arrived at our site here at the base of Las Mitres in Monterrey at about 11:45. Immediately as we turned into the gravel road to drive up to our site, a light was seen on the slope of the mountain, on the sheer cliff where there is nothing but forest and sheer cliff. There is no home there; there are no power lines there; there was not light there last night. After we arrived—and jumped out of the car immediately,—Steven sending thoughts to it. Then a very huge light illuminated and has signalled to us repeatedly in very precise signals. They would do three flashes, but each flash would be timed either very short or very long. I would match their flash with the light; they would then signal to us in another sequence. This has gone on now until 1:00. It is a very round, brilliant light, greenish colored through the night-vision scope. At one point when I was watching it, while the light was very brilliantly illuminated another beam, a darker beam moved independently across the face of the lit beam. I think it was a being walking in front of the light beam. The beam from this round light was so large that it illuminated all the way down the slope of the very steep mountainside, all into the foothill area. The light has moved. It has changed direction, it has changed the angle of the beam, its very large.

When it first appeared, I must say this, first of all we saw this steady small light which actually has been on through the duration of almost this entire event so far. There formed to the left of the little star-like light a small bank of clouds. As I had the night vision scope on this small, little puff of cloud, probably over one of the caves that ET craft are believed to use, a strobing light appeared in the cloud. It was from this strobing light that this very large lit craft then manifested. Not strobing, but signalling, moving sweeping the ground. There is also a very dense, very low cloud all the way over covering the base of the mountain. This is unusual, last night the clouds were at the top of the mountain. We have felt their presence extremely near. We sense that the craft is definitely still here in the cloud bank that is directly in front of us.

Present tonight are only Sandy Houghton, Steven Greer and Shari Adamiak. Tom Tuliene decided not to come out with us tonight. We have sent Jose, the driver, and Fernando, Lisa's husband down the road because we were concerned they might panic in the face of an ET event.

December 15, 1994 (SG)

This is further dictation addendum to the night of the 14th, early morning of the 15th when my microcassette recorder failed. This entry is taking place after the event. On the night of the 14th at approximately 11:45 P.M., we arrived on a site outside Monterrey where we had been doing research. Almost immediately, I saw a starlight-type object on the side of the mountain, quite high and obviously in an area where there could not have been houses or cars. It was artificial, it looked like the brightest star in the sky, except it was resting on the side of the mountain. Literally as the Suburban rolled to the site, I was out of the car as it was still moving because I knew this was an anomalous object. I went to it and we began to signal as we all gathered. It then began to signal to us with a massive light similar to a helicopter search light. It did this from 11:45 P.M. until 2:00 A.M. This is over two hours. Some of this we have on video tape. This was the night that Tom Tuliene, who was our videographer who had the correct equipment decided he would stay in Monterrey.

Around the time that we first arrived a weird mist, fog, cloud-like formation formed. It did not move into the area, but formed around the base of the mountain and into the area where this object was seen. During the course of the signalling to this object, we saw small humanoid figures moving outside in front of the lights. It appeared it was on a high ridge up on the side of the mountain and apparently near some of the caves that are on this mountain, Las Mitres. Of course, we were all stunned to have this happen for two and a half hours. It is unprecedented. As we were signalling to this object the object would move slightly back and forth. At one point there were two sources of these lights and, I should say, that this was extremely close. It was up high on the side of the mountain, but certainly well within a mile distant. Later, when we returned on the 16th in the evening with Santiago Yturiia and others, they said there were absolutely no roads or other means of conveyance up to that point on the mountain. Nothing was heard. There was no sound of motors or anything of this sort. The light was a brilliant white color and sometimes yellow. They signalled congruently with us for over two hours. When we would signal, for example three flashes, they would return it three times and so on. If we would stop signalling for a while, they would try to initiate the signalling with us and start the signalling again, which is very unusual. The area is extremely rough and steep. These mountains are virtually vertical. It was not at the top of the mountain, but about a third of the way up the ascent or the slope in an area where there is no access either by road or other means. Interestingly, when we left the site at about 2:00, after the object went out in a spectacular fashion, it seemed to follow us to the other side of the mountain.

I should comment on the manner in which the object disappeared. Through the night scope binoculars, we could see the light dim and then Sandy and Shari saw a red light emit from this object, and then through night scopes I could see a brilliant, bright lightening-like flash that occurred. This lightning-light flash was the final event and after this point, the object and the lights ceased. This was about 2:00 A.M. Interestingly, from the perspective where the driver and Fernando were located, they had gone down the mountain from our location to give us privacy, they could see an outline of the shape. It was a disc that was domed. We could roughly make out its shape, but there were some trees obscuring that specific shape from our area. However, it should be noted that these shaped objects have been filmed in daytime and nighttime in that area within the last month.

34

Rapid Mobilization Investigative Team Report, Southern England—July 1995

By Shari Adamiak

From July 24 through August 1, 1995, six CSETI members from the United States included Steven Greer, M D., International Director of CSETI, Shari Adamiak, Executive Director of CSETI, Ron Russell, Denver CSETI, Jon Groves, coordinator of a San Diego, California working group, Joani Gulino, Santa Fe, New Mexico working group coordinator, and Louise Olivi, CSETI member from Connecticut. We also had Alison Tredwell, Northern England working group, and joining us on several of the nights were Mark Haywood and Nick Nickerson, also of the Northern England team.

CSETI teams have been traveling to Wiltshire County in southern England for four years to do real-time research, coinciding with crop circle season. This year, however, was the hottest summer in twenty years, and very dry. The wheat was stunted compared to previous years and early harvesting reduced the number of crop formations in our vicinity. A bang-up spring season and major formations in Wiltshire, Hampshire and northern counties of England did produce some astonishing formations.

The hot weather did, however, allow us a far greater degree of comfort for our night-time field work. We are generally swathed in layer upon layer of winter clothing to withstand the extreme chill and damp we have historically faced during our midsummer projects in England

Team member Jon Groves, coordinator of one of the San Diego working groups, summed it up this way:

> "The RMIT could not have asked for better weather conditions during the week of 24 July to 31 July 1995. The week was during a New Moon phase and offered us moonless nights, which when combined with the lack of cloud cover,

made for extraordinary viewing of the night skies. Almost every evening was completely clear from "horizon to horizon", presenting the Milky Way in its full luminous glory. Being approximately 75 miles west of London, between Calne and Marlborough, we didn't have big city light pollution interfering with visibility."

A number of events highlighted this year's trip. For two nights, we had exceedingly high numbers of so-called satellites that traversed the sky. The first of these nights, we tracked 32 objects within 90 minutes; the next night we counted 27 in the same time span. on all remaining nights, the satellite traffic was the usual four or five over a period of five to seven hours. Another anomaly was the fact that our radar detector was active on several different occasions during our nights of field work. With nothing visible in line sight, we had sporadic beeps coming from the radar detector. One night this lasted over an hour. We were never able to locate any visible source that would repeatedly trip the radar detector.

One warm night when we were encamped near Morgan's Hill, near the Cherhill White Horse and within view of Furze Knoll where a commemorative obelisk marks the spot where Marconi sent his first radio signals, the team observed the following: A military plane was flying low and slow, apparently in pursuit of a large white ball of light. The plane and light were flying at approximately the same speed and attitude, with the plane behind and slightly above the UFO. We had a clear and unobstructed view of this chase through our binoculars. The two objects were directly in front of us, perhaps two miles distant. Through the glasses we could clearly make out the details of the military plane; yet we could see no features on the ball of light. It was simply a glowing orb. As the plane approached closer to the orb, the light just appeared to vanish, leaving only the military plane in sight. As often happens when multiple individuals observe the same event, our teammate who didn't see this entire sequence (because he attempted—unsuccessfully—to get a video camera into position in time to tape) thought he saw the plane and white light in opposite positions and flight patterns. Also this night we had been having our radar detector which was plugged into to a vehicle nearby go off randomly for over an hour with no known source in line sight of us. Regarding the sighting, team member Alison Tredwell stated:

> "I was initially facing in the opposite direction and did not see the start of this incident. When I turned around I saw what appeared to be a plane following and catching up on a slower-moving light—both moving parallel to our position. As the plane caught up with the light, the light disappeared. I had no remote view or any sense that would lead me to believe the light was an ET craft. I wondered whether it was not a military exercise in which a plane pursued a remote-controlled target. However, in some ways this was similar to the incident we observed during the RMIT at Furze Knoll in 1993, when a very bright anomalous light was approached by a helicopter: the light initially went out, but as the helicopter reached the spot, the light flared up enormously, and the helicopter was not seen again."

An unusual close encounter occurred on the night of July 28/29. We were helping to coordinate a large meditative project planned by Dr. Joachim Koch, a surgeon from Berlin, and his fellow researcher, Hans-Jergen Kyborg. The event was a follow-up to a smaller scale but similar project carried out in 1994, and written up by Ron Russell and myself for two English magazines. We had teams of people at several sacred sites around Wiltshire, including Silbury Hill, The Sanctuary, Knapp Hill, Windmill Hill, West Kennett Long Barrow, Barbury Castle, and Avebury. Avebury was to be the locus for the energy, with the satellite groups visualizing beams of light being projected at a 30° angle towards Avebury, and all groups were to then envision a large column of light arising from Avebury (the largest stone circle in England). Two groups were in the focal area of Avebury, arranged at the direction of Dr. Koch and Mr. Kyborg; three women were in the Cove (including myself, Louise Olivi from Connecticut who was a member of our RMIT, and Mary Bennett, CSETI member from England); and three men were in the obelisk (Steven Greer, Colin Andrews—English crop circle researcher, and Jon Groves—CSETI member from California). Our group meditation was to last from midnight until 1:00 A.M.

When the six of us arrived at the car park in Avebury, we were dismayed to discover that the Red Lion Pub had been rented for a private party, complete with very loud live band. Pubs in England are required to close at 11:00 P.M., which is why our project was to start at midnight.

However, a special dispensation for this party had been granted so we prepared our sites and began our work amidst a lot of noise. It seemed so incongruous to me that such a sacred and special spot as Avebury would have to be the unwitting host for the only party taking place in Wiltshire that night, and the only night of the year the pub had been booked for a late event. An interesting side note—the final song played by the band was "Wild Thing", and Steven Greer, Colin Andrews and I had been on Silbury Hill earlier in the evening with Reg Presley and his wife. Reg Presley wrote and sang the song "Wild Thing" during his days with The Troggs. After the hoopla came to an end, the revelers poured out of the pub and staggered into the large stone circle, where the men's team was attempting to do their meditative work.

At five minutes to midnight, when all groups were preparing to begin the meditation, a huge and colorful fireball fell from very high in the sky, seen by all the teams on all the sites. It came close to the Earth and from our viewpoint, seemed to explode in sparks directly over Avebury.

In the women's group, Mary Bennett agreed to be the watcher since she lives in the area and can visit Avebury at any time. This allowed Louise and I to feel free to go deeply into meditation; Mary would keep check on the times and what was occurring around us. After just minutes, Mary softly said, "just look around us. "I opened my eyes to see thick white mist swirling from the ground upward about three feet, forming on particular sides of the huge, ancient standing stone sentinels in the Cove. Gradually the mist became thick all around Avebury. We learned later that the mist engulfed many of the groups. Those at a high vantage point stated that it seemed to be thickest over and emanate from Avebury. It had been a hot dry day and the following day was hot and dry. The night was not damp. It was not the typical atmosphere for this type of mist to form.

We proceeded with our meditative work, including surrounding the planet with a veil of peace and healing energy. At the next morning's debriefing, several people stated they had images of weapons being dropped and fights stopped in mid-swing with the participants not even knowing why or what had happened. All the 30–40 participants felt that we had effected a positive force for the planet in that moment.

Near the end of our hour, while deep into the portion of the meditation for peace for the universe, Mary spoke once more. Quietly she said, "look just there." I opened my eyes to see an amazing aura of pink-red intense light of a hue I had never seen. It was just to the left of the ancient tree that stands but a few yards away from the two huge canti-levered stones beside us. The light came from a brilliant point on the ground and made a perfect, sharp semicircle that arose about three feet from the ground. We were astonished but barely moved a muscle as we watched the light contract towards the ground, changing to turquoise, then golden, then yellow-white. I observed gold and yellow lights to flash in random sequence at ground level, taking up about three feet of width. From where I was sitting, the lights were at a slight angle and I perceived an elliptical dome shaped top through the lights. Mary and Louise did not see a solid object, although Louise reported seeing a dome shape; indeed, Mary suspected that the entire event may have been a hologram.

The lights gradually subdued and faded. We softly spoke to one another, saying, "is that what we think it is?" We ruled out prosaic explanations one by one. We quickly decided to do what we were doing just prior to the appearance to see if it would respond and return. Although I thought I spoke a request that if it were an extra-terrestrial object, to please turn the red light back on, my two teammates said I never uttered those words. So it was a thought request only. Yet instantly, the red light came back on. It glowed at ground level, pulsing like a gigantic red ruby. Slowly the gold and white reappeared, and the lovely pink-red intense glow returned and created another arc of light. Then it contracted and vanished.

Moments later Louise called our attention to a faint red streak of light moving upwards at an angle into the sky. But before the red streak of light, in the vicinity where this object had been, an unusually shaped bank of mist suddenly appeared. This mist was a block about the size of a car, only taller—perhaps six to eight feet high. And the mist was shaped like a parallelogram. We all compared notes to check if we were seeing the same thing and all three of us agreed. The mist stayed for several minutes. When the red light did streak upward, it went at the same angle as the sides of the parallelogram. Moments after the red streak of light, a golden faintly strobing light appeared. We learned the next day at our debriefing that two of the other teams had also observed the gold strobing light. No other groups could have seen the object, including the men in the other part of Avebury. However, Ron Russell from atop Windmill Hill reported seeing a cloud of mist descending directly towards Avebury and stated that within the mist was a small point of red light. Was this the same object that landed in the Cove? Unknown, but an interesting correlation.

Louise Olivi RMIT team member present with me in the Cove, stated:

> "...I saw what appeared to be a brilliant golden circle of light just above the ground about 90 feet from our position (which Steven Greer later measured out). The light was diffused into a lighter shade of yellow in a dome shape all around it. Because of the fog that had set in, I had difficulty discerning any solid shape. The glow changed from gold to blue-green to rose red, then disappeared. The display lasted no more than 10–15 seconds. The gold ball then appeared again in the same area and [we watched] it turn from half gold, half red to all red before disappearing a second time. The feeling I had was one of being surrounded by an all-encompassing love energy. Mary later told us she had telepathically sent universal love to the area just prior to the lights reappearing."

To me, the object appeared solid. It appeared to be some sort of remotely piloted vehicle. Some such RPVs have been filmed on previous years in this area, but this was unlike the ones I had seen on video. Those had all been silvery discs with no visible features approximately one foot in diameter. What I saw in the Cove appeared to be about three feet in diameter with multicolored lights that could perform some different functions. It actually seemed to me like a smaller version of the structured craft seen by our CSETI team not far from Avebury in July 1992.

On July 30, we made our encampment on Giant's Grave in Oare. We had learned of a sighting in this area on the previous night. Nicki and Charlie, village residents, climbed the hill in search of their dog and stopped to visit. They were unaware of the sighting the previous night. At 12:20 A.M., we were watching through the night vision a round ball of light just to the left of Woodborough Hill. Through the regular binoculars I could see that it was amber colored. Now it appeared as a column of light vertically. It had obviously changed. We then noticed that the wind had become quite warm. Also, Steven and I both felt strongly at the time that we should go to the Woodborough Hill area. We did so and approached from the Woodborough side, walking up the trail and standing upon the ancient curved bridge over the River Avon. This is a magical spot that is very special to all of us. We watched and signalled to lights in the WSW, low to the ground, flickering, moving. Although we could not discern anything definite in our night vision equipment, we felt their actions were quite unusual. We learned the next day that a UFO had been videotaped in Swindon that night. Swindon is not in the vicinity where we saw the lights, however.

The following night was our last one for the entire team and was a quiet one. Many of us were staying on in England and continued to have some occasional sightings during night-time skywatches. After I returned to the States, I learned of two separate sightings of a large triangular craft which happened just days after our departure. one event was reported to me over the Internet by the witness who lives in Glastonbury.

He and his family saw the object as they were approaching the town of Glastonbury after a weekend holiday. The second sighting occurred to Karen Douglas, Northern England CSETI, and Steve Alexander, well-known crop circle photographer, in Avebury. Steve reported that his cameras were in the boot of the car at the time of the occurrence.

35

Ambassadors to the Universe Training, Crestone, Colorado—June 1997

A Perspective by Shari Adamiak, September 1997

In mid-June, 37 people arrived in the alpine oasis-like town of Crestone, Colorado to study and participate in CSETI's Ambassadors to the Universe Retreat. This was the fourth year in a row that CSETI held a training retreat in Crestone. Crestone is an anomaly. Nestled against the massive Sangre de Cristos Mountains, this unique town is home to twelve different spiritual centers representing most of the world's major religions. From nuns to Tibetan monks, all dwell harmoniously together in their respective spiritual centers. Sangre de Cristos means "blood of Christ." The mountains are thus named because on rare occasions, when the clouds are just so, the sun setting behind the San Juan Mountains to the west turns the snow-capped Sangres a blood red.

Crestone is located in the world's largest, highest and most pristine alpine valley—the San Luis Valley, also cryptically known as the Mysterious Valley. It is also known historically as "The Bloodless Valley." Not only were no battles ever fought here, but those who drew weapons were asked to leave. The valley was revered by native tribes as a place for good medicine, vision quests and learning from nature. The San Luis Valley runs 200 miles from north to south. Midway, along the Sangres, can be found The Great Sand Dunes. These are the highest dune fields in North America and moreover, are the site of some of the highest and lowest magnetic fields in the country. The visible result is a very shallow, wide creek, flowing at the base of the dunes and boasting undulating waves. The enigmatic dunes are visible for many miles. From the distant past to the present, numerous accounts of UFO sightings—indeed, even a crashed disc—have been reported.

Towering just south of the Great Sand Dunes looms Mount Blanca and its many slopes. Revered by many Native American tribes as one of the sacred mountains, this "Sacred Mountain of the East" is considered the keeper of knowledge. An apt title, as many UFO's have been seen around the Blanca Massif. A revered and respected colleague of CSETI's, a medical doctor, clearly saw from his plane some years back a metallic disc literally vanish into Mt. Blanca. Needless to say, this was not in this man's usual paradigm and he was very taken aback by the sight. During CSETI's 1994 retreat, we were searching for a field site near dusk at the northern edge of the Great Sand Dunes. We had pulled up in a caravan of cars and were reconnoitering the site for its merits. In the clear flat light before the sun began to set, we all saw a small plane flying low and slow. It attracted our attention as it was headed straight towards a crevice in the Blanca Massif (the sloping mountains that border Mt. Blanca on the north). We were afraid the pilot was having difficulty—it appeared that we were going to unfortunately witness a dreadful crash. The pilot kept flying on a beeline straight for the crevice, through which no plane could physically pass. We watched in anticipated horror for the inevitable crash. But the plane flew directly to the crevice and continued going! It seemed to slice through the rock with the same ease it had just been passing through thin air. We had witnessed for ourselves one of the mountain's many legends. What we had assumed was a small plane surely was either a masked ship or a holographic projection. It certainly was not simply a small airplane. Interestingly, our team observed the "plane" in many different ways. Although all agreed that it appeared to be a private prop plane, there was no agreement on its color. We have noted this discrepancy often during events of high strangeness.

We had another unusual "plane" event occur at our training retreat in June of 1997. During our second night of field work, we were approached by a military-looking plane flying rather low on a course that took it directly over our team. Professional pilots in the group noted that the lighting configuration was unusual; it had lights on only one of its two wings. CSETI's webmaster, Tony Craddock, was quick to video the overflight. When he analyzed the footage frame-by-frame, he noted something else. A small, green light or probe appeared. As Tony describes it: "It came from nowhere, flew right by the fuselage, and then flew out of the picture in an almost linear track, slowing slightly only as it passed the plane. "He verified that it appears on video for two seconds at the most. CSETI teams have seen this in Mexico as well, when a red-light probe accompanied the huge triangular craft that visited our five-person team near Mt. Popo in early 1993.

We spent time each day in remote viewing training. Dr. Steven Greer, CSETI's founder and director, has developed a technique we call RV2—Remote Viewing and Remote Vectoring. In each CSETI training, the team members are surprised and pleased to see that they can soon begin to develop this innate skill, and this Crestone training was no exception. We had some remarkably accurate hits when team members were asked to remote view events that would transpire in upcoming field work, and in areas where the team should be located to have contact experiences. On our second night of field work, a very distinct orange orb of light was observed by several team members, including Dr. Greer and Tony Craddock.

The team's growing proficiency at RV2 was particularly accurate the afternoon we spent at the Great Sand Dunes in finding a field site for that night. After much discussion and pouring over maps, we decided to go to Mt. Blanca that evening. The journey to the picnic area and Zapata Falls revealed several hits that teammates had picked up remotely, so many that we knew this was the spot for us to be that evening.

As we all began to pull out our dinnertime snacks, the sky grew ominously black. Soon lightning was flashing over the San Luis Valley sprawled out before us in our 100-mile view. As lavender streaks reached down to the nearby dunes, Dr. Greer asked everyone to stay in their vehicles. We knew this was killer lightning, and Colorado has one of the highest death rates from lightning strike. Again, Tony Craddock's videotaping proved Dr. Greer correct—frame -by-frame viewing reveals lightning originating with a streamer from the ground up first—from the very road on which we were parked.

We were fortunate to be treated to an hour and a half of one of the most spectacular displays of nature as lightning almost continuously struck far and near. During the light show, Dr. Greer and I were looking directly out in front of us, across the northern half of the valley. Suddenly, a large, metallic disc appeared momentarily in an opening in the clouds directly in line with our Jeep's windshield.

Yellowish-white, it was absolutely crystal clear for the fractions of seconds that it was visible. After the lightning ran its course, it began to rain. Another hour and a half inside the stuffy vehicles produced some interesting events.

One gentleman who was near the far end of the string of cars was standing outside for a few minutes when he saw a large dark disc materialize momentarily. Another man sensed someone standing close to him, although he knew no one else was nearby in the rain. Other team members reported sensing and feeling energy forms close by. After the rainfall, everyone piled out of their vehicles and began observing flashes of colored light occurring randomly around the mountain top. Brilliant colors would flash momentarily and were seen by all of us. Soon, an event began to unfold on the rocky path towards Zapata Falls. More than just light flashes began to manifest. Forms of light, balls of light, short columns of light, scintillating shimmers and more were reported. The events began to be reminiscent of what we experienced in Monterrey, Mexico in December of 1994. We picked our way in the dark up the path to a clearing in which close encounters ensued. Some teammates said they felt a shortness of breath during this event and the time leading up to it, which ended once the encounters concluded. I saw a brilliant blue neon-like light appear in a very precise geometrical arrangement. Many of us observed light forms standing in front of us. It appeared that a meeting was to occur between Dr. Greer and other life forms. Before the rest of the team was called to join, we heard invisible moccasin-clad feet softly walking around us.

There are human operations occurring on and perhaps inside Mt. Blanca at present. The airspace over Mt. Blanca is now restricted. If there are military or quasimilitary projects here, it would be very dangerous indeed for ET craft and life forms to make an overt, lengthy appearance. Something very real, albeit not solidly physical, occurred on Mt. Blanca that night and many people witnessed it.

But, a very solidly physical trace remained. Dr. Greer had his compass with him, in the breast pocket of his jacket. This is the same compass he has carried in all of his field work for the past six years. It is the same compass which in the course of an hour rotated around magnetic north 360° during the near-landing event in Alton Barnes, England in July 1992. After the hour of aberrant behavior, the compass in 1992 returned to its completely normal, functioning state. It had stayed that way since 1992. Here, the next time Dr. Greer looked at his compass was two days after the events on Mt. Blanca. We were stunned to see that the compass was altered. It no longer registered north as true. It was approximately 140-160° turned and registered north as somewhere near due south. In July of 1997 at our training in England, the compass was still altered, and has not returned to normal functioning to this day. We have photographs to preserve this data.

Our final night together as a team in Crestone was spent at a lovely hot springs facility. We met at our lodgings to caravan to the hot springs, with Dr. Greer and I leading the way since we knew how to get there.

When we pulled out of our lodgings and continuing for twenty miles, the radar detector in our vehicle kept sounding. It would register on X and K bands both. There was no regularity to the signal or the time between signals. Only our team's vehicles were behind us and we were in the vast emptiness of the San Luis Valley as we traveled. We drove straight into a thunderstorm and thought we would have to call off the event due to lightning danger. As we came near the hot springs, twin streaks of lightning shot down to touch the Earth in brilliant lavender light on each side of the highway. Our vehicle drove between them, through the crossing point of light created by the lightning. It was a poetic and enigmatic moment.

As we pulled into the hot springs, the rain began to stop and we all enjoyed a beautiful night under the moon and stars together.

A number of events occurred while we were all in the hot springs. Unusual satellite-like objects originated from the handle of the Big Dipper, began to travel south or west across the sky and then vanish in a streak as they shot vertically out of sight. However, one of our team members has since researched the objects and they were indeed satellites, their trajectories and times of appearance correlating with satellite chart print-outs. Several of the satellite passes terminate with what is designated "Shadow Entry" on the chart, giving the appearance of "shooting vertically out of sight." However, two other items that cannot be explained were seen from the hot springs.

Webmaster Tony Craddock clearly saw a black flash whizzing by at an altitude of several hundred feet coming from the direction of Mt. Blanca. I observed a dark or black object which streaked across just feet over our heads directly over the hot springs pool. Other sightings were registered that night, both in the hot springs and afterward when some of the team journeyed once more to Mt. Blanca, gifting us with some beautiful events as we ended our 1997 Crestone training retreat.

36

Ambassadors to the Universe Training, England—July 1997

by Linda Willitts
with Introduction by Shari Adamiak

For the first time, CSETI held an Ambassadors to the Universe Training Retreat in England. We selected the time to coincide with the five-year anniversary of the near-landing in 1992 in Alton Barnes. (See "CE-5 In Southern England— July 1992" on page 210.) This same week in 1992 was also when the CSETI team projected and meditated upon a specific crop formation to appear. The precise design appeared in a wheat crop that same night and consequently has become the CSETI logo.

Ron Russell, CSETI member, had arranged for a country home where the training participants would stay and where he was hosting guided crop circle tours. After his first group left, Ron was concerned about whether he had chosen proper lodging to accommodate the entire CSETI retinue. The house was a lovely 18th-Century house, but with some 18th century problems. Although the plumbing had been modernized, it proved less than ideal for Ron's tour group. Ron told us that the night his first group left, he was outside in part of the lovely lawns and gardens ruminating on whether the house would be adequate for the CSETI team. He said that he sent a thought to the universe, asking if he had done the right thing in securing this house for our use. Ron said that immediately three lights appeared in the perfect shape of the CSETI triangle. Moreover, there were beams of light connecting all three orbs, making it a perfect depiction of the CSETI crop circle and logo. Ron felt that he indeed had received confirmation that all would be well. Soon, one of the lights flew off into space at a high speed. Then another sped off in another direction and then the third vanished in like manner. It was a fascinating CE-5 experience for Ron. And, indeed, all went well. Our group had no problem with the plumbing, like the groups before us had.

After all fifteen people participating in our retreat converged in southern England from their various corners of the world, Ron and Neil Cunningham led us all to a magnificent crop formation in Alton Barnes. The crop formation had chosen the area called North Field for its appearance. This is a steeply sloped field of wheat which allows one to view the crop circle in its entirety from the road—a rather rare and most welcome occurrence. Somewhat similar to a torus ring, thin intersecting lines surrounded a central circle. Even though the crop circle had been there for at least two weeks and was somewhat trampled, the beauty of this perfect, enigmatic formation was not dimmed. One of the major London newspapers sent a reporter to Wiltshire County within the next few days who photographed crop circles and wrote an article. The reporter stated that he had visited the Alton Barnes formation and did not see how any human agency could have hoaxed it due to the fact that it lay on a steep slope.

We walked all around in the center of the crop circle and in the rings, which were approximately three feet wide. It radiated a very peaceful energy. Our group sat in a circle around the center point and meditated in the afternoon sun. Eventually, we left that location and drove to Oliver's Castle, where we had heard a new crop circle had appeared that morning. From the top of a grassy green hill with a gorgeous view of the surrounding area, we looked down on a lovely crop circle, not quite as large as the Alton Barnes circle, but perfect and new. The geometric design seemed to have a signature—the letter "S" at the bottom left of the design. A policeman was nearby and said that the farmer did not want people walking into his field, so we left for a pub dinner.

The English summer sun didn't set until around 10:00 P.M., so our night research commenced fairly late each night. This night, our second of the training, was exciting because we had permission from the Alton Barnes farmer, Tim Carson, to spend it in the large torus crop circle that we had visited earlier that afternoon. Our group was alone in the center of the circle. Around 12:30 A.M., a couple of us decided to walk through the wheat field towards Woodborough Hill to get a closer look at a low-lying fog bank that had partially obscured a distant group of trees. We walked down a tram line into the dark, watching the fog bank to our left. It seemed to move as we approached it. I thought it might be an optical illusion, but the group back in the circle said it actually moved back and forth, first obscuring the trees; then allowing them to become visible again.

The next morning brought news from Ron that another major crop formation had appeared overnight. Since the appearance of new formations had only recently picked up, and since we had just landed in the country, we took this as a most agreeable form of welcome. That morning, we drove to Silbury Hill which many of us climbed to see the formation. It was a huge Koch fractal executed in the wheat—a large multipointed snowflake shape with star-point edges and many small circles around its perimeter. We had been warned not to attempt to enter the formation; the farmer was disagreeable and would simply mow through it and ruin it. As we watched, we could see a handful of people within the circle and no sign of an irate farmer.

We decided to find the tram line that connected with the formation and visit for ourselves. Once inside, we noticed a decided lack of unusual or heightened energy that is common in most intricate formations. However, our exploration revealed that the energy was extending outward and was most noticeable in the small circles on the edges. We had not gotten a vantage point from which we could see the entire design as a whole. When we returned home, Ron had pictures hot from the developers. We could scarcely believe our eyes. The formation near Silbury Hill was a most complex, lovely and huge design— an accurate representation of a Koch fractal.

We spent the late afternoon at the house while rain fell outside. Dr. Greer decided to cancel a night trip to Stonehenge because of the rain, so we had a training session indoors and watched a video of UFO's. He and Shari decided to go upstairs and do some healing treatments. The rain stopped, the sky cleared, and most of the rest of the group went outside to the large back yard to do our research. Dr. Greer had told us to be outside for the 10:30 to 12:30 "sighting window." At 11:34 P.M. (the same time that 5 of us had an anomalous "shooting star" sighting in the yard the night we arrived in England), we all saw a bright white ball shoot from behind the big tree in the back yard in an arc, ending at the bay window corner of the house at the second floor level. It was clearly not a shooting star— it kept its round shape and didn't leave a trail, and to all of us it appeared to have entered the house through the bay window. Ron said "That's where Steven's room is!" The next day, when we told Dr. Greer about our sighting, he said that an ET in the form of a lavender/white ball of light had come in through his window at 11:34 P.M. while they were doing healing work! The ball of light entered his window, then appeared as a softly lit ET form about 3 to 3.5 feet tall, by the fireplace in his room. It was of humanoid shape and a sort of soft electronic/hologram type form. It was very kind, and Dr. Greer and Shari could tell that the ETs were excited about their work and hoping that they could continue.

The last few of us stayed outside that night until 2 A.M., and we had many sightings of smaller things: satellite-type lights that moved quickly across the sky, and many alleged shooting stars over the house. The house was clearly the site of most of the activity. Several times we saw anomalous light activity in the house— flashes and glows.

A special night research event was planned for July 26— the fifth anniversary of the CSETI sighting of the craft in the field at the Carson farm in Alton Barnes. We planned to meet a group of Colin Andrew's people there, and another UK CSETI group was doing research at a site on the other side of Woodborough Hill from us. It rained most of the day, but stopped by dinner and we headed for the field. We drove past the farmer's house and onto the paved farm road along the field where the '92 sighting had occurred. It was a Saturday night, but soon the local military began dropping flares. It was good to see the flares, because the Phoenix, AZ lights last March 13 had been called flares, and we could see that there is no mistaking flares for anything else— they linger in the sky for only a few seconds and then drop, leaving obvious smoke trails. Besides the 15 people in that training group, there were at least 15 people in Colin Andrew's group, so there were a lot of people milling around that night. We all settled down on the paved farm road, since the grass along the side of the road was wet and muddy from the rain. Dr. Greer led the whole group in one of his wonderful meditations. Afterwards, we started seeing very suspicious white and amber lights to our left. Soon, the military started dropping flares to our left, as though trying to chase away any ETs or confuse our group. This event had been publicized, so was no secret. At one point our security team, Ron, Neil, and Carl, saw a woman walk robot-like from out of the field and through our group. They spoke to her and she spoke back the same words they had said (hi, hello, etc.). Ron said they recognized that there was something very weird about her, but they were somehow made powerless to act on their suspicions. A woman in our group, Kay, also noticed her and thought she seemed very robotic. The next day, in discussing her, we determined that she was not a member of Colin's group. Another report will be written later by the members of our group that noticed this strange woman.

Towards the end of the night, we were standing around on the road next to the vehicles, and it appeared that someone had flashed a flashlight beam horizontally through our group from behind us. Dr. Greer turned around and asked the people behind us if they had done it. No one had used a flashlight. No sooner than we turned back around, a similar light flashed from behind us. Again, no one had done it!

The next afternoon, after our morning debriefing, we went to the Tumulus we had visited earlier. On top of the hill, under the canopy of tree branches, Dr. Greer led us in a powerful meditation using the distant sacred site of Silbury Hill as a focal point. When we walked back to our locked van, he discovered that his seat had been moved up close to the steering wheel, but that was not the way he had left it when he locked the van. Later, during dinner, the van's alarm went off spontaneously several times. Dr. Greer noticed that the skylight was open when he went out to silence the alarm, but we all had made sure that the windows and skylight were closed before we went in for dinner.

After dinner we went back to the house to get our gear together for the night's research. Some of the group were tired and wanted to stay in the back yard; the other nine of us, including Shari and Dr. Greer headed for the Koch snowflake crop circle where we had planned to go this next-to-the-last night in England. It was dark when we got there, and the landmarks had been changed by the people who had visited it in the days since we first walked into it when it was brand new. We chose a tram line we thought would lead us to the edge of the snowflake, and started walking through the dark, quiet wheat field. It seemed to be taking longer than it should have to reach the circle, so I walked ahead, leaving the others to rest with their gear. I soon found myself in the center of the large, silent crop circle. I called to the others, and Dr. Greer and Shari soon appeared. We were the only people in the crop circle for 10 or 15 minutes, so we walked around its entire periphery, in and out of every point, feeling its peaceful energy under the dark sky. Dr. Greer chose a point at the tip of the snowflake, and we spread our tarps and began to settle down as the other members of our group arrived in the circle. Ron soon joined us, and several strangers entered the circle and quietly found their own corners in which to settle down, a few of them intending to sleep there. It was very peaceful and the weather was mild, though damp. We saw quite a lot of activity in the sky, most notably a boomerang/arrow shaped alleged shooting star that was quite spectacular and observed by all of us. Around 1:30 A.M., someone drove up to the edge of the wheat field and shined a large spotlight over the crop circle. It looked as though we were going to be chased out, so we hurriedly packed up our gear and headed out down the tram lines. As we reached the end of the field near the base of Silbury Hill, we stopped and looked with amazement at the mist and moon over the Hill. It was very ethereal, like a scene from another planet.

We all understood that we had participated in another communication with ET intelligence.

37

Nighttime UFO/ET Phenomena Observed By CSETI Field Teams

Compiled by T. Loder (Dec. 4, 1998) and updated May 11, 1999 with help from L. Willitts, T. Guyker, T. Craddock, D. Foch and others

Introduction

When observing in the field, it is important for a CSETI field team to be alert for a significant variety of phenomena that are associated with ET activity. These include phenomena that impact on the full range of senses including visual, remote viewing, hearing, touch, smell, and emotional. It is sometimes possible to determine the efficacy of a suspected craft by using CE-5 protocols including light/laser signals or thought/mind requests for a response signal indicative of a true ET craft. The following list includes phenomena and responses that have been observed by many CSETI working groups in the field at many locations throughout the world. Any additional information on phenomena would be welcome and will be added to the list.

Visual - Sky - Night-time sightings

Alleged meteorites

Incoming ET craft can often appear to look like a meteor, however, sometimes they act very differently than a normal meteor.

They may move more slowly than a normal meteor.

A second meteor follows the same path through the sky within seconds.

They move across the sky in a horizontal manner.

Their flight path changes directions sometimes by as much as 90 degrees or they zigzag in flight.

A number of meteors fall along the same path during the evening.

They respond to thought command to change direction.

They just feel different (hard to really describe or nail down).

They are larger, brighter, and more spherical.

They don't have a tail.

They flash bright or get dimmer on their own or in response to being signaled at with a spot light or laser light.

They may enter a building through a window. This phenomenon was seen by a CSETI team in England in July 1997. A distinct blue-white sphere moved through the sky in an arc from behind a large tree and entered the window of the house where Dr. Greer and Shari Adamiak, inside, saw it appear as a small, shimmering ET.

They may be huge, brightly colored, and streak directly down from the apex of the sky and go into the ground with no explosion, disturbance of the ground, etc. A CSETI team witnessed a bright teal object do exactly this in Joshua Tree National Park in November 1996.

Alleged satellites

Satellites move at a constant speed across the sky and are usually seen during the first few hours after sunset. They may appear with a constant brightness or may pulse in a regular fashion as the satellite rotates reflecting sunlight. Some satellites (i.e. Iridium types) may flash very brightly as the sun glint from their solar panels reflects to the ground. Constant speed and course characterize real satellites. Low level satellites usually traverse the sky from zenith to horizon in 2-4 (?) minutes. ET craft or ARVs (Alien Reproduction Vehicles—made on Earth) can travel at speeds ranging from virtually standing still (hovering) to speeds allowing them to traverse the width of the sky in a fraction of a second to several seconds. They also can change speed and direction more rapidly than conventional aircraft.

Satellites are visible until they gradually fade from view. Anomalous "satellites" suddenly disappear, or if viewed through powerful night-vision binoculars, can be seen to dart swiftly into space at an angle perpendicular to their earlier trajectory.

ET craft may change direction or speed or may change brightness sometimes in response to a directed thought or signal such as a powerful flashlight or laser.

ET craft may also appear at any time of the night unlike normal satellites.

Starlike UFOs

Here we refer to objects that appear to be stars at first observation, but act differently in the following manners.

They blink off and on, sometimes randomly, sometimes moving slightly between the blinks. We observed a whole "squadron" of craft one evening in Sedona that blinked off and on for 10-15 minutes in one area of the sky. When a laser was pointed at one of the craft it glinted off the craft. Night vision scopes can be useful in determining the number of craft if they are far away.

A starlike object appears on or near the horizon (most common though they can be most anywhere) and remains there motionless for a long period of time (minutes to hours). These are often dismissed as a star until it suddenly flies off, changes brightness, or fades out in a cloudless sky. It may also change its appearance in response to signals.

Some stars twinkle actively and change colors, twinkling white, green, and red, especially when they are near the horizon. So do some UFOs. A star-like object may be seen in the sky, and over a period of a few hours, may be observed to move east while all the other stars in the sky move west. This phenomenon was observed by a CSETI team in England in 1997. A large, twinkling "star" was seen to move from behind one large tree and travel 30 degrees across the sky and disappear behind another tree, while all the other stars moved in the opposite direction.

(Air) Planelike UFOs

Here we refer to airplane-like objects that are lighted and fly like planes, but are not planes. They may be either ET craft or ARVs (Alien Reproduction Vehicles—made on Earth).

Although all planes are required by the FAA to flash or strobe lights at night, some planes and some UFOs do not. (Is this true?) In Sedona, AZ, a CSETI team watched a probable ARV fly by silently, with no flashing lights in the company of military reconnaissance jets. Its speed, odd lighting and silent behavior made it appear very anomalous, although at first glance it looked like another plane in the night sky. Usually flashing or strobing planes that sound like jet or prop engines are normal planes, however totally silent planes may be UFOs (or ARVs), note the sound of other "planes" in the same area of the sky. Any plane that appears to be silent should be watched very carefully even though it may appear to be a perfectly normal plane. ET craft can be cloaked to appear perfectly normal. In Crestone, CO, several years ago, a group of CSETI workers observed a small private plane fly very low right over the group in total silence, and then proceed into a mountain canyon and just disappear. Many of the witnesses later reported seeing the plane in different colors.

Orbs and Lights

Distant orbs

Depending on their size and proximity to the observer, these objects may appear as single star-like objects up to round glowing objects of varying sizes. They are often a uniform amber or gold in color though they can appear in various colors. Airplane landing lights are often mistaken for orbs, but can usually be differentiated by noting the light's location (such as proximity to an airport), strobing lights and/or associated red and green navigation lights.

Orbs often will remain stationary for a period of time though they do move about as well. Lights may be any color and can appear singly or in groups. Group lights may be either individual craft flying together or a single large craft with lights on the outer edges such as observed over the Santa Barbara channel or Phoenix, AZ. Flares, often dropped by the military to confuse observers after a genuine sighting, have occurred and float downwards at different rates and give off smoke seen above the floating lights. Since they fall at different rates, a line of flares will often have a jagged appearance after several minutes.

Close orbs

These often appear as small spots of light (like a laser spot) or small globes that may appear within several 100 meters or as close as touching a working group member. These are often considered to be probes and either contain intelligence or are under intelligent control (the difference may be academic). They can move about, change intensity and just appear and disappear.

They can also appear as amber-colored "street lights," and may even be mistaken for street lights until they suddenly disappear, or are seen in rural fields where there are no street lights (e.g. the "golden orbs" often seen in Wiltshire, England).

Close orbs can also be very misleading when they are initially observed and mistaken for people with flashlights or other simple explanations. For example a small group of very experienced CSETI team members described the following observations in Sedona one night in November, 1998.

S: "I saw four lights behind J. which I thought at the time were shining from the road. There were three lights, light amber in color, roughly the size of an average flashlight, in an uneven row. To the right of the 3 amber lights was a dull red light at least twice the size of the others. In the red light there seemed to be a small grid-like pattern. There were no beams coming from the lights. The four lights then moved rather irregularly to the right and out of my sight. I then commented to the others that I had seen some lights and perhaps there were people on the road. Every one commented that they hadn't heard anything and there certainly was dead silence on the site.

"I kept thinking about the lights that I had seen and finally asked D. to shine the big light in the direction I had seen the lights. When she shined the light it did not illuminate the road - the road was too far down the ramp to be seen - it illuminated the edge of the mesa at least 20 feet behind the truck. That's where I had seen the lights, no more than 40 feet (roughly) from where we were sitting! The lights had moved to the right behind the truck out of sight and had not reappeared."

Very Large orbs.

Observers (CSETI and others) in England in 1998 twice saw a very large (3X full moon) orange globe rise above the horizon, then dip back below, then rise again before it suddenly disappeared. This object was observed on two nights, in different directions each night. The second night, after it rose above the horizon for the second time, it "dissolved" as it disappeared, and several British military jets and helicopters appeared in the area within 30 seconds even dropping a flare in the vicinity of where the object had been seen.

Although orb appearances may be for extended time periods (minutes to hours) sometimes they appear so quickly, one has to be looking in just the right direction to see one. In Joshua Tree in 1997, 5 to 6 CSETI team members observed a globe-like object 1/4 to 1/3 the diameter of the nearly full moon appear to the left and below the moon and travel to the right and below the moon and then just vanish all in just a few seconds.

Dark objects

These objects (craft) are often observed under starlit skies with minimum moonlight and may be moving or still. They may appear as rapidly moving black objects (unlit) that stand out against the star field and can range in size from small to apparently huge.

For example, in 1997, a group on Mount Blanca, CO, watched a rectangular cloud form over the top of the mountain on a cloudless night. A few minutes later a black object was seen to fly up, out of the cloud, which then disappeared.

More examples of these darting black objects were seen by a CSETI team in Hawaii in 1998 through a foggy mist.

Distorted Sky

There are times when a craft hovering just beyond the crossing point of light will cause a distortion in the star field. It will appear as though there are heat waves or shimmering even though no object can be seen. There are other times when a small portion of the sky may appear darker than the surrounding sky. This may be indicative of a hovering cloaked craft. These distortions have been observed both at a distance and close to an observing group when a craft was either just above a group or surrounding a group.

In England in 1998, the beam of a powerful laser directed at an area approximately 25 feet from the group was distorted/bent when it hit the edges of a cloaked object on the ground (and partly on a river).

Grids and energy fields

Some observers have reported seeing a manifestation of energy grids in the sky which appear as lines of light which may sparkle or fade in and out. These can often be very subtle and therefore not seen by every member of the team. However, on Mt. Blanca several years ago nearly everyone in the group was able to see energy sparkles all over the mountain, appearing like lightening bugs from a distance.

Flashlight or Camera-like Flashes

Flashes of light have appeared in mid-air, with no apparent source.

In England in 1997, two flashlight-like streams of light burst horizontally amid a group of people, but others surrounding the group were not using their flashlights.

In Hawaii in 1998, four CSETI observers witnessed two flashes within a few feet of the group, as though flash photos had been taken, but there were no cameras nearby.

Close proximity events with a craft beyond the crossing point of light

There are a number of signs to look for in the event that a craft has approached a group in the field and is just beyond the crossing point of light. We will assume that there may also be ETs on the ground nearby or among the observing group. Although a craft or ETs may be observed at any time by someone skilled at remote viewing techniques, we will deal here with phenomena observed more typically with the "usual" senses. The use of slightly out-of-focus or "soft eyes" will often aid in seeing. Different observers will observe some, none, or all of the following. Seeing with both your physical eyes and the mind requires practice.

If the craft is close to the crossing point of light there may be "bleed through" and the craft may be partially visible, or perhaps just a sparkling is apparent to some. This sometimes appears as a faint glow or even a scintillating full form of a ship. Craft may appear either whitish or in soft colors. Keep in mind that craft may also become totally visible to everyone on the team. Both types of phenomena have been observed numerous times by CSETI field teams.

During an event, members of the group may sense or observe some, none, or all of the following:

- A sense of body warming.
- A sense there is an increase in the surrounding temperature.
- An apparent change in atmospheric pressure, which can be felt in observers' ears.
- A decrease in wind—a stillness or quietness feeling perhaps leading to the feeling of warming mentioned above.
- Body vibrations from barely detectable to full-out shaking.
- Hair on head, arms or legs stands up (pilo erection)
- Sounds including: buzzing, humming, clicking, or strange, other-worldly screeching (sometimes heard by only some of the observers).
- Radar detectors setting off for no obvious reasons.

- Animals in the area will respond with howling, barking, etc. Animals will often respond to ET presence before humans are aware of it.
- Scents or smells including ozone and flowers scents such as violets, roses, carnations, sage, etc.
- Emotional feelings especially that of warmth and love, sometimes so strong that people are moved to tears.

If ETs are on the ground nearby or among the CSETI team, which has happened many times, the following additional phenomena have been observed:

- Shuffling sounds on gravel or rustling branches, leaves, or grasses.
- Strange breathing or coughing sounds.
- Soft and gentle touches;
- Sparkling lights moving around and within the group. The lights can appear as small probes or as vertical forms or shapes of light often greenish or white.
- When a bare hand is moved though the light forms the hand will sparkle as though there was an electrical discharge

The appearance of the ETs may range from just areas of faint sparkly light to indistinct shapes to fully visible entities with clothing, facial features, and hands, etc. all fully distinguishable. It should be noted that different people will see the ETs very differently, even when the people are standing beside each other, so that some report seeing nothing, others a slight shimmering or shadows, and others can describe the ET in detail. often however, what is observed is just dark or fuzzy forms near the group as described by this team member observing in a small group in Sedona. "We had been visiting for about an hour when I noticed a fairly tall form to the right of the tree. It was upright and the same shade as the tree. I kept having a running conversation with myself that went, "Is that part of the tree or is that a life form" and "It really looks familiar but it can't be a life form, so it must be part of the tree. "It didn't move, but I kept an eye on it. I have no idea why I didn't tell the others what I was seeing. She later described: "We decided to call it a night and started to pack up at which point I looked to see if the form by the tree was still there - it was gone. I stood in the spot where I had seen the form and estimated that it must have been at least six to seven feet tall. "She added that she has seen this type of very tall form at least four other times.

If the ETs are being "projected" into the area and a person walks into the projection area or "energy field", there is a distinct feeling of soft pleasant warmth as one passes into the "field."

Interactions between ETs and individual group members range from just a sense of presence to loving personal acknowledgment to full telepathic conversations. The sense of love is almost always present, no matter the level of the interaction, and is truly wonderful and unforgettable. The conversations are typically non-verbal. Field observers have reported shimmering-light ETs that have stood in front of them or sat at (on) their feet for prolonged times.

The ground around the group may appear colored such as emerald green or red. Some observers have noted complex geometric shapes and forms or beautiful unusual pictures while interacting with the ETs. These colors, forms, pictures may occur with the observers eyes both open in the "soft eyes" mode or closed. one observer described the experience as though the ETs were sharing beautiful art with him.

If the field team has been surrounded by a craft, partially in the ground and partially above, members can sometimes see structural parts of the interior of the ship depending on how visible the ETs make it and the persons ability to 'see.' This is when there is a feeling of quiet, warmth, the star fields may appear to distort and there is often a strange sense of time distortion. often when the craft leaves there is a distinct brightening around the group.

Some or all the above interactions may also occur in this situation and when they do, it is truly a wonderful "out of this world" experience.

Group members may bi-locate.

In England in 1998, seven people sitting in a circle in a pasture were engulfed by a craft. The air became still, as though the wind were blocked, the temperature rose 10–15°, and many ETs were perceived among the group of people. While remaining ever conscious of sitting in the pasture, the group was also conscious of looking down at Earth from space (through a window in the bottom of the craft) and joining the ETs in a meditation for the healing of the planet.

Other "Strangeness" Happenings added by the CSETI Webmaster

These happenings by themselves appear as isolated "funny things that happened to me the other day while out observing or at home "yet taken as a group they may indicate some sort of interaction or communication by someone with perhaps a sense of humor. This is just a sample of some of the types of things that have happened.

Randy's flashlight being disassembled in his lap during CTS and the pieces scattered round him and his sleeping bag.

The ETs insistence in locking Pat's door on my car. Being a Metro, it is 100% mechanical. We were at the job site a couple of weeks ago, and she heard a click as it was locked once again while she was standing next to it. Doors were locked and interior lights were turned on SG's car while we were in Hawaii.

Smells. After the last night at Sedona had an overpowering smell of sage in my room all night (no, it was not toilet freshener!).

C. —being on-line the day after a field trip, her phone rings, and she carries on a conversation while still logged on to the Internet. She only has one phone line, and it is not dedicated.

C. —Washing machines, dryers turning themselves on, and their doors being left open.

Microwaves turning on. VCRs turning on and off and locking up. Squawking noises being broadcast through pocket dictaphone, and machine locking up.

Logged on to Internet, and while in Quicken, program skips to an entry two years back and highlights a check written to someone whose name Pat was trying to remember of course this could also have been a mental feat.

Pieces of toilet paper appearing to flutter around the sky in the dark of night (of course this could have been toilet paper if the night was windy!)

Being touched on site or having a sleeve tugged.

Having pictograms beamed into your head - half inside, half outside, the bedroom pulsating with light visible with eyes open and closed...AJC

SG sees UFOs while we are chatting on the phone.

And many more.

38

The CSETI Earth/Near-Earth Extraterrestrial Survey

Research Proposal

Recent scientific research has verified the existence of a number of star systems with planetary bodies, as well as the existence of molecules in space which may provide the essential components necessary for life.

According to the Drake Formula, it is likely that thousands of intelligent life forms have evolved within our own galaxy alone, which is only one of billions of such galaxies. The question then presents itself of whether or not intelligent life actually exists outside of Earth, and if so, how such life might manifest itself.

The SETI project (Search for Extraterrestrial Intelligence) has focused on surveying space for non-Earth originating electromagnetic signals using radio telescopes and a billion-channel computerized monitoring system. The assumption used by SETI is that intelligent, artificial and repeating electromagnetic signals originating from outside of Earth or human derived near-Earth technologies would be evidence of other intelligent life in the universe. But would it be the *only* evidence?

While the SETI effort represents one rational approach to the question of discovering intelligent life in the universe, there are additional strategies which are herein presented which will augment the SETI project and test a number of hypothesis which are related but separate from that of SETI.

It is a commonly held view that, in a universe containing billions of galaxies each with billions of star systems that, somewhere, higher intelligent life forms are likely to have evolved. However, what is frequently left out of this analysis is the question of how such life-forms might utilize laws of physics not currently known to twentieth century Earth scientists, how such a utilization may appear to humans and how we might regard it should we encounter such technologies.

While it is possible that electromagnetic signals, propagating at the speed of light, may be detected from civilizations using *those* technologies, it is equally likely that such technologies of ET origin may be utilized in a manner very foreign to humans. Moreover, it is possible, if not likely, that there are communication and transportation technologies which utilize laws of the universe, physics and applied technologies which altogether transcend current human understanding.

In this regard, it is important to consider that the universe (as we currently understand it) is 15-20 billion years old. In a universe so vast and ancient it is likely that, if there are intelligent life forms outside of the Earth, they are at points of technological and social evolution different from our own. Moreover, once a civilization reaches a certain point in social and technological evolution it is likely that their further development becomes virtually quantum in nature.

Consider how rapidly society and technology have changed and evolved since the human scientific revolution, and especially since the late 1800s. In the span of one human's life, we have gone from horse-and- buggies to inter-planetary probes, the Internet, lasers, holograms and fiber optics. Extrapolating such exponential growth into the future 10,000 years one can see that the technology of that future time would seem virtually like magic to humans of today.

Alternatively, consider a human of 200 years ago confronting the technologies of 1997: It would all seem like a fantasy, a dream or manifestations of the supernatural to someone of the late 1700s. And in a universe 15-20 billion years old, 200 years is like a nanosecond.

Thus, as we consider the likelihood of ET intelligent life, it is important to avoid an overly anthropocentric view of such life, and to remember how quickly technological change may happen— and how bizarre to us it may appear.

As a number of scientists and Arthur C. Clarke have pointed out, any civilization sufficiently advanced to travel through interstellar space will, by definition, appear with technologies which will look like magic to *us*.

This then brings us to a fundamental dilemma: Advanced ET life forms may very well utilize laws of physics and technologies which are completely beyond the known electromagnetic spectrum. Hence, if we are looking *only* within that spectrum, as SETI is doing, we are likely to altogether miss the existence of such civilizations.

Indeed, it may be that as intelligent civilizations evolve technologically, other spectra are discovered, mastered and utilized which altogether bypass (or transcend) the currently known electromagnetic spectrum. Is it possible—if not likely—that the current human use of the EM spectrum is a technological phase of relatively short duration, and that within a few hundred years other spectra will be utilized for communications? Could our looking for advanced ET civilizations in the EM spectrum be the equivalent of a civilization at the evolutionary level of cavemen looking for our civilization by trying to detect smoke rings rising from the jungle?

Extraterrestrial civilizations which may be thousands to hundreds of thousand of years ahead of us technologically will, by definition, not be using twentieth century Earth technologies. And while current human scientists insist that the speed of light cannot be exceeded, we must remember that only a few decades ago eminent scientists were insisting that the sound barrier could not be exceeded by any aircraft. Perhaps advanced ET civilizations capable of interstellar communication and travel have evolved technologies which do exceed the speed of light. And while this may seem impossible to us today, the world of today would seem impossible to someone a brief 200 years ago.

Therefore, an alternative hypothesis in the search for intelligent life elsewhere in the universe must be considered: That such life, if sufficiently advanced beyond current Earth technologies, may be capable of interstellar travel and communications at multiples of the speed of light, or in altogether non-linear modes, which simple EM monitoring will never detect.

Central to this hypothesis is the concept that any sufficiently advanced civilizations attempting interstellar communication and travel will, perforce, develop *trans-luminal* technologies which permit real-time communication and travel beyond the light (EM) barrier. As many scientists have pointed out, interstellar space is so vast that even the speed of light is too slow to accommodate communication and travel across it. (A hundred light years is virtually in our galactic neighborhood, and yet at the speed of light, a 'round-trip' conversation needed for communication will take 200 years; that is, one would be deceased before the 'conversation' could be completed.)

If ET civilizations capable of interstellar travel exist, their technologies will not only look like magic to us, but will very likely bypass or transcend current EM spectrum monitoring attempts.

In a universe 15-20 billion years old, how likely is it that some of the ET civilizations which exist are thousands to millions of years more evolved technologically (and socially) than twentieth century Earth? Very likely it would seem. Because if, for argument sake, one assumes that- of the thousands of likely ET civilizations estimated by the Drake formula- half are less developed and half are *more* developed than current Earth civilization, we are left with many thousands of civilizations which could be thousands—or millions—of years further down the path of technological evolution. And some of them could have interstellar communication and travel capabilities which go beyond the light barrier.

Of course, the next dilemma is the real limitations of current human technologies. If we cannot project communications at multiples of the speed of light, nor receive them, what chance do we have of detecting ET civilizations using current technologies? This dilemma is in part rooted in the arbitrary assumption that, should ET civilizations exist, they are only 'out there'. However, it is also possible that they are 'here.'

The hypothesis that we are not alone and, in fact, may already be receiving visits from advanced ET civilizations cannot be dismissed out of hand. In light of the above analysis and hypothesis, human civilization could be visited by advanced ET life-forms and be missing the events due to anthropocentric views of technology and scientific prejudices regarding what may be possible in terms of trans-luminal space travel and communications. Human history, and that of modern science in particular, are rife with examples of such myopia. And yet a review of scientific, military and intelligence cases dealing with extraordinary aerial phenomena would suggest that a near-Earth survey may be of more value than electromagnetically scanning the distant galaxies.

The CSETI retrospective review of scientific cases, photographs, video-tapes, top-secret government documents and reported landing-trace cases would suggest that a phenomenon exists in near-Earth proximity which could constitute ET monitoring and reconnaissance of the Earth. Moreover, the identification and interviews by CSETI of over 100 top-secret government, military, intelligence and aerospace employees who have worked in so-called "black" super-secret projects strongly suggests that there is an on-going ET phenomenon, albeit bizarre in terms of technological manifestations.

While many such reports which exist in the general culture certainly represent misidentifications of prosaic atmospheric, man-made or celestial phenomenon—if not outright hoaxes—there is a residua of very convincing data which the objective scientist cannot ignore. Included in this body of evidence are nearly 500,000 cases in the so-called UFOCAT computerized system, over 4000 landing trace cases in which unexplained craft have landed and left physical trace evidence, over 3500 military and civilian pilot reports, many with corroborating radar confirmation and hundreds of pages of unambiguous government documents. There are also dozens of scientifically analyzed photographs and videotapes which show objects which cannot be explained by conventional phenomenon or human-made craft.

While the interpretation of the data may be debated, there is no question that a real, scientifically measurable aerial and near-Earth phenomenon exists which may constitute ET activity.

Unfortunately, due to the sensationalizing and subsequent dismissing of the subject in toto, no global scientific, civilian, independent survey of this phenomenon has ever been conducted. In light of the substantial body of scientific evidence which now exists, we feel that the time has come for a serious scientific global survey of this unexplained Earth/near Earth activity to begin. Even if all of the current data only suggests a 10% likelihood of ET activity, the implications of near-Earth ET activity are so profound that a serious independent (non-governmental) scientific survey is warranted.

Due to the well-documented history of official and covert governmental machinations related to this subject, it is necessary that this global Earth/near-Earth ET survey occur independent of government, military or government aerospace contractor control or influence.

CSETI (The Center for the Study of Extraterrestrial Intelligence) is a 501-C-3 scientific research organization and proposes a three year initial scientific research project which would conduct a *global real-time survey* of this phenomenon which would, for the first time, scientifically attempt to measure this phenomenon. Research would occur in passive/observation and active (interactive) modes as described below. Phase I of the Proposal is a Global Scientific Symposium to formally collect and present in one place all of the best, credible retrospective data on the subject currently available. This part of the survey will enable the current state of knowledge of the subject to be formally organized and publicly presented at a serious scientific gathering of researchers from all over the world. It will enable the real-time research project described below to proceed with maximum data of past events and the identification of areas of on-going anomalous aerial activity which may be ET in nature.

Research Concepts, Logic And Design For Phase 2

Unexplained phenomena and craft near to the Earth have been reported for over 100 years. An analysis of these phenomena results in several patterns of events which have been repeating throughout much of the twentieth century:

- Aerial objects observed transiently by multiple credible observers. These objects have been seen at close range and are variably described as discs, spheres, triangles etc. and invariable maneuver in non-aerodynamic ways. An object seen within 500 feet has been termed a close encounter of the first kind (CE-1).
- Objects or craft which are landed or very near the ground hovering and which have left physical trace evidence (a landing area which is indented, burned etc.) or electromagnetic anomalies. This has been termed a close encounter of the second kind (CE-2).
- Objects or craft at which humanoid life forms have been observed. This has been termed a close encounter of the third kind (CE-3).
- Events during which observers claim to have been on-board such objects (close encounter of the fourth kind or CE-4).
- Interactive events with craft or objects which may involve voluntary human signaling followed by deliberate communicative responses from the object. This is termed a close encounter of the fifth kind or CE-5.
- Importantly, any combination of the above may occur in a given geographic region persistently over a period of time, in what has been called a 'wave' of sightings. For example, persistent waves of anomalous aerial activity has been reported during the 1990s in Belgium, Mexico, parts of the USA, Brazil, Russia, Japan and the United Kingdom.

The identification of credible areas of anomalous aerial activity which are either acutely or chronically persistent allows for the most promising setting for real-time, serious scientific research and observation.

An informal network of organizations and individuals studying the subject exists which allows for the rapid identification of an on-going wave of events to which a scientific team could be deployed. Over the past 7 years, CSETI has observed that at any given time there are areas of anomalous aerial activity being reported by credible observers, pilots the military and others to which a properly equipped scientific team could be deployed. These areas of chronic and/or acute activity, which may persist for days to weeks to years, are prime targets for scientific research and real-time observation.

The following nine research components are required for an effective real-term survey of potential ET activity in near-Earth proximity:

1. Effective global monitoring of anomalous aerial events (AAE) followed by
2. Rigorous analysis of AAE to eliminate conventional explanations (mis-perception of celestial activity, experimental military aircraft, hoaxes, natural aerial phenomenon etc.) resulting in
3. Determination of genuine anomalous aerial events which are persisting, followed by
4. Deployment of rapid response teams (RRT) to the area, with fully portable scientific detection, measurement and recording equipment and personnel trained in observation and interactive protocols; followed by
5. Processing and analysis of resulting data, evidence, materials and events, followed by
6. Determination of validity of RRT evidence and events:
7. IF events are deemed likely ET in nature, further analysis of data, evidence and events by separate, independent and impartial scientific review panel (SRP)
8. IF events and data confirmed by SRP, notification of appropriate scientific and governmental authorities, followed by
9. Full scientific media briefing and release of data and findings to the public.

Each of the above components are described below.

1. Global Monitoring of AAE

Currently, there are no non-covert, professionally funded and staffed entities monitoring AAE globally. However, we have identified a network of reliable researchers, scientists and organizations who monitor the phenomenon and these could be professionally linked at a central data center. Also, the Internet increasingly allows for rapid reporting of such events.

The Global AAE Data Center would monitor current AAE around the world via a substantial network of volunteer researchers and organizations and would also create reporting networks with the following:

- NORAD, NRO and NSA
- Air Traffic Control Centers (globally)
- Select Military points of contact
- Civilian Airline Pilots
- NASA
- Local and regional police forces
- News media (both passive scanning of the media for reports and requests to media for active reporting of events)
- others

2. The Global AAE Data Center will be staffed with personnel who will collect reports, analyze and prioritize validity of reports, further investigate raw data as needed and identify events which warrant close scrutiny for possible RRT deployment.

This analysis phase of collected data and reports is key since the assessment of AAE from these reports will determine whether or not the RRT is deployed.

A scientific staff with expertise in the following will be needed to make this determination:

- Atmospheric Physics
- Astronomy
- Data analysis and imaging analysis (photographs, videotapes, satellite images etc.)
- Experimental military aircraft and covert military capabilities
- Aerospace/Orbiting debris and re-entry phenomenon

other

Reports of current AAE will be analyzed and assigned a rank-order classification which lists the event in a fashion that allows for rapid determination of the quality of the event. Events which have multiple credible witnesses (military, pilots, police, scientists etc.) and for which other corroborating evidence exists, such as landing traces, photographs, radar confirmation or material evidence, will have the highest ranking.

3. Once an AAE is analyzed, verified and authenticated, a determination will be made as to whether the event was transient and non-repeating or part of a larger pattern of ongoing and persistent activity.

For example, an AAE of high quality may be part of a chronic background pattern of activity in the general geographic area and could indicate an intensification of the phenomenon. If so, the RRT may then be considered for deployment and on-site, real-time research.

Ranking of these events, then, will be twofold: by quality of the event itself on a 1-10 basis (1 indicating the weakest supporting evidence and 10 the highest) and by degree of persistence of the phenomenon in that region. Persistence ranking will be as follows: T = transient, non-repeating;

AP = acute persisting phenomenon (that is sudden onset but repeating and persistent phenomenon in a given geographic area); CP = chronic, persisting phenomenon (that is an event which is part of an historical area of chronic, background activity and reports of AAE); and SAP = AAE which are persistent but intermediate between chronic and acute waves of activity.

The determination of the validity of the report, its relative rank and persistence factor will determine whether or not the RRT is deployed.

4. Deployment of the Rapid Response Team (RRT) will be decided on the above factors, plus the feasibility of getting a team rapidly into the geographic region in question. This will be decided by the Project Director in consultation with the RRT members and the scientific advisory board.

Given current AAE activity, it is likely that multiple RRTs will be needed for multiple, simultaneous research projects in varying geographic areas.

Each RRT will need the following specialists:

- Team Coordinator
- Equipment and technical specialist for equipment set-up and maintenance
- Imaging specialist(s) for photographic, videotape, film and other imaging tasks
- AAE identification specialists trained in early detection and observation of AAE

- ET communication specialist proficient in high-level contact protocols
- others

Equipment used on-site for the RRT:

- Magnetometers
- GPS
- Night-vision equipment (third generation)
- Regular, infrared, ultraviolet and starlight-scope cameras, video cameras and film
- Portable DAT (digital audio tape) recording equipment
- electronic sensors for laser, microwave and other energy forms
- landing configuration strobes and markers
- communications equipment
- radio-transmitters for anomalous tone projection (see below)
- TV transmitters for projection of data to AAE (see below)
- High powered light and laser signaling equipment
- Data, landing trace and material evidence collection and storage equipment
- Portable Radar Unit
- other

Activities of the RRT include:

- General observation and reconnaissance of the AAE area
- Collection of information from local sources regarding times, places of recent AAE events
- Obtaining optimal research site which is secure and in center of AAE
- Passive observation and scientific measurement and recording of any AAEs
- Active, peaceful engagement of AAE once it is determined that the AAE is a presumptive ET object under intelligent control
- Communication with ET object and / or occupants if possible using Contact Protocols

- Full recording of all passive and active / interactive events and collection of scientific measurements
- Collection and safeguarding of any objects/materials of ET origin

Extensive preliminary field research during global CSETI CE-5 experiments has enabled CSETI to develop protocols for signaling to and engaging AAE/presumptive ET objects. While these experiments to date have been unfunded and lacked professional scientific equipment or staff, as preliminary events they have afforded CSETI remarkable opportunities for experimenting with engagement and contact protocols.

Since a component of the hypothesis to be tested is that these objects are under intelligent control by advanced intelligent life forms, it is important to note that in addition to passive observation and recording, protocols will be used for active engagement, active vectoring of AAE to the research site and interactive communication, should events evolve to that point.

Vector protocols include the use of projected images, projected beeping tones previously recorded during AAEs high luminosity lights and lasers and ground landing strobes.

In the event an object approaches at close range and engages the RRT in active signalling and/or communication, the event will continue to be recorded if possible and the RRT will advance to protocols for higher level contact with presumptive ET life forms and/or objects.

Since an event theoretically could evolve to the point of open contact and communication with non-human life forms, it is necessary that the RRT be fully cross-trained in diplomatic and communication protocols so that such an event may proceed optimally.

For this reason, no weapons or objects which could be construed as weaponry will be allowed during any RRT activation.

For classification purposes, the following Levels of Contact with AAE/Presumptive ET Objects will be used:

Level I Contact: Clear and confirmed contact which lasts less than 60 seconds

Level II Contact: Clear and confirmed contact which lasts more than 60 seconds and which is clearly interactive (responding to RRT interactive protocols)

Level III Contact: Near Landing or Landing event during which object approaches at less than 500 ft. and under 100 feet AGL (above ground level) altitude

Level IV Contact: Landing/near landing event with signalling or substantive communication lasting more than 60 seconds

Level V Contact: Prolonged landing and interactive event lasting over 60 seconds

Level VI Contact: Prolonged landing and interactive event lasting over 60 seconds with subsequent contact with or communication with observed ET life forms

Level VII Contact: Event which results in one or more members of the RRT entering presumed ET object

Level VIII Contact: Event which results in RRT member(s) departing with presumed ET object and/or life forms

Level IX Contact: Return of RRT members from Level VIII Contact above with substantive information and evidence, OR exchange of substantive information, evidence and technologies.

Every effort will be made to conduct full scientific measurements, recording and retrieval of data at every level of contact. Manual recording (still and motion picture cameras) which is not dependent on electrical or electronic energy systems will be also used since past experience with the phenomenon by CSETI CE-5 teams indicates that anomalous EM interference may render electronic devices inoperable.

Should a Level VI Contact or higher event transpire, communication of this fact will be made as soon as practical to the United Nations Secretary General, the UN Security Council and the United States President through secure points of contact already developed by CSETI.

5. Processing and analysis of data resulting from RRT events.

Depending on the degree of contact and type of evidence recovered, a multi-disciplinary team of scientists will be utilized for analysis of the event. The data from regular, infrared, ultraviolet and star-light cameras and videotape as well as electronic data will be processed and analyzed by scientists specializing in those areas.

Should materials be retrieved which are of presumptive ET origin, these will be secured and then analyzed by experts in metallurgy, biology, histology etc. as warranted. Should a landing/near landing occur, the landing site will be secured and thoroughly studied and analyzed, and soil and vegetation samples will be retrieved for later laboratory analysis.

6. At the completion of the analysis of the event and all evidence, a determination will be made regarding the nature of the event and the validity and usefulness of the evidence. This final in-house determination will be made by the Event Determination Team. If the event is regarded as ET or very likely ET in nature, it will be referred to scientists independent from the project.
7. The Scientific Review Panel (SRP) will consist of impartial scientists from multiple disciplines who will review all evidence, materials, recordings, measurements etc. and perform independent analysis of same. The SRP will be asked to make an independent determination regarding the event(s) in question. Should the SRP make a determination which differs from the in-house scientific team's, a third analysis will be performed by another separate scientific panel. Should the event continue to be regarded as indeterminate by this team, the event will be reported publicly in a manner which reflects the differing assessments.
8. Should the SRP concur with the CSETI EDT regarding the validity of the event and make an assessment that it was likely or definitely ET in nature, appropriate scientific and governmental authorities will be notified by CSETI and the SRP jointly. Entities to be notified include:

   The UN Secretary General and UN Security Council
   The International Astronomical Union
   The UN Office of Outer Space Affairs
   The US National Academy of Sciences
   The National Science Foundation (US)
   The Russian Academy of Sciences
   NASA
   Other nations' academic institutes
   The Executive Office of the President (US) the Science Advisor to the President

9. After an appropriate interval to allow for review by the above authorities, a full scientific media briefing will be conducted at which the data and findings will be released to the public. A reputable and competent media relations firm will be engaged to coor-

dinate the media briefing and subsequent media inquiries, which would be substantial.

Part III

Disclosure: CSETI Project Starlight

This section elucidates perhaps the most beguiling aspect of the UFO/ET subject: how has the secrecy been maintained, who knows what, where are the key facilities related to the subject and what should the legal components of our government do about it.

Beginning in 1993, CSETI began an ambitious undertaking to brief world leaders on this subject, encourage their support and active participation in disclosing the facts—and push forward a definitive disclosure, with or without governmental help if needed.

We have always preferred that the UN and the major world governments take an active role in such a momentous event. This section includes briefing papers written for the CIA Director, President Bill Clinton, UN Secretary General Boutros Boutros Ghali and many others.

You will find a summary of a few of the top-secret military and government witnesses who are willing to come forward to tell the truth about this subject. As of this writing, we have identified approximately 200 such witnesses.

You will read the summary of the historic CSETI briefings for members of Congress in April of 1997. And you will read a frank discussion of the risks to our national security presented by the out-of-control black budget world of secret projects. Some of these papers were written specifically for senior Pentagon officials with whom I have met and who are supportive of disclosure, but who, like CIA Director Woolsey, were out of the loop.

The dangers to world peace and security presented by an out of control, unauthorized and powerful project dealing secretively with this subject cannot be overstated. When very senior UN, US national security, Congressional, Pentagon and British Ministry of Defense officials *all* tell me personally that they are sure such projects exist but are powerless to penetrate or control them, we should be deeply concerned.

CSETI Project Starlight has labored for over 5 years to provide the world's leadership with advice, information, perspective and evidence related to UFOs/ETI. Ultimately, it is up to 'we the people' to force this issue and see that the governments which represent our interests regain control of this subject and begin to forge ahead with efforts to create a time which is open, peaceful and honest.

If the people will lead, the leaders will follow....

39

Unacknowledged

21 May 1996

Can the government keep a secret?

A really big secret—the biggest of all time? When the peccadillos of every politician and government leader are prime time news, could the government hide from us the most astounding discovery in the history of the world—the existence of ET life?

Well, yes—and no.

First, the concept of government must be redefined, because there exists the government of "we the people," elected and appointed officials, public representatives, the executive, legislative and judicial branches, etc., à la your standard junior high civics course.

But then, there is also the unacknowledged "government": the "government" of deep cover, deep black projects, contract agents and companies, and shadowy mid-level functionaries whose task it is to ensure that the government of "we the people" knows little or nothing about the unacknowledged "government."

The right hand does not know—or often want to know—what the left hand is doing....

But we're getting a little ahead of ourselves now. First some background.

For nearly six years I have quietly researched how real secrecy is maintained, in the latter half of the twentieth century. What I have found is astonishing, and frankly unbelievable. What you are about to read is the truth—but I admit that I would not have believed it had someone told me this three years ago. You may want to read the rest of this article as if it were a fictional story. You may feel more comfortable looking at all of this from a distance. But let some part of you know that this is the truth.

This article is not about whether UFOs/ETs are real, or are visiting Earth. Let's get this out of the way first, since it is the easy part: UFOs are real; they are of ET origin; they have been around for decades (if not centuries); there is no evidence that they are hostile; there is probably more than one type of life form visiting us; and aspects of the "government" have known this for 50 years, at least.

The more difficult part of this subject is getting your mind around the fact that something this extraordinary is real, and yet remains somehow unreal, hidden, secret, enigmatic. That the official government—and the official keepers of truth in the media and science- have been deceived for this long is a tribute to the sophistication, depth, breadth and ubiquity of a secret program unparalleled in history.

Indeed, the story of how—and why—this deception has existed exceeds the ET phenomenon itself in bizarreness, mystery and incredulity. In fact, it seems that the effectiveness of the secrecy is itself related to the stunning incredulity of the nature of the secrecy. Put another way, the whys, hows, and wherefores of these secret projects are so bizarre and unbelievable, that they provide their own best cover: no one would believe it even if they came upon it. It is absolutely over the top.

To be honest, my own first reaction to what you are about to read was, "yeah, right...". But then confirmation after confirmation, and independent corroboration after independent corroboration convinced me of it. And then I was saying, "Oh God..."

Space here only permits me to share with you the highlights of six years of intense, behind-the-scenes research. Someday, I hope the entire story can be told, names and all, but for now allow me to paint for you a broad picture, and some of the details. This information comes from personal, private and exquisitely sensitive meetings and long discussions with very senior and relevant military, intelligence, political and private corporate sources. The search for truth regarding these secret projects has brought me to heads of state, royalty, CIA officials, NSA operatives, US and foreign military leaders, political leaders and high-tech corporate contractors. The process has been exhaustive, relentless and mind-blowing. Safety and prudence requires that I leave their names out of this for now; by the time you finish reading this, the reason will be obvious.

This phase in the CSETI project began in earnest in July of 1993, when a small group of military and civilian people involved with the UFO matter met at my request to discuss how to best liaison with the government and military. From an operational point of view, CSETI needed a senior point of contact (POC) within the chain of command who knew what we were doing to contact ET civilizations. We wanted to ensure that our efforts were safe from intentional or unintentional military/intelligence/government interference. And we wanted to be clear that our effort should be regarded as a citizen's-diplomacy effort and that a stand-down order should exist protecting us from any interference, in the US or abroad. In the previous year, CSETI had facilitated two near-landing events in England and Mexico, and we wanted to be sure, given these developments, that we could proceed with safety for both our teams and for the ET visitors, whom we regard as our guests.

Over the following few months, members of our team had had discussions and briefings with a wide array of government, military, intelligence, political, international and private leaders around the world. What we learned seemed surreal, unimaginable and bizarre.

Beginning at least as early as World War II, we found that certain officials in the US government knew that we were not alone, that there were advanced machines flying around in certain regions of the WWII conflict which were not ours, and not theirs. A medical colleague and friend, whose relative was a celebrated WWII pilot, has told me that this pilot was sent to Europe by the president to figure out what these so-called "foo" fighters were. He reported back to the president that they were ET spacecraft.

From there on, it gets more and more strange. A retired general, who later became right hand man to a certain CIA director, told me this: That as a military officer in 1946, he was responsible for writing "non-responsive" letters regarding a series of day time sightings of UFOs over Idaho. He said people knew the UFOs were real, but soon a Cold War was on, and later a few hot wars ensued, and everyone was concerned with global thermonuclear war—so who had time to worry about these enigmatic but harmless ETs?

Who indeed.

Multiple new, independently corroborating witnesses told us of the crash and retrieval of ET spacecraft in 1947 in New Mexico and in 1948 in Kingman Arizona. Now *this* really got someone's attention, and the name of the game was, henceforth, *advanced ET technology.*

How does it work; what can it be used for; how will they use it; what if the Soviets figure it out before we do; what if it leaks out and some new Hitler uses it to dominate the world; what if people panic when they learn of it; what....

And a million more questions, at the time all unanswered.

And thus was born the secret project of the millennium.

After all, at the time, we were working on the development of the hydrogen bomb—and our arch-enemy the Soviets were hot on our tail. What could be more destabilizing to an already fragile world order than the introduction of inter-stellar propulsion technology to a world of vacuum tubes and internal combustion engines? To say we were facing a quantum leap in technological capability is an understatement. And we wanted it safely for ourselves.

So, "National Security" demanded that this entire matter be kept quiet at all costs. And no cost was spared in doing so.

But there was one very large and busy fly in this ointment: The ETs were flying, sometimes in formation, with thousands of witnesses, over the skies of America, and the rest of the world. Now, how do you hide that?

The mind hides it. In an Orwellian twist, it was found from past psychological warfare efforts during WWII that, indeed, if you tell a lie often enough, especially if told by "respected" authority figures, the people will believe it. It appears that one of the masters of psychological warfare during WWII was put in charge of this in the late 1940s. General Walter Bedell Smith helped coordinate the psychological warfare components of this problem, and helped launch the big lie: UFOs, even though millions have seen them, do not exist.

For every sighting which made its way into public awareness, there would be official denial and, worse, ridicule of the event and the observers. Harvard Astronomer Donald Menzel was trotted out to tell the world that it was all hysteria, that UFOs were not real, that it was all poppycock.

So well into the 1950s, a relatively small group of people knew the truth, and kept the truth to themselves. When an event occurred which got the media's attention, authority figures would deny and ridicule it. Since humans are generally insecure social creatures, and more like lemmings that we would like to admit, it became clear that if you wanted to avoid embarrassment, ridicule and social estrangement, you kept quiet about UFOs, even if you had seen one up close and personal. Add to this the active encouragement of wacky stories and bizarre tall tales within the civilian UFO subculture, aided by the naturally occurring level of crazies and crack-pots in society generally and, well, you get the picture. Any respectable person—and especially the "respectable" media, scientists and political leaders—would have to view this as the "topic non grata" to avoid.

(Having gone through what I have in the past 6 years, I really can't say I blame them...)

But this is all very conventional stuff, really. The bizarre twists began in the 1950s, when a new model for covert projects evolved; a frankenstein was created, but now it has gotten a will of its own, has gotten up off the table, breaking all restraints, and is moving around amongst us.

In late 1993 and into 1994, 1995 and 1996, from one meeting to another, a shocking truth emerged. Somehow on the way to the 90s, something awful had happened: The entire matter had been largely privatized, was 10 levels deep black and was operating outside the constitutional chain of command of the US or any other government. Now, I know what you are thinking—I thought the same at first—but hear me out.

Within a few months of that initial meeting in July of 1993, I and / or members of our team had met with very, very senior officials of the CIA, Congress, the Clinton Administration, the UN, the Joint Chiefs of Staff, the military in England and elsewhere. Our initial logic was first to make the case to these folks that since the Cold War was over, a window of opportunity had opened through which a major disclosure on this matter could be made. The time had come to return this matter to the international community. Right? Wrong! Virtually without exception, leaders in the military, intelligence fields, politics and national security areas agreed that the time had come for the truth to be told. Problem is, they had no access to the truth, or the data, or the cases, or the technology or the deceased ET bodies in storage (yes we know where they are and it is not Wright Patterson Air Force Base any longer).

Those who I thought would be in the loop were out, and the ones running the show were a strange combination of covert operatives and private corporate interests. From then on it was through the looking glass we go.

My ancestors fought in the American Revolution in North Carolina. They fought for the establishment of a constitutional, representative form of government; now I wondered what had happened to the constitution. Like a very bad dream, I kept hoping to awaken to find it was not true. How could I share this with others? Who would believe it? It was bad enough for a doctor in NC to maintain that we were being visited by advanced ET life forms, but this?

I asked a friend who was on the staff of President Reagan's National Security Council how this could be true. How could some of the most powerful people in the world—in government, in the military, the senior intelligence and national security areas—not only not know about this, but have *no access* to this information? I asked him if we let the President know exactly who out there really does know about this and he called them into the Oval Office and said, "I am the President of the United States and I want you to tell me everything you know about this matter", what would they do?

He laughed and said, "Steve, if they don't want the President to know, they will simply lie to the president and say no such thing exists. Its done all the time...." I was stunned by the cynicism of this, and by the clear breech in constitutional law.

Under the ruse of "plausible deniability" to "protect" senior government officials, this apparently is done in certain sensitive areas, and the UFO matter is the most sensitive of all.

In a meeting with a very senior leader in the intelligence community, whose position any one in the public would assume allowed him to know every bit of important secret information, I discovered that, even though this official knew the matter was real, that the UFOs were real, he had no access to either past or current information or projects dealing with the ET subject. Again, I was stunned.

Ditto for very senior Senate investigators with subpoena power and top secret clearance. Ditto for people at the Joint Chiefs of Staff. Ditto for senior UN people. Ditto for senior Ministry of Defense officials in Great Britain. Ditto for heads of state.

And so it went, on and on. No deception this; these meetings were arranged by personal, back-door contacts and friends. Ironically, these leaders were turning to us for information, analysis and, strangely, action, to get this secret mess fixed. My pointing out that I am only a country doctor from North Carolina, with a wife, four kids, a mini-van and a golden retriever did not change this reality. So in my "spare" time, I have done what I could.

Unacknowledged Special Access Projects. USAPs. This term—concept, really—took some time to take hold. Call me naive, but I really believe in democracy and the constitution, the office of the president, the importance of a congress and so on. But such quaint notions at some point had to be assimilated in my mind and reconciled with this new reality: That the president, and congress and the courts and the UN and all the other world leaders exist. They worry about taxes, money, programs of this sort or another. But the really big stuff—leave them out of it. After all, these people come and go every 2 or 4 years. What they don't know won't hurt them; besides, we're doing them a favor by keeping them innocent of any knowledge of these secret projects. At any rate, these projects are *unacknowledged*, and they don't really exist at all...

In working with people on the inside of these projects, you must understand that I had to endure a very steep learning curve. Having never been in the military, the government or the intelligence field, this was all new to me. Please understand that I cannot betray the confidence of those who risked so much to share this information with me. People have been killed—and recently—for less, much less.

What is a USAP? It is a top-secret, compartmentalized project requiring special access even for those with a top secret clearance, AND it is unacknowledged. This means that if someone -anyone- including your superiors, including the Commander-in-Chief, the President, asks you about it, you reply that no such project exists. You lie.

People in these USAPs are dead serious about keeping their project secret, and will do nearly anything to keep the story covered, and to keep both other officials and the public disinformed.

And the grand daddy of all USAPs is the UFO/ET matter.

Remember that a top-secret Canadian document written by Wilbur Smith in 1950 ("Wilbur Smith Document" on page 441) stated that he had found that a secret US group was working on the UFO matter, including the technology behind the UFOs, and that this was the most secret undertaking in the US government, exceeding even the secrecy surrounding the development of the H-bomb.

Now imagine if you will, this project 50 years later. A lot of water has gone beneath the bridge. There has been 50 years and countless billions spent on various aspects of the project: reverse engineering ET technology to figure out how it works; experiments with non-linear propulsion and communications systems; massive public disinformation efforts and the deceit of constitutionally elected and appointed officials and bodies; and more.

Add to this active disinformation—the hoaxing or simulation of false ET events to deceive the public and serve as decoys, thus taking peoples' attention away from the real action. Abductions. Mutilations. Hybrid babies floating in space and in underground bases. Secret pacts between one-world-government forces and the sinister aliens. And so forth ad nauseam. Tragically, the tabloid media, book publishers, the UFO subculture/industry and the general public eat this stuff up by the gallon measure.

Not only does this nonsense serve as effective decoys to the unfunded and unprofessional civilian UFO subculture, it creates the patina of craziness and tawdriness needed to keep "respectable" scientists, mainstream media and public officials silent. It keeps the whole matter safely off their radar screens.

From the mid 1940s to the mid to late 1950s, as these matters go, this secret group was somewhat conventional. A number of officials in the Truman and Eisenhower administrations knew about it and were involved. It was genuinely felt to be imperative to the national security that this matter be kept quiet for a while. And I believe they were acting in good faith, and within the reasonable limits of our constitutional democracy.

But apparently sometime in the mid- to-late Eisenhower years, a pattern developed where those who legally should be in the loop were shoved out. We have more than one corroborating source that this was the case in the late Eisenhower years and the Kennedy Administration.

First hand witnesses have told us that Eisenhower was furious that he was being kept in the dark about a number of important aspects of the UFO/ET matter. He had seen the ET spacecraft and bodies, and yet he found that extraordinary projects were under way, and he was out of the loop. Is it any wonder then that, notwithstanding the fact that he was a 5 star general and conservative Republican, he warned of the "military-industrial complex" in his last address to the nation as president? People forget that it was this five-star general—and not Abby Hoffman—who coined the term military-industrial complex, first warning us of the dangers of its excesses. Why? Because he had seen those excesses up close and personal.

Fast forward to June of 1963. Kennedy is flying to Berlin to deliver his famous speech proclaiming "I am a Berliner". On board Air Force One is a military man who relates the following: Kennedy, on the long flight, at one point began discussing the UFO matter with this military officer. He admitted that he knew the UFOs were real, had seen the evidence, but then astonished the officer by stating that "the whole matter is out of my hands, and I don't know why...." Kennedy said that he wanted the truth to come out, but that he couldn't do it. And this is the President of the United States, the Commander in Chief of the armed forces, stating that the matter is out of his hands, and he doesn't know why. I wonder if he found out before he was killed later that year.

Eisenhower, Kennedy, Clinton Administration figures, military leaders, intelligence leaders, foreign leaders. All out of the loop. But all know it's real. What is going on?

USAPs are only part of the story. The smaller part. Remember Eisenhower warning of the military-industrial complex? Operative word: industrial, private, privatized. In discussing this matter with a former head of the Ministry of Defense in Great Britain in July of 1995, I found that he was similarly kept out of the loop. We found once again that the really secret stuff was kept from even a man who was head of MI5 and the MoD. The answer existed in part with USAPs, but more largely with private contract entities.

The US government builds almost nothing (thank goodness...). The B-2 Stealth bomber is not built by the US government, but *for* the US government by private industry. And private industry keeps secrets even better than USAPs. It makes sense: after all these years nobody knows the formula for Coca Cola. Not even the President of the United States can get it. The formula is secret, and private.

Now if you will, combine the proprietary power of private secrets with a combined liaison with USAPs and you build a covert fortress which is virtually impenetrable. Because if you try to get at it through the private sector, it is protected by proprietary privilege. And if you try to get to it through the public sector—government—it is hidden in USAPs, and the "government" as you and I ordinarily think of it is clueless.

And from personal experience I can tell you that if you inform the leaders of this, they will hold their heads in their hands and say, as I once did, "Oh my God..."

So, what is the essential profile of this covert operation? Below is my current assessment, based on the degree of penetration and research as of the spring of 1996:

Last code name related to me by reliable sources: PI-40

Meaning of code name: Unknown

Description: PI-40 is a quasi-governmental, USAPs related, quasi-private entity operating internationally/transnationally. The majority of operations are centered in private industrial "work for others" contract projects related to the understanding and application of advanced ET technologies. Related compartmentalized units, which are also USAPs, are involved in disinformation, public deception, active disinformation, so-called abductions and mutilations, reconnaissance and UFO tracking, space-based weapons systems, and specialized liaison groups (for example to media, political leaders, the scientific community, the corporate world etc.). Think of this entity as a hybrid between government USAPs and private industry.

PI-40 consists primarily of mid-level USAPs-related military and intelligence operatives, USAPs or black units within certain high-tech corporate entities, and select liaisons within the international policy analysis community, certain religious groups, the scientific community and the media, among others. The identities of some of these entities and individuals are known to us, though most remain unidentified.

Approximately 1/3 to 1/2 or those comprising the decision-making body of PI-40 are now in favor of a public disclosure of some type on this matter; these are, in general, the younger members who have less complicity in past excesses. The remaining members are opposed or ambivalent regarding a near-term disclosure.

Actual policy and decision-making seems to rest predominantly at this time in the private, civilian sector, as opposed to USAP-related military and intelligence officials, though some information indicates that there is significant relative autonomy in certain areas of operations. It is our current assessment that a rising degree of debate exists within PI-40 regarding certain covert operations and the advisability of a disclosure.

Many compartmentalized operations within "black" or USAPs projects are structured so that those working on the task may be unaware that it is UFO/ET related. For example, some aspects of the so-called "Star Wars" effort, or SDI, are intended to target ET spacecraft which come into close proximity to Earth, but the vast majority of scientists and workers in the SDI program are unaware of this.

We have learned from three separate, corroborating sources that since the early 1990s, at least two ET spacecraft have been targeted and destroyed by experimental space-based weapons systems.

The vast majority of political leaders, including White House officials, military leaders, congressional leaders, UN leaders and other world leaders are not routinely briefed on this matter. When and if inquiries are made, they are told nothing about the operations, nor is the existence of any operation confirmed to them. In general the nature of this covert entity ensures that such leaders do not even know to whom such inquiries should be addressed.

International cooperation exists to a wide extent, though some witnesses state that certain countries, particularly China, have aggressively pursued somewhat independent agendas.

Major bases of operations, apart from widely diversified private sites, include Edwards Air Force Base in California, Nellis Air Force Base in Nevada, particularly S4 and adjacent facilities, Los Alamos New Mexico, Fort Huachuca Arizona (Army Intelligence Headquarters), the Redstone Arsenal in Alabama, and a relatively new, expanding underground facility accessible only by air in a remote area of Utah, among others. Additional facilities and operations centers exist in a number of other countries, including the United Kingdom, Australia, and Russia. Numerous agencies have deep cover, black, USAPs related units involved with these operations, including the National Reconnaissance Office (NRO), the National Security Agency (NSA), the CIA, the Defense Intelligence Agency (DIA), the Air Force Office of Special Investigations (AFOSI), Naval Intelligence, Army Intelligence, Air Force Intelligence, the FBI, and others. An even more extensive list of private, civilian and corporate entities have significant involvement. The majority of scientific, technical and advanced technology operations are centered in the civilian industrial and research firms. Significant—and lethal—security is provided by private contractors.

The majority of personnel as well as the leadership of most if not all of these agencies and private groups are uninvolved and unaware of these compartmentalized, unacknowledged operations. For this reason, sweeping accusations related to any particular agency or corporate entity are wholly unwarranted. "Plausible deniability" exists at many levels. Moreover, specialization and compartmentalization allows a number of operations to exist without those involved knowing that their task is related to the UFO/ET subject.

Both positive inducements to cooperate and penalties for violating secrecy are extraordinary. A senior military source has related to us that at least 10,000 people have received $1 million or more each to ensure their cooperation, over the past few decades. Regarding penalties, we know of more than one credible case where individuals have had their families threatened should they break the code of silence, and we have learned of two recent alleged "suicides" at a private contract industrial firm which occurred after the victims began to violate secrecy on a reverse-engineering project related to ET technology.

Funding: A senior congressional investigator has privately related to us that "black budget" funds apparently are used for this and similar operations which are USAPs. This "black budget" involves conservatively $10 billion, and may exceed $80 billion per year. The amount dedicated to the UFO/ET operation specifically is unknown at this time. Additionally, significant funds are derived from overseas sources and private and institutional sources. Amounts deriving from these activities are also unknown by us.

This is part of what we know at this time. Obviously, there are more questions than answers here, and what is unknown exceeds what is known. Nevertheless, we have, I believe, made significant and historic advances in understanding how this entity operates. I have presented this general assessment to a number of important military, political and policy institute figures, and was surprised that it was regarded as quite accurate and in agreement with independent assessments arrived at separately by them.

But the larger question is why? As in life in general, the whats, whos and hows are always easier than the whys. Why the continued secrecy and deception?

I am reluctant to go too much further out on this limb, because here we get into questions related to ultimate motive and purpose, which is always a rather squishy area, ill-defined in the best of cases. And this, I am afraid, is no ordinary matter, and the emotions, motives and purpose behind such extraordinary and high-stakes actions are likely complex and dissonant. Indeed, such motives are likely a very mixed bag, ranging from the initially noble and well-intentioned, to the depraved.

Sen. Barry Goldwater told me in 1994 that the secrecy surrounding the ET subject was "a damn mistake then and a damn mistake now...".

I am inclined to agree with the senator here, but the drive for secrecy was not and is not altogether rooted in stupidity. Rather, I see it rooted in fear and a lack of trust.

While I generally dislike psycho-babble, I believe the psychology of all of this is important. It is my belief that secrecy, especially extreme secrecy of this degree, is always a symptom of illness. If you have secrets in your family, it is a sickness, born out of fear, insecurity and distrust. This, I feel, can be extended to communities, companies, and societies. Ultimately, the drive for secrecy is a symptom of a deeper malaise derived from a fundamental lack of trust, and an abundance of fear and insecurity.

In the case of UFOs/ETs, the early days of the 1940s and 1950s were, I sense, a time of fear bordering on panic. We had just emerged from a devastating world war, and unleashed the horror of nuclear weapons. The USSR was expanding its empire, and arming itself to the teeth with bigger and deadlier nuclear weapons. And they were beating us in the race into space.

Now along come ET spacecraft, which are retrieved along with deceased (and one living) life form. Panic. Fear. Confusion. Countless unanswered questions arise, all tinged with fear.

Why are they here? How will the public react? How can we secure their technology—and keep it from our mortal enemies? How can we tell the people that the most powerful air force in the world cannot control its airspace? What will happen to religious belief? To the Economic order? To Political stability? To the keepers of current technology? To....

It is my opinion that the early days of secrecy were predictable, even understandable, and possibly even justifiable.

But as the decades rolled by, and especially with the end of the Cold War, fear alone does not fully explain the secrecy. After all, 1996 is not 1946—we have been to space, landed on the moon, detected planets around other star systems, found the building blocks of life in far-away space, and about 50% of the population believe the UFOs are real. And the Soviet empire has collapsed.

I believe two other significant factors are at play now: Greed and control, and the inertia of decades of secrecy.

Greed and control are easily understood: Imagine being involved with a project unraveling and then applying advanced ET technology. The power and economic impact—and thus value—of such technology exceeds the combined significance of the internal combustion engine, electricity, the computer chip and all forms of telecommunications. We are talking about the technology of the next millennium. You think the computer/information age revolution is big? Fasten your seat belts, because down the road—sooner or later—will be the non-linear, zero point technological revolutions based on advanced ET technologies.

No wonder the corporate, military-industrial complex interest and secrecy exceeds even that of the government related USAPs. The formula for Coca Cola has nothing on this.

The bureaucratic inertia of large secret operations is yet another matte. After decades of operations, and of lies, public deceptions and worse, how does such a group unravel all the webs it has weaved? There is a certain addictive allure to secret power for some types of people; they are charged by having and knowing secrets. And there is the specter of a sort of cosmic Watergate, with all manner of people calling for this head or that. It becomes easier to maintain the status quo, something all bureaucracies are adept at doing.

And even now there is fear. Not just fear of being exposed in the age of Watergate, this-gate and that-gate, but a rather xenophobic and primitive fear of the unknown. Who are these humanoids, why are they here; how dare they enter our airspace without our permission! Humanity has a long tradition of fearing—and hating—that which is different, unknown, from elsewhere. Witness the still-rampant racial, ethnic, religious, and nationalistic prejudice and hatred which ravage the world of humanity. There is an almost ingrained xenophobic response to the unknown and that which is different. And it is certain that the ETs are more different from us than, say, Protestants are from Catholics in Ireland.

I once asked a physicist involved with military and intelligence operations related to UFOs why we were attempting to destroy these spacecraft with advanced space-based weapons. He immediately became agitated and said, "Those cowboys running this thing are so arrogant, so out of control, that they view any entry by a UFO into our air space as an offense worthy of a hostile response. And they are going to get us into an inter-planetary conflict if we are not careful..."

And so it goes. Fear. Fear of the unknown. Greed and control. Institutional Inertia. These are a few of what I see as the current animating forces driving the continued secrecy of PI-40.

But where to from here? How to transform this situation from extreme secrecy to disclosure?

There is an old Chinese proverb which says, "Unless we change directions, we are likely to end up where we are going." How true. And where we are going in this area is immensely dangerous. Extreme secrecy, especially on something this far-reaching and important, undermines democracy, subverts the constitution, concentrates enormous technological power in the hands of the unelected few and puts the entire planet in harms way. This must end.

CSETI Project Starlight has been working for nearly 3 years to collect evidence, identify current and former government, military, intelligence and corporate witnesses, and brief various world leaders. Much has been accomplished, with no paid staff, no significant funding and the dedication and volunteer efforts of a persistent team. But much remains to be done. Here is a partial list:

In June of 1995, we convened a meeting of important military and government witnesses from the US and Russia, and we all signed a letter asking President Clinton to issue an executive order permitting such witnesses to speak without penalty or retribution. I suggest that the Administration, in cooperation with Congress, sponsor open hearings where these witnesses, who now number over 2 dozen, could openly testify to what they know about the UFO/ET matter. This would constitute a definitive disclosure, I assure you. In this regard, you can help in two ways: 1) Write the President and ask that he issue an executive order permitting these witnesses to safely come forward, and at the same time write your Senator and Congressman and request that they sponsor open hearings where these witnesses may speak. 2) Contact me immediately if you or someone you know may be a current or former government, military or corporate witness. We have protective measures in place, and the more witnesses we have, the stronger the case—and the greater the margin of safety for all concerned. Please help us if you can.

The international community and the United Nations should similarly hold open hearings on this matter. We have witnesses from all over the world, and ideally, an international disclosure and evidence gathering effort should begin immediately.

The world community should not sit by passively, thus abdicating responsibility to secret operations. CSETI has for 5 years been involved in a citizens diplomacy effort, and made significant breakthroughs in developing protocols to contact these ET visitors. Rather than passively watching this as some distant "phenomenon," we should attempt to establish communication with these life forms, and begin the early stages of an open inter-planetary relationship. If you are interested in learning more about how you can be involved in such a research and diplomacy effort, contact us.

Lastly, we must be prepared to forgive. There is nothing to be gained by calling for severe retribution for those involved with either current or past secrecy. Many may have felt they were doing the right thing at the time, and even currently. We do not need a cosmic Watergate, and we must collectively renounce it. We should be willing to look to the moment and to the future, and forgive the past. There is precedent for this: In the early days of the Clinton Administration, there were sweeping disclosures about past excesses and crazy experiments within the Department of Energy, and the former Atomic Energy Commission. We learned of plutonium being put on the oatmeal of kids in orphanages, of deliberate radiation releases in populated areas to see "what would happen," and so forth. This truth came out, and the world did not end. Nobody had to go to jail. The government did not collapse, and the sky did not fall. Let us move forward, with some real compassion and forgiveness, and begin the next century anew.

Ultimately, if the people will lead, the leaders will follow. Courage, vision and perseverance are needed to transform this situation, and create a time of openness, trust and to lay the foundation for both global and inter-planetary peace. If our leaders currently lack this courage and vision, then we must manifest it for them. The stakes are too high to look the other way while our future is stolen from us. The future of life on Earth, and our place in the cosmos, are at risk. Together, let us work to secure it, for our children and our children's children.

40

Understanding UFO Secrecy

14 April 1999

Introduction

Over the past few years I have had the responsibility of briefing senior government and scientific leaders both in the US and abroad on the UFO/ET subject.

The evidence regarding this subject is clear and overwhelming: It has not been difficult to make a compelling case for the reality of UFOs per se. What is a greater challenge is elucidating the architecture of secrecy related to UFOs (see the exposition of this matter contained in the paper entitled "Unacknowledged" by this author). But the greatest challenge is explaining the "why." Why all the secrecy? Why a "black" or unacknowledged government within the government? Why hide the UFO/ET subject from public view?

The "what" or evidence is complex but manageable. The "how" or nature of the secret programs is more difficult, much more complex and Byzantine. But the "why"—the reason behind the secrecy"—is the most challenging problem of all. There is not a single answer to this question, but rather numerous inter-related reasons for such extraordinary secrecy. Our investigations and interviews with dozens of top-secret witnesses who have been within such programs have enabled us to understand the reasons behind this secrecy. They range from the fairly obvious and straight-forward to the really bizarre. Here, I wish to share some key points regarding this secrecy, why it has been imposed and why it is so difficult for the controlling interests within covert programs to reverse policy and allow disclosure.

In The Beginning

In the early days of the ET/UFO phenomena, military, intelligence and industrial interests had concerns regarding the nature of the phenomena, whether it originated from our human adversaries and once it was determined to be ET, how the public would react.

In the 1930s and 1940s this was no small matter: If these UFOs were of terrestrial origin, they would be evidence of an earthly adversary with technological devices far in advance of US aircraft. And once it was determined to be ET (some quarters knew this prior to the end of WWII) there were many more questions than answers. To wit: Why were the ETs here? What are their intentions? How do the devices travel at such fantastic speeds and through the vastness of space? How might these technologies be applied to the human situation—both in war and in peace? How would the public react to this knowledge? What effect would the disclosure of these facts have on human belief systems? Political and social systems?

From the late 1940s through the early 1950s, a concerted effort was made to figure out the basic science and technologies behind these spacecraft, primarily through the direct study and reverse-engineering of the retrieved ET objects from New Mexico and elsewhere. It was immediately recognized that these objects were using laws of physics and applied technologies far in advance of internal combustion engines, vacuum tubes and the like. In the climate of the Cold War and in a world where a relatively minor advantage technologically could tilt the balance of power in the nuclear arms race, this was no small matter.

Indeed, the theme of human geo-political dysfunction appears as a recurring feature of the secrecy related to UFOs—up to the present hour. More on this later.

From the Wilbur Smith top-secret Canadian government document of 1950, we know that this subject was held in greater secrecy than even the development of the hydrogen bomb. There was a tremendous effort underway by the late 1940s to study ET hardware, figure out how it operated and see what human applications might be made from such discoveries. Even then, the project dealing with this subject was extraordinarily covert.

It became much more so by the early 1950s when substantial progress was made on some of the basic physics behind the ET craft energy and propulsion systems. The best we can estimate, it was then that the entire project became increasingly "black" or unacknowledged.

The compartmentalization of the project dealing with UFOs was exponentially increased by the early 1950s when it was realized what it was that these covert projects actually had: Devices displaying physics and energy systems which—if disclosed—would forever alter life on Earth.

By the Eisenhower era, the UFO/ET projects were increasingly compartmented away from legal, constitutional chain-of-command oversight and control. This means that—while we know from witness testimony that Eisenhower knew of the ET craft—the president (and similar leaders in the UK and elsewhere) were increasingly left out of the loop. Such senior elected and appointed leaders were confronted with (as Eisenhower called it) a sophisticated military-industrial complex with labyrinthine compartmented projects which were more and more out of their control and oversight. From direct witness testimony we know that Eisenhower, Kennedy, Carter and Clinton were frustrated by their attempts to penetrate such projects.

This is also true of senior congressional leaders and investigators, foreign leaders and UN leadership. This is indeed an equal opportunity exclusion project—it does not matter how high your rank or office, if you are not deemed necessary to the project, you are not going to know about it. Period.

Contrary to popular myth, since the 1960s concern over some type of public panic when faced with the fact that we are not alone in the universe has not been a major reason for the secrecy. Those in the know—notwithstanding the fantastic tales spun in UFO circles and on the X-Files—understand that fear of hostile ETs has also not been a significant factor. While there has been continued confusion in some covert circles over the ultimate purpose behind the ET phenomena, we know of no knowledgeable insiders who regard the ETs as a hostile threat.

By the 1960s—and certainly by the 1990s—the world was very familiar with the concept of space travel and the popular science-fiction industry had thoroughly indoctrinated the masses with the idea of ETs from far away being a possibility. So why the continued secrecy?

The Cold War is over. People would hardly be shocked to find out that we are not alone in the universe (the majority of people already believe this—in fact most people believe the UFOs are real).Besides, what could be more shocking than to live through the latter half of the

20th century with thousands of hydrogen bombs aimed at every major city in the world? If we can handle that, surely we can handle the idea that ETs are real.

The facile explanations of fear, panic, shock and the like do not suffice to justify a level of secrecy so deep that even the President and his CIA Director could be denied access to the information.

A Current Estimate

Continued secrecy on the UFO subject must be related, then, to on-going anxiety related to the essential power dynamics of the world and how such a disclosure would impact these.

That is, the knowledge related to UFOs/ET phenomena must have such great potential for changing the status quo that its continued suppression is deemed essential, *at all costs*.

Going back to the early 1950s, we have found that the basic technology and physics behind these ET spacecraft were discovered through very intensive reverse-engineering projects. It was precisely at this point that the decision was made to increase the secrecy to an unprecedented level—one which essentially took the matter out of ordinary government chain of command control as we know it. Why?

Aside from the possible use of such knowledge by US/UK adversaries during the Cold War, it was immediately recognized that these devices were not your dad's Oldsmobile. The basic physics behind the energy generation and propulsion systems were such that they could easily replace all existing energy generation and propulsion systems on the Earth. And with them, the entire geo-political and economic order.

In the 1950s, there was no great concern over global warming, ecosystem collapse, ozone depletion, rain forest loss, bio-diversity degradation etc. In the wake of WW II, what was needed was stability, not a new convulsion of the world economic, technological and geo-political order. Remember: those in control like to stay in control. They are risk-averse, do not like significant change and do not give up control and power easily.

The disclosure of the existence of ETs, with the inevitable disclosure related to these new technologies soon to follow, would change the world forever—and they knew it. This was to be avoided at all costs. Besides, that was the era of "what is good for GM is good for America," and the same would be true of big oil, big coal and the like.

The inescapable fact is this: The disclosure of the ET presence would bring with it the certain release of these technologies -and that release would sweep away the entire technological infrastructure of the planet. The changes would be immense—and sudden.

Fifty years later, as we prepare to turn the page to a new millennium, this is more true now than then. Why? Because avoiding the problem in the 1950s—while convenient at the time—means that the situation is more tenuous now. For example, world dependence on oil and internal combustion technology is greater now than in 1955. And the world economy is larger by orders of magnitude now, so any change would be exponentially greater—and potentially more chaotic.

And so this is the conundrum: each decade and generation has passed this problem on to the next, only to find any path but continued secrecy more destabilizing than it would have been a decade earlier. In a maddening circle of secrecy, delay of disclosure and increasing world complexity and dependence on out-dated energy systems, each generation has found itself in a greater squeeze than the one before. As difficult as disclosure would have been in the 1950s, disclosure now is even more difficult. And potentially Earth-shaking in its consequences.

The technological discoveries of the 1950s resulting from the reverse-engineering of ET craft could have enabled us to completely transform the world economic, social, technological and environmental situation. That such advancements have been withheld from the public is related to the change-averse nature of the controlling hierarchy at the time—and to this day.

And make no mistake, the changes would be immense.

Consider: A technology which enables energy generation from the so-called zero point field and which enables every home, business, factory and vehicle to have its own source of power -without an external fuel source. Ever. No need for oil, gas, coal, nuclear plants or the internal combustion engine. And no pollution. Period.

Consider: A technology using electro-gravitic devices which allows for above surface transportation—no more roadways to cover fertile farmland since transportation could take place totally above the surface.

Sounds great. But in the 1950s, oil was plentiful, nobody worried too much about pollution, global warming was not the faintest concern and the powers that be just wanted stability. The status quo. And besides, why risk the tectonic changes related to such a disclosure? Let a later generation take care of it.

But now, we are that later generation. And 1999 is not 1949. The Earth is straining under the burden of a growing population—now 6 billion people—all of whom want cars, electricity, TVs and the like. Everyone knows that we do not have 50 more years of oil—and even if we did, the Earth's ecosystem could not withstand 50 more years of such abuse. The risks of disclosure are now much *less* than the risks of secrecy: If secrecy continues much longer, the Earth's ecosystem will collapse. Talk about a big change and global instability...

Many people will consider the technological and economic impact of such a disclosure as the central justification of continued secrecy. After all, we are talking about a multi-*trillion* dollar per year change in the economy. The entire energy and transportation sectors of the economy would be revolutionized. And the energy sector—the part where non-renewable fuels are purchased and burned and have to be replenished—will utterly vanish. And while other industries will flourish, only a fool would dismiss the impact of such a multi-trillion dollar segment of the economy disappearing.

Certainly the "vested interests" involved in the global industrial infrastructure related to oil, gas, coal and internal combustion engines and public utilities is no small force in the world.

But to understand UFO secrecy you must consider what all that money represents at its core. Power. Massive geo-political power.

One must consider what will happen when every village in India (or Africa or South America or China) has devices which can generate large amounts of power without pollution and without spending huge sums of energy on fuel. The entire world will be able to develop in an unprecedented fashion—without pollution and without billions spent on power plants, transmission lines and combustible fuels. The have-nots will have.

This would widely be considered a good thing: after all, much of world instability, warfare and the like is related to mind-numbing poverty and economic depravity in a world of great wealth. Social injustice and extreme economic disparity breeds much chaos and suffering in the world. These decentralized, non-polluting technologies would change that permanently. Even the deserts will bloom...

But it must be remembered that geo-political power flows from technological and economic prowess. India has over 1 billion people and the US about one-fourth that, but who has the greater geo-political power?

As these new energy systems proliferate, the so-called third world will *rapidly* reach parity with the industrialized world of Europe, the US and Japan. This will cause a massive shift in geo-political power. And the industrialized world will find that it must then actually share power with the now down-trodden third world.

Those in the cat-bird seat currently (and in 1950) have no interest in doing any such thing. We can hardly even support and share power in the United Nations.

The release of information on the UFO / ET subject will lead to the global proliferation of new energy systems which will rapidly result in an equalization of power in the world. The US and Europe have around 600 million people. That is only 10% of the world's population. Once the other 90% rise in technological and economic standing, it is clear to see that the geo-political power will shift—or equalize—to the rest of the world. Power will have to be shared. Real global collective security will be inevitable. It is the end of the world as we know it.

When you combine the economic and technological impact with the geo-political impact, it becomes obvious that the changes related to ending secrecy are truly tectonic—massive, world-encircling and transformative. It is not to be regarded lightly.

But 50 years after the world *could* have had these new technologies—and 50 long years of ecological degradation, social and economic chaos and disparity—we find that we are the last generation in the long line of passing the cosmic hot potato known as the UFO secrecy problem.

And here we stand, holding this hot potato, but what shall we do about it?

To end the secrecy means vast and profound changes in virtually every aspect of human existence—economic, social, technological, philosophical, geo-political and so forth. But to continue the secrecy and the suppression of these new energy and propulsion technologies means something far more destabilizing: the collapse of the Earth's ecosystem and the certain depletion of the fossil fuels on which we depend. And the growing anger of the have-nots, who are needlessly being deprived of a full and dignified life. There are no more generations to which we can pass this cosmic hot potato: we must deal with it and do what should have been done in 1950.

The Webs We Weave

As if the foregoing was not enough to justify secrecy, recall that extraordinary things have been done to maintain this secrecy. The infrastructure needed to maintain and expand the level of secrecy which can deceive presidents and CIA Directors and senior congressional leaders and European Prime Ministers and the like is substantial—and illegal. *Let me be clear, the entity which controls the UFO matter and its related technologies has more power than any single government in the world or any single identified world leader.*

That such a situation could arise was forewarned by President Eisenhower when, in January 1961, he cautioned us regarding the growing "military-industrial complex." This was his last speech to the world as president—and he was warning us directly of a frightening situation about which he had personal knowledge. For Eisenhower had seen the ET craft and deceased ET bodies. He knew of the covert programs dealing with the situation. But he also knew that he had lost control of these projects and that they were lying to him about the extent and full nature of their research and development activities.

Indeed, the current state-of-the-art in secrecy is a hybrid, quasi-government, quasi privatized operation which is international—and functions outside of the purview of any single agency or any single government. "The Government"—as you and I and Thomas Jefferson may think of it—is really quite outside the loop. Rather, a select, tightly controlled and compartmentalized "black" or unacknowledged project controls these matters. Access is by inclusion alone and if you are not included, it does not matter if you are CIA Director, President, Chairman of Senate Foreign Relations or UN Secretary General, you simply will not know about or have access to these projects.

Indeed the situation is so dire that senior Joint Chiefs of Staff leaders in the Pentagon whom I have briefed have no more access to such projects than any other civilian—unless they are on the "inside" for some reason. But this is rare.

Essentially, the covert management of this matter operates as part super-secret international government program, and part privatized organized crime operation: It is more like a secret Mafia than government as one would normally think of it.

To acquire and maintain such power all types of things have been done. We are reminded of that Robert Frost poem in which he describes "the webs we weave...." But how does such an entity extract itself from such a web of secrecy, deceit, lies and insubordination?

To be specific, this group has usurped power and rights not legally granted to it. It is extra-constitutional, both in the US and in the UK and other countries around the world. It is, therefore, a criminal enterprise and a conspiracy of the first order. Additionally, it has committed crimes which include assassinations, murder, kidnaping, theft of technology and so forth.

I will grant the possibility that, at least initially, this covert undertaking was designed to maintain secrecy and avoid instability. But the risks of inadvertent leaks—or a national or world leader deciding legally that it was time for disclosure—made it essential to weave a web of greater and greater secrecy and of illegal operations. *And now the web has closed in on the operation itself.*

That is, the complexity of the compartmentalized projects, the degree of unconstitutional and unauthorized activity, the "privatization" (or theft) by corporate partners (the "industrial" part of the military—industrial complex) of advanced technologies, the continued lying to legally elected and appointed leaders and to the public—all of these and more have contributed to a psychology of continued secrecy -*because disclosure would expose the greatest scandal in recorded history*.

For example, how would the public react to the fact that the degradation of the entire Earth's ecosystem and the irretrievable loss of thousands of species of plants and animals now extinct due to pollution, has been utterly unnecessary -and could have been avoided if only an honest release of this information had occurred in the 1950s?

How would society react to the knowledge that trillions of dollars have been spent on unauthorized, unconstitutional projects over the years? And that these tax-payer dollars have been used by corporate partners in this secrecy to develop spin-off technologies based on the study of ET objects which were later patented and used in highly profitable technologies? Not only have the taxpayers been defrauded, they have then been made to pay a premium for such breakthroughs which were the result of research paid for by them! And this does not address the intellectual property theft of such technologies from the ETs. While the basic energy generation and propulsion technologies have been withheld, these corporate partners have profited wildly from other breakthroughs and benefits in electronics, miniaturization and related areas. Such covert technology transfers constitutes a multi-trillion dollar theft of technologies which really should be public domain since taxpayers have paid for it.

And how would the public react to the fact that the multi-billion dollar space program, using internal combustion rockets and the like, has been a primitive and unnecessary experiment since much more advanced technologies and propulsion systems were in existence before we ever went to the moon? NASA and related agencies have, for the most part, been as much a victim of this secrecy as has the rest of the government and the public. Only a small, very compartmentalized fraction of NASA people know of the real ET technologies hidden away in these projects. Certainly my uncle, who helped design the lunar module which took Neil Armstrong to the moon, was as much a victim an anyone insofar as he was denied access to these technological breakthroughs. He had to rely on the old physics and the old internal combustion jet thruster technologies just like everyone else. What a shame.

The inescapable reality is this: This secret project, no matter how well intentioned initially, got carried away with its own secret power. It abused this power. It has hijacked our future for fifty years. And the scandal of this fact would result in such consternation in society and in government that its consequences can hardly be imagined. Indeed, it could well be cataclysmic from a social and political perspective.

In fact, the quiet coup d'état of the late 1940s and early 1950s, once exposed, could result in real instability today.

But the situation is actually much worse than this. All that is written above is dwarfed by a larger problem: The covert group running these UFO-related black projects has also had exclusive sway over the early days of an embryonic ET-human relationship. And it was been tragically mismanaged—nearly to the point of genuine global catastrophe.

For what happens when an unelected, unappointed, self-selecting, militarily oriented group alone has to deal with inter-species relations between humans and ETs? Well, as in most areas, if you wear rose-colored glasses the entire world looks red. And if you are wearing military glasses, every new and uncontrolled development will be seen as a potential or real military threat.

The nature of such a group—which is inordinately controlled and incestuous—is that it is homogenous in world-view and mind-set. Power and control are preeminent qualities. Such extreme secrecy creates a very dangerous milieu in which checks and balances, give and take, are utterly lacking. And in such an environment, very dangerous decisions can be made with inadequate feedback, discussion or insight from needed perspectives which are, per force, excluded.

In such an environment of extreme secrecy, militarism and paranoia, we have found that immensely dangerous actions have been taken against the ETs. Indeed, we have multiple inside sources who have described to us the use of increasingly advanced technologies to track, target and destroy ET assets. If there is even a 10% chance that this is true (I am convinced it is 100% accurate) we are dealing with a global diplomatic and social crisis which is utterly out of our control but which puts the entire planet at risk.

Remember, covert reverse-engineering projects have resulted in huge quantum leaps forward in technologies which, once applied to military systems, could be a real threat to ETs who may be here peacefully. The attempts to rapidly militarize space is likely a result of a myopic, militaristic and paranoid view of ET projects and intentions. If left unchecked, it can only result in catastrophe.

Indeed this group, no matter how well-intentioned, is in urgent need of exposure so that global statesmen with a new perspective can intercede in this situation. While we see no evidence that the ET civilizations are at all hostile, it is also clear that it is unlikely that they will allow unfettered and growing interference with their operations. Self-defense is likely a universal quality. And while tremendous restraint has been shown by the ETs thus far, might there be a "cosmic trip wire" if human covert technologies begin to reach parity and we are using such advanced technologies in a bellicose fashion? The prospect is sobering.

We need our Jimmy Carters and Dalai Lamas and other international statesmen involved with so vast a problem. But if access is denied—and the subject remains undisclosed and off the global radar screen—we are left with the unelected few to decide our fate and act on our behalf. This must change, and soon.

In the final analysis, while the changes attendant such a disclosure related to UFOs and ETs would be massive and profoundly impact virtually every aspect of life on Earth, it is still the right thing to do. Secrecy has taken on a life of its own—it is a growing cancer which needs to be cured before it destroys the life of Earth and all who dwell on her.

The reasons for secrecy are clear: global power, economic and technological control, geo-political status quo, the fear of scandal surrounding the exposure of such projects and their behavior and so forth.

But the one thing more dangerous than disclosure is continued secrecy. The Earth is dying because we are killing her. The top 250 people and families in the world have the net worth of 2.5 billion of our poorest citizens. The promising relationship between humanity and people from other planets is being militarized and strained by failed thinking and failed programs run completely in secret.

As daunting as disclosure may be, with all its potential for short-term instability and change, continued secrecy means that we will destroy the Earth through our folly and greed. The future of humanity, which has been delayed and hijacked for the past 50 years, cannot be hijacked for 50 more. For we do not have 50 more years—the Earth's ecosystem will collapse before then.

There are no easy choices. But there is one right one. Will you help us make it?

41

Projects And Facilities Related To the UFO/Extraterrestrial Matter

30 August 1996

Edwards Air Force Base And Related Facilities

Government Facilities:

- Edwards AFB
- Haystack Butte
- China Lakes
- George AFB
- Norton AFB
- Table Top Mountain Observatory (NASA)
- Blackjack Control

Aerospace Facilities

- Northrop "Anthill" (Tejon Ranch)
- McDonald Douglas Llano Plant
- Lockheed-Martin Helendale Plant
- Phillips Labs (North Edwards facility)

The Nellis Complex

- Area 51/S4
- Pahute Mesa and Area 19
- Groom Lake

New Mexico Facilities

- Los Alamos National Laboratories
- Kirtland Air Force Base
  - Sandia National Laboratories (SNL), Defense Nuclear Agency
  - Phillips Labs

Manzano Mountain Weapons Storage Facility, and underground complex

Coyote Canyon Test Site (N. end of Manzano)

White Sands Complex

Arizona

Fort Huachuca, underground storage facility, NSA and Army Intelligence complex Near Ft. Huachuca underground storage of ET spacecraft and previously autopsied ET life forms

Others

Utah underground complex southwest of Salt Lake City, accessible only by air

Redstone Arsenal underground complex Alabama

Lawrence Livermore Labs

Cheyenne Mountain Colorado Deep Space Network, dedicated console for tracking UFOs

US Government Agencies With Current or Past Involvement

(activities are compartmentalized into super-secret USAPS -Unacknowledged Special Access Projects, which means that they are not acknowledged to anyone, even those senior in the chain of command)

NRO (National Reconnaissance Office)

NSA (National Security Agency)

CIA

Military Intelligence divisions (Army, Air Force, Navy)

Air Force Office of Special Investigations (AFOSI)

DARPA

FBI

Space Commands

others

Private Corporate Entities Believed To Be Involved

Northrup Aerospace

Boeing Aerospace

Lockheed Martin (various facilities including Denver research center)

BDM
E Systems
EG&G
Wackenhut Corp.
Village Supercomputing, Phoenix AZ
Phillips Labs
McDonnell Douglas Corp.
TRW
Rockwell International
Booz-Allen and Hamilton, Inc.
MITRE Corp.
SAIC (Science Applications International, Inc.)
Bechtel Corp.
others

RECOMMENDATIONS

We recommend that the Congress pursue this matter as follows:

- By making directed inquiries to contacts and chairmen of the House and Senate Intelligence Committees;
- By inquiring directly to the various facilities, agencies and entities listed;
- By pursuing other contacts known to the Congress which may be able to assist in identifying points of control for these operations;
- We recommend that the Congress pursue this matter further by convening Congressional hearings whereby direct witnesses to these projects may testify. We believe more than one member of Congress should be located to co-sponsor such an inquiry.

Thank you for your assistance in this important matter.

42

An Open Letter To PI-40

12 September 1996

Dear PI-40[1],

The time has come for us to discuss directly and openly plans related to a disclosure on the existence of ET life forms.

As you know, we are working with important world leaders regarding a near-term disclosure on this matter which is intended to be factual, evidence-based and non-alarming. We have become aware of a number of your operations, both historically and currently, related to ET reconnaissance, research and reverse-engineering. Since capability on our part for disclosure has been reached, we feel it important to proceed with a dialogue with those controlling current covert operations so that an optimal and safe outcome occurs.

Certainly, you are aware of the profound and far-reaching implications of this subject, and it is our desire for this information to come out in as positive and in the least-destabilizing manner possible. Ideally, this disclosure would occur:

With the cooperation, whether explicitly or tacitly, of your operations

- Without recriminations or vilification of your operations or people, provided non-interference is assured
- Without the application of 'false or deceptive indications and warnings' related to this matter
- While avoiding either the demonization or deification of the ET life forms

1. PI-40 is the acronym last mentioned to me as the code for the group controlling covert operations dealing with the UFO/ET issue. It is not known if it is accurate or currently in use.

I have asked the President to provide for amnesty for your group and its personnel, provided there is cooperation and non-interference, and restraint on your part is observed. Neither the United States, nor the world, can afford a conflict over this issue.

But we are aware of certain projects of your group which we feel run counter to a safe and effective resolution of this problem. We are requesting that a 'stand-down' order be issued regarding these types of destabilizing and dangerous projects, including:

- Tracking with intent to target, and targeting with intent to destroy, ET assets
- Covert human-controlled 'abduction' programs and related genetic, biological and psychological disinformation projects
- Development and implementation of 'false and deceptive indications and warnings', which intend to stage false or hoaxed ET events of a violent nature, for the purpose of consolidation of control and other manipulative purposes
- The continued general disinformation and denial control points in the scientific, political, academic and media communities.
- There are a number of areas where I feel healing and resolution are needed, especially the conflict and estrangement between:
- Various ET groups and your entity
- Your operations and those of the traditional military and governmental operations and leadership, as well as the public
- The ET groups and humanity in general.

How may we help?

Personally, I am exquisitely aware of the time in which we live and the unprecedented risks and changes of the coming one to two decades. And while in the short term I know we are bound to encounter the general turbulence and chaos of a global phase transition, in my heart I am certain that the intermediate and long term future is exceedingly hopeful. I feel we must look to that far-horizon, while yet being mindful of the current exigencies.

There is a Chinese proverb: Unless we change directions, we are likely to end up where we are headed.

I feel where you are headed with this issue is currently very dangerous, and it will take vision, courage and some faith to change it. Not every power which can be acquired should be, and not all acquired power should be used. It is time for restraint and wisdom; perhaps together we can find the safest path to the next century.

Presently, we are aware of certain covert projects which, if pursued further, could result in a worst-case scenario and outcome for the entire planet. There is no point in pursuing a scorched earth policy, or should I say an interplanetary version of the old Mutually Assured Destruction (MAD) policy of the Cold War.

The misunderstandings, fears and suspicions of the past need to be suspended, for the sake of all of us. The recent targeting and destruction of ET spacecraft, while no doubt demonstrating a certain sophistication and prowess, may lead to catastrophic consequences in the future. Can we work together to find a safer and more sustainable way to deal with our differences with other life forms?

We should begin working together now, throughout the world, to establish the foundations of global and universal peace. The means for doing so are available to us; it is our responsibility to act and implement this plan.

With the establishment of universal peace, then and only then will we be able to disseminate the infrastructural and technological means of creating a high technology, sustainable civilization on this planet. A civilization which will be using advanced, zero-point and related technologies for peaceful purposes, and which will no longer need to destroy this extraordinary planet on which we all depend for our survival.

Surely, we cannot establish world peace, and continue to have conflicts with our planetary neighbors. And yet without world peace, and the peaceful use of these new technologies, we lack a civilization capable of surviving yet another century.

Ultimately, then, we are in a crisis of spirit and vision, and only secondarily of outward circumstance. I would like to offer to you to help work on this issue, to come together to find a resolution to this most challenging problem.

We would like to help you in creating a dialogue with the ET peoples which would lead to resolution and peace. And to bring about a truthful and hopeful disclosure on this subject which would serve as the catalyst to the establishment of global and universal peace. And then to plan the eventual dissemination of the technological means to create a truly sustainable civilization on this planet.

I know this can be done. Yes, there will be some turbulence along the way, but it will be worth it. It will not be easy, but the rewards are so great, no effort can be too much.

I would invite you to contact me, at any time and at any place of your choosing, to pursue this further. We have many people on our team who can help us create a future civilization on Earth which can grow in peace for hundreds of years. This future is waiting for us to create it.

My roots are humble here in North Carolina; I am no saint, and lay claim to no nobility. But my father was part Cherokee, and there is a Cherokee teaching which says that all that we do should be done with consideration for seven generations to follow.

For the sake of our children, and our children's children's children, I hope we can work to establish a time of peace on Earth, and beyond.

I look forward to hearing from you soon.

Sincerely,

Steven M. Greer, M.D.
Director of CSETI

43

CSETI Project Starlight

The Center for the Study of Extraterrestrial Intelligence (CSETI) Project Starlight is a global effort designed to effect a definitive disclosure on the detection of ET intelligence (ETI). Begun in 1993, the Project now encompasses a world-wide network of researchers, government liaisons, military and intelligence personnel, media leaders, leaders in society generally and important official witnesses to covert operations dealing with the UFO/ETI subject.

Substantial evidence has been collected dealing with the existence of ETI in proximity to the Earth, including video tape footage, movie footage, photographs, government documents, case reports, pilot encounters, landing trace events and witness testimony. It is the intent of Project Starlight to convene a disclosure event where the best of this collected evidence, data and testimony will be presented to the world's population.

The over-arching philosophy of the Project is that the time has come for this information to be presented in a scientific and credible manner to the public, and that this must be done in a manner which is non-threatening, hopeful and, to the extent possible, not destabilizing to society generally. The end of the Cold War presents a window of opportunity for this disclosure, and the world community has reached the point generally so that such a disclosure could not only be assimilated, but could prove beneficial in a number of areas, including:

- Geopolitics, insofar as such a disclosure would cause people and governments around the world to realize that we are not alone and that the Earth is the basic homeland of all the peoples of the world.

- The environment, since a disclosure would set in place the eventual public application of advanced ET technologies, which are non-polluting.
- Global economic development, since these advanced technologies mentioned above would remove the world from the current relative scarcity of energy, which fundamentally drives economic development world-wide.
- Government integrity, since a disclosure would return the most important covert project of the twentieth century to the national and international community, hence ending the destructive and erosive effects which extreme secrecy exerts in constitutional democracies.

Key to this process is an integrated, multi-phase strategy which includes evidence and witness testimony collection, preliminary briefings to world leaders and leaders of society, a world-encompassing disclosure event, and the management of the post-disclosure era so that maximum benefit to humanity would occur. Ultimately, this will enable the world to develop the capacity to enter into intentional communication with ET civilizations and the advent of the early stages of inter-planetary relations in the next century.

Since actual deceased ET bodies and retrieved ET spacecraft are not available to the Project Starlight briefing team, special emphasis is being placed on the identification of credible first-hand witnesses to covert programs dealing with this subject. We have identified a significant number of such witnesses and are obtaining their testimony. Their testimony before Congress, the UN or other suitable body is currently being actively sought.

As of June of 1996, CSETI Project Starlight has successfully completed the initial evidence and witness testimony gathering phase, and has briefed a number of world leaders, including important US government leaders in the Clinton Administration, members of Congress, senior military and CIA officials, senior UN figures, and leaders in Europe and Japan, among others There is widespread agreement among these figures that the time has come for the truth to come out regarding the UFO/ETI subject, although none of these officials, no matter how senior, have had direct involvement with the covert programs dealing with matter. This is because the management of this subject has been so-called "black" in nature and operates as an unacknowledged "special access" project, the existence of which is not disclosed to any one outside the project, no matter how senior the person is in the chain of command.

Assistance to CSETI Project Starlight is invited from the public in the following areas:

- Obtaining new and important credible evidence.
- Identifying important new witnesses from the government, military, intelligence or corporate sector who have first-hand knowledge of projects (current or past) dealing with the UFO/ETI subject. An effective strategy protecting such witnesses is in place.
- Networking with various sectors of society to gain support for such a disclosure and for arranging preliminary briefings to various leaders.
- Identifying funding sources, since at this point the main impediment to completing the project's goals is a lack of significant funding. (CSETI is a 501-C3 nonprofit scientific and educational organization, and donations are tax-deductible to the extent allowed by law.)

CSETI Project Starlight welcomes your input, involvement and assistance.

44

Summary of Points Regarding Project Starlight for the Clinton Administration

Hand-delivered by Dr. Greer to CIA Director James Woolsey—13 Dec 1993

Project Starlight is a program spearheaded by CSETI to educate the world leadership and the world's population regarding the reality of UFOs/ETI. Key points include:

- It is our sincere intention to cooperate with the U.S. government, the United Nations, and other governments, and to conduct the briefing process and the Announcement so that neither the Administration nor the government in general is harmed. We invite active U.S. government participation in this process and feel that for a number of reasons it is in the best interests of the Administration to do so.
- Project Starlight has commitments of assets, both evidential and in the form of key first-hand, credible witnesses to make an undeniable case for the ET origin of these objects. These assets include day and nighttime videotape footage, photographs, radar tapes, pilot cases, landing trace cases, and the important testimony of former government and military officials from the U.S., Europe, and Russia who have knowledge of this subject, in several instances including knowledge of spacecraft wreckage and ET bodies. These witnesses are willing to testify publicly before major media.
- Project Starlight has access to and offers of cooperations from major media, both print and electronic. These are respected mainstream media sources, not "tabloid" type.
- We are working with other leaders in society, here and abroad, who concur that now is the time to change current government policy to one of increasing openness and disclosure of evidence on this subject.

- The ending of the Cold War and the beginning of a new Administration provides a unique "window of opportunity" for such a change in policy and for the cooperative disclosure of evidence (See "Strategies And Rationale For Changing Government Policy" on page 353.)
- To reduce the potential for a panic reaction in society, the Announcement should be spearheaded by civilian researchers and scientists. A government announcement alone may appear abrupt and alarming.
- Failure to effect a change in policy and to provide disclosure on this subject by the end of 1995 may result in regrettable outcomes for the Administration because:
    1. The window of opportunity will have been lost, insofar as the end of the Cold War would be a relatively distant event and the new President and his appointed officials would have lost the protective aspect of being new to their responsibilities.
    2. Given the current increasing trend in ET activity and increasingly successful CSETI attempts to establish contact with these spacecraft (See "Brief Summary Of Some CSETI Research Results" on page 187.), there is a very high probability that a major UFO event of a publicly undeniable nature will transpire before the current President's term expires in January, 1997. A controlled and well thought out Announcement and disclosure of evidence is much preferred over an uncontrolled and surprising event. While the former, if handled wisely, could have a unifying and beneficial effect on humanity, the latter would very likely have a negative and very destabilizing effect. Therefore, the highest risks are associated with non-disclosure.
    3. By 1995, re-election concerns and other factors would make this process of disclosure increasingly risky due to the competitive and divisive nature of political campaigns.
    4. Other governments are moving in the direction of disclosure on this subject, and the Japanese government is funding and has plans to open a major museum on UFOs/ETI in 1996, before the current President's term expires.

5. Other civilian UFO groups who have a decidedly confrontative approach to the U.S. government are building a base of both congressional and grass roots support which may prove embarrassing to the government and military in the U.S. In contrast, Project Starlight is committed to working cooperatively with the U.S. government and avoiding language or evidence which would be harmful or embarrassing.
6. There are other civilian groups which are framing this topic in alarmist, xenophobic and potentially conflict-oriented ways which will prove harmful to world stability and to the world's "consciousness." This potentially harmful trend would be contained by Project Starlight, which is committed to presenting this information in a scientific, nonalarming and hopeful manner.

- We have learned that the other nations of the world are looking to the U.S. for leadership on this subject. Providing that leadership on a subject this important would strengthen the Administration's stature in the Post-Cold War era.
- Insofar as a majority of Americans hold that UFOs are real and are probably interplanetary spacecraft, the President would be viewed in a positive, courageous and possibly even heroic light for cooperating with such an Announcement and briefing process. Similarly, the public would become convinced that a new era had truly begun where government could be trusted to tell the truth; such a perception could go a long way towards erasing the cynicism and mistrust which has developed since the assassination of Kennedy, the Vietnam War, Watergate and other scandals. It would certainly be convincing evidence that the Administration is sincere about building a "new covenant" with the people and would fulfill the promise of a new openness in government. Mr. Woolsey's comment on *Larry King Live* On November 30, 1993, that the Administration wished to "disclose historical material" in a spirit of new openness would be fulfilled by a cooperative relationship with Project Starlight.
- We are sincerely dedicated to fulfilling this project in a way which would be a positive event for humanity. We are acutely aware of the profound implications this project might have, both positive and negative, on humankind, in general, and on economic and other systems, in particular, and are therefore making all efforts to prevent a negative or alarmist tone from creeping into the message.

U.S. government cooperation in this project would assist us in this goal, and specifically could serve to calm the financial markets in the period of the Announcement.

- A major media project, plus a major east coast U.S. newspaper will probably be completing large scale investigative reports on this subject in the next 12 months. These projects, which are very high quality and credible, will be seen by millions and probably hundreds of millions of people. Along with Project Starlight, which will conduct briefings and an Announcement with or without government cooperation, this subject and the U.S. government's connection to it, will be known by a very large segment of the population. The Administration would be best served by positioning itself in a cooperative, open, disclosing manner during the process. To do otherwise would be to increase suspicion and mistrust of government in general and the Administration in particular.
- Government cooperation and involvement with Project Starlight would afford government valuable input into the process, content and timing of these events. A passive or non-cooperative stance would of course have the opposite effect.

In any case we do not desire, nor do we recommend, the disclosure of certain valid secret projects which are vital to national security or to future defense readiness, including projects at Nellis Air Force Base in area S4, which apparently deal with reverse engineering ET technology for human applications.

Irrespective of the level of U.S. government involvement or cooperation, we wish to assure you that we intend to conduct this project in a way which will not harm the President, the military, the government or the society in general. However, due to the high likelihood of ET-human interactions in general, and ET contact by CSETI research teams specifically, which may be imminent, we are committed to fulfilling this project within the coming year. Furthermore, we are carefully and systematically thinking through what needs to be included in an extended effort that will assure that the response to this Announcement is positive and full of hope. We welcome and invite your participation.

45

Letter to Those Working Closely with Project Starlight

1 November 1994

Dear ____,

I would like to update you on recent significant developments regarding the Project Starlight effort and the CSETI initiative in general.

First, however, I would like to thank you for your support and advice over the past year or so, and wish to assure you that your contribution to this effort has been important to its success. Your support and contributions to this initiative are always deeply appreciated, even if overwhelming demands on my time have not permitted my conveying this to you often enough.

The past six months in particular have enabled us to thoroughly assess the situation presently operating regarding a potential disclosure to the public sector of the detection of ET life forms. Some of these findings have been rather extraordinary, perhaps even briefly overwhelming for me personally, but they have contributed greatly to our knowledge of the truth on this subject. This era of fact-gathering and "testing the waters" must now give rise to significant forward movement in the Project, and we have been given a large green light to move boldly forward over the next year.

Meetings with various military, governmental and intelligence sources, as well as on-going CSETI research efforts in general, have resulted in the following information and assessments:

- Through more than one source, including a recent meeting with a relevant government/intelligence liaison, we have learned that our efforts over the past 9-10 months have "had an effect in government way beyond anything you can imagine or could have hoped for", and that semi-official and indirect support exists and will be forthcoming in the direction of disclosure.

- Support exists for a civilian, external overt process to gradually replace the "internal control group" on this subject. Apparently, this decision was made in the past 2-3 months. We have been strongly encouraged to move forward as a civilian effort to collect evidence, perform briefings, and in about 1 year, bring all of this to the direct attention of major media.
- White House/ official governmental support will be indirect at this stage, but later acknowledgment will be forthcoming, and a commission will be appointed following media involvement.
- A direct announcement by the White House or government is not desirable at this stage because, while certain data of superior quality may be available to them, they are not equipped, nor is it appropriate for them, to place this data in a workable cosmology or new paradigm. This is what we must do, in concert with a significant number of other people. As I have felt all along, the barrier is not evidential or strategic (since the end of the Cold War); it is philosophical and paradigmatic. Government bureaucracy is not good at this, and this leadership initiative should rightly come from the civilian sector, with increasing indirect, and then direct support.
- We should be very wary of presentations of data devoid of an adequate elaboration of a paradigm and cosmology to contain it. Information is not knowledge, and knowledge is not wisdom; all three must be operating if this subject is to be assimilated by our civilization. Certain military, scientific or intelligence entities and individuals may be able to present the data—but what of the paradigm, the understanding, the knowledge and wisdom which must go with it? Now is the time for all of us to join to put this all together in a coherent fashion.
- While "semi-official support" apparently is in place, I was warned of "renegade factions" which may not be so supportive. While undaunted, I am cautious of this factor, a significant wild card which must be anticipated, since this renegade faction has significant resources at its disposal.
- However, it appears that legal and constitutional support exists for this effort, and this is a major plus.

- It was stated to me that adequate data exists in the civilian research community to constitute definitive evidence for the existence of ETI; this we have known for some time. We are encouraged to move decisively in collecting this data, and completing a comprehensive briefing document containing the Best Available Evidence. This must be a very high priority, and funding needs to be secured soon for this unprecedented research project.
- The BAE briefing document must be presented along with a framework, or paradigm, for understanding this subject. The White House, the National Security Council and apparatus, the Joint Chiefs of Staff, the U.N. Secretary-General and U.N. Security Council, and select other foreign heads of state must be fully briefed with this BAE briefing document. Further, at the time this data is conveyed to them, we must not fail to present two other essential assessments:
    1. A frank but brief discussion of the disinformation process, and how they and others may be targeted for disinformation on this and related matters. In particular, we must be concerned for the potential of data devoid of a framework being later placed by certain entities into a false framework, which is specifically designed to prompt a negative, hostile or violent military reaction to the presence of a false "ET threat." (See below)
    2. A comprehensive assessment and framework for evolving future inter-planetary relations, to be implemented as world integration and unity progresses. We must not assume that these matters have already been thought out, since many if not all of these leaders have been largely not informed of the subject matter.

In general, we must not assume that key policy makers have been accurately briefed on this matter. We can assume, however, that they have directly or indirectly, at least through mass population psychological conditioning, if not more personally, been dis-informed. A responsible approach to this, it is my opinion, requires that we present the scientific data along with a well-conceived assessment and set of recommendations.

- Recent meetings with a foreign head of state, as well as with certain military and intelligence personnel, reveals that a 1989 Announcement attempt apparently failed because:

1. The announcement itself was ill-conceived and alarmist, and would have presented a spin indicating a false "ET threat."

2. A covert entity, operating with advanced psycho-electronic capabilities, created a false but convincing ET intervention, which ended the announcement process.

In any case, the lesson from this is clear: This information must be presented in a truthful, positive framework, and we must be aware, and inform various leaders (see above) of the risk of retrograde factions attempting to derail the process.

I do not feel that it is productive to dwell on these matters, and they certainly do not need to be gone into with any detail publicly. But we must be aware of them.

We have learned (and I have experienced on at least one occasion first hand) that certain covert entities possess technological means for inducing programmable experiences electronically. The so-called MK ULTRA and other psycho-electronic mind control technologies are fully operational. A reliable navy source informs me that off-the -shelf capability exists that, if desired, an individual could be induced remotely to "have a personal conversation with their personal God, and he would believe it was real." We should, therefore, be aware of the extent to which disinformation and psychological warfare may be applied, and not be deceived by it. Moreover, we must quietly assure that our leaders and policy makers are not misled.

We have also learned that capability exists to launch a false but convincing ET hostile action, which could result in certain unfortunate actions by the military, the NSC, the U.N., and others. This must be averted at all costs, since such an event would send us down a path of unwarranted conflict.

Finally, we have learned that, unfortunately, advanced and classified weapons are operational and have been already used to fire upon, and in at least one event destroy, ET spacecraft. I would dismiss this account, except it has come to me from more that one source deemed reliable. If there is only a 1% chance that this could be true, we must assemble a few elder statesmen to ensure that a "stand down" order is in place to stop these actions. I have recently asked about whether such a stand down order is in place, and was told that it now is, but we must confirm this and assure that no future events of this type occur.

- A significant scientist and astronomer with excellent contacts in the physics, astronomy and SETI fields will be lending his considerable support to our effort, and will arrange briefings within senior ranks of these areas. He will also assist us in pulling together significant new evidence, some from new and important sources within the above mentioned fields of study.

The following comments are personal reflections which I wish to share with you.

The past year has been interesting, to say the least, but it has not been always easy. I have made mistakes, and there have been successes. I hope that you will overlook my shortcomings, and will understand that your help and support is needed, now more than ever.

I must confess that at one point earlier this summer, I was rather inclined to withdraw from this effort altogether, and indeed would have had an extraordinary personal experience not occurred. But it is clear that for whatever reasons we may grasp with our minds, heart and spirit somehow require that we go forward. We are humans, and therefore will make mistakes, but the larger Plan is unfolding and will be fulfilled, notwithstanding our frailties. A largeness of Spirit must inform our every word and action, and only inner guidance will enable us to steer this ship through the turbulent waters ahead.

This is an effort which we must love deeply. Somewhere, deep within us, and within the heart of the universe, a call has gone forward, and somehow we must answer it. I cannot escape this movement within the heart, though perhaps at times I wish I could. We will be tested, but I believe never beyond our capacity. For if we look to the great, universal Spirit, guidance will be there, within our selves and mysteriously appearing in the world around us.

We must not look to our own, finite selves, but to the great Spirit which is informing and quickening this process. No power on Earth, covert or otherwise, can transcend this guidance. We must be assured of the ultimate goodness of our future here on Earth, and keep our vision on the bright, far horizon, while yet being attentive to the path before our feet.

The most, the best, we can do is to allow our individual, finite selves to be at the service of a rapidly unfolding Plan, the Architect of which is infinitely wise and skillful. In a true sense, we need only to get out of our own way, to forget self and follow guidance. Even as it is said in the Mathnavi, a mystical writing: "The death of self is needed here, not rhetoric: Be nothing, then, and walk upon the waves." When we die to self, the Divine will shine through and guide us.

Indeed, we are entering a Day which shall not be followed by night, an era the likes of which the Earth has never seen nor even been capable of visualizing until now. The onset of universal peace is at hand, and the light of this Day is young, and growing. Nor should we be dismayed by the onset of intervening clouds, for they are as nothing and will be burned away with the growing warmth of this light.

We have the blessing and the burden of living in the most potent decade of the most momentous century in the history of Earth. Let us not doubt the vast potential of this time and place, for it has been anticipated for millennia, and Providence will assure its fulfillment. We can only ask ourselves "what can I do to assist in the birth of this new era?" and then strive to fulfill the guidance which follows. And it will follow.

Whenever I try to flee this responsibility, it meets me around the next corner, and demands an answer; and I am sure others of you have had a similar experience. The only answer that I have found is to give myself to it as selflessly as possible, to forget all limitations and move positively forward.

And even those who fear a threat should know this: No threat can overcome the future which awaits the Earth, and no threat, real or imagined or contrived, will deter the Divine Plan. And if real, no threat will be overcome by the old ways, but only a new way of creating peace will succeed in this new time. Forget the missiles. Forget the many means of conflict, for only the heart filled with the spirit of love will ensure the undying peace which assuredly awaits us.

Let no doubt deter you; let no fear detract you. This is not the time for timidity or withdrawal, but for action, rightly guided. Ten years from now, we will not recognize the Earth, so great will be its transformation. With strength and yet with humility, let us move together into the light of this new world, unfettered by either our own failings, or the sounds from the fading night.

Personally, this has presented something of a crisis for me, and for my family. The crushing hours spent in my medical practice, the long and exhausting hours spent on CSETI work, and the usual family responsibilities, altogether are overwhelming. Something simply must go, and we have decided that, at least for a couple of years, it should be my medical career. Hence, I am resigning my position at the hospital, and rather on faith, will move forward full time with this effort. Emily and I are willing to make this sacrifice, and while we are unsure where our personal means of support will come from, we have always believed that "Where God guides, God provides..."

Let us pray for one another, and look always to what is possible. Knowing that there is one Mind shining from the brow of every life form in creation, let us work towards the fulfillment of a universal peace, where indeed there will be one universe, inhabited by one people.

I look forward to working with you in this effort, and hope you will let me know how you can assist in this important undertaking.

Assuring you of my prayers and abiding affection,

Faithfully,

Steven M. Greer, M.D.
Director of CSETI

46

Operational Readiness And The UFO/ETI Subject

22 August 1998

Why Military And National Security Leaders Have A Need To Know

Abstract:
Key military and national security leaders have been inadequately informed on the UFO/ETI subject due to its management under Unacknowledged Special Access Projects (USAPS). This lack of information has resulted in substantial national security risks. The risk of inadequate and/or dangerous actions by uninformed or misinformed leaders is greatly increased by the lack of in-depth briefings and discussions on this subject. Key areas of operational readiness are thus placed "at risk" by these leaders being dangerously uninformed or misinformed on such matters as the following:

- Use of Alien Reproduction Vehicles (ARVs) in false indications and warnings (I &W) scenarios.
- The unexpected appearance and disappearance of ET vehicles with super-luminal speed (faster than light) capabilities.
- Unanticipated ET concern over deployment of space-based military and other assets.

Senior military leaders and senior national security leaders, including the Joint Chiefs of Staff, the National Security Council, Senior Watch Officers in the National Military Command Center, key Congressional leaders, the President, the Secretary of Defense, the Director of Central Intelligence, among others, clearly have a need-to-know regarding the issues above.

Background and Introduction:

Since 1990, CSETI, a non-profit research organization based in the United States, has been conducting original research into the subject of UFOs and Extraterrestrial Intelligence (ETI). In 1991, an initial Comprehensive Assessment was completed and since that time CSETI has been investigating the subject through real-time field expeditions throughout the world and through the identification of scientific evidence and information sources with direct knowledge of the subject. Sources for our information and subsequent assessments include:

- Direct, real-time observation of UFOs/ET Objects via field research teams deployed throughout the world
- Collection of retrospective evidence with thousands of case reports, including military and civilian pilot encounters, military and civilian radar contact with these objects, landing trace cases, photographic and videotape evidence and thousands of pages of declassified government documents.
- Extensive interviews with several dozen scientists, military and civilian witnesses in intelligence and other programs and civilian research witnesses who have been involved in covert programs. These witnesses have had direct, personal knowledge of UFO/ETI events and covert programs, including the retrieval and reverse-engineering of ET spacecraft and the covert applications of technological breakthroughs resulting from possession of these spacecraft.

The above sources and research have resulted in a number of assessments regarding the subject in general and national security implications in particular. These are provided as separate attachments to this document.

Overview of UFO-Related USAPs

While tight compartmentalization of intelligence and programs is often needed to maintain security of sensitive operations, excessive classification and compartmentalization poses a threat to national security and military readiness and is contrary to Presidential directives. In the case of the UFO/ETI subject, extreme secrecy and multiple levels of special compartmentalization have existed since the 1940s. This extreme secrecy, together with the special nature of the technologies involved, has resulted in a potentially dangerous situation with respect to lack of oversight of actions not in the national interest, significant degradation in military readiness to deal with events related to ETI/UFO and total lack of Congressional oversight.

The nature of the covert entity/USAP which currently manages the UFO matter is described in the attached paper (See "Unacknowledged" on page 285.) Briefly, this unusual USAP has the following characteristics:

- Global in scope
- Multiple levels of sub-compartmentalization
- Primarily based in the civilian, privatized contracting/work-for-others sectors
- Runs parallel to and generally separate from conventional government, military and intelligence programs, including other sensitive USAPs/black projects
- Exists as a hybrid entity which draws from high technology corporations and compartmented, government, intelligence and military operations, but which in effect functions as an independent, separate entity
- Apparently, is controlled by no single branch of conventional government, military service or agency
- In general, access to this project is by project-controlled inclusion and access has little to do with the individual's position in government, military rank or position in the traditional (constitutional) chain of command
- After nearly 60 years of studying advanced ET technologies from retrieved ET devices, the group which controls this USAP possesses substantial technologies which may present a threat to conventional military assets and to world security in general.
- Funding for these operations is derived both from the so-called "black budget" and from "creative," non-governmental sources.
- Maintenance of secrecy/control over this project has been at all costs and has consistently violated legal, constitutional oversight and checks and balances and the rights of U.S. citizens.

Discussions with a sitting Director of Central Intelligence, senior White House staff, senior members of Congress serving on key, relevant committees, senior military staff in the US and UK, among others, has shown that access to projects related to UFOs/ETI is not related to position or constitutional law. Five star Admiral and former UK Minister of Defense, Lord Hill-Norton has confirmed that a similar arrangement exists in the United Kingdom. Directed inquiry by such officials has not resulted in disclosure, even when the request originated from the office of the President of the United States.

Why Key Military and National Security Leadership Need to Know

There are several inter-related aspects of the UFO/ETI issue which necessitate key military, intelligence and national security leaders knowing about this matter. Failure by such leaders to be adequately informed has resulted in a situation wherein important decisions and actions may be made which could result in extremely undesirable outcomes. The capabilities of the UFO/ETI USAP allow for widespread deception of chain-of-command leadership and for surprise scenarios which could be catastrophically misinterpreted.

Moreover, while there is no objective evidence that the non-human life forms behind the genuine ET events are at all hostile towards the Earth or humanity in general, events could be—and more importantly we understand have been—negatively misinterpreted, leading to unwarranted human military actions against such ET assets. Such actions constitute a genuine world security threat about which conventional military and civilian leadership is unaware. In order to avoid the potential for future human military actions which could lead to a dangerous escalation of events, it is imperative that military and national security leadership be adequately informed on this subject.

Below is a brief summary of scenarios and activities which illustrate why such leaders have an immediate need to know on this matter:

- Misidentification of UFO/ET assets. Since there are both genuine ET and look-alike human engineered ARV (Alien Reproduction Vehicle) assets, the risk for confusion and misidentification is real. Such confusion could result in actions which could then lead to unintended results. (See also False Indications and Warnings below.)

Surprise by ET object. In the past, senior military commanders have been surprised by the sudden appearance of ET objects and have taken hostile actions towards them. For example, in October of 1981, such an object appeared off of the eastern seaboard, triggering pandemonium in the U.S. Atlantic Fleet (CINCLANTFLT) Command Center. This object, estimated 300 feet in diameter and disc shaped, was able to rapidly move, in one radar sweep from an area off the coast of Newfoundland to off the coast of Norfolk, Virginia. During this daylight event, the U.S. Atlantic Fleet Command Center went to Condition Zebra alert ("Stripes") and orders were given by NORAD to the CINC, ADM Harry Train, to identify this object and even force it down if necessary. Fighters were scrambled from land and sea-based forces and, while one fighter got close enough to clearly photograph the object, it moved in the span of one radar sweep from off the coast of Norfolk, Virginia to an area in the Atlantic Ocean near the Canary Islands, turned upward at a 60 degree angle, and left the Earth's atmosphere. This situation, which resulted in surprise to the CINC, chaos on the Command Center Floor, and orders to force down the object (which could have had catastrophic consequences) could have been avoided with concept and scenario briefings to top military leaders and the development of clear "Special Rules of Engagement" (ROEs) for these unique situations.

- Misinterpretation of ET Actions. It is our assessment that more that one ET civilization is involved in reconnaissance of the Earth and in surveillance of global military developments. In the past, ET concern over weapons of mass destruction has led to technological demonstrations at certain strategic sites, such as SAC ICBM facilities at Minot ND in November of 1975, which had its strategic launch capabilities inerted. Similar neutralization, we understand, occurred in the USSR. While such an event would understandably generate human military concern, it is important for such events to be interpreted in a broader context which is non-anthropocentric. While one view may hold that this action demonstrated ET hostility, it is more likely that, given the event's non-violent nature, that it was intended to be a message of great concern over such globally destructive weapon systems. Unless leadership is adequately briefed on this subject, the potential for a catastrophic misinterpretation of ET actions and intentions exists.
- Extraterrestrial concern over space-based military assets. It is our understanding that the ET view of human military assets being placed in space is very unfavorable and that in the recent past certain events have taken place which underscore this ET viewpoint. U.S. Space Command and other military entities dealing with space or which interface with and depend upon space-based assets

need to be aware of this concern. It appears that ET concern is based on the increasing militarization of space, combined with a continued high level of human warfare and violence and the proliferation of weapons of mass destruction. There is also reason to believe that covert USAP programs are targeting ET assets with increasing frequency and efficacy (see below).

- *Multiple* credible first-hand military and intelligence program witnesses have described covert USAP utilization of advanced weapons systems to track, target and destroy ET spacecraft. Such events have apparently increased in frequency and accuracy since the 1980s. If true, this constitutes a grave national and world security crisis about which key leaders have an urgent need to know. In light of the testimony which we have heard, simple denials that such events are not occurring or are somehow justified are not sufficient grounds to dismiss these reports or take a hands-off approach. Key military and national security leaders need to fully investigate this matter and produce a full assessment of the situation for the National Command Authorities (NCA), the Chairman, Joints Chiefs of Staff (CJCS), and key congressional leadership.
- Multiple, military and civilian witnesses involved in covert programs dealing with this subject and having first-hand personal knowledge have corroborated reports of UFO/ETI related USAPS' intent to utilize reverse-engineered ET based technologies to stage (hoax) ET events of a violent nature. The existence of a very powerful covert USAP which possesses extraordinarily advanced technologies capable of materialization/dematerialization, faster-than-light travel, antigravity propulsion and related systems is in itself a direct threat to conventional and constitutional military and national security leadership and control. Such an entity, unless fully under direct, legal and constitutional chain of command oversight, and control, has great potential for abuse, deception and manipulation of traditional governmental leadership. For example, an important intelligence witness has described the planned use of ARVs in a false indications and warnings scenario in which the ARVs would attack conventional military assets to make it *appear* that we were being attacked by hostile ET life forms. If military and national security leaders do not know of such covert human capa-

bilities, they could be deceived by such a scenario and could then issue orders for unwarranted and potentially catastrophic countermeasures against genuine ET assets.

- Sub-electromagnetic, non-linear communications systems of ET origin which interface directly with consciousness and thought have been reverse-engineered by covert USAPs and can be used against civilian and military leadership in False I and W scenarios. Information directly from a foreign head of state suggests that this has already occurred. Such non-linear telemetry systems, which bypass linear time/space and interface directly with mind and thought can be modified to induce hoaxed but very real experiences in target subjects. Senior military and civilian national security leaders need to know about the potential of these systems, thus minimizing the deceptive value of such systems should they be directed against them. (Alleged "Alien Abduction" experiences are largely the result of the misuse of these systems by covert USAPs.)
- NASA, civilian astronomers and other scientists are increasingly concerned about the possibility of an Earth orbit-crossing asteroid or comet impacting the Earth. Teams at JPL and elsewhere have already detected thousands of such Earth orbit-crossing objects within our solar system. Large impacts in the past have created what is now the Gulf of Mexico, Hudson Bay and other geological features on the surface of the Earth. Most scientists agree that it is not a question of "if," but "when," such an impact will take place. Conventional scientists have discussed using nuclear weapons and other conventional means to avert such an impact. However, it is clear that UFO related USAPS possess technologies which are far more advanced and which could be brought to bear on this problem. This is especially true of gravity-altering technologies which could be used to change the mass effect of such an object and move it off of an Earth intersecting course. Since such an impact could potentially terminate human civilization as we know it, senior military and civilian national security leaders should have knowledge of and *access to* such UFO USAP related technologies. Moreover, use of such technologies in space for such a critical and beneficial purpose may be dependent on the perception by ETs that such space deployment would be only for peaceful purposes. We understand that this is not the current perception.

Conclusions

- Disclosure of the reality of the UFO/ETI subject and associated technologies would certainly alter many aspects of life on Earth, including geopolitical relations, technology, economics and the general social order. Military and national security leaders unaware of the subject cannot adequately anticipate the far-reaching implications of such a disclosure and would therefore be unprepared. Since CSETI and others are actively pursuing such a disclosure in the relatively near future, it is important that leaders understand these implications fully and are able to respond to the challenges of such a disclosure in an orderly manner. Should a sudden, undeniable ET event occur, it is even more important that military and national security leaders be informed and are prepared to respond properly to the situation.
- The energy and propulsion technologies associated with ET spacecraft utilize the zero-point field of energy, do not rely on nuclear or internal combustion engines and are therefore non-polluting. One of the great "wild cards" facing the military and national and world security leaders is the eventual exhaustion of fossil fuels and the concomitant decay in the Earth's ecosystem. With the rapid industrialization of China, India and much of the third world, the damage to the Earth's ecosystem will only accelerate exponentially, even as the fuel sources are more rapidly diminished. Currently, we exist as a terminal technological civilization - a serious long term security issue indeed. However, the covert USAP responsible for UFO/ETI matters has already reversed-engineered energy and propulsion systems which render the internal combustion engine obsolete. We estimate that this breakthrough occurred between 1954 and 1957. Ben Rich of Lockheed Skunkworks, prior to his death, confirmed to a CSETI consultant that "we already have the means to travel among the stars, but these technologies are locked up in black projects and it would take an act of God to ever get them out to benefit humanity...." Long term national security planning necessitates the eventual (and preferably near-term) release of these technologies for the benefit of mankind and the preservation of the planet. Certainly national security and military leaders should understand these technologies, which will replace the entire global energy and internal combustion infrastructure. More-

over, they should anticipate the implications related to the release of such technologies so that the transition to sustainable energy systems can be as smooth and peaceful as possible.

These are a few of the national security and military implications of the UFO/ETI subject - any one of which justifies a full briefing to leadership on the subject.

Recommendations

We recommend senior military and national security leaders take the following actions:

- Receive a thorough briefing on the subject by CSETI leadership and military/civilian witnesses
- Fully brief CINCS, and develop special ROEs for ETI/UFO encounters.
- Independently investigate the subject and penetrate USAP operations related to the subject
- Become fully involved in covert projects related to the subject to ensure that such projects are adequately supervised and are under the direct and continuous control of the constitutional chain of command
- Correct and/or restrain any USAPS's covert misuse of advanced technologies or weapon systems related to UFOs.
- Attempt peaceful, cooperative engagement of these life forms and assiduously avoid violent military engagement. CSETI has a prototype project which was been peacefully engaging ETI for over 7 years and suggests that national and international leaders adopt a similar approach
- Carefully consider the deployment of space-based military assets in light of the above information and avoid actions which may be viewed as bellicose or hostile by ET life forms.

CSETI Contact:

- Steven M. Greer, M.D., International Director, CSETI - (540) 456-8302; email: 103275.1472@compuserve.com

This paper was presented at a briefing of very senior Pentagon officials in September, 1998.

47

UFO/ETI Disinformation

November 15, 1994

Implications for National Security and International Security Policy Makers

A Confidential Briefing

Abstract

In advance of a confirmed announcement concerning the detection of ET life forms, it is important for national and international security policy makers to be aware of the risks to the decision-making process created by certain types of sophisticated disinformation and covert interventions. These include, but are not limited to: induction of psychoelectronic experiences; mass psychological conditioning with false information; targeting of certain key leaders with individualized disinformation; the staging of a false yet convincing ET threat. Awareness of these forms of disinformation by key policy-makers would help minimize the risk of unfortunate events resulting from decisions influenced unduly by covert interventions.

Background

CSETI Project Starlight efforts directed towards the public confirmation of the detection of ET life forms have resulted in the discovery of a number of covert activities which may jeopardize decision-making within the national and international security communities. Since some of these decision-making processes may be adversely affected well in advance of a public announcement on the subject, we at CSETI feel morally bound to issue this briefing to advise policy-makers of certain risks. Failure by certain key policy-makers (especially the White House, the National Security Council, the Joint Chiefs of Staff and the U.N. Security Council) to compensate adequately for these risks could result in the adoption of policies and actions harmful to global security and to the future of interplanetary relations. This briefing is designed to provide information regarding specific disinformation processes and their related risks to national and international security.

Overview

Disinformation is false information which is deliberately provided to groups or individuals for the purpose of obfuscating an issue and/or effecting a specific psychological response (such as denial, disbelief, fear, ridicule, et cetera). Covert attempts designed to minimize accurate knowledge of UFOs and ETI have used disinformation and psychological warfare techniques for over 40 years, and these techniques and related technologies have become increasingly sophisticated and effective, especially since the 1960s. The most effective disinformation is information which is related to a truth, at least in part, but which is then embellished and deliberately distorted by combining disinformation with the information. The presence of a minimal but adequate degree of truth enables the false information to be more readily accepted, or for the intended psychological response to occur.

Disinformation may be divided into two broad categories: Passive Disinformation, which is false information placed into individual or public awareness via conventional communication means; and Active Disinformation, which involves false experiences which are induced and which result in a very sophisticated manipulation of individual and group perspectives and experiences. Examples of each types are given below.

Passive Disinformation

Denial of UFO Reports

Providing false data concerning UFO events

Engaging certain scientists or authorities to ridicule the subject matter and its proponents

Providing false, misleading or slanderous information about UFO researchers and organizations

Providing information to the public which induces fear, denial, skepticism, repulsion, etc.

Active Disinformation

Hoaxing of certain events to entrap or embarrass researchers or organizations

Use of active psychoelectronic devices to induce false abduction experiences which control individual and public attitudes towards ETI

Use of technologies to simulate false ET hostile action, to affect both policy-makers and the general public

Early covert operations relied primarily on passive disinformation. However, in the 1960s and 1970s, as more evidence of ETI activity made its way into the public domain and awareness, active disinformation began to play a more dominant role. Most of the active disinformation currently in use is designed to:

1. Create a scenario which induces fear or rejection of the phenomenon
2. Bury real UFO/ETI activity under a mountain of superficially similar yet qualitatively different false events, especially so-called abductions and cattle mutilations
3. Influence public perception and governmental policy-makers to conclude (falsely) that there is an "ET threat" which we must fight

Active disinformation has become more effective as increasingly sophisticated technologies have been developed and perfected in the US and Russia.

Covert special operations, funded by "black budgets" and private sources, have effectively dominated and polluted the database in two popular areas: abductions and cattle mutilations.

Abductions:

Alleged abductions of humans by UFOs have been reported since the 1960s. We at CSETI doubt that "abductions" as they are currently understood are actually occurring, but that a very small number of people *have* been taken on board ET craft for reasons not yet fully understood. No evidence exists to suggest that such events are harmful or of a hostile nature. Unfortunately, the real on-board cases have been buried beneath a large volume of human-induced pseudo-abduction events, designed to negatively affect public perception and credibility of the phenomenon. These "events" are being induced by a advanced psychoelectronic technologies which can remotely target an individual or group and create a convincing but false ET experience.

The existence of psychoelectronic and other technologies has been confirmed to CSETI by certain military, intelligence and high-technology sources who contract with government agencies. These psychoelectronic devices are much more advanced and operational than most would imagine, and have gone through several generations of evolution and improvement. Policy-makers must not be deceived by these reports, nor should decisions be influenced in any way by them. Since the currently available information is hopelessly distorted by these falsely induced events, it cannot be relied upon as a source of truth for policy formulation. CSETI has learned that a number of researchers in this area have similarly concluded that 80-90% of abduction events are disinformation or misidentification of other unusual phenomena.

Cattle Mutilations

Alleged cattle experiments by ET craft (misnamed "mutilations" for disinformation purposes) have been reported since the 1960s. The primary scientists and researchers in this area have confirmed that at least 80% of these cases are actually decoy cases created by covert operations and have nothing to do with UFO/ETI activity. CSETI's assessment is that the real cases are environmental and genetic research related to radiation and chemical pollution and their effect on advanced mammalian systems. We seriously doubt a sinister or hostile motive behind these relatively rare actual occurrences, and feel that the false decoy cases are designed to create disinformation, to conceal the actual cases, and to create an atmosphere of fear around the subject. Policy-makers should not be adversely influenced by these reports, or be deceived by them in any way.

Policy-makers need to be aware of the potential for advanced technological disinformation, both as it affects databases and as it could potentially be targeted towards policy-makers themselves. CSETI would caution against undue fear in this regard, but do feel that senior policy-makers should be aware of the potential for this type of disinformation and how it could be directed at them, including both active and passive targeting.

We have also learned that technologies exist to support the simulation of false hostile ET events, designed specifically to influence policy-makers in a time of crisis, or to "spin" any announcement and disclosure process in the direction of uniting the world against a "common alien threat." Military and civilian policy-makers must not be deceived by such events, since decisions based on such pseudo-UFO events would likely result in negative actions which would be unwarranted. The vast and profound implications of our future relations with ET civilizations must not be influenced by this type of disinformation, since it would be designed to place the Earth on a path of inter-planetary conflict and would subvert the potential for future peaceful and beneficial relations.

In summary, a number of advanced disinformation modalities exist which policy-makers need to take into consideration as they evaluate data or receive briefings from traditionally covert sources. CSETI and its affiliated scientists and researchers are committed to obtaining reliable data by way of direct, real-time observation of and interaction with the ETI phenomenon. We feel that empirical research of this type is more useful, accurate and reliable than other secondary means which are prone to disinformation contamination.

48

Project Starlight Update: Failed 1989 ET Announcement

A very important development has occurred which I believe directly impacts our strategy regarding Project Starlight.

I first learned of the following series of events in July, 1994, and have delayed writing this so that sufficient analysis and confirmation could be attempted. This information underscores the urgent need to complete the collection of evidence and for this evidence to be presented in a framework of pursuing peaceful inter-planetary relations. As you will see, my early fears that a cult of secrecy surrounding this issue would result in a conflict-oriented response to ETI appear to have been well-founded.

The source for the following information, while known to me, will remain unspecified in this written memo. He is a foreign head of state, however, and has intimate and personal knowledge of the events described here. Parts of his account have been independently confirmed by me. I have no reason to believe that this person is fabricating this account, although I will admit that accepting it on face value is difficult.

The events are as follows:

In 1989, a group of world leaders numbering about 80, were planning an announcement concerning the detection and confirmed contact with ETI. These leaders included President Bush, the Secretary General of the U.N. Perez de Cuellar, President Gorbachev, and others. Apparently the tone for this event was set back in 1986 when President Reagan stated to Gorbachev, in effect, that "wouldn't our job to create world peace and unity be easier if we had a common alien threat to unite against and fight." President Reagan repeated this sentiment publicly on 5-6 occasions, and it was cited in the NY Times at least once in 1986.

Tragically, from what I can gather, the "spin" which was going to be placed on this event was decidedly alarmist, perhaps even a call to arms, and a number of world leaders were convinced of there being an "alien threat" by the same secret group which has been controlling this subject for a number of years. It appears that the alarmist tone attending this Announcement assured its ultimate failure, and was motivated by an attempt to create world unity out of fear of a "common alien threat." It was, I believe, also motivated by a desire to prop up the collapsing defense, technology and intelligence infrastructures of the U.S. and U.S.S.R., which were headed for an obvious melt-down in light of peace between the two superpowers. Even more alarming, it appears that the alarmist tone of the announcement, as well as that of most civilian sources of information on this subject, has been orchestrated by this secret group so that a certain religious cosmology and paradigm would be reinforced. More on this latter.

After a very late night meeting on this planned announcement, a certain world leader, known to us but left unnamed here, was en route home in a motorcade with a number of other officials when he was suddenly taken on board an ET spacecraft, this being witnessed by a number of other people involved with the announcement. This occurred in fall 1989 in New York City.

While on board this spacecraft, the world leader was told that the planned announcement must not go forward, and that if necessary other world leaders would be taken on board, in significant numbers if necessary. It was made very clear to this person that the ETs would not allow this announcement to occur as planned.

According to my source, this event "blew up in the Bush White House like an atomic bomb", and while Bush was NOT the person taken on board and given this information, apparently some fear existed that he would be next. As a result, the plug was pulled on this planned announcement, and apparently, the control group in charge of this subject buried it into even deeper levels of secrecy and deception, where it remains today.

Predictably, the response to this event was decidedly negative, so much so that my source for this account has used it to try and dissuade us from pursuing the goals of Project Starlight. He earnestly believes that the ETs themselves will stop any attempt to announce their presence to the world's population, and that anyone who attempts it is in grave danger. He is convinced that the ETs do not want their presence known by the world, and will subvert any attempt to reveal it.

My own analysis of all of this is quite the opposite:

- This source is likely a member of PI-40, or whatever the current code is for the secret control group;
- The announcement was halted by the ETs because its basic premise and ulterior motives were inherently flawed. Wisely, they do not want an artificial world unity created out of an alarmist and conflict-oriented Announcement which would serve only the worldview and control issues of PI-40. An announcement which serves to justify a world-wide arms race to face-down the "common alien threat," or which would demonize the ETs to serve a certain religious cosmology and paradigm, should not be allowed. We should all be grateful that the ETs intervened and aborted this scheme.
- Concurrent with the 1989 Announcement and so-called abduction of the world leader, a massive and well documented ET wave began over Belgium, which happens to be NATO headquarters, and the center of European unity. This peaceful series of low altitude sightings, early in the evening and with thousands of military, police and civilian witnesses, would contradict the assessment that the ETs do not wish to be known to the world. The issue is *not* if their presence should be known, but *how* it should be announced. What they are saying to us is that it should not be used as a pretense for propping up the military industrial complex, nor should it be used as a negative source of focus, around which an artificial and fearsome world unity can be contrived.
- PI-40, by being the primary source of information on this subject to certain world leaders, is able to "spin" the data in such a way as to convince these leaders of the "ET threat," even though there is no evidence to support such an assessment. This creates a dynamic where either these leaders agree to keep this subject secret since they have been manipulated into thinking that the "truth is just too awful for the world to take," or if they go forward with an announcement, as they did in 1989 at the close of the cold war, it will be artificially infused with alarm and conflict, and the ETs themselves will stop it!
- Similarly, I have confirmed that the paradigm and motives operating in the civilian UFO community are primarily controlled by this same group, and that the so-called abduction research and other areas of UFO research are manipulated by and are in large part funded by representatives of this entity. By injecting fear and conflict based concepts and "research" into the civilian mass con-

sciousness, an effective psychological warfare program has assured that any announcement would be introduced into a general environment friendly to the assumption of an ET threat.

Recommendations

1. We should continue to assemble the best evidence on this subject for briefing purposes; funds must be located so that a professional evidential package can be created.

2. However, it is clear that evidence alone is useless if it is regarded in a framework of threat and inter-planetary conflict. Therefore all briefings must be accompanied by a review of the principles of interplanetary relations and diplomacy, and the pitfalls of jumping to threat-oriented conclusions must be emphasized. A frank discussion of the historic use of disinformation and psychological warfare must be explored, since I am convinced that any world leader looking into this subject will be targeted by direct and indirect means. We must be reminded also that the data available in the pop culture is hopelessly tainted with the intended spin of PI-40, and that any leader will have been already indirectly "targeted" by this mass consciousness psychological warfare, which is at once insidious and very effective.

3. We will need to overcome objections to any future announcement by emphasizing that the failed announcement of 1989 was flawed in both its premises and ulterior motives, and that a scientifically oriented announcement which avoids alarmist undertones and which presents a hopeful future based on increasing inter-planetary relations will be effective and a positive event for humanity. The risk of any ET intervention in the announcement process will be minimized by avoiding the errors of the 1989 attempt.

4. We must urgently pursue an end to the dysfunctional secrecy and disinformation surrounding this subject. I believe a senior team of elder statesmen must be assembled to avert any further inter-planetary conflict. In the darkness of secrecy, I am afraid the seeds of inter-planetary warfare have already sprouted and have grown into small weeds. If we do not eliminate them soon, we will see them grow to choke off the potentially brilliant future of Earth. I have very good reason to believe that we have already traveled quite far down the path of inter-planetary conflict, and that only level heads and a clear vision towards a peaceful future will avert disaster in our time. Your suggestions in this regard are welcomed.

5. This information directly impacts CSETI research and RMIT efforts. Obviously, so long as PI-40 is determined to spin information in the direction of fear and conflict, and can infiltrate the minds of world leaders and mass consciousness with this perspective, any evidence gathered through RMIT efforts must be disclosed carefully, lest it become the window through which PI-40 launches a campaign of world wide fear and disinformation. Our research results must not be allowed to become the trigger point for unleashing fear and conflict-oriented disinformation from this group.

6. We must inform the President of the United States, the U.N. Secretary General and other world leaders of not only the existence of ETI, but of the disinformation surrounding this subject. We cannot allow these leaders to be the victims of the sort of disinformation and "spin" which others have fallen prey to, and if we do not provide information to them which is truthful, I am convinced others are ready to provide the worst sort of disinformation. In short, if we do not act, others will, and with disastrous results. As an example: The head of state with whom I met in July is so convinced of the malevolence of the ETs, and has demonized them so extremely, that he has blamed them for every world conflict, every set-back in human history since the beginning of life on Earth. This person has access to and rapport with many world leaders. I shudder to think that this perspective is being privately shared with other leaders, and that others are being recruited into a realm of unbridled fear, superstition, and virulent hatred. The fear and hatred which was evinced by this person was so deep and firmly held that I was immediately reminded of the scapegoating and hatred which the Nazis held for the Jewish people in WWII. Unless good and level-headed people act soon, and boldly, we will all live to witness an era of inter-planetary conflict. This possibility is real, and it must be averted. Please convey to me your suggestions of how to proceed at this point.

In closing, I will admit that we have an uphill battle before us. But I believe in the innate goodness of all people, and that there are sufficient people of good-will and vision who can help the truth along and join with us. We cannot afford to allow this most important subject be controlled by a secretive few. But it is up to us to act, or we will cede the dialogue to those who favor conflict over peace, and prejudice over truth.

Wishing you the best of all worlds,
Steven M. Greer, M.D.
Director of CSETI

49

Strategies And Rationale For Changing Government Policy

1994

It is recommended that current government policy on UFOs/ ETI be changed to one of increasing disclosure, openness, and cooperation with civilian researchers. Failure to effect a review and policy change within the next 12–24 months may result in significant unfortunate outcomes insofar as it is likely that both civilian research initiatives (e.g., CSETI RMIT research projects) and imminent ET events will overtake current policy.

A "window of opportunity" exists for the Administration to effect such a change. This unique window exists as the result of the confluence of two significant events:

1. The existing policy of secrecy exists, in part, because of justifiable concerns during the Cold War, which included the control of possible developments *vis-a-vis* ET technology, as well as more general psychological and sociological concerns. The ending of the Cold War provides for a plausible rationale for changing current policy at this time, and would provide the current Administration with an excellent explanation for the public so that past secrecy could be justified, thereby minimizing any embarrassment to past administrations, or to career government, military, and intelligence employees. Since some time has already elapsed since the end of the Cold War, this rationale is highly time sensitive.
2. Since the Clinton Administration is less than one year old, the President, the Secretary of Defense the Director of Central Intelligence, the new Chairman of the Joint Chiefs of Staff and other key government figures will have "plausible deniability" on this issue, so long as a policy change occurs in the first one to two years of the term. After that time, the Administration could be harmed by a late, uncontrolled disclosure since such

> an event would play to the public in one of two equally unacceptable ways: If the Administration claims ignorance on a subject this important, it will be accused of incompetence. And if the Administration admits to knowing about this subject, it will be subject to accusations of unwarranted secrecy, and possibly even "cover-up" by the media and public. At this point in time, the Administration would not be faulted for a one-to two-year delay in disclosure, and may even be viewed heroically by a majority of the American people, inasmuch as a majority of Americans already believe that UFOs are real and are most likely interplanetary craft.

We believe that this "window" provides for an historic opportunity to change current policy and enter a new era of openness on this important subject.

Beyond this, such a policy of openness, with the resulting disclosure of the existence of ET life, could be a world unifying event which would serve the over-arching goal of world peace. Suddenly, the Earth would indeed appear as one homeland inhabited by one people.

In advance of any change in policy, and subsequent disclosures, we would advise a concerted effort to confidentially brief select world leaders, leaders in society (including media, religious, business and academic leaders) and scientific leaders. CSETI, in cooperation with other researchers and organizations, has already begun this process, and welcomes cooperative initiatives from the current Administration.

Furthermore, it is our sincere desire that this matter be handled in such a way that neither the government of the United States nor world society in general will be harmed. We would like to extend our offer to help in this process to the fullest extent possible, and recommend that a dialogue on this subject proceed in a thoughtful yet somewhat urgent manner.

We also recommend that the international community be encouraged to support and expand a worldwide diplomatic and research initiative to establish increasingly open contact between Earth civilization and ET civilizations. CSETI has already established such an initiative and is willing to work openly with the international community to advance this process.

50

List of Government and Military Witnesses to UFO Events and Projects

1998

The following is a brief summary list of some of the top-secret witnesses identified by Dr. Greer. Approximately 150 such military and government witnesses to UFO/ETI events exist.

Witness A: Captain of a navy contract vessel in charge of retrieving ICBM test missiles in the south Atlantic, August 1963. During one evening, UFO seen on radar and then abruptly disappeared. Following morning, the captain was vectored to the place where the UFO vanished and they found an ejection pod, approximately 6 feet by 6 feet, containing three ET biological entities (EBEs): Each ET was clad in a one piece flight suit, was about 40 inches tall, olive complexion, 4 digits, etc. This witness handled the EBEs and has detailed information concerning their morphology, how they were taken off of his ship by a navy nuclear submarine and how the ET ejection pod was transferred to another surface ship.

Witness B: MSM; a naval worker at Atlantic Command, Norfolk, with a top-secret, SCI (Special Compartmentalized Intelligence) clearance, October 1981. Present during a prolonged encounter off the eastern US seaboard of a 300-foot UFO, disc shaped, which came in from space, and was monitored on radar (multiple) and KH-11 spy satellites. This witness was in the control room at Atlantic Command during the entire event. The UFO was confirmed (by hotline) to be neither Soviet nor US. Admiral X (known to us) then gave the order to force down or destroy the object, and military jets were scrambled from land and sea-based carriers in the Atlantic. The UFO propulsion was so extraordinary that in ONE sweep of the radar screen, the disc would move from off the coast of Newfoundland, to the area of Jacksonville Florida. One jet briefly got close enough to photograph the object (clear conditions, unlimited visibility). This photograph was later enlarged and shown on large screen in the Atlantic Command for Admiral X. This witness was present throughout the encounter and chase, and subsequently saw the photograph of the huge metallic disc.

Witness C: Major GF, Air Force Intelligence (21st Air Force Intel) at McGuire Air Force Base NJ, November 1978, came in to work one morning and found the control room in chaos. He was informed that a UFO had violated the perimeter of the base the previous night, and that an ET was shot and killed outside on the tarmac. He was informed that he was to brief the general of the base that morning. Major GF collected information on the event and prepared to brief the general, but subsequently "Blue Berets" from Wright-Patterson AFB in Dayton Ohio flew in and took over the operation. An Air Force C-141 transport came and took the ET body (deceased) to Wright-Patterson AFB. Witness D is an MP who guarded the ET body prior to disposition and stood near the body (Witness D is NOT known to Witness C).

Witness E: Edwards Air Force Base Air Traffic Controller, present during long and detailed encounter with up to seven UFOs over the Edwards facility in 1965. Controller had UFOs on radar for over FOUR HOURS and had jets scrambled to pursue. Each time "lock-on" occurred with on-board jet radar, the UFOs would disappear and instantly reappear in another area of the sky. Also noted landing event of UFO at one point. We have located and possess the previously scrambled tape recording of the air traffic control conversations with jet pilots and others about the encounter. The tape recording corroborates the account of this important witness.

Witness F: Soviet Cosmonaut PP, most decorated Soviet cosmonaut, has had multiple UFO encounters and sightings as both a pilot and cosmonaut. He is willing to describe these in detail.

Witness G: Sandia National Laboratories Engineer who directly worked with and knew of programs studying ET materials and technologies for reverse-engineering tasks. This witness also has knowledge of security surrounding such ET technology transfer projects and specifics of types of devices studied with applications.

Witness H: Captain GB, a navy pilot and captain who in 1951 was flying a group of Navy VIPs across the north Atlantic when he and his co-pilot saw what looked like a small city in the middle of the ocean. They contacted Gander radar which confirmed the object on radar. The UFO moved in 1-2 seconds from a distance of 25 miles to directly in front of the plane. Auto-pilot was disengaged to avoid a collision. Object flew along beside them and them took off at extraordinary speed and was out of range very quickly. Substantial electromagnetic effects from the craft occurred, including gyroscope spinning wildly out of control when the UFO was very near. Estimated size about 300 feet diameter. Corroborating official government documents and report of the events have been obtained by the pilot and are now in our possession.

Witness I and Witness J: TWO separate witnesses, unknown to each other, who at different times and at different places, saw NASA photographs with UFO or ET facilities (moon). Witness I was present at Johnson Space Center, working under contract with Ford Aerospace, and directly saw clear day time photograph from a satellite with a disc shaped UFO, which cast a shadow on the Earth beneath it. When she asked what they would do with the photo (she wrongly assumed it would be released to the public) she was told that it, like others, would be altered and the UFO would be removed from the image prior to release to non-secure NASA or other agency use. Witness I saw strips of film showing extensive artificial structures on the dark side of the moon which were there result of the Lunar Orbiter overflights.

Witness K: Major SL, a respected lawyer, was an Army cryptographer in the Pentagon 1959-61. He was shown metal samples of debris from the crash of an ET craft in New Mexico in the late 1940s, and it was demonstrated to him the extraordinary properties of the material. He saw the ET writing on the debris and was told it was being studied by Army cryptographers, but that they had not (in 1959) broken the code. He also had confirmed to him then President Eisenhower's interest in the subject, that he knew of the subject, but that he was being left out of substantial information dealing with ET technology programs. Major SL had a top-secret clearance and continues to possess a top secret clearance as an Army reserve Major.

Witness L: Counter-Intelligence Corp (CIC) officer from the 1940s who was directly at the site of a crashed ET device and who directly saw the device and the EBEs which had died at the site of the event.

Witness M: DD, Air Force Office of Special Investigations, very decorated officer with detailed knowledge of recent covert programs related to the subject of UFOs and who has been in an underground storage facility at Fort Huachuca AZ (Army Intelligence Headquarters) where he has personally seen multiple retrieved ET craft and ET bodies in storage. He has knowledge of the nature of the ultra-secret group which manages the UFO matter. Witness M is a very credible witness who is seriously afraid of being identified and whose identity will need to remain secret (disguised).

Witness N: Lt. Col. JW, a highly respected Air Force officer and public relations official, present at NE air force base in 1969 during a prolonged encounter with large, silent triangular UFOs which overflew area of base with strategic nuclear assets. Was on base radar and seen by others in the area. As public information officer, has knowledge of how such events were/are denied, covered up and "spun."

Witness O: Cosmonaut MP, USSR, highly decorated test pilot and cosmonaut with multiple unmistakable sightings and encounters while working as a test pilot and cosmonaut.

Witness P: Air Force Colonel PC, involved with covert programs related to retrieval and study of crashed ET craft, including extensive knowledge of applications of reverse-engineered ET technologies and covert management and disinformation on the subject. Also had assignments with the National Security Council and other intelligence and military programs, and has impeccable credentials.

Witness Q: KS, US Air Force career air traffic controller and radar operator with top secret clearance, present at Minot ND Strategic Air Command (ICBM) base who had multiple extraordinary encounters with UFOs on radar and documented maneuverability of shocking proportions such as instant vertical accelerations to >5000 m.p.h. straight up, against the force of gravity, etc.

Witness R: Mercury Astronaut and American hero Gordon Cooper, had clear sighting of disc shaped UFO 1950s and also had his squadron film a landed UFO at Edwards Air Force Base. Film was flown on the general's plane to the Pentagon and was never seen again.

Witness S: Admiral LHN (five star admiral) and head of British Ministry of Defense (MOD) and MI-5, MI-6, is an inverse witness. That is, he is willing to go on record that he knows the subject is real but that as MOD head he was kept in the dark about projects related to the subject, even though he knows now that they were on-going during his term in office. This inverse witness provides extraordinary insight into the depth of secrecy surrounding the subject. As one of the most decorated military officers of the 20th century, his insights are historic and compelling and expose the unprecedented level of secrecy related to this subject.

Witness T: MS, USAF Radar operator and air traffic control officer present during multiple UFO craft over-flights at the Klamath Falls OR Keno site in 1972; confirms that NORAD at Cheyenne Mountain CO would "hand-off" the UFOs routinely and provide a "heads up" warning that they were coming, and ask that military traffic be routed around the path of the speeding UFOs. Also later present at a very low altitude event, on radar, in Ohio, which resulted in police car chase of the UFO through the countryside.

NOTE: There are multiple additional witnesses equal to those listed above, but we have listed these as they represent various military and intelligence operations over a wide span of time and place. All witnesses are willing to sign statements that their information is truthful and that they would be willing to testify under oath before Congress regarding these events and programs. —SG

51

Evaluating The Validity Of National Security Oaths Related To UFOs/ETs

21 October 1996

A number of first hand military, intelligence and government-associated witnesses to covert projects dealing with UFOs and Extraterrestrial Intelligence (ETI) have been identified by CSETI's Project Starlight effort. Over the past three years, we have located several dozen such potential witnesses as part of a comprehensive strategy to collect adequate evidence for a global, definitive disclosure on this subject. The story which these important government witnesses can tell will make a credible, undeniable case for the reality of UFOs and the existence of ET life forms in proximity to the Earth.

One of the persistent obstacles to this testimony coming out into the public arena has been the issue of so-called national security oaths and restrictions placed on these witnesses. Some feel that they are not free to speak unless "released" from these national security oaths and restrictions, and so we have been working to encourage Congress and the White House to take actions which would remove these restrictions.

In the summer of 1995, a number of these witnesses gathered at a witnesses summit, and we all signed a letter to President Clinton asking him to take actions leading to the release of these restrictions. While receipt of this letter was acknowledged by a special assistant to the President, we still await specific action from the executive branch of the US government.

With this said, it is important to visit the question of whether or not such national security oaths and restrictions are themselves legally valid.

We have compelling witness testimony that the operations dealing with this subject currently exist, and have existed for several decades, outside of normal governmental projects. Members of the Project Starlight Team have met with very senior members of the Administration, Congress, the Joint Chiefs of Staff, the CIA and other relevant government agency operatives. The picture which emerges from these discussions is that of an operation dealing with UFOs which is functioning outside of the normal channels of government, as it is usually considered. Indeed, we have found that the most senior levels of the executive branch, Congress, the military etc. are totally out of the loop on this extraordinary matter.

This then brings up the sobering question of who is in the loop, and under what authorization are such projects operating? It is our assessment that for the large part, these operations do not fall under any constitutionally sanctioned avenues of authorization, and as such are, perforce, illegal.

Aside from the lack of oversight and authorization from the executive branch and Congress, these operations have, from time to time, engaged in deceptive practices which have frustrated the organs of constitutionally legal inquiries and democratic processes. Any such operation which behaves in this fashion unilaterally removes itself from the inherent legality and protection which exists for projects which are consonant with constitutional law.

This being the case (we are eager—nay, desperate—for someone to prove otherwise...) all of the so-called "national security oaths" and other "restrictions" placed on military, intelligence and government contract workers are null and void. That is, they appear to have no legal validity since the operations for which they were obtained are themselves illegal. In a constitutional democracy, it is a basic requirement of law that such operations be constitutionally legal, and if they are not, then all that flows from them—including such "oaths"—are illegal and therefore non-binding. *If* these operations are legal, nobody in the Congress, executive branch or senior military with whom we have spoken knows of it. The production of a single current executive order or congressional directive authorizing these projects, which can be independently verified, would convince us otherwise.

More than one covert contact has told us that, indeed, any such witnesses can and should speak out at the right time and place since no legal entity would—or legally could—do anything about it. We agree.

Beyond this, it is the legal, moral and patriotic duty of such witnesses to come together, and at the highest, best and most credible venue possible, speak out in unison regarding the truth on this matter. Granted, if only one or two such persons come forward, the case will be weak, and the risk will be unacceptable. But if ten, twenty or more such witnesses come together, and united, resolve to share their information and experiences on this subject, then a definitive case will be made, and a great service to the world and their country will be fulfilled.

The return of this matter to the legal channels of government and the deliberation of the people is one of the great unfulfilled tasks of the post cold war era. Over half a decade has elapsed since the end of the cold war, and there can no longer be a justification (if there ever was) for this type of extraordinary secrecy and covert agenda. Both national and world security requires that this matter be returned to the world community as soon as possible.

We recommend that men and women of vision, courage and dedication join with us in fulfilling this task. Far from being a legal violation of "security oaths," the public testimony by such witnesses is a highly moral and legal act. Further, is it not true that the continuation of this secrecy itself is illegal and immoral, given the inherent unconstitutionality of such programs? Credible witnesses, joining together and providing their testimony in a united strategy can return this subject to legal oversight and control, and thereby enable the people of our country and of the world to begin the public deliberations which should have occurred 50 years ago.

52

Points Supporting An Executive Order

To Release Witnesses From National Security Oaths And To Declassify Documents Related To UFO/ET

March 1995

I. Such an Executive Order (EO) would permit witnesses to speak openly about the historical aspects of the subject without fear of legal action against them. If no substantive information is forthcoming from such witnesses, then at least the "air would be cleared" on this issue, and if major disclosures are forthcoming then an end to inappropriate secrecy would be effected.

II. Should significant disclosures occur without an EO the President would be viewed in one of two equally damaging ways:

If the President and Executive Branch of the US Government maintain that they did not know anything about a subject this important, Presidential stature and credibility would be significantly damaged.

If the President and Executive Branch maintain after such an unsanctioned disclosure that they knew of the subject, but were not connected to the disclosures, the President may be accused of supporting a cover-up, which would be unfair in light of the actual facts of how this subject has been covertly handled.

III. An EO would restore public faith in government in the long run, since such an order would be seen as an act of support of democratic principles, as opposed to the maintenance of the covert status quo.

IV. The EO would fully utilize the powers of the Presidency to terminate certain "black projects" activities which appear to be operating out of the constitutional chain of command. While certain aspects of reverse engineering of ET technology (and other matters) may not be fully accessed through this EO it would enable definitive witness testimony to be disclosed. Efforts to keep the President, the Executive Branch in general and the Congress "out of the loop" would thereby be neutralized.

V. Provided that the disclosure process (as conceived by Project Starlight) avoids xenophobic, fear-inducing and militaristic overtones, the EO would set events in motion which would usher in a new era of global awareness and unity. The world community could begin the long awaited dialogue on the implications and promises of initiating early interplanetary relations.

VI. In summary, the risks of not providing an Executive order on this issue far outweigh the risks of doing so. The benefits of such an issuance are numerous and far-reaching, and would be viewed as a just and moral Presidential act by peoples around the world.

53

Unless Otherwise Directed

15 November 1996

To: President William Jefferson Clinton
Vice President Al Gore
National Security Advisor Tony Lake
Secretary of Defense William Perry
Secretary of State Warren Christopher
DCI John Deutch
General Shalikashvili,
Chairman, Joint Chiefs of Staff
Mr. Arlen Specter,
Chairman, Senate Intelligence Committee
Mr. Larry Combast,
Chairman, House Intelligence Committee
Mr. Strom Thurmond,
Chairman, Senate Armed Services Committee
Mr. Floyd Spence,
Chairman, House National Security Committee
Dr. Daniel Golden, Director of NASA
FBI Director Louis Freeh
Attorney General Janet Reno

From: Steven M. Greer, M.D.,
Director of CSETI

Re: Planned Disclosure on the UFO/ET Subject and National Security Oaths

The CSETI Project Starlight initiative has now identified several dozen former and current military, intelligence and defense contractor related witnesses to UFO/ETI events and projects. As set out in a number of documents and briefings (see enclosures) it is our intention to have these important witnesses provide open, public testimony on this matter in the very near future.

In the summer of 1995, we requested that the President take appropriate steps to allow these witnesses to speak openly, without civil, military or other penalties. Since then, there has been an exponential growth in the number of such witnesses who wish to come forward. Some of them are elderly, and suffering from serious medical conditions. We feel that these patriotic and courageous heroes of our country—who very much wish to tell their fellow citizens the truth on this matter—must not take this information to their graves. Therefore, we are asking from you a clear determination regarding their freedom to speak openly on this subject.

Over the past three years, we have found that members of Congress, the Executive Branch, military and intelligence leaders have not been briefed on this important matter, and that operations related to the subject exist as 'unacknowledged' special access projects. Most operations exist in the private aspects of the military industrial sector, with apparently extra- constitutional funding and oversight.

As such, and until established otherwise to our satisfaction, we regard these operations, and all so-called 'security oaths' derived from them, as illegal, and therefore non-binding for these witnesses mentioned above.

Therefore, *Unless Otherwise Directed By 1 January* 1997, we will move forward with a series of events whereby these witnesses may provide open, public testimony. If we do not hear from you, or if we hear that you concur, we will proceed with a public disclosure after that date. Only if you notify us specifically that such witnesses to UFO/ETI related matters are still bound to silence will our plans for a disclosure by them be altered. As mentioned in previous briefings and documents to members of the Administration, the military, the Congress and others, it is our intent to effect this disclosure in a way which is scientific, forward looking and hopeful. It is not our intent to cause instability for our nation or the world, but, rather, to mitigate the clear dangers which current covert management of this issue presents. We invite your advice, assistance and support in this process of disclosure on a matter which is arguably the most important of the twentieth and early twenty first centuries.

Testimony from these witnesses will include but not be limited to:

- Retrieval of disabled ET devices and ET life forms
- Reverse-engineering projects related to ET technology
- Reconnaissance and tracking of UFO/ET vehicles
- Covert projects related to the subject
- Confirmation of military/UFO encounter cases
- The nature and scope of disinformation programs related to the subject

We hope to hear from you regarding this matter as soon as possible.

Thank you for your attention to this request for a determination on the status of these witnesses as it relates to providing public testimony during 1997.

Respectfully,

Steven M. Greer, M.D.
Director of CSETI

54

Letter of January 1, 1997

1 January 1997

At 12 A.M. 1 January 1997, the deadline expired for US Government correction of our previously stated position that military, intelligence and other government related witnesses to UFO events/projects were free to speak openly of their knowledge and experiences.

In a letter dated 15 November 1996, CSETI Project Starlight stated the position that, since projects related to UFOs exist and have existed outside legal constitutional oversight and control, that all security oaths related to such projects are null and void. The letter stated that, *unless otherwise directed*, that this assessment would be regarded as accurate and that all such government witnesses would be free to speak openly as of 1 January 1997.

This letter was sent to, and acknowledgment of receipt has been obtained, from:

President Bill Clinton
Vice-President Al Gore
National Security Advisor Tony Lake
Secretary of Defense William Perry
Secretary of State Warren Christopher
Director of Central Intelligence John Deutsch
Chairman, Joint Chiefs of Staff, General Shalikashvili
Chairman Senate Intelligence Committee Arlen Specter
Chairman House Intelligence Committee Larry Combast
Chairman Senate Armed Services Comm. Strom Thurmond
Chairman House National Security Committee Floyd Spence
Director of NASA Daniel Goldin
FBI Director Louis Freeh
Attorney General Janet Reno

Additionally, this document has been sent to the US Supreme Court and acknowledgment of receipt is pending.

The letter is attached to this file. Numerous background and position papers were enclosed with this letter, including a detailed listing of agencies, entities, corporations, and covert facilities associated with the UFO/ETI subject.

The *unless otherwise directed* (UNOD) format is routinely used in governmental and military situations and indicates that unless otherwise instructed, the position and described actions are approved implicitly.

This letter clearly stated that we intend to assemble as many bona fide government officials and witnesses as possible, and that they will speak publicly and openly about their knowledge of UFO/ET events and covert projects.

Since the letter was issued, senior and reliable intelligence sources have stated that no response or interference would be forthcoming vis a vis plans for government witnesses to publicly come forward with their testimony.

Significantly, as of 1 January 1997, no government entity, official, agency, department or office has contradicted this assessment or stated that such government witnesses are any longer bound to silence.

CSETI Director Dr. Steven Greer has been meeting with various government officials, including members of the US Congress (House and Senate) to discuss this matter and ask for open hearings on the subject of UFOS/ETI.

In preparation for these disclosures, and in light of the expiration of the above deadline, a meeting of such military, intelligence, government and corporate witnesses will be held later this winter. Bona fide witnesses, or contacts to such witnesses, should contact Dr. Steven Greer immediately concerning participation in this event. A similar, but smaller, event was organized by CSETI in 1995, and was attended by US Astronauts, US and Russian military officials and others.

The meeting this winter will assemble a significant number of such government UFO witnesses to meet with congressional and other public officials and to request open hearings within the Congress, so that they may testify openly about their knowledge and experiences related to UFOs/ETI.

Should Congress not agree to open hearings, other venues, such as the United Nations or a private disclosure event, will be pursued to effect a pubic acknowledgment of the reality of UFOs/ETI.

This notice may be distributed freely among all newsgroups, media and interested parties, without further permission or restrictions.

55

Letter to the Clinton Administration

17 March 1995

MEMO

TO: The Clinton Administration

FROM: Steven M. Greer M.D.,
CSETI Project Starlight

RE: Executive order
Releasing UFO/ETI Witnesses and Documents

We have received approval from Mr. Laurance Rockefeller for the sponsorship and funding for a high-level meeting of military, astronautic and government witnesses concerning the Unidentified Flying Object/Extraterrestrial Intelligence matter.

This meeting will take place in May 1995 in the United States, and will be designed to obtain first-hand testimony from senior military and government witnesses.

We have received commitments from various participants, including a well-known astronaut with first-hand exposure to the subject.

In advance of this meeting we feel that it would be prudent to explore the implications of this meeting and subsequent disclosures with the Administration, and to secure an Executive Order releasing these witnesses from their National Security oaths/obligations.

We feel that these developments should go forward in a cooperative manner with the Executive branch of the U.S. Government, and thus are requesting a brief initial meeting with relevant members of the Administration.

Please advise as soon as possible concerning how we should proceed with this matter.

Respectfully,

Steven M. Greer, M.D.
Director of CSETI

56

Memo to Prospective Participants

MEMO:

To: Prospective Participants
Re: The Witness Meeting (TWM)
From: Meeting Organizer

Purpose: To gather in a confidential and supportive environment high-level, first-hand witnesses of the Subject. This meeting which is closed to the public and media is designed to enable the participants to consult and cooperate on strategies related to a disclosure on the Subject. It is also felt that such a gathering would enable the witnesses to be supported in a unified front. Both the credibility and the safety of this process is enhanced by multiple witnesses cooperating towards disclosure. Any testimony obtained at this meeting or subsequently will only be used with their express consent and through an appropriate and dignified venue.

Participant Criteria:

- Credible, senior, first-hand witnesses to the subject, especially those with direct involvement with manufactured or biological evidence, documents, etc.
- Other witnesses with authenticated corroborating evidence, such as documents, films, artifacts, objects or other witnesses.
- Contacts to the witnesses may come to the meeting ONLY if they bring witnesses who meet the above criteria.

Release from National Security Oaths (NSOs):

- An oral agreement in principle was secured in March 1994 from a senior Administration official to release all such witnesses from the NSOs on this subject.

- A senior member of the Coordinating Group can obtain release from NSOs for individuals who can produce the signed oaths relevant to The Subject.
- Currently, a request is pending at an appropriately senior level of the Administration to obtain a blanket release for all such witnesses (prior to 1975 or 1980) via Executive Order. We hope to receive a definitive answer to this request prior to TWM.
- Similarly, a request for an Executive Order to declassify official documents related to the Subject is pending.

Logistics:

Contacts who have Witnesses who meet the above criteria should submit the names of these witnesses and the type of events, evidence, programs or material which they witnessed. If the name of the witness is too sensitive to submit, the individual's position or rank must be listed. These should be conveyed to ______ by FAX or FedEx as soon as possible at the below location.

The organizers of TWM will contact you regarding these witnesses and will convey to you those who are confirmed for participation. This procedure is necessary to insure that participation is limited to senior, first hand Witnesses.

The site of TWM will be disclosed once the participants are confirmed AND the enclosed non-disclosure form is signed and returned to the below address. For obvious security and privacy purposes, only confirmed participants should be informed of the site and subject matter.

______ will provide follow up and logistical assistance related to confirming participants, travel arrangements and accommodations.

57

Report On The CSETI DC Briefings April 7-11 1997

15 April 1996

Background

CSETI founded Project Starlight over three and a half years ago as an initiative to identify the best scientific evidence related to UFOs and ET Intelligence. Of particular importance is the identification of bona-fide military, intelligence, government contractor and other government agency employees with direct, first-hand knowledge of the UFO/ET subject.

The goal of the CSETI Project Starlight initiative is to present the best available evidence and witness testimony in a manner which would constitute a definitive disclosure regarding the reality of the UFO/ET subject. This is to be done in a scientific, non-sensational and hopeful manner, assiduously avoiding an alarmist tone or emphasis.

Since 1993, Dr. Steven Greer, CSETI Director, and other CSETI Project Starlight team members, have provided preliminary briefings for White House staff, a sitting Director of Central Intelligence, senior military leaders, senior United Nations leadership, members of the Senate and House of Representatives, international leaders, and leaders in foreign governments, among others.

It has always been our intent to effect this disclosure in cooperation with the United States and other governments, if possible. We are acutely aware of the vast and profound implications of this matter and for this reason have carefully included key government figures and offices in our deliberations and plans. From the start, it was made clear that, while we desired a cooperative effort leading towards disclosure, the matter would be disclosed through a civilian-led initiative should the government choose to be uninvolved.

Through exhaustive and repeated private briefings with various government leaders, we learned that this subject was being managed in a way which kept the majority of our constitutional leadership uninformed on the subject. It became clear that we should collect the best evidence and witnesses and provide unmistakable and unambiguous information to these leaders so that they could make a decision on how to proceed. Obviously, unless the leadership was informed, there could be no chance of their disclosing any information to the public, or of even convening an open hearing and inquiry.

On 15 November 1996, a letter was sent to all pertinent offices of the United States Government asking for a determination on the validity of national security oaths related to the UFO/ET subject. In this letter, which is available on the CSETI website (www.cseti.org) it was stated that it was our assessment that these oaths and restrictions were null and void, since the oversight of the projects related to this subject was improper, illegal and extra-constitutional.

Further, it was stated that, *unless otherwise directed* by 1 January 1997, we would regard all military, intelligence and other government-related witnesses to UFO/ET projects and events as free to speak openly about what they know concerning this topic.

No corrective measures or statements—oral, written or otherwise—were submitted to us by 1 January 1997. Through back-door channels it was conveyed that we would be allowed to move forward, and that our progress was being noted by various military, intelligence, government and private groups connected to the subject.

Pursuant to the above letter, since no instructions stating otherwise were sent by the US Government, CSETI proceeded to plan a Washington DC Briefing for this spring, as promised.

During the week of April 7-11, the CSETI Project Starlight team convened a gathering of nearly 20 first-hand government witnesses to UFO/ET events. These events principally took place at the Westin Hotel in Washington DC, although separate briefings took place at the Pentagon and elsewhere in the Washington vicinity.

All of the US government witnesses who were present signed a statement that they are willing to testify *under oath* before an open hearing in the US Congress concerning the UFO/ET projects and events which they personally and directly witnessed. These government UFO witnesses spanned from the early 1950s to the 1990s, and represented events and/or projects observed while these witnesses were in the Air Force, Army, Navy, NASA, private industry and intelligence operations.

Most of these witnesses had top secret clearances and were testifying regarding events which took place while they had those clearances.

It should be noted that the witnesses who were assembled during the week of April 7-11 are the courageous tip of a much larger iceberg: There are 107 such first-hand government UFO witnesses who have been identified to date, and who should be subpoenaed by the Congress to testify in open hearings. Conceptually, these witnesses may be divided into three levels:

- Level One Witnesses. These are witnesses who are ready and willing to come forward today, as a unified coalition, to disclosure what they know about the subject. There are 44 such witnesses thus far identified.
- Level Two Witnesses: These are witnesses who have been identified but feel intimidated about coming forward and request the protection of Congressional hearings and the protective effect of a Congressional subpoena. They number 55.
- Level Three Witnesses—These are witnesses who are known to us but who are considered probably hostile or uncooperative witnesses. They would need to be subpoenaed and treated as potentially hostile witnesses. There are at least 8 such witnesses in this category.

The Washington Briefings of April 7-11, 1997

The purpose of the events of April 7–11 were as follows:

- To gather together bona-fide first hand government UFO witnesses to further solidify the coalition of such witnesses who are willing to come forward with definitive, unambiguous information concerning the UFO/ET subject.
- To convene a closed, confidential briefing for members of Congress, congressional staff, White House staff, military leaders and other Washington leaders on the subject, and for these leaders to hear the direct testimony of the US government and military witnesses. This briefing was designed to present the best scientific evidence and witness testimony to establish the reality of the subject matter, and to specifically ask for open congressional hearings on the matter.

- To conduct a background educational briefing for interested members of the media.
- To provide private briefings to other military, intelligence and political leaders as needed.

All of the objectives listed above were met.

(All members of Congress, the President, Vice-President and key cabinet officials, as well as key military and intelligence leaders, were invited to the briefing. Further, they were offered the opportunity to receive private briefings at their convenience during the week.)

Chronology:

April 7, 1997: Various CSETI support staff arrive, as well as early arrival of some of the US government witnesses. En route with one of the Eisenhower era witnesses, Dr. Greer et al discuss witness' contacts to the president of a Latin American country which may be helpful in obtaining a United Nations symposium on the subject.

April 8, 1997: Arrival of all US Government witnesses, CSETI staff and others. During a lunch meeting, Dr. Greer, Shari Adamiak and one of the US government witnesses meets with a producer for a major investigative TV program, to provide background information and an overview of the subject. At 6 A.M., all witnesses, along with Apollo Astronaut Edgar Mitchell and CSETI staff, gather for dinner. Introductions and an overview of the project's plans and goals were provided. At 10:30 A.M. CSETI support staff gather to discuss logistics, security and other issues related to the events of April 9 and 10.

April 9, 1997: 7:45 A.M. breakfast meeting between Dr. Greer and an influential former member of Congress who offers to help us move this subject forward in the Congress.

9 A.M.–1 A.M.: Gathering of US Government Witnesses, with statements recorded. This is a closed meeting for the witnesses and senior CSETI staff, at which detailed accounts of the witnesses experiences related to their US government service or employment is shared. It is also a time of bonding and support for the witnesses as a coalition.

1 A.M.: Lunch with the witnesses and CSETI team. Dr. Greer also briefs during lunch an important Washington figure who offers to help network this subject to various points in the Washington leadership.

2:30 A.M–5 A.M: Continuation of US Government Witness testimony and recording of statements.

5–5:45 A.M.: Dr. Greer meets with new witness who relates definitive testimony related to Los Alamos and other facilities. (This is a Level Two Witness)

7 A.M.–7:40 A.M.: Reception for members of Congress, Congressional staff, foreign embassy staff and other Washington VIPs and leaders.

7:45–about 10 A.M.: Closed Briefing for members of Congress and Congressional staff, etc. Nearly 30 congressional offices were represented by either members of congress or staff members. Also present were VIPs from the executive branch, foreign embassy staff, government scientists, representatives sent to the briefing by 2 state governors' offices, and many other dignitaries.

During the briefing, participants were introduced to a substantial Briefing Document which contains numerous scientific cases and over 250 pages of definitive and unambiguous US Government documents related to the subject. The government documents were selected from a larger collection of several thousand. Many were provided to CSETI by the CIA in 1994.

These participants also viewed a collection of excellent photographic, video and movie footage evidence spanning over 40 years and from every continent.

Eleven first-hand government and military witnesses were selected to testify before this group of government leaders. For over one and a half hours, they provided definitive and unambiguous testimony regarding UFO/ET events. Their testimony ranged from a world-renown astronomer who was present when an apparent ET signal was received at the Harvard observatory (SETI) facility, to an Eisenhower military top-secret witness who saw ET metal debris from a UFO crash, to a NASA employee who saw a picture with a UFO clearly in broad daylight which was destined to be air-brushed out before release, to a Navy employee with a top secret clearance who was present in 1981 during a major encounter off the eastern seaboard, which was tracked by satellite, radar, and chased by military planes with a resulting clear day- time photograph.

The richness of detail of this testimony, and the down-to-earth sincerity of these witnesses, was very moving to the gathered officials.

At the end of the briefing, one of the Congressional staffers came to the podium and, unsolicited by us, appealed to those congressional staffers and members of congress gathered to take definitive steps to let this information out to the public.

Numerous congressional offices represented at this historic briefing expressed a sincere desire to move this subject forward and to work with us in obtaining open congressional hearings as soon as possible. There was great enthusiasm for this, and one staffer from a congressional office has volunteered to coordinate these efforts in Washington with CSETI.

The combination of the extensive briefing materials, videotape evidence, first-hand witness testimony and the participation of so many congressional offices and other Washington leaders and dignitaries certainly constitutes the most historic civilian gathering in UFO/ET history.

In planning this event, we had hoped for positive RSVPs from 5-10 Congressional offices. The participation of nearly 30 such offices, as well as representatives from the executive branch and 2 state governors, certainly exceeded our expectations.

Each congressional office and VIP was provided with:

- The CSETI Briefing Document and related case materials
- The Videotape summary of photographs, videos and movie footage of UFOs
- A copy of the 1965 Edwards Air Force Base Air Traffic Control Tower tape of multiple UFO encounters, with transcript

Following the presentation, a number of congressional staffers remained to discuss this subject with the witnesses and CSETI staff and leaders.

April 10, 1997: 10 A.M.—Briefing at the Pentagon for very senior military staff. The CSETI team present included five members: Dr. Steven Greer, Astronaut Edgar Mitchell, Shari Adamiak, CSETI's military advisor and an Eisenhower-era first hand UFO/ET witness. This historic briefing lasted nearly one and one half hours and was enthusiastically received by senior Pentagon staff present.

During the afternoon of April 10, follow up with various congressional staffers, other Washington VIPs and the media took place.

7 A.M.: Reception for invitation-only media briefing. Note: Uninvited media were not allowed into this meeting. For example, long time debunker Phil Klass appeared without an invitation and was politely removed from the reception area. Similarly, had tabloid media appeared, they too would have been asked to leave. This meeting was a background educational briefing for major media only.

7:30 A.M.: Media Background briefing begins. Present are UPI, The Boston Globe, NBC, ABC the BBC and others. Seven first-hand witnesses provided statements to the media, and a general overview of the subject was provided by Dr. Greer. Following the briefing, a question and answer period took place, and the media all had excellent and insightful questions.

It should be noted that the above meeting was a background press briefing, *not* a press conference. The purpose of the meeting was to provide scientific background materials, and to introduce the invited media to the concept of open congressional hearings on the subject. The CSETI media team felt that such a meeting would be an important step towards preparing the mainstream media for a future disclosure, and would encourage them to cover the subject in an informed and serious manner.

Future Strategic Considerations:

Much work remains to be done to follow up with the considerable interest generated by these briefings. We will be forming a DC Coordinating Committee of congressional staffers, members of congress and other Washington area leaders to facilitate the educational and networking process needed to realize open Congressional hearings on this subject.

Strategically, we sense the need to move quickly with consolidating any interest in Congress on this subject, and to call for open hearings in the near future. In a parallel and therefore complementing effort, we are working with points of contact to other nations and the UN to facilitate an open symposium on the subject at the UN in the near future. We have been advised that the best route to achieve this is to secure the support of other nations with missions to the UN and have them directly ask for such an inquiry and symposium. Anyone with contacts to other nations which may be helpful in this regard should contact Dr. Greer as soon as possible.

Unless there are positive results from these efforts within a reasonable amount of time, it is our intent to move forward with a civilian disclosure process independent of any governmental involvement. We feel that the subject must be placed on the national and international agenda, and that we must have the resolve to move forward with or without specific governmental support or involvement.

However, the gravity of the subject, together with the far-reaching and deep ramifications of such a disclosure, necessitates a cautious, deliberate and inclusive policy for the present. We feel that it is imperative to provide excellent scientific cases, evidence and witness testimony to appropriate government leaders, in the US and elsewhere, thus empowering them to take the subject seriously, and to provide positive leadership. Only after such efforts, which are nearing completion, can we feel that we have done all that is possible to empower the democratic institutions which are the bedrock of our society.

As a civilian group taking a leadership position in this matter we feel that it is essential that we also move towards a global civilian multi-media educational project. Even should the Congress or UN take up this subject, it will be necessary for us to continue to provide perspective, a framework of understanding on the subject, and accurate information and evidence.

The concerned and interested public are encouraged to do the following to assist us in this historic undertaking:

- Write *and* call your congressional representative and members of the Senate from your state asking them to support open congressional hearings on the UFO/ET subject.
- Help us in identifying further first-hand US and other government UFO witnesses who may join in the historic and courageous witnesses coalition.
- Help us identify more of the best available evidence on the subject, including scientific cases, photographs, movie footage, videotape footage, government documents, and ET artifacts (such as metal samples and biological samples).
- Assist us in networking this project to national and international leaders who can further assist in establishing a global disclosure on the subject.
- Help us identify sources of funding for this historic effort. We urgently need a full time staff to pursue the momentum already created; we have clearly gone beyond the point where an all-volunteer effort can be effective.

The time has come for the world to know that we are not alone in this vast universe. The era of excessive secrecy, which is so corrosive to a free and democratic society, must end. Working together, we can create a truly open and free society, which through much deliberation and wise efforts, may someday take its place among other planetary civilizations.

58

Letter to Friends of Project Starlight

17 December 1997

Dear Friends of CSETI Project Starlight,

This letter is to bring you up to date on developments since the historic CSETI briefings in Washington DC for members of Congress and other leaders held on 9 April 1997.

The past 6–8 months have witnessed a number of promising developments, with increasing interest from key congressional leaders and congressional committees, as well as leaders in other countries. Additionally, senior scientific leadership who direct major operations at nationally significant scientific institutions are now looking into the ET question in a serious and thorough fashion.

Last month, we concluded preliminary meetings with these scientific leaders and congressional staff, and are optimistic that the subject of UFOs/ETI is finally being taken seriously.

Members of several Congressional committees, as well as the chairman and chief of staff of a key House committee, have stated that they are now convinced that the subject is "real" and of importance. We are continuing our dialogue with these and other leaders and encouraging them to hold open hearings in the Congress during the next term which begins in January.

This month we are sending a full briefing package, including videotaped witness testimony, government documents, UFO photos and film footage and other evidence to the chairmen of 15 major Congressional committees which are relevant to this subject (see enclosed letter). In this letter they are asked to reply to our formal request for hearings.

Additionally, we are completing a proposal for a major new global survey of ET intelligence. This proposal, called The CSETI Earth/Near Earth ET Survey, calls for a major scientific real-time survey of UFO/ET activity using state-of-the-art technology and rapid response capability. Properly funded and executed, it would scientifically study and document in real-time UFO events globally. Scientists and institutions of the highest caliber are currently consulting with us on this project. (See "The CSETI Earth/Near-Earth Extraterrestrial Survey" on page 269.)

Regarding future strategic plans to effect a global disclosure on the existence of UFOs/ET Intelligence, we are at a significant crossroads: While continuing to provide briefings, evidence and advice to the Congress, White House and other national and world leaders, we must now make good on our promise to disclose fully what is know about this subject to the public. To "privatize" the disclosure of top secret witness testimony and other evidence will require several world-class documentaries and books coordinated with a world scientific gathering and press conference.

While we certainly have the materials, evidence and witnesses in place to fulfill such a plan, funding is another matter. Most likely, these documentaries and books will need to be funded through a business endeavor since it is clear no benefactors exist to fund such an undertaking through a non-profit entity.

From a practical point of view, the minimum required to effect such a privatized disclosure, including a broadcast quality 2 hour documentary, two books, the world press briefing and a scientific gathering to review the evidence is approximately $2 million.

If you know of any individuals or entities who could help with such an undertaking, please contact me as soon as possible.

The release of definitive evidence and top-secret testimony through such a multi-media plan - if done properly - would constitute a disclosure of significant proportions. It would very likely then lead to the congressional investigations and hearings for which we have been calling.

Strategically, it is unwise to continue to allow governmental foot-dragging to delay any longer the release of information and top-secret witness testimony. The obvious advantage to Congressional hearings is that they would be taken seriously, seen widely and would be funded by the Congress. If we must, as a civilian group, achieve much the same goals through a private multi-media effort, then substantial business and financial support will be needed. The resulting products must be first-rate and be positioned to avoid the tabloid, lower-end media.

Certainly, we are ready to move into the public domain with this disclosure process and look forward to your comments, ideas, networking and general assistance in this important global undertaking.

Wishing you the best of all worlds and a time of Universal Peace,

Steven M. Greer, M.D.
Director of CSETI

enclosures

59

The CSETI Project Starlight Disclosure Strategy

8 April 1998

Update And Clarification

For over four and one half years, CSETI has been diligently implementing a strategic plan to effect a disclosure on the UFO/ETI subject. Recent misinformation and disinformation regarding this process which has appeared on the Internet and elsewhere necessitates a reiteration of that strategic plan and an update on the process.

In the summer of 1993, a group of CSETI advisors and military consultants met to discuss how to best develop a reliable point of contact (POC) to the US government. This was felt necessary after a number of CSETI CE-5 encounter incidents had occurred which resulted in team members expressing concerns about covert attempts to interfere with the CE-5 diplomatic initiative. It was felt a reliable POC was needed for communication and briefing purposes, thus reducing the likelihood of an undesired outcome or event.

Ultimately it was decided that we should pursue various POCs within the Executive Branch of the US government and the military and to approach congressional leadership at a later point in the process.

A strategic plan was devised to 1) collect and identify the Best Available Evidence related to UFOs/ETI; 2) identify top-secret military and intelligence witnesses to the matter who were willing to come forward and disclose what they knew; 3) create a team of briefers and advisors to Executive Branch officials and military officials who would conduct briefings and recommend near-term disclosure of the subject and the end to secrecy related to the subject.

By September of 1993 this plan was in action, and with the assistance of a senior official at the Joint Chiefs of Staff, a meeting was set up at Wright-Patterson Air Force Base with the top-secret Foreign Aerospace Science and Technology Center located there (this had previously been the Foreign Technology Center to which the 1940's New Mexico UFO crash remains had been sent; it is now called the National Air Intelligence Center—NAIC). The discussions at Wright-Patterson AFB were cordial and constructive.

Eventually, a number of consultants became involved with the briefing and disclosure process, including national security think tank heads, friends of the President and others. Continued networking resulted in briefings for senior Clinton Administration officials, including CIA Director James Woolsey.

During these briefings, we recommended decisive government action to end the secrecy surrounding this subject and that the Administration should work to disclose substantial facts about the UFO/ETI issue as soon as possible. In the materials provided for senior White House, CIA, DOD and other officials we set out the rationale for the timeliness of this disclosure and the dangers associated with continued secrecy. *We also clearly stated in writing that if the government did not coordinate this disclosure, that we would bypass the government and work to disclose these secrets unilaterally*. However, we made it clear that it was in the nation's (and world's) best interest to have so weighty a matter disclosed cooperatively by the government.

Unfortunately, very senior Executive Branch officials, including the CIA Director, senior Presidential advisors and Pentagon officials found it difficult to penetrate the ultra-secret 'black' programs dealing with this subject. As CIA Director Woolsey pointed out to me, they cannot disclose what they do not know or have access to.

It is now a matter of public record that Assistant Attorney General and close Presidential friend Webster Hubble had been asked officially by the President to look into the UFO issue (see Hubble's book *Friends in High Places*). Hubbell stated that they were not satisfied with the answers they were getting from NORAD and elsewhere. It is disturbing to think that the President—our Commander-In-Chief—and his inner circle may not have high enough clearances to be briefed fully on this matter...

After a period of extensive briefings for US, foreign and UN leaders, it became obvious that 1) these leaders were deliberately being kept in the dark on the subject and 2) that they did not possess the courage or political will to take on the covert apparatus managing the UFO/ETI matter. In fact, they were visibly shaken by the situation.

As more and more top-secret witnesses, documents and other evidence was identified, it became clear that—unless a Presidential executive order effectively ended the secrecy and resulted in disclosure—that our next best option would be to identify a member of congress who would call for and hold open congressional hearings on the subject.

At this point, a number of old wags in the UFO subculture stated that we should just come forward with what we knew, identify the top-secret witnesses and let it all come out. This facile strategic recommendation overlooked three major problems:

1. The foundation of the disclosure process is the pool of dozens of top-secret military and intelligence witnesses to unambiguous UFO/ET events and programs. These courageous witnesses have asked for a safe, effective and official means of coming out with their testimony, if at all possible. CSETI felt a moral responsibility to vigorously pursue an officially sanctioned venue for so momentous a disclosure, if at all feasible. To this end, CSETI has—for 4.5 years—attempted to secure the highest, safest official venue possible for this disclosure. These courageous military witnesses have asked this of us, and we have faithfully pursued that request. Some of these witnesses are in fear for their lives; others fear other sanctions and punishment. All of them would prefer to come forward in an official setting, freed from the restraints of their national security oaths etc.

2. The disclosure of the reality of UFOs and ETI is no small matter. Neither the CSETI leadership nor our witnesses wanted to appear to be upstaging the US government, the UN or other concerned governments. It was *imperative* that we make good-faith efforts to get our national and world leaders to deal with this subject officially, prior to a unilateral privatized disclosure. The implications of such a disclosure are so vast and so profound that only a very reckless person or group would attempt to effect this disclosure without first offering to work cooperatively with our governments. We have assiduously created a paper trail which fully documents these efforts, lest we later be accused of disclosing the ultimate secret without first consulting with the government. While this process has been in turns tedious, rewarding, exasperating, expensive and time-consuming, we are certain that it was the right thing to do.

3. In the absence of significant funding for a privatized disclosure, the best and most cost-effective way to achieve this goal was to convince the government or the Congress to take on this task. A congressional hearing, obviously, would be funded by the Congress. A private disclosure will need to be funded by—whom? Those who think that you simply hold a press conference with the witnesses (arranging that—including flying into one place, lodging etc. dozens of witnesses-would alone cost tens of thousands of dollars, if not hundreds of thousands) have never dealt with big media on this subject. We are not willing to expose these witnesses unless it is strategically effective. There is no point in taking such risks unless there is a reasonable likelihood that the status quo will be changed. To privately see that this is the case -with no support from Congress or the government—will be a very complex and expensive undertaking, far outside the resources of the UFO community at this time (or at any time in the past).

In light of the above, from 1995-1997 CSETI pursued a number of briefings with members of Congress. One year ago, on April 9,1997, we convened the historic CSETI briefings for members of Congress, White House figures and senior military figures, among others (see the CSETI Report on the DC Briefings). Since April of 1997, we have continued to provide briefings and recommended to key congressional committee chairmen that open hearings be convened as soon as practical. Hundreds if not thousands of CSETI supporters have written these key congressional leaders recommending open hearings on the UFO/ETI subject.

I have personally met with numerous members of Congress. Key committee chairmen have been fully briefed and given unambiguous evidence and top-secret witness testimony, in person and on videotape. And everyone is tossing this hot potato to someone else's committee. Not unlike the refrain Not In My Backyard, it appears our leaders are saying Not In My Committee.

To recap, we have over the past four and a half years assiduously fulfilled a strategy to identify the best scientific evidence and government witnesses, brief and advise world leaders, members of Congress, the Pentagon, the UN and others and have fully documented this process. We have done everything humanly possible, at immense cost in funds, time and human life, to see that this process was done properly. In good faith to our witnesses we took no shortcuts and have consistently asked the President, the Congress and others to allow this disclosure to take place officially and safely through proper channels.

While we are willing to continue to brief members of Congress, Pentagon leaders and other government leaders when called upon, and while we still prefer official government involvement in this disclosure, the time has come to begin these disclosures without the government. We cannot allow this process to be delayed indefinitely by bureaucrats or timid politicians who will not take on this responsibility. The opportunity has been offered to them, and we continue to offer our cooperation should Congress or the President decide to do the right thing and become involved in this disclosure process.

Ultimately, however, the time comes when closure is needed regarding the government briefing process, and 'we the people' should exert our rights to free speech and come forward with the truth as we have found it.

Without the cover of a congressional subpoena, many witnesses may be reluctant to step forward. However, we know that the most courageous and resolute government witnesses will come forward with us, independent of the government. They, more than we, are weary of the excessive secrecy and ridiculing which surrounds this subject. With these courageous witnesses, we will come forward with a privatized, civilian-led program to disclose the truth of this subject, in the most credible, highest and most effective manner possible.

This will consist of a world news conference, multi-part prime time expose documentary series, compendium books and a world scientific summit. This process, once begun, must be relentless, high quality, serious and thorough.

Ironically, numerous members of Congress, White House staff, and very senior Joint Chiefs of Staff personnel have recommended that we bypass the government altogether and come forward with the evidence and witnesses. Of course, this is somewhat self-serving, since it gets them off the hook and ignores the fact that many of our best witnesses will not come forward without officially sanctioned approval and immunity from prosecution for violating national security regulations. Nevertheless, after four and half years of thorough strategic implementation, the time has come to see that the truth comes out via a civilian, privatized multi-media process. And we have been told by members of Congress that once this happens, the likelihood of open Congressional hearings will be significantly enhanced.

These are the crossroads at which we find ourselves: The Congress, like Caesar's Senate, pursues trivialities while Rome burns, and the main stream news media regards the pursuit of sexual peccadillos as the summit of investigative reporting. How tragic.

Meanwhile, it is left to the people to resolve one of the most important issues of our time: That we are not alone, that intelligent life is visiting this planet, and that a cabal of covert programs and entities are hiding the truth from our leaders and from the people. And the means for generating immense amounts of pollution-free energy is hidden away in black projects, while the Earth's geophysical equilibrium is increasingly upset.

I suggest we move on.

Steven M. Greer, M.D.
Director of CSETI

60

Criteria For The Privatization Of Disclosure Of UFOs/ETI Information

10 April 1998

A number of people have asked for clarification of plans and criteria related to the disclosure of top-secret government witness testimony and other evidence related to the UFO/ETI matter.

The privatization of this process, which would by-pass the currently non-responsive US government, requires a carefully planned and executed strategy in order for this disclosure to be effective, safe and meaningful. Clearly, there is no justification in exposing multiple top-secret government witnesses and sources unless the risk of doing so is surpassed by a reasonable expectation of benefit.

The expected goals and benefits of such a privatized (civilian led) disclosure are:

- To establish for the international community- including mainstream scientists, politicians, religious leaders, media and others- the reality of the UFO/ETI matter, thus altering the current status quo which largely dismisses the subject as fictional;
- By achieving the above, engaging the international community in a serious discussion regarding the evidence related to the ETI matter, its implications and what actions should be taken to further study the issue. This would also end the exclusive covert management of the subject which has been on-going for over 50 years and which is a threat to world and national security;
- Effect this disclosure in a manner which will avoid unnecessary panic, anxiety and xenophobia by conducting the disclosure strategy in a manner which is hopeful, scientific and neutral.

Components of the disclosure are:

- A multi-part prime time major network documentary series which would present the best available scientific evidence and top-secret witness testimony to a global audience; this series will be restricted to major mainstream media and will not be available to the minor and tabloid media
- Compendium books and other educational materials to the documentaries
- A well-organized, main-stream press conference and briefing to coincide with the release of the materials mentioned above
- A global scientific conference to be convened following the disclosures which would look at all of the evidence and make recommendations for further study and action

Criteria of evidence to be included in the documentaries, books and other materials listed above:

- Top-secret government witnesses and aerospace witnesses to unambiguous UFO/ETI events and programs. These witnesses will be vetted and include ONLY first-hand witnesses with documented involvement with the military or government and who have a clean legal/criminal record;
- High-quality government documents which demonstrate the reality of the UFO /ETI matter and which demonstrate the reality of long-standing covert interest in the matter;
- Independently analyzed photographic, video and movie images of unambiguous UFO/ETI objects;
- Objects of ET Origin (OEO) which have been independently analyzed by qualified scientists who have no financial interest in the verification of the OEO.
- Other cases and evidence which are not anecdotal and which have multiple points of corroboration
- Audio tape, radar tapes and other electronic evidence which has been independently verified.

Exclusion Criteria: The following types of cases will not appear in the disclosure materials:

- Anecdotal cases such as idiosyncratic personal sightings and experiences, alleged contactee/abductee cases and rumors of events;
- Second hand government witnesses unless extremely compelling and of VERY high rank and credibility
- Unverified and non-analyzed images, documents, tapes, OEO etc.
- Wildly speculative cases, theories and belief systems

Features of the international press conference and briefing:

- To be held contemporaneous to the airing of the disclosure documentaries
- To be held at a suitable venue with adequate credibility and gravitas commensurate with the importance of the event, in Washington DC
- Participants restricted to:
    - First-hand top secret government and military witnesses to UFO/ETI events
    - Respected aerospace and aeronautics figures
    - Mainstream and credentialed scientists
    - Noteworthy political figures and leaders
- All others will be observers
- Invited media restricted to:
    - Major mainstream media (print, radio, TV etc.)
    - Science and political reporters for specialty areas (astronomy, geo-politics etc.)
    - Major International media
- Tabloid and minor media will not be invited

The Global Scientific Conference on UFO/ET Phenomena will include the presentation of the best scientific evidence and top-secret first-hand government witness testimony. Participants are restricted to the following:

- Scientists and researchers with Ph.D. or minimum Masters degrees
- Top-secret government UFO / ETI witnesses
- Select Scientific leaders

- Select Think-Tank leaders and officials
- Science reporters from mainstream and specialty media and journals

Proceedings will focus on:

- The presentation of evidence and testimony
- Analysis and Discussion of same
- Recommendations from the Scientific Advisory Board to scientific, academic and governmental leaders

The above plans are contingent on the identification of sufficient funding to properly fulfill these plans. Inadequate funding and/or attempts to diminish the disclosure by identifying it with tabloid and fringe venues and media outlets will result in non-disclosure and/or postponement of the disclosure process. We see no point in putting forth important and top-secret witness testimony and other critical evidence in a venue (or through a process) which would be obviously ineffectual from the outset.

The maintenance of these high standards is critical to the success of the disclosure process.

Part IV

Official Government Documents And The Project Starlight Paper Trail

Quite simply, this section presents the tip of a very large iceberg: official government documents and the substantial CSETI paper trail dealing with the government.

The official government documents presented here are nearly all officially released documents which came to us after a request to the CIA in 1994 (after my briefing for CIA Director Woolsey). In addition, there are a few government documents—such as the Marilyn Monroe wiretap summary(see "Marilyn Monroe Document" on page 455)—which came from inside contacts at the NSA or elsewhere. These are only presented since we have had them authenticated by the best experts in the field. The documents here represent only a tiny percentage of the documents which we have obtained. Space and publishing costs would not allow more.

I should make a few comments regarding some of the documents: The Marilyn Monroe Document came to me by way of a contact with access to NSA officials. It has been authenticated by the best document researcher in the world—a man who for years sat outside General Odom's door as his senior aide when Odom was NSA head. It is a smoking gun, especially when put together with the other documents. The reader will note that the document is signed by James Angleton, one of the main CIA counter-intelligence figures of the 1960s and fanatical "mole hunter" who ruthlessly tried to stop any leaks of sensitive intelligence. Note that the document, which has very important project code names and numbers on it, is a summary of CIA wiretaps of Marilyn Monroe. After the Kennedy brothers distanced themselves from her she felt hurt and began to call Bobby Kennedy and some of her friends, threatening to hold a press conference to tell the world what President Kennedy had privately told her about some very sensitive matters.

The most sensitive of these matters was the ET issue. Note the section of the document which refers to telling all regarding what President Kennedy told her about "the visit by the President at a secret air base for the purpose of inspecting things from outer space." Later, the document refers to "secret effort by the US and UK governments to identify the origins of crashed spacecraft and dead bodies" and that Dorothy Kilgallen believed the story may have come from the New Mexico crash in the late forties..."—a clear reference to a Roswell-type incident. The document also refers to Monroe's "secret diaries and what the newspapers would do with such disclosures."

This document is dated 3 August 1962—around the time of Marilyn Monroe's mysterious death. Actor Burl Ives, a personal friend and CSETI life time member, told me at his home in Anacortes, Washington, that he had been friends with Marilyn Monroe before her death. He told me quite clearly that he and all her close friends knew she had been murdered. But they did not know why. Perhaps now we do...

The reader will also note the important documents which describe the CIA's involvement with alleged impartial scientific reviews of the UFO matter which took place in the 1960s. Of particular note are those documents, starting on page 505, which describe the CIA's attempts to keep secret and cover-up its involvement and manipulations of the Condon committee report. The Condon committee was a group funded by the Air Force at the University of Colorado to allegedly do an impartial scientific review of the UFO evidence. Instead, it was controlled and infiltrated by the CIA from the outset, and its negative findings on the UFO matter were anything but impartial.

Similarly, there are documents dealing with the Roberston committee from the 1950s which also show clear CIA involvement, and attempts to hide that involvement. ("Letter to Lloyd Berkner" on page 503.)

So when you hear "objective" scientists debunking and ridiculing the UFO matter, you may be excused if you ask yourself, "I wonder who is paying them to say that...". Covert projects lie. And they pay others to lie. All the time, every day.

The CSETI/Greer Project Starlight letters give the reader a sense of the scope and gravity of the historic Project Starlight effort. This section also contains documents which show the activities of Project Starlight—for all the world to see.

We have many, many letters from world leaders which we have not reproduced here for both personal and strategic reasons—not to mention we are doubtful that they would give permission for such publication. But the reader will get a sense of the magnitude of the Project Starlight disclosure effort and will see that we have made every effort to obtain the faithful cooperation of the world's leadership.

They know. Now the rest of the world must know.

Our next step must be to get all of the evidence and the dozens of government and military witnesses out in front of the world. Then the truth will be known and the world can at last do what Barry Goldwater told me in 1994 it should have always done: dealt with this subject openly and honestly, for all the world to see.

Plate 1. Lago de Cote, Costa Rica, September 4, 1971.

Plate 2. Vancouver Island, British Columbia, Canada, October 8, 1981, 11:00 A.M., Hannah McRoberts, courtesy of the McRoberts/Fortean Picture Library

Plate 3. Wichita Falls, TX. ©1993 Ron Russell

Plate 4. Santa Fe, NM, August, 1992. Taken by Ivy Blank.

Memo to President Clinton—8 May 1995

FROM CSETI Project Starlight, Steven M. Greer M.D.

RE: Meeting and Executive order

Please find enclosed several documents previously conveyed to the Administration via the Director of Central Intelligence (James Woolsey), the President's Science Advisor and Mr. Bruce Lindsey regarding the UFO/ETI subject.

As mentioned previously, we feel that a strategy leading to disclosure on this subject should be urgently pursued, and we are requesting a meeting with relevant Administration officials as soon as possible. Astronaut Gordon Cooper, Apollo Astronaut Dr. Brian O'Leary, John F. Kennedy Chief Steward for Air Force One, ______, a prominent NASA scientist, and others could attend such a meeting.

Our team has had recent conversations with former Air Force office of Special Investigations and Naval Intelligence officers and other senior military personnel which indicate that current handling of this subject constitutes a threat to the national security, to the basic structures of constitutional democracy, and specifically to the integrity of the United States Constitution.

Long term trends towards increasingly covert, quasi-privatized, 'black-budget' management of this subject, combined with a concomitant increase in disinformation and public deception, must be arrested and reversed. Neither the Congress nor relevant and responsible military, intelligence and Administration officials are receiving honest and reliable information and assessments of this situation. Legal and constitutionally sanctioned control over this subject appears to have been diminished, if not completely lost, and this has created a dynamic of covert activities and programs which threaten the national security.

Multiple military intelligence sources have independently confirmed to us the use of experimental, SDI related weapons against extraterrestrial spacecraft, with at least two successful hits. If this has even a remote chance of being true, it would indicate the dire need for a reversal of the covert management of this subject, and the need for the public and the international community to dialogue on this subject in a sane and rational manner. Very senior members of the U.N. community with whom we have met concur with this assessment.

Who speaks for Planet Earth? We feel that the people of Earth should, not a small covert operation which, without consultation, controls a subject which affects the entire planet in vast and profound ways.

We feel that the Administration should take decisive steps to regain constitutional and accountable control over this matter, and that a strategy should be developed to effect a well-thought out disclosure.

We have located a number of military and intelligence witnesses to this subject who require a Presidential Executive order releasing them from their national security oaths and obligations on this subject. We are urgently requesting that this be done as soon as possible. If there are no substantial disclosures resulting from these witnesses, then the subject may be put to rest. However, if what we have learned in confidence is true, then these witnesses can confirm the existence of extraterrestrial life forms visiting this planet, and help to move this matter into the public domain for dialogue and international consultation, thus effectively ending the exclusive covert control.

CSETI, Mr. Laurance Rockefeller, Astronaut Gordon Cooper, as well as several other prominent astronauts and military figures will be convening a meeting of witnesses on June 2, 3 and 4, 1995, and we invite the Administration to send an observer or participant to this meeting. If this would be possible, please contact Dr. Steven Greer or ______.

A subject this profound in its implications for life on Earth must not be allowed to be the exclusive domain of a covert group which is accountable to neither the public nor recognized governmental authorities. For secret and covert processes are at great risk for taking on a life of their own, and in doing so threaten the security of our nation and of the world. We appeal to the President, the National Security Advisor and others in the Administration to take decisive steps to effect disclosure on this subject prior to the 1996 election year. In doing so, a great service will be rendered to the world and its peoples, and this important matter will rightly become the focus of the world community. We are acutely aware of the courage needed to face this challenge, but we are equally aware of the risks to world peace and democracy of doing nothing.

Please be assured that our hopes and our prayers are with you.

Sincerely,

Steven M. Greer, M.D.
Director of CSETI

Letter to President Clinton from Participants at the Asilomar Conference

June 4, 1995
William Jefferson Clinton President of the United States
The White House Washington, D.C.
Dear Mr. President:

We, the members of the Project Starlight Coalition, a group of American and international citizens working to effect a public disclosure on the UFO/extraterrestrial issue, respectfully request the following:

That appropriate members of the administration meet with members of the Project Starlight Coalition to review significant evidence and witness testimony related to the subject.

That the President issue an executive order to release U.S. government witnesses from their national security obligations/oaths related to the subject so that they may provide public testimony.

That the President issue an executive order to declassify and release currently classified materials, documents and evidence related to the subject.

We feel that these requests are consistent with recent administration actions which resulted in the release of classified information related to the Department of Energy, intelligence satellite photographs, and other documents. We recommend that this matter be handled expeditiously and we respectfully look forward to your reply.
Sincerely,

24 signatories,
Names not included for reasons of confidentiality

Letter to Mr. Dorskind

10 August 1995

Dear Mr. Dorskind,

Thank you for your letter of 3 August 1995

Mr. Laurance Rockefeller and I have been working together on this issue for over 18 months, and he will be seeing the President at his ranch in Jackson WY soon (I have very fond memories of being there with Laurance in the fall of 1993— it is a wonderful and spiritually refreshing spot). At his request, I have conveyed to him a package of evidence, assessments and other documents to share with the President.

Please know that I am available to answer any questions regarding this evidence or the subject in general, and am willing to come to the JY Ranch on very short notice, should this be helpful to the President or his staff. Be assured that our entire network of scientists, astronauts and researchers are at your service.

I will be with the family in Palm Beach FL from 12 August-19 August and can be reached at _____.

Also, I will be in Washington D.C. August 30-September 3 for the 50th anniversary of the U.N. meetings going on there and will be staying at the conference site, the D.C., Grand Hyatt.

Wishing the President and First Family a renewing and much deserved vacation at the Ranch,

Sincerely,

Steven M. Greer, M.D.,
Director of CSETI

Letter to President Clinton—19 October 1995

Dear President Clinton,

Thank you for your letter of August 3, 1995, written by Mr. James Dorskind on your behalf, and for your consideration of our request to meet with relevant members of the Administration on the UFO/ETI subject.

We feel that the time has come to permit a number of our witnesses to speak openly about their involvement with U.S. government military and intelligence operations dealing with extraterrestrial spacecraft and related matters. Our witness pool continues to grow, and we would like to meet with relevant members of the Administration as soon as possible to discuss protection for these witnesses.

It is our opinion that it is in the best interests of the Administration, and of the American people, to have these witnesses disclose their information in the context of a cooperative effort with the government. At a minimum, these heroic witnesses deserve protection from prosecution for violating national security oaths, and need specific protection from all civil and military prosecution. A few of them need physical protection, since some of them sense that they and/or their families may be in real physical danger.

I am enclosing a briefing on the national security implications of the UFO/ETI subject, which is being distributed to certain figures in the US and abroad who are connected to national and international security concerns. It is intended to be a brief summary of national security implications for the President, the National Security Advisor and other relevant members of the US national security apparatus.

Please let us know how we may proceed with a meeting with members of your Administration on this important and pressing issue.

Respectfully,

Steven M. Greer, M.D.
Director of CSETI

Letter to President Clinton—23 May 1996

Dear President Clinton,

It has been several months since hearing from your special assistant Mr. Dorskind, and I would like to update you on some important developments concerning the UFO/ET issue and to make a few suggestions.

We have continued briefing select leaders both in the US and abroad concerning plans for a disclosure of evidence and witness testimony related to the UFO/ET subject. To date some two dozen former and/or current government, military, intelligence and private corporate witnesses have been identified. As mentioned to CIA Director Woolsey and others in your Administration, we are in need of some degree of protection for these witnesses so that they may openly testify without fear of reprisals.

I have briefed a number of members of Congress concerning this issue, as well as officials in the United Kingdom and Russia. There is wide agreement that we should move forward with such a disclosure. A consensus is growing that joint Executive Branch and Congressional action is needed, and that the international community should be involved via the United Nations.

We are preparing to go forward with private briefings for members of Congress and other national leaders, as well as important military leaders at the level of the Joint Chiefs of Staff. Additionally, we will be pursuing a preliminary briefing for members of the UN in New York. Both the Washington and New York briefings will be closed to the media and public, and will allow us to introduce these leaders to several of our witnesses and to an overview of the scientific evidence. We certainly welcome any input from you or your assistants, and would hope that a member of your staff could attend the Washington meeting. We will inform you when the dates for these meetings have been set.

Separately, we are pursuing liaisons with current covert operations dealing with this matter. An enclosed paper describes the basic characteristics and operations of the covert organization (here called PI-40 which we have found is currently responsible for deep cover projects dealing with the UFO/ET matter. Briefly, this entity is operating covertly as an unacknowledged special access project, USAP (so-called 'black project') and does not typically respond directly to the chain of command. We feel that the avoidance of conflict with this group is critical at the time of a disclosure, and to this end recommend the following:

Careful channels of communication with this group's leadership should be pursued as soon as possible; we have identified certain points of contact which may help facilitate this.

- It should be clearly communicated to this group that the current administration of their projects are in need of modification and should be returned to direct chain of command control and congressional and executive branch oversight. This would apply to both deep cover military and intelligence USAPS and to private contract/corporate activity. A date should be negotiated for this, and for complete cooperation with the elements of a disclosure.
- In exchange for cooperation in this manner, and assistance and non-interference at the time of a disclosure, this group, in all its aspects, should be given complete amnesty and full immunity for any questionable activity which may have occurred prior to that time.
- Those involved in this group, in addition to amnesty, should be granted complete confidentiality, should they request it.
- The intent of these recommendations is to reduce the risk of conflict with this group, and to increase the margin of safety for the President, the Congress, the witnesses and, generally, the United States government.

Recent meetings which I have had with important members of the Aspen Institute, former Ministry of Defense head and five star admiral Lord Hill-Norton, congressmen from both sides of the aisle and members of the aerospace and astronautics programs convince me that the time has come for a disclosure, and that joint cooperation among civilians, the White House Congress and the UN is urgently needed. We hope you will provide important leadership for this critical global issue.

I wish to assure you of my prayers for your guidance and for your success in the cause of universal peace.

Respectfully,

Steven M. Greer, M.D.
Director of CSETI

Letter to President Clinton—15 November 1996

Dear President Clinton,

Congratulations on your historic re-election for a second term as President of the United States.

As the first president of the next millennium, you will have the opportunity and challenge of helping to guide both America and the world into a new era of great promise. As a descendent of people who fought in 1776 to secure the freedom of America, I believe, as they did, that America is the great hope of the world, and that our vision and spirit—more so than even our immense material wealth—must lead the world into a brighter future.

In the past six years, I have endeavored to discover the truth about the UFO/ET matter. We have consulted some of the best minds in the world on whether—and how—this matter should be disclosed to the public. There has been wide agreement that the time has come for the secrecy surrounding this subject to end, and for the people of the world to know that, indeed, life exists beyond our beautiful home, the Earth.

I believe that you can leave a lasting and historic legacy, for America and the world, by facilitating the confirmation of this fact to the public. A scientific, evidence driven and hopeful disclosure of this information will be one of the seminal events of this century, and I feel that your support and involvement in so weighty a matter is imperative.

We are moving forward with setting up an historic meeting at the United Nations in February to coordinate this disclosure. We have identified substantial evidence and important government and military witnesses to accomplish this goal. I would like to ask you to please consider a meeting, however brief and at any time or place, where we might discuss these plans, and obtain your advice and input. Would you consider such a meeting before the end of this year?

Can we work together on this, for the sake of our children, and the generations which follow?

I would be honored to meet with you and your staff, either alone, or with a small and senior group of astronauts and military witnesses, including Dr. Edgar Mitchell, who walked on the moon in Apollo 14, Astronaut Gordon Cooper, and _____, a military aid to President Eisenhower.

We are eager for this disclosure to be accomplished in a manner which is cooperative with you and the Congress, and which redounds to the benefit of all of humanity. To achieve this, I feel we must discuss this matter at the earliest possible time.

Please be assured of my prayers for your guidance and success, and of my abiding respect and support.

Wishing you and your family the best of all worlds,

Steven M. Greer, M.D.
Director of CSETI

Letter to President Clinton—6 February 1997

Dear President Clinton,

From April 8–10 1997 CSETI Project Starlight will convene a closed, confidential meeting in Washington DC for top secret military and intelligence officials who are witnesses to UFO/Extraterrestrial events and programs.

Along with astronaut Ed Mitchell, there will be individuals who are heroes of our country and who are courageously willing to come forward publicly with their testimony regarding UFOs

We are requesting that you and the Vice President agree to meet with these patriotic American veterans to hear their testimony. Even a brief meeting, with follow up with appropriate Administration officials, would show these courageous individuals the respect and concern which they deserve.

These are honest witnesses who are willing to testify under oath before an open hearing in Congress about what they know. Their testimony will establish unequivocally that we are not the only intelligent life in the universe.

We sincerely hope that you and others in the Administration will be able to meet with this coalition of government UFO witnesses. Ideally, we would like to see your administration actively involved in the facilitation of the disclosure of this information to the world by hosting a White House meeting on this matter with key Congressional leaders.

Please let me know at your earliest convenience if you will be able to meet with this coalition of government UFO witnesses. We will be happy to provide a list of these witnesses to your staff if this meeting can be arranged.

I wish to assure you and your family of my best wishes and of my sincere prayers that you may be instrumental in securing for the people of the world a future which is open, peaceful and ever advancing.

Respectfully,

Steven M. Greer, M.D.
Director of CSETI

Letter to Mr. & Mrs. Boutros Boutros Ghali— 15 June 1995

Dear Mr. and Mrs. Ghali,

I hope that this letter finds you well and in good health as you continue to work for international peace and cooperation.

We have finally completed a packet of initial briefing information and a draft video which I had promised to send to you when we last saw Madame Ghali in New York in December. The printed materials have been shared with senior White House Staff, the President's Science Advisor, the former Director of Central Intelligence Jim Woolsey, members of the US Joint Chiefs of Staff and others. This preliminary briefing information is preparatory to a later full briefing which will include the testimony of senior military and intelligence operatives who have handled extraterrestrial materials directly.

As you can see, there is a letter signed by two astronauts, members of the military associated with former US Presidents Eisenhower and Kennedy, and others requesting President Clinton to sign an Executive order releasing a number of witnesses from their national security oaths so that they may openly testify on the subject.

There is wide consensus that the time has come for this information to be released, and we recently received a letter from five star Admiral Lord Hill-Norton, former head of the British Ministry of Defense, supporting this effort. We are hopeful that a major disclosure on this matter can be effected within the next 12 months, if not sooner.

We have heard from your friend Dr. _____ and hope to visit with him in Paris while we are there this summer.

The CSETI research team met with remarkable success in May in Colorado where we held an 'Ambassadors to the Universe' training program, and had a near landing of an extraterrestrial craft near Crestone Colorado. It would appear that the visitors are increasingly ready for open contact.

Please feel free to contact me personally if you have any questions about the enclosed materials, and be assured of my prayers for your success in creating universal peace and understanding.

Respectfully,

Steven M. Greer, M.D.
Director of CSETI

Letter to Vice-President Gore— 23 August 1996

Dear Vice-President Gore,

We have learned of the Administration's plans to host a 'Space Summit' this fall, as a response to the likely discovery of primitive extraterrestrial life forms from Mars. We applaud your initiative to bring this issue into the forefront of people's awareness and are encouraged by these developments.

The CSETI Project Starlight effort has assembled an impressive amount of evidence regarding the existence of extraterrestrial intelligence in near-Earth proximity, as well as witness testimony from military, intelligence and aerospace leaders concerning covert projects dealing with this matter as far back as 1946. This evidence includes:

- over 3,000 military and civilian pilot encounter cases
- hundreds of landing trace cases
- verified photographic, videotape and movie evidence of extraterrestrial spacecraft
- government documents describing certain projects dealing with the UFO/ET matter
- over two dozen important government, military, intelligence and astronaut witnesses to either covert projects dealing with this matter, or of actual extraterrestrial events

We are providing briefings regarding these findings to numerous leaders in advance of a public disclosure of this evidence and witness testimony. To date, we have briefed Director of Central Intelligence Woolsey, U.N. leadership, military leaders at the Joint Chiefs of Staff, Air Force leaders at Wright Patterson Air Force Base, and numerous members of Congress among others. Important members of the Clinton Administration have received materials through secure channels concerning this project, beginning with DCI Woolsey in December of 1993.

It is our feeling that the time has come to present these materials, in part, to both the public and scientific community. We would like to offer to work with your office to develop a strategy to accomplish this, and would suggest that the Space Summit is an appropriate venue for this matter to be seriously discussed and for some of these witnesses to provide information.

Please let me know if you have any questions or comments regarding these ideas. Certainly, with the end of the Cold War, the time has come for the world to know the facts about this subject, and for these covert projects to begin to be returned to public knowledge and oversight. We have met with numerous leaders, including five star admiral and former Ministry of Defense head Lord Hill Norton of Britain, Astronaut Edgar Mitchell, Sen. Barry Goldwater and Laurance Rockefeller, who feel the time has come for a clear and definitive disclosure on this subject.

I am enclosing; some briefing materials for your information, and hope that you will consider the Space Summit as an appropriate setting for this subject to be honestly explored and discussed.

We look forward to hearing from you at your earliest convenience.

Respectfully,

Steven M. Greer, M.D.
Director of CSETI

Letter to Dr. Kohlenberger, Scientific Advisor to Al Gore—22 August 1996

Dear Dr. Kohlenberger,

Your brother Steve and I recently had lunch together in Newport Beach California, and after checking with your wife he suggested that we send you some initial briefing materials. They are enclosed.

My interest in the subject of extraterrestrial intelligence goes back to when I was a child and my uncle was designing the Lunar Module which took Neil Armstrong et al to the moon. I can assure you that 90-95% or more of everything said, written and seen on this matter is a combination of nonsense, fantasy, hoaxes, covert disinformation and conjecture. With that said, I also wish to assure you that there is a core of data, evidence, photographs, videotape, government documents and, most importantly, first hand government witness testimony which establish the fact that we are being visited by advanced extraterrestrial life forms. obviously, they are not using 20th Century Earth technology, and therefore their existence has been largely overlooked by the non-covert scientific community due to paradigm insufficiency and the nonsense and disinformation mentioned above.

We hope you and Vice President Gore will give serious consideration to this matter. Select members of our team, including NASA scientists and first hand covert witnesses to projects dealing with the extraterrestrial issue, are willing to come to Washington to personally brief you and Mr. Gore, and to seek your advice and insight on the best way to publicly disclose this information. The implications of such a disclosure are vast and profound, and span not only science and technology, but also geopolitics, national and world security, theology and the environment. Regarding the latter, we know that the technologies which have been reverse-engineered from retrieved extraterrestrial objects are operational and would obviate the need to use polluting energy systems such as oil, gas, coal or nuclear power. To borrow from Mr. Gore's book, Earth indeed is in the balance.

Please feel free to contact me should you have any comments, questions or suggestions.

Respectfully,

Steven M. Greer, M.D.
Director of CSETI

Letter to Prince Charles—15 November 1996

Dear Prince Charles,

At the suggestion of actor and CSETI member _____, I have prepared a few articles for your perusal on the CSETI project. In particular, they describe on-going processes related to a proximal disclosure on the existence of extraterrestrial life forms.

You may already be aware of some of this work, courtesy of a mutual friend, Lady____ of _____, Scotland. _____ and I have spent some time discussing these matters and she may have previously mentioned this to you.

The Project Starlight disclosure process is entering a critical stage, and, confidentially, we will soon be convening a summit for briefing various world leaders at the United Nations in February, 1997. If you wish, we will notify you of full particulars as soon as they are determined.

Since briefing Director of Central Intelligence James Woolsey in December of 1993, we have located a substantial amount of evidence related to this subject, as well as over 60 first hand military and intelligence witnesses who have been, or are, involved with projects related to UFOs/ETI There is wide agreement among past and current leaders that the time has arrived for a disclosure of the facts related to this matter. Our team has briefed members of Congress, White House staff, members of the Joint Chiefs of Staff' UN leadership, as well as your Lord Hill-Norton, and there is consensus that the time for a disclosure has come. Certainly you, the Queen, and your Prime Minister should also be briefed on these developments.

It may be possible for me to accompany Mr. _____ on his visit to the United Kingdom in December. If so, I would be honored to have the opportunity to share with you further details concerning this matter, as well as a briefing packet which has been provided for President Clinton. Please feel free to contact me at any time should you have any questions.

Wishing you always the best of all worlds,

Respectfully,

Steven M. Greer, M.D.
Director of CSETI

Letter to Various UN Ambassadors—6 February 1997

Dear Ambassador

The Center for the Study of Extraterrestrial Intelligence (CSETI) Project Starlight is an international research initiative which has identified compelling evidence regarding the existence of UFOs/Extraterrestrial Intelligence.

This evidence consists of:

- Excellent scientific cases from around the world over 4,000 landing trace cases of UFOs
- Dozens of scientifically analyzed photographs and videotapes of these objects. Hundreds of pages of official government UFO documents
- And most importantly, several dozen government witnesses from around world who have first hand knowledge of UFO events or projects

In previous discussions with the staff of Secretary General Boutros Boutros Ghali, it has been determined that the time has come for an open scientific conference at the United Nations on this subject.

We are not asking that anyone believe in the reality of UFOs only that they be willing to consider the scientific evidence which exists on the subject.

Because the UFO/ET phenomenon is truly global, we feel that the UN is the most appropriate venue for a conference of this type. There are vast and profound implications to this matter, and no single nation can adequately respond to the challenges of this issue.

Since there has been significant, well-documented UFO activity in your country, we are respectfully requesting that you agree to sponsor or co-sponsor this UN conference on UFO/Extraterrestrial Intelligence. We have learned from the staff of Boutros Boutros

Ghali, that in order for this conference to be held, we need a letter supporting this conference from one or more of the missions to the UN. We hope that your mission will consider doing this.

Please feel free to contact me at your earliest convenience to discuss this further.

Respectfully,

Steven M. Greer, M.D.
Director of CSETI

Letter to Congressman Christopher Cox—30 August 1996

Dear Congressman Cox,

Thank you for taking the time from your busy schedule to meet with Mr. _____ and me on the 19th. We hope you have had a chance to review some of the materials related to the UFO/ETI matter. Please feel free to contact us should you have any further questions or comments.

We also very much appreciate your offer to make some directed inquiries into the matter through appropriate points of contact with the intelligence committees of the Congress. As you requested, since our meeting I have been collecting information on a number of projects and facilities where advanced research and development related to extraterrestrial technology are located. We hope that this information will be useful and will enable you to make as specific an inquiry as possible.

Sources with whom I have spoken indicate that no official oversight and knowledge of these programs is likely to be found, even through intelligence committee briefings in secure settings ("the tank"). Of course, this then brings up the question of how such expensive R and D could be effected. A few possibilities are listed below, and are considered likely avenues of funding by military and intelligence people with whom we have worked on this matter.

I am not optimistic that any official and legal oversight of these projects is occurring. This is based on the following:

- Director of Central Intelligence Jim Woolsey was not briefed on any such projects. I was asked to come to Washington to brief him because he knew the matter was real but was unable to officially get any information of these projects.

- Dick D'Amato, chief counsel and investigator for the Senate Appropriations Committee, told us in 1994 that even with a top secret clearance and subpoena power he could not penetrate these operations, even though he knew they were ongoing projects, and he knew basically where to look. He said "This is the varsity team of all covert projects. Good luck..."
- A four-star general on the Joint Chiefs of Staff knew nothing of these projects, but after a briefing by a member of our team he made an inquiry through channels, and was assured nothing was there. Then he made a private inquiry to a former military colleague with whom he had attended Westpoint and who currently works for a major military contractor. He was told that such projects do exist and was told the locations. He was justifiably astonished and disturbed.
- Similar lack of information exists at very senior levels of the White House.
- Lord Hill-Norton, a five star admiral and former head of the Ministry of Defense in Great Britain has assured us that, even though he now knows such projects exist, he was never informed about them as head of the MOD or MI5.

Of course, we have not queried the congressional intelligence committees, and will do so as you suggested. But given past experiences we would be surprised to find that they have been briefed on this matter, although this remains a possibility.

Alternate Means of Funding

An Air Force source has told us that deep black projects can escape any direct oversight by having funds "hidden" in other projects. For example, $1 billion may be allocated for secret aerospace research and development, with certain projects cited as beneficiaries of this funding. In reality, however, $600 million may be used for those 'acknowledged' secret projects while the remaining $400 million is used for 'unacknowledged' projects.

Many of these projects have been largely 'privatized' by multi-billion dollar military contractor corporations. R & D on the extraterrestrial matter is funded through 'profits' or revenue built into lucrative contracts with the government on 'acknowledged' projects. This, then, creates an indirect source of government funding inasmuch as the funds used for UFO/ET research is derived from 'profits and overhead' related to legitimate projects.

These projects are global in scope and transcend both the boundaries and control of the US government. Similarly, funding is from global, i.e. foreign, sources, as well as domestic public and private sources.

One member of the 'control group' dealing with this matter has told us that there are 'creative' ways of funding such things out of the international monetary system, including the process of rounding off transactions so that the far decimal amounts (.00099) are placed in secure accounts for such funding purposes. This individual, who runs a major global supercomputer firm, states that this is easily done with current supercomputing technologies.

More than one source has stated that certain illegal activities by the military and CIA, such as drug trafficking, have been used to generate revenue for deep black projects.

I hope the enclosed list of facilities and projects will be helpful to your inquiry. It is by no means exhaustive, but reflects the best information to date which our team has been able to collect.

Please feel free to contact me at any time should you have any questions or comments.

Sincerely,

Steven M. Greer, M.D.
Director of CSETI

Invitation to Members of Congress to the D.C. Briefing—31 March 1997

Dear Member of Congress,

The Center for the Study of Extraterrestrial Intelligence (CSETI) wishes to invite you to a closed briefing on UFO/Extraterrestrial Intelligence at which definitive evidence will be presented and first hand government witnesses to UFO/ETI events will be present.

The purpose of this meeting is to present you and your staff with the scientific evidence related to this subject and for you to meet first-hand government witnesses to UFO/ETI events and programs. We are asking for open hearings in the Congress at which these witnesses may testify.

The evidence which will be presented includes:

- Well-researched cases of significant scientific integrity from around the world
- A substantial collection of official government documents related to the matter
- Numerous scientifically verified photographic and videotape cases of these objects
- And most importantly, numerous first-hand United States military, intelligence and other government workers who are willing to testify openly regarding what they know about the UFO/ETI matter.

These government witnesses are heroes of our country who know first hand about extraordinary events of an unambiguous nature related to UFOs. The time has come for these witnesses to be heard by our nation's leaders.

Through meetings with Clinton Administration, Congressional and Military officials we have learned that this subject is being managed covertly outside of recognized and constitutional oversight and control, and there are significant national security and world security risks and implications related to this covert management (please see enclosed documents). We feel it is imperative to the national security of the United States that you, as a leader in our government, be properly briefed on this matter, and that steps are taken to facilitate a disclosure in the near future. The military and intelligence witnesses who wish to come forward are ready to testify before a select open hearing in the Congress.

You and your staff are invited to attend this briefing and to meet these witnesses at the Westin Hotel, 2350 M Street NW, Washington, D.C, from 7pm to 9:30pm on Wednesday, April 9. This briefing will be closed to the media and public. At this meeting, you will be given an extensive briefing document of some of the best available evidence which we have collected. If you are unable to attend the entire meeting, please feel free to stop by for as long as your schedule permits. Please have your staff RSVP to me by 7 April 1997.

We certainly do not expect you to believe in the reality of UFOs, but we do request that you be willing to consider the evidence and listen to these courageous military and intelligence witnesses who are moved on a deep personal and ethical level to come forward.

In 1966 and 1968, Congress held hearings on this matter. Now that definitive evidence and multiple first-hand government witnesses have been identified, we are recommending that Congress again hold hearings to objectively investigate this important subject.

We look forward to seeing you at this briefing on Wednesday, April 9.

Respectfully,

Steven M Greer, M.D.
Director of CSETI

enclosures

Memo to Participants at D.C. Briefing—25 February 1997

From: Steven M. Greer M.D., Director of CSETI
SENSITIVE AND CONFIDENTIAL
Re: Planned DC Briefing for US Government Leaders

The CSETI Project Starlight initiative, designed to effect a definitive disclosure on the UFO/ETI subject, has reached a critical stage in its strategic implementation.

For the past three years we have been meeting with senior Clinton Administration, Congressional, Military and Intelligence officials regarding a disclosure on the reality of UFOs. It is clear that the best outcome would be an open hearing in Congress where both scientific evidence and important first- hand military and government witness testimony could be presented. We have learned through numerous first-hand meetings with relevant congressional and administration officials that the constitutionality of the control and oversight of this matter is apparently not intact. As a service to our country and the world, it is imperative that this subject be disclosed and placed back on the appropriate national and international radar screens.

Therefore, we are inviting you to attend an historic gathering of first- hand military, intelligence and government-related witnesses to the UFO subject, beginning on 8 April 1997. The purposes of this meeting are:

- To assemble as many first- hand, bona- fide and credible US military, intelligence and government-related witnesses to UFO events and projects as possible. By gathering a significant number of such witnesses together, a dynamic of mutual support will be created so that, as a coalition, we may come forward in unison to provide open, public testimony regarding the reality of UFOs. Numerous witnesses coming forward at the appropriate time and setting not only augments the credibility of each witness, but increases the security for each witness and for the process as a whole. While the testimony of one witness may be questioned, that of several dozen cannot and will not be doubted.

- To brief members of Congress, the White House and other relevant government leaders regarding the scientific evidence for UFOs, and for these leaders to meet the witnesses first hand. At this briefing, the members of Congress and others present will specifically be asked to hold open, public hearings at which both the scientific evidence and the witness testimony may be presented.

We wish to emphasize that both the meeting of the government UFO witnesses and the briefing for members of congress will be closed to the public and the media. Only pre-approved participants will be allowed into these meetings.

It is essential that these witnesses have an opportunity to meet each other, bond, and form a coalition with the resolve and support to come forward on this very important issue. It is their testimony which alone can definitively establish the reality of the UFO/Extraterrestrial matter, and return this subject to the democratic process, where it certainly belongs. Moreover, unless our congressional leaders have an opportunity to meet the witnesses first hand, they will continue to doubt the reality of the subject. We must give them the opportunity to choose to do the right thing.

The proposed agenda is as follows:

8 April 1997

Afternoon arrivals in Washington DC 8 April 1997

Evening. Dinner together and introductions, until 10 P.M.

9 April 1997 9 A.M.-5 P.M..: Closed gathering of US government UFO witnesses

9 April 1997 7 P.M.-9:30 P.M.: Confidential Briefing for US government leaders, with presentation of evidence and introduction of witnesses

10 April 1997

Morning and afternoon. Select private meetings with government, military leaders in the DC area, follow up (with select witnesses participation)

Should the Congress choose not to hold open hearings at which these witnesses may provide public testimony, then we will move towards a disclosure event through the United Nations or a similarly appropriate venue. It is clear that no official policy changes will be forthcoming unless we possess the resolve to move forward with a disclosure, regardless of Congressional action.

As you can see from the various enclosures, we have taken all prudent and appropriate steps to inform the President, the Director of Central Intelligence, the Secretary of Defense, the National Security Advisor, Congressional leaders and others of these plans. In personal meetings with senior administration, congressional, CIA and DOD officials, we have made it clear that the witnesses will testify publicly given an appropriate venue and circumstances. We are gratified that on the official level there has been wide support and no opposition voiced regarding this. Indeed, most are relieved that a civilian group is taking this on, since many of these leaders have known that the matter is real, but have had no access to those covert operations that deal with it. We feel that this dangerous and unconstitutional situation must be corrected, and we are confident that the disclosure strategy we have been implementing has the potential to do so.

Working together, we are certain that a safe and definitive disclosure can be effected in the coming months. This action is needed by our nation and the world. Thank you for your courageous and historic participation in this project. I look forward to hearing from you soon.

enclosures:

UNOD letter and return receipt requested forms,
National Security Implications,
Implications,
Project Starlight overview

Memo of Confirmation of Attendance at D.C. Briefing—30 March 1997

To: Members of Congress and Staff attending 9 April Briefing
From: Steven M. Greer M.D., Director of CSETI
Re: Confirmation of Your Attendance

This is to confirm your attendance at the 9 April 1997 Washington briefing convened by CSETI.

Each congressional office present will receive an extensive briefing package including a videotape summary of UFO photographs, movie and videotape footage, over 250 pages of US Government UFO documents, scientific case evidence and air traffic control tape and transcripts.

We are honored that you will be attending this meeting. A reception between 7 pm and 7:30 pm will provide an opportunity for you to meet the numerous first-hand government and military UFO witnesses, as well as Astronaut Edgar Mitchell and the CSETI staff. The briefing will begin at 7:30 pm.

Should you or your staff wish to have a subsequent private meeting on this subject, please do not hesitate to contact me. The CSETI staff and several of the government UFO witnesses will be in the DC area on 10 and 11 April to accommodate your needs in this regard.

Please feel free to contact me directly if you have any questions or comments.

We look forward to seeing you on 9 April 1997.

Letter to Senator Bryan—27 November 1996

Dear Senator Bryan,

Thank you for the opportunity to meet with and your staff in Las Vegas last week. As you requested, I am enclosing a number of briefing documents and materials which have been provided to the White House and some other members of Congress, as well as the UN leadership.

I very much appreciate your patriotic concern over the management of the NRO and related covert operations. The difficulties which you have encountered with the NRO are really only the tip of a somewhat disconcerting iceberg of extensive covert operations which lack adequate oversight by the executive and legislative branches of our government.

While it is true that most information in the public domain on the UFO/ETI subject is nonsense, it is also true that there is a core of data and, now, government witness testimony, which establish the reality of this matter. Indeed, this subject is the most deeply held secret operation in the history of the US government, far exceeding the secrecy surrounding the development of the hydrogen bomb and other important programs involving national security.

I have enclosed a descriptive list of former government, military, intelligence and related witnesses to UFO/ETI programs and operations who can testify to the significance of this issue. Given the fact that both the White House and Congress have been misled about the scope and importance of these secret projects, we feel that the only way for this situation to be corrected is for the Congress to hold open hearings at which these bona fide government witnesses may testify concerning their direct, first hand knowledge of these operations.

We ask that you and other members of the Senate Intelligence Committee begin this process by meeting with a small group of these witnesses, and review the other evidence which has been identified as valid. We would be happy to arrange for such a briefing at your earliest convenience.

A wide range of leaders, both in the US and abroad, feel that the time has come for this matter to be returned to proper and legal oversight and control, and for the public to know about the subject generally. From Sen. Barry Goldwater, to Mr. Laurance Rockefeller, to former British Ministry of Defense Head and five star Admiral Lord Hill-Norton, to former Secretaries of Defense for the US - all feel that this subject should be disclosed and returned to public knowledge and oversight.

We feel it is a matter of national and world security that this be done in the near future. We look forward to working with you, your staff and other members of Congress to achieve this goal, which is so important to the integrity of our constitutional democracy.

Please let me know how we may work with you in the future to provide adequate briefings to you

Respectfully,

Steven M. Greer, M.D.
Director of CSETI
enclosures

Letter to Congressman Newt Gingrich—January 2, 1998

Congressman Newt Gingrich
Speaker of the House
2428 Rayburn HOB
Washington, DC 20515

Dear Congressman Gingrich,

For the past seven years, CSETI (The Center for the Study of Extraterrestrial Intelligence) has been collecting scientific evidence on the matter of extraterrestrial intelligence and so-called UFOs.

We have identified a substantial amount of irrefutable evidence as well as the testimony of over 100 military, intelligence agency and civilian government witnesses who have held Top Secret (TS) clearances, many of whom were additionally cleared for access to Sensitive Compartmented Information (SCI). These people have personally witnessed or been involved in covert operations related to this subject or events of an unambiguous extraterrestrial nature (see enclosures).

The implications of this matter transcend the interests of any given branch or agency of the US government, and impact numerous interrelated areas, all of which affect national security, governmental function and finances and government accountability.

In general, the US government and its legal representatives are excluded from briefings and developments impacting this important area—a situation which we feel is unconstitutional, dangerously avoids Congressional oversight, and which must be corrected as soon as possible.

In meetings which I have had with a sitting CIA Director, members of the Senate and House of Representatives, the Executive

Branch and senior military representatives in the Pentagon, I have found that, while there is interest in the subject and general support for a disclosure regarding the existence of extraterrestrial life forms, there is an almost universal absence of information available to these leaders.

The implications of excessive and undue secrecy surrounding this issue should concern every member of Congress who is charged with upholding the integrity of the U.S. Constitution and the rule of law. The subject itself has vast implications for world peace, science and new technologies, the environment, the economy and geopolitics (see enclosed paper "Implications of an Extraterrestrial Disclosure" [see page 3]).

CSETI is hereby formally asking your committee to convene open hearings on the subject of extraterrestrial intelligence beginning with the next term of Congress. We are prepared to provide you with a substantial body of detailed briefing materials in addition to those enclosed, as well as the names of bona-fide first hand military and intelligence witnesses who wish to testify under oath before Congress. These heroes of our country are eager to inform the Congress and the American people of what they know first-hand regarding this matter.

We respectfully ask that you reply to this request and answer the following questions:

Is your committee willing to receive a preliminary briefing on this subject?

If not, why?

Is your committee willing to allow open, publicly accessed hearings on this subject?

If not, why?

CSETI and its worldwide network of military witnesses, scientists and researchers are ready to provide you with a full briefing on this subject at your earliest convenience. We feel the American people, and the people of the world, deserve to know the truth of this matter.

We request that our elected representatives assert their constitutional rights on behalf of the American citizen to be provided a full, reasonable disclosure on this matter in the next term of Congress.

Sincerely,

Steven M. Greer, M.D.
International Director of CSETI
enclosures

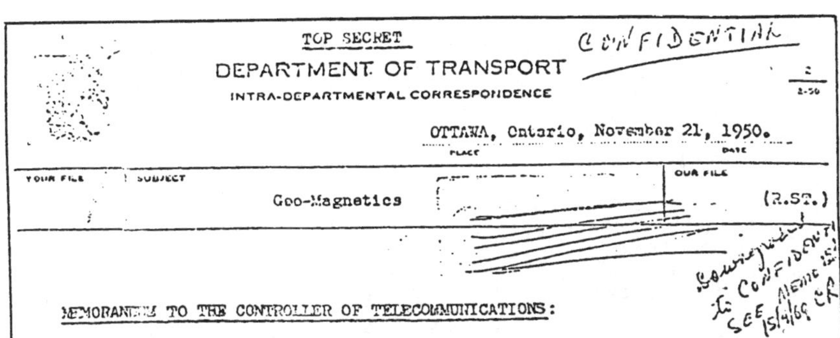

TOP SECRET

CONFIDENTIAL

DEPARTMENT OF TRANSPORT

INTRA-DEPARTMENTAL CORRESPONDENCE

OTTAWA, Ontario, November 21, 1950.

PLACE DATE

YOUR FILE SUBJECT OUR FILE

Geo-Magnetics (R.ST.)

Downgraded to CONFIDENTIAL SEE MEMO 15/4/69 CR

MEMORANDUM TO THE CONTROLLER OF TELECOMMUNICATIONS:

For the past several years we have been engaged in the study of various aspects of radio wave propagation. The vagaries of this phenomenon have led us into the fields of aurora, cosmic radiation, atmospheric radio-activity and geo-magnetism. In the case of geo-magnetics our investigations have contributed little to our knowledge of radio wave propagation as yet, but nevertheless have indicated several avenues of investigation which may well be explored with profit. For example, we are on the track of a means whereby the potential energy of the earth's magnetic field may be abstracted and used.

On the basis of theoretical considerations a small and very crude experimental unit was constructed approximately a year ago and tested in our Standards Laboratory. The tests were essentially successful in that sufficient energy was abstracted from the earth's field to operate a voltmeter, approximately 50 milliwatts. Although this unit was far from being self-sustaining, it nevertheless demonstrated the soundness of the basic principles in a qualitative manner and provided useful data for the design of a better unit.

The design has now been completed for a unit which should be self-sustaining and in addition provide a small surplus of power. Such a unit, in addition to functioning as a 'pilot power plant' should be large enough to permit the study of the various reaction forces which are expected to develop.

We believe that we are on the track of something which may well prove to be the introduction to a new technology. The existence of a different technology is borne out by the investigations which are being carried on at the present time in relation to flying saucers.

While in Washington attending the NARB Conference, two books [illegible], one titled "Behind the Flying Saucer" by Frank Scully, and the other "The Flying Saucers are Real" by Donald Keyhoe. Both books dealt mostly with the sightings of unidentified objects and both books claim that flying objects were of extra-terrestrial origin and might well be space ships from another planet. Scully claimed that the preliminary studies of one saucer which fell into the hands of the United States Government indicated that they operated on some hitherto unknown magnetic principles. It appeared to me that our own work in geo-magnetics might well be the linkage between our technology and the technology by which the saucers are designed and operated. If it is assumed that our geo-magnetic investigations are in the right direction, the theory of operation of the saucers becomes quite straightforward, with all observed features explained qualitatively and quantitatively.

I made discreet enquiries through the Canadian Embassy staff in Washington who were able to obtain for me the following information:

a. The matter is the most highly classified subject in the United States Government, rating higher even than the H-bomb.

b. Flying saucers exist.

c. Their modus operandi is unknown but concentrated effort is being made by a small group headed by Doctor Vannevar Bush.

d. The entire matter is considered by the United States authorities to be of tremendous significance.

I was further informed that the United States authorities are investigating along quite a number of lines which might possibly be related to the saucers such as mental phenomena and I gather that they are not doing too well since they indicated that if Canada is doing anything at all in geo-magnetics they would welcome a discussion with suitably accredited Canadians.

While I am not yet in a position to say that we have solved even the first problems in geo-magnetic energy release, I feel that the correlation between our basic theory and the available information on saucers checks too closely to be mere coincidence. It is my honest opinion that we are on the right track and are fairly close to at least some of the answers.

Mr. Wright, Defence Research Board liaison officer at the Canadian Embassy in Washington, was extremely anxious for me to get in touch with Doctor Solandt, Chairman of the Defence Research Board, to discuss with him future investigations along the line of geo-magnetic energy release. I do not feel that we have as yet sufficient data to place before Defence Research Board which would enable a program to be initiated within that organization, but I do feel that further research is necessary and I would prefer to see it done within the frame work of our own organization with, of course, full co-operation and exchange of information with other interested bodies.

I discussed this matter fully with Doctor Solandt, Chairman of Defence Research Board, on November 20th and placed before him as much information as I have been able to gather to date. Doctor Solandt agreed that work on geo-magnetic energy should go forward as rapidly as possible and offered full co-operation of his Board in providing laboratory facilities, acquisition of necessary items of equipment, and specialized personnel for incidental work in the project. I indicated to Doctor Solandt that we would prefer to keep the project within the Department of Transport for the time being until we have obtained sufficient information to permit a complete assessment of the value of the work.

It is therefore recommended that a PROJECT be set up within the frame work of this Section to study this problem and that the work be carried on a part time basis until such time as sufficient tangible results can be seen to warrant more definitive action. Cost of the program in its initial stages are expected to be less than a few hundred dollars and can be carried by our Radio Standards Lab appropriation.

Attached hereto is a draft of terms of reference for such a project which, if authorized, will enable us to proceed with this research work within our own organization.

W.B. Smith

(W.B. Smith)
Senior Radio Engineer

WBS/CC

Concur
22/11/50

Go ahead with it & keep me posted from time to time G.P. Edwards 2/12/50

WASHINGTON INSTITUTE OF TECHNOLOGY
OCEANOGRAPHIC AND PHYSICAL SCIENCES

DR. ROBERT I. SARBACHER
PRESIDENT AND CHAIRMAN OF BOARD

November 29, 1983

02

Mr. William Steinman
15043 Rosalita Drive
La Mirada, California 90638

Dear Mr. Steinman:

I am sorry I have taken so long in answering your letters. However, I have moved my office and have had to make a number of extended trips.

To answer your last question in your letter of October 14, 1983, there is no particular reason I feel I shouldn't or couldn't answer any or all of your questions. I am delighted to answer all of them to the best of my ability.

You listed some of your questions in your letter of September 12th. I will attempt to answer them as you had listed them.

1. Relating to my own experience regarding recovered flying saucers, I had no association with any of the people involved in the recovery and have no knowledge regarding the dates of the recoveries. If I had I would send it to you.

2. Regarding verification that persons you list were involved, I can only say this:

John von Neuman was definitely involved. Dr. Vannever Bush was definitely involved, and I think Dr. Robert Oppenheimer also.

My association with the Research and Development Board under Doctor Compton during the Eisenhower administration was rather limited so that although I had been invited to participate in several discussions associated withthe reported recoveries, I could not personally attend the meetings. I am sure thatthey would have asked Dr. von Braun, and the others that you listed were probably asked and may or may not have attended. This is all I know for sure.

300 BRAZILIAN AVENUE PALM BEACH, FLORIDA 33480 305-833-1116

Mr. William Steinman
November 29, 1983 - Page 2

3. I did receive some official reports when I was in my office at the Pentagon but all of these were left there as at the time we were never supposed to take them out of the office.

4. I do not recall receiving any photographs such as you request so I am not in a position to answer.

5. I have to make the same reply as on No. 4.

I recall the interview with Dr. Brenner of the Canadian Embassy. I think the answers I gave him were the ones you listed. Naturally, I was more familiar with the subject matter under discussion, at that time. Actually, I would have been able to give more specific answers had I attended the meetings concerning the subject. You must understand that I took this assignment as a private contribution. We were called "dollar-a-year men." My first responsibility was the maintenance of my own business activity so that my participation was limited.

About the only thing I remember at this time is that certain materials reported to have come from flying saucer crashes were extremely light and very tough. I am sure our laboratories analyzed them very carefully.

There were reports that instruments or people operating these machines were also of very light weight, sufficient to withstand the tremendous deceleration and acceleration associated with their machinery. I remember in talking with some of the people at the office that I got the impression these "aliens" were constructed like certain insects we have observed on earth, wherein because of the low mass the inertial forces involved in operation of these instruments would be quite low.

I still do not know why the high order of classification has been given and why the denial of the existence of these devices.

I am sorry it has taken me so long to reply but I suggest you get in touch with the others who may be directly involved in this program.

Sincerely yours,

Dr. Robert I. Sarbacher

P. S. It occurs to me that Dr. Bush's name is inccorrect as you have it. Please check the spelling.

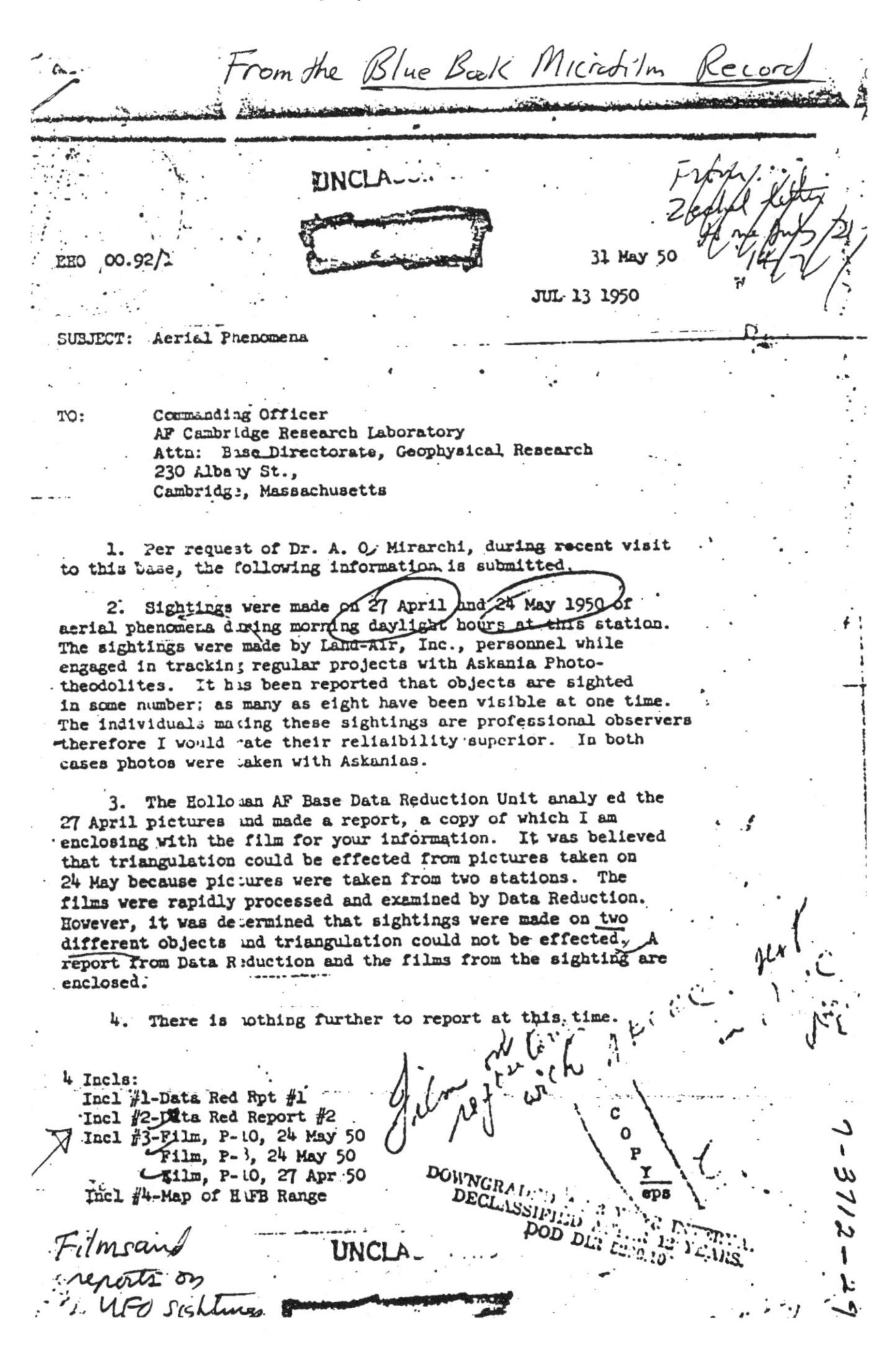

From the Blue Book Microfilm Record

UNCLA...

EHO 00.92/2

31 May 50

JUL 13 1950

SUBJECT: Aerial Phenomena

TO: Commanding Officer
AF Cambridge Research Laboratory
Attn: Base Directorate, Geophysical Research
230 Albany St.,
Cambridge, Massachusetts

1. Per request of Dr. A. O. Mirarchi, during recent visit to this base, the following information is submitted.

2. Sightings were made on 27 April and 24 May 1950 of aerial phenomena during morning daylight hours at this station. The sightings were made by Land-Air, Inc., personnel while engaged in tracking regular projects with Askania Photo-theodolites. It has been reported that objects are sighted in some number; as many as eight have been visible at one time. The individuals making these sightings are professional observers therefore I would rate their reliaibility superior. In both cases photos were taken with Askanias.

3. The Holloman AF Base Data Reduction Unit analyzed the 27 April pictures and made a report, a copy of which I am enclosing with the film for your information. It was believed that triangulation could be effected from pictures taken on 24 May because pictures were taken from two stations. The films were rapidly processed and examined by Data Reduction. However, it was determined that sightings were made on two different objects and triangulation could not be effected. A report from Data Reduction and the films from the sighting are enclosed.

4. There is nothing further to report at this time.

4 Incls:
Incl #1-Data Red Rpt #1
Incl #2-Data Red Report #2
Incl #3-Film, P-10, 24 May 50
Film, P-3, 24 May 50
Film, P-10, 27 Apr 50
Incl #4-Map of HAFB Range

COPY
eps

DOWNGRADED ... DECLASSIFIED ... DOD DIR 5200.10

Films and reports on UFO sightings

UNCLA...

7-3712-29

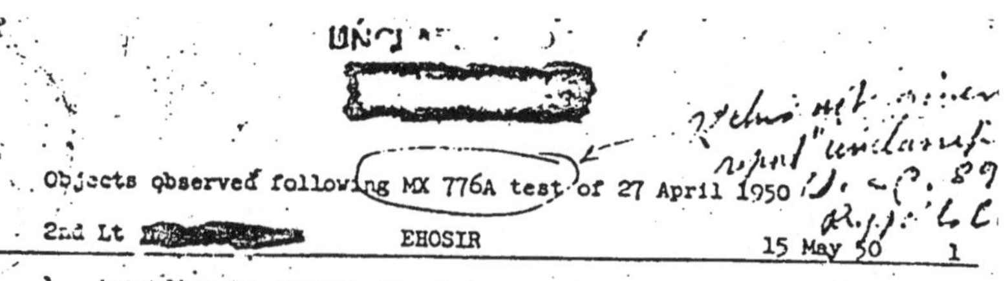

UNCLASSIFIED

Objects observed following MX 776A test of 27 April 1950

2nd Lt [redacted] EHOSIR 15 May 50 1

1. According to conversation between Col. Baynes and Capt. Bryant, the following information is submitted directly to Lt. Albert.

2. Film from station P10 was read, resulting in azimuth and elevation angles being recorded on four objects. In addition, size of image on film was recorded.

3. From this information, together with a single azimuth angle from station M7, the following conclusions were drawn:

a. The objects were at an altitude of approximately 150,000 feet.

b. The objects were over the Holloman range between the base and Tularosa Peak.

c. The objects were approximately 30 feet in diameter.

d. The objects were traveling at an undeterminable, yet high speed.

WILBUR L. MITCHELL
Mathematician
Data Reduction Unit

WLM/rd
ext 172

The other two movies were made at the White Sands Proving Grounds with Askania Cine theodolites—scientific tracking cameras for following guided missiles. The first was made on April 27, 1950. Shortly after a missile was fired and had soared into the stratosphere and fallen, someone spotted an object in the sky. The theodolites were hooked up by an intercom system, and several stations were instructed to try to get pictures. Unfortunately only one camera had film. The pictures showed a smudgy, dark object, not very well defined. It was moving.

EXTRACT RUPPELT TRUE MAG ARTICLE

COPY
eps

DECLASSIFIED AFTER 12 YEARS.
DOD DIR 5200.10

UNCLASSIFIED

DC – III/37

WED ENTERPRISES • A Division of Buena Vista Distribution Co., Inc., subsidiary of Walt Disney Productions

Imagineering

November 9, 1978

Ambassador Griffith
Mission of Grenada to the United Nations
866 Second Avenue
Suite 502
New York, New York 10017

Dear Ambassador Griffith:

I wanted to convey to you my views on our extra-terrestrial visitors popularly referred to as "UFO's", and suggest what might be done to properly deal with them.

I believe that these extra-terrestrial vehicles and their crews are visiting this planet from other planets, which obviously are a little more technically advanced than we are here on earth. I feel that we need to have a top level, coordinated program to scientifically collect and analyze data from all over the earth concerning any type of encounter, and to determine how best to interface with these visitors in a friendly fashion. We may first have to show them that we have learned to resolve our problems by peaceful means, rather than warfare, before we are accepted as fully qualified universal team members. This acceptance would have tremendous possibilities of advancing our world in all areas. Certainly then it would seem that the UN has a vested interest in handling this subject properly and expeditiously.

I should point out that I am not an experienced UFO professional researcher. I have not yet had the privilege of flying a UFO, nor of meeting the crew of one. I do feel that I am somewhat qualified to discuss them since I have been into the fringes of the vast areas in which they travel. Also, I did have occasion in 1951 to have two days of observation of many flights of them, of different sizes, flying in fighter formation, generally from east to west over Europe. They were at a higher altitude than we could reach with our jet fighters of that time.

I would also like to point out that most astronauts are very reluctant to even discuss UFO's due to the great numbers of people who have indescriminately sold fake stories and forged documents abusing their names and reputations without hesitation. Those few astronauts who have continued to have a participation in the UFO field have had to do so very cautiously, There are several of us who do believe in UFO's and who have had occasion to see a UFO on the ground, or from an airplane. There was only one occasion from space which may have been a UFO.

If the UN agrees to pursue this project, and to lend their credibility to it, perhaps many more well qualified people will agree to step forth and provide help and information.

I am looking forward to seeing you soon.

Sincerely,

L. Gordon Cooper
Col. USAF (Ret)
Astronaut

LGC:jm

NOV 15 1978

Air Intelligence Report No. 100-203-79

ANALYSIS OF FLYING OBJECT INCIDENTS IN THE U. S.

Air Intelligence Division Study No. 203
10 December 1948

Directorate of Intelligence and Office of Naval Intelligence

DISTRIBUTION "C"

WARNING: This document contains information affecting the national defense of the United States within the meaning of the Espionage Act, 50 U.S.C., 31 and 32, as amended. Its transmission or the revelation of its contents in any manner to an unauthorized person is prohibited by law. Reproduction of the intelligence in this publication, under the provisions of Army Regulation 380-5, is authorized for United States military agencies provided the source is indicated.

Directorate of Intelligence
Headquarters United States Air Force

Office of Naval Intelligence
Navy Department

Washington, D. C.

DECLASSIFIED
Authority AF INA Memo 5 Mar 85
By [illegible] NARS Date 3/[illegible]

SECRET

APPENDIX "C"

SELECTED REPORTS OF FLYING OBJECT INCIDENTS

1. A NUMBER of reports on unidentified flying objects come from observers who, because of their technical background and experience do not appear to be influenced by unfounded sensationalism nor inclined to report explainable phenomena as new types of airborne devices. Some of the details of their reports are presented in this appendix, along with those from possibly less reliable sources who have reported evidence which is of such a nature that it cannot be entirely ignored.

2. DESCRIPTIONS OF significant incidents, arranged chronologically, follow:

a. During April 1947, two employees of the Weather Bureau Station at Richmond, Virginia reported seeing a strange metallic disk on three occasions through the theodolite while making PIBAL observations. One observation was at 15,000 feet when a disk was followed for 15 seconds. The disk appeared metallic, shaped something like an ellipse with a flat bottom and a round top. It appeared below the balloon and was much larger in size. The disk appeared to be moving rather rapidly, although it was impossible to estimate its speed. The other observations were made at 27,000 feet in like manner.

b. The following month, [redacted] a field engineer for Radio Corporation of America, reported a disk flying near his home in Oklahoma City, Oklahoma. The object was thought to be at an altitude between 10,000 feet and 18,000 feet, and was moving toward the north at a high rate of speed, leaving no trailing effects.

c. While flying at 10,000 feet on a course of 300 degrees, 30 miles northwest of Lake Meade, Nevada, an Air Force lieutenant reported seeing five or six white circular objects in close formation and traveling at an estimated speed of 285 miles per hour. This sighting occurred on 28 June 1947.

d. The following day a party of three, two of them scientists, were motoring along Highway 17 toward the White Sand, New Mexico, V-2 firing grounds and reported seeing a large disk or sphere moving horizontally at a high speed and an estimated altitude of 10,000 feet. It was of uniform shape and had no protruding surfaces such as wings. The object was in sight for about 60 seconds before it disappeared to the northeast. The three observers agreed on the details of the sighting except that one thought he had seen vapor trails.

e. On 7 July 1947, five Portland, Oregon police officers reported varying numbers of disks flying over different parts of the city. All observations were made within a minute or two of 1305 hours.

f. On the same day, [redacted] of Phoenix, Arizona allegedly saw a disk circling his locality during sunset and took two photographs. The resulting pictures (page 9) show a disk-like object with a round front and a square tail in plan form. These photographs have been examined by experts who state they are true photographic images and do not appear to be imperfection in the emulsion or imperfections in the lens. (See Figs. 1, 2, 3 and 4.)

SECRET

g. On 10 July 1947, Mr. [redacted] a Pan-American Airways mechanic reported a circular object flying at high velocity, paralleling the earth's surface and leaving a trail which appeared as a "burning up" of the cloud formation. The sighting occurred near Harmon Field, Newfoundland. Two other persons also saw the trail which remained in the sky for about an hour and was photographed by another PAA employee. The resulting photographs support Mr. Woodruff's observation as far as the sky cleavage is concerned. (See Figs. 5 and 6.)

Fig. 5

SECRET

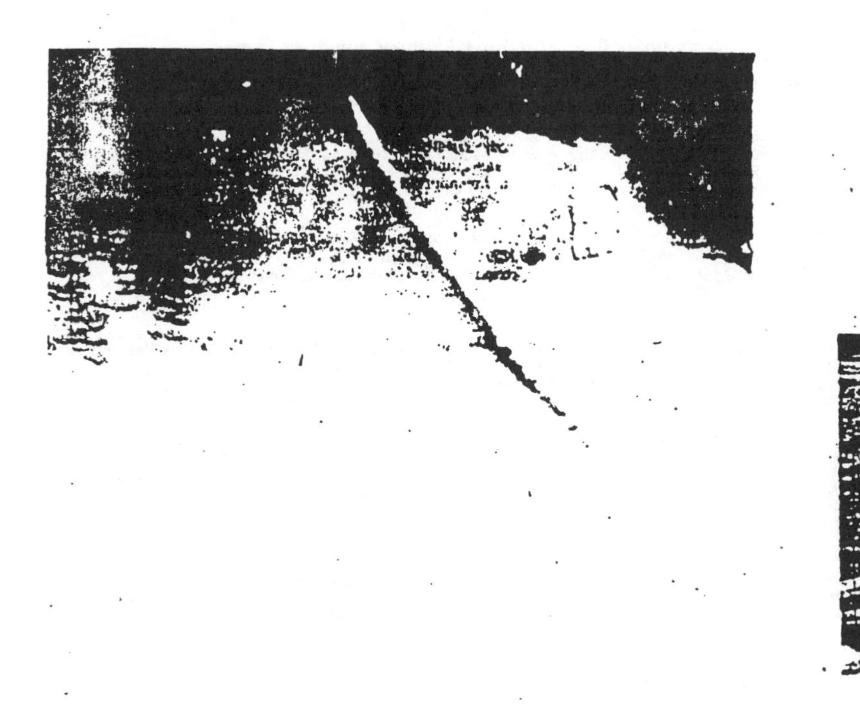

Fig. 6

h. On 29 July 1947, [redacted] while flying near Tacoma, Washington, reported a formation of flying objects. His sketch of their shape corresponds closely to that shown in the photographs made by Mr. [redacted] On the same day, two U. S. Air Force pilots at Hamilton Field reported two flying disks trailing a P-80, following it toward Oakland, California.

i. On 4 August 1947, the pilot and co-pilot of a DC-3, flying for one Al Jones, near Bethel, Alaska, reported a flying disk larger than their aircraft. This disk crossed their path at about 1,000 feet and they turned to give chase. The DC-3 was flying at 170 mph, but the disk flew out of sight in four minutes.

j. On 12 November 1947, two flying disks trailing jet-like streams of fire were reportedly sighted from the bridge of the tanker Ticonderoga, according to the second officer. The Ticonderoga was 20 miles off the Oregon shore. This officer said the disks were in sight 45 seconds, moving at a speed estimated at 700-900 mph, curving in a long, low arc.

SECRET

k. On 7 January 1948, a National Guard pilot was killed while attempting to chase an unidentified object up to 30,000 feet. While it is presumed that this pilot suffered anoxia, resulting in his crash, his last message to the tower was, "it appears to be metallic object..... tremendous size....directly ahead and slightly above....I am trying to close for a better book."

l. On 5 April 1948, three trained balloon observers from the Geophysical Laboratory Section, Watson Laboratories, N.J. reported seeing a round, indistinct object in the vicinity of Holliman Air Force Base, New Mexico. It was very high and fast, and appeared to execute violent maneuvers at high speed. The object was under observation for approximately 30 seconds and disappeared suddenly.

m. A yellow or light colored sphere, 25 to 40 feet in diameter was reported by Lt. Comdr. Marcus L. Lowe, USN, just south of Anacostia Naval Air Station, D.C., while he was flying on 30 April 1948. It was moving at a speed of approximately 100 miles per hour at an altitude of about 4,500 feet. Although winds aloft were from the north-northwest, its course was to the north.

n. On 1 July 1948, twelve disks were reported over the Rapid City Air Base by Major Hammer. These disks were oval-shaped, about 100 feet long, flying at a speed estimated to be in excess of 500 mph. Descending from 10,000 feet, these disks made a 30-degree to 40-degree climbing turn accelerating very rapidly until out of sight.

o. On 17 July 1948, a report from Kirtland Air Force Base describes a sighting in the vicinity of San Acacia, New Mexico, of seven unidentified objects flying in a "J" formation at an estimated height of 20,000 feet above the terrain. The formation varied from "J" to "L" to circle after passing the zenith. Flashes from the objects were observed after passing 30 degrees beyond the zenith but there was no smoke or vapor trail. If the reported altitude is correct the speed was estimated at 1,500 miles per hour, according to the report.

p. Other sightings of lights and trails, rather than disks, have been reported, viz:

(1) On 12 September 1947, the pilot and co-pilot of a Pan American aircraft, en route from Midway to Honolulu, saw a blue-white light approaching, changing to twin reddish glows upon withdrawal. The pilot estimated the speed of the light at about 1,000 knots.

(2) On 15 June 1948, Mr. [redacted] territory manager for the B.F. Goodrich Company, observed a reddish glow with a jet exhaust in the vicinity of Miles City, Montana. This glowing light made no sound, traveled about twice the speed of a conventional aircraft and flew from noth to south several times in a wide arc, finally disappearing over the horizon.

q. During the early morning of 25 July 1948, two Eastern Airlines pilots reported having seen a huge flying craft similar to a V-2 pass their aircraft in flight. (See Figs. 7 and 8.) The attached drawings made by these two observers very closely resemble a flying object reported to have been seen on 20 July 1948, by [redacted] chief investigator of Court of Damage Inquiry, and his daughter at Arnham, Netherlands. This object appeared to be a wingless aircraft having two decks. The craft, sighted four times through scattered clouds and unlimited visibility, was traveling at high speed at a high altitude. A sound similar to that made by a V-2 was reported.

r. An object, similar in shape to the one in the preceding incident was reported by an experienced American newspaper reporter about 25 kilometers northeast of Moscow on 3 August 1948. A Russian acquaintance identified it as a rigid airship but the reporter disagrees because it flew at a high, but not excessive speed.

s. On 1 October 1948 at approximately 2030 hours the pilot of a F-51 aircraft, 2nd Lt. George F. Gorman (North Dakota Air National Guard), flying near Fargo, North Dakota, sighted an intermittent white light about 3,000 feet below his 4,500 feet cruising altitude. The pilot pursued the light which appeared to then take evasive tactics. The object or light out-turned, out-speeded, and out-climbed the F-51 in every instance during the attempt to intercept. The pilot lost contact 27 minutes after the initial sighting. The same light was observed by three other witnesses from the ground: Mr. [redacted], Air Traffic Controller, Mr. [redacted] Assistant Traffic Controller, and Dr. [redacted], Oculist. A comparison of all testimony revealed that one object was sighted and that it consisted only of a small round ball of clear white light with no apparent shape attached. It was about 6 to 8 inches in diamter. At times it traveled faster than the F-51 and performed maneuvers in an evasive manner. When first sighted the ball of light was traveling at an estimated 250 miles per hour. Under this condition, the light was not continuous but blinked off and on. At high performance the white light was continuous. Subsequent investigation eliminated the possibility that this incident may have been another aircraft or a meteorological balloon.

t. On 18 November 1948 at approximately 2145 hours, three reserve pilots, 2nd Lt. Kenwood W. Jackson, 2nd Lt. Glen L. Stalker, and 2nd Lt. Henry G. Combs, flying near Andrews Field, Maryland, encountered an unidentified flying object. When first sighted, it appeared to be lighted and flying at about 1,700 feet. Three or four passes were made in an attempt to identify it. The pilot of the aircraft stated that while diving his aircraft at approximately 240 miles per hour, the object would climb vertically and then would drop below the aircraft from behind and continue to circle. On the last pass, the landing light was switched on and momentarily a dull gray glow from the object was observed. Lt. Combs stated he maintained contact for about ten minutes with the object flying between the lights of Washington, D. C. and his aircraft. All that could be observed was an oblong ball with one light, no wings and no exhaust flame. It finally made a very tight turn and headed toward the east coast at an estimated 500 to 600 miles per hour. At the same time Staff Sergeant John J. Kushner observed from the ground an unusual object in the air over Andrews Field. He stated that it was not very high and that it did not look like an aircraft.

3. REPORTS OF radar intercepts point to unusual air activity which may be related to flying objects.

a. On 1 July 1947, a GCA radar at Hokkaido, Japan picked up an unidentified target at 16 miles, with a speed in excess of 500 mph. This target split into two targets, each estimated to be larger than a P-51.

b. On 16 September 1947, an MEW radar at Fukuoka, Japan, picked up a target at 89 miles and trailed it to 19 miles, where it faded. Speed was 840-900 mph. The speed measurement, made by a good crew through a 70-mile track, is believed accurate.

4. Investigations conducted by Headquarters, Air Materiel Command, have definitely established the identification of 18 of approximately 210 so-called flying saucers which have been reported. Approximately nine per cent of the total number of incidents are, therefore, eliminated from further specific consideration. Among those incidents positively explained, three were hoaxes, two were from unreliable witnesses. In the remaining 13 eliminated incidents, objects were actually seen but investigation has shown that they were celestial bodies or phenomena, meteorological and carnival balloons, and airborne cosmic ray experimental equipment. The following examples are presented for comparison of the information reported by witnesses and true identification of the object involved:

a. On 22 July 1948, Captain Henry Glover (Ordnance Reserve) and his wife observed at Van Nuys, California, an object which they were unable to positively identify. Object at first appeared to be round and looked like a weather balloon at about 2,000 feet but there was no characteristic bobbing. The wind was blowing on the ground but the object was quite steady. During the time it was under observation, about an hour, it traveled through a vertical arc of about twenty-five (25°) degrees or more. The observer concluded that it was not a celestial body. It has a bluish luminescence and as the sun set, the object's color gradually changed to orange at dusk and ceased to be illuminated almost instantaneously. The outline was clear and the air was clear with visibility unlimited. The object traveled from the east to the west.

This object was determined by investigation to have been a balloon carrying cosmic ray equipment.

SECRET

b. On 19 August 1948, at approximately 1050 hours an unidentified flying object was visible from the ground at Godman Air Force Base, Kentucky. This object was estimated to be at about 30,000 to 40,000 feet altitude, spherical in shape, bright silver color and gave a bright reflection from the sun. An F-51 was dispatched from Standiford Air Force Base, Kentucky, to observe the object. During observation from the ground, there was no change in the elevation of the object and it seemed to be moving southwest from Godman Air Force Base. The F-51 which was flying over Godman AFB at an altitude of 30,000 to 35,000 feet reported that it was unable to locate the object although it was still visible from the ground with the naked eye. Azimuth and elevation readings were taken by theodolite every minute and the path of the object was charted.

The object was determined to be the planet Venus by Mr. Moore, the head astronomer at the University of Louisville, Louisville, Kentucky. It is believed that earlier incidents at Godman Field (reference paragraph 2k, page 12, Appendix "C") may also have been observations of the planet Venus.

5. AMONG THOSE incidents still not positively explained, reported observations differ to some extent, but three general categories of sightings emerge -- the flying disk, the ball of fire and the large jet rocket. Interesting observations that were noted are:

a. Most of the objects are a thin disk, round on top and flat on the bottom. The front half of the disk is often circular, sweeping back to a square tail across the full width.

b. A high rate of climb as well as the apparent ability to remain motionless or hover for a considerable length of time is indicated.

c. Reported sizes have varied from that of a 25-cent piece to 250 feet in diameter, and from the size of a pursuit plane to the bulk of six B-29 airplanes.

d. Speeds have been estimated throughout the entire range from very slow or hovering to supersonic.

e. Sounds and visual trails are not normally associated with the sightings.

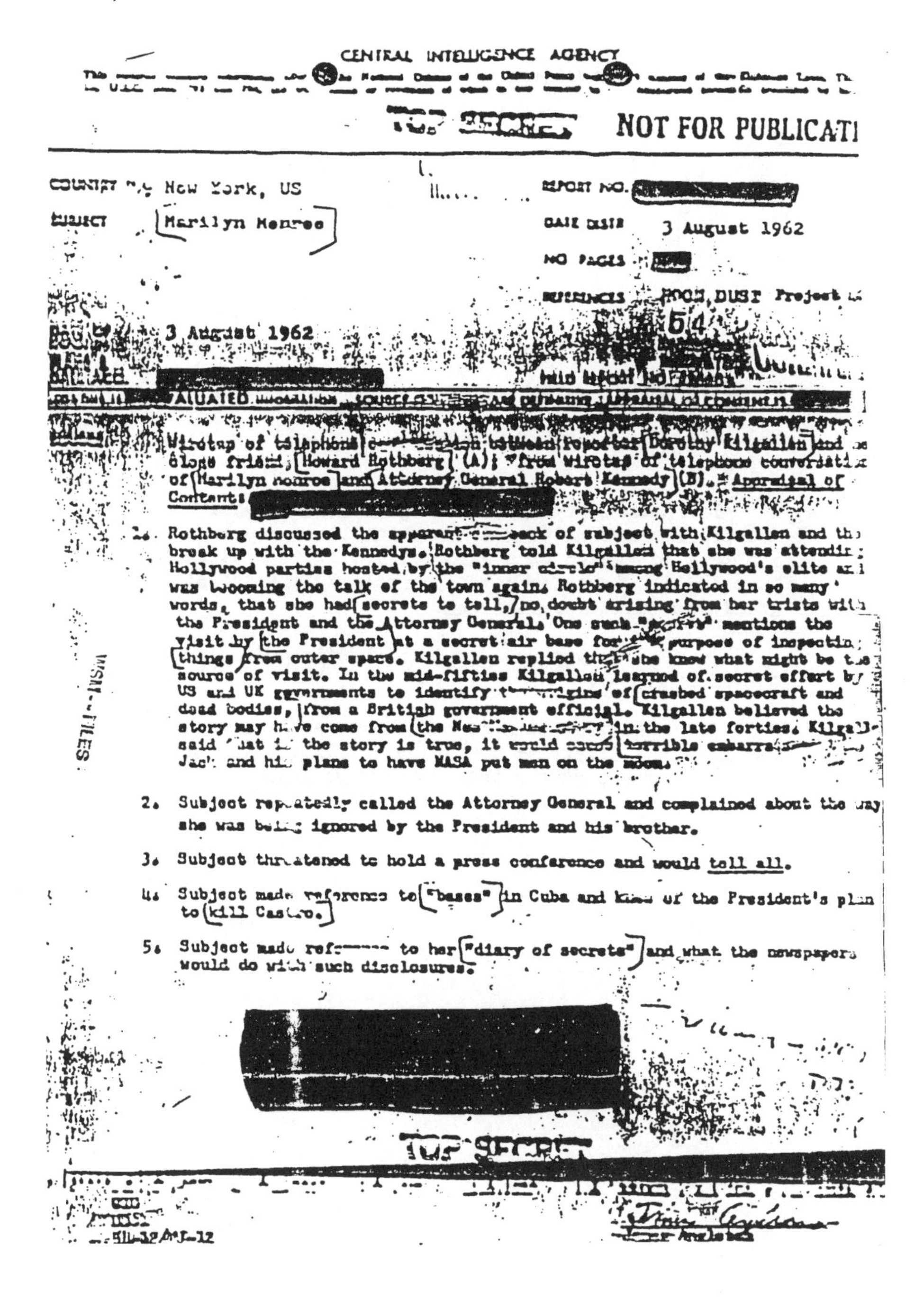
CENTRAL INTELLIGENCE AGENCY

TOP SECRET NOT FOR PUBLICATI

COUNTRY New York, US

SUBJECT Marilyn Monroe

REPORT NO.

DATE DISTR 3 August 1962

NO PAGES

REFERENCES MOON DUST Project

3 August 1962

Wiretap of telephone conversation between reporter Dorothy Kilgallen and close friend, Howard Rothberg (A); from wiretap of telephone conversation of Marilyn Monroe and Attorney General Robert Kennedy (B). Appraisal of Contents:

1. Rothberg discussed the apparent comeback of subject with Kilgallen and the break up with the Kennedys. Rothberg told Kilgallen that she was attending Hollywood parties hosted by the "inner circle" among Hollywood's elite and was becoming the talk of the town again. Rothberg indicated in so many words, that she had secrets to tell, no doubt arising from her trists with the President and the Attorney General. One such "secret" mentions the visit by the President at a secret air base for the purpose of inspecting things from outer space. Kilgallen replied that she knew what might be the source of visit. In the mid-fifties Kilgallen learned of secret effort by US and UK governments to identify the origins of crashed spacecraft and dead bodies, from a British government official. Kilgallen believed the story may have come from the New Mexico in the late forties. Kilgallen said that if the story is true, it would cause terrible embarrassment to Jack and his plans to have NASA put men on the moon.

2. Subject repeatedly called the Attorney General and complained about the way she was being ignored by the President and his brother.

3. Subject threatened to hold a press conference and would tell all.

4. Subject made reference to "bases" in Cuba and knew of the President's plan to kill Castro.

5. Subject made reference to her "diary of secrets" and what the newspapers would do with such disclosures.

TOP SECRET

MSM--FILES

CENTRAL INTELLIGENCE AGENCY

WASHINGTON 25, D. C.

OFFICE OF THE DIRECTOR

000014

MEMORANDUM TO: Director, Psychological Strategy Board

SUBJECT: Flying Saucers

1. I am today transmitting to the National Security Council a proposal (TAB A) in which it is concluded that the problems connected with unidentified flying objects appear to have implications for psychological warfare as well as for intelligence and operations.

2. The background for this view is presented in some detail in TAB B.

3. I suggest that we discuss at an early board meeting the possible offensive or defensive utilization of these phenomena for psychological warfare purposes.

Walter B. Smith
Director

Enclosure

RELEASED 5/9/94

See next page for translation

DEC 10 1952

MEMORANDUM FOR: The Director of Central Intelligence

THROUGH: Deputy Director (Intelligence)

SUBJECT: Unidentified Flying Objects

REFERENCE: Request of the Director of 10 December 1952

1. The following is a summary of the current situation with respect to the investigation of unidentified flying objects. Recent incidents include:

a. Movies of ten (10) unidentified flying objects (unexplained on the basis of natural phenomena or known types of aircraft), near Tremonton, Utah, on 2 July 1952.

b. A very brilliant unidentified light over the coast of Maine for about four hours on the night of 10-11 October at a height computed to be two or three times that which can be sustained by any known device.

c. Alleged contact with a device on the ground in Florida late this summer which left some presently unexplained after-effects.

d. Numerous other sightings of lights or objects which either in configuration or performance do not resemble any known aerial vehicle or explainable natural phenomena.

2. In furtherance of the IAC action on 4 December, O/SI has been working with Dr. H. P. Robertson, consultant (former Director of Research, WSEG), toward establishing a panel of top scientists and engineers in the fields of astrophysics, nuclear energy, electronics, etc., to review this situation. Wholehearted cooperation has been assured by DI/USAF and ATIC, and a visit by AD/SI, Dr. Robertson, and Mr. Durant of SI to ATIC is planned for Friday. It is hoped to organize the panel and undertake substantive scientific review of this subject within the next two to three weeks.

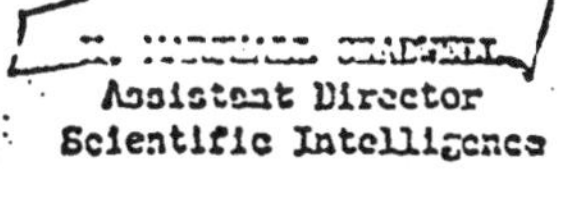

Assistant Director
Scientific Intelligence

Distribution:
DD/I - 1
Opns/SI - 1
Prod/SI - 1
AD/SI - 2

OSI:RLC/ntw (10Dec52)

3c

Pertinent Parts Retyped For Readability

Memorandum For:The Director of Central Intelligence
[illegible]:Deputy Director (Intelligence)
SUBJECT:Unidentified Flying Objects
[illegible]:Request of the Director of 10 December 1952

1. The following is a summary of the current situation with respect to the investigation of unidentified flying objects. Recent incidents include:

a. Movies of ten (10) unidentified flying objects (unexplained on the basis of natural phenomena or known types of aircraft), near Trementon, Utah on 2 July 1952.

b. A very brilliant unidentified light over the coast of Maine for about four hours on the night of 10-11 October at a height computed to be two or three times that which can be sustained by any known device.

c. Alleged contact with a device left on the ground in Florida late this summer which left some presently unexplained aftereffects.

d. Numerous other sightings of lights or objects which either in configuration or performance do not resemble any known aerial vehicle or explainable natural phenomena.

2. In furtherance of the I/C action on 4 December, O/SI has been working with Dr. H.P. Robertson, consultant (former Director of Research, [illegible] establishing a panel of top scientists and engineers in the fields of astrophysics, nuclear energy, electronics, etc., to review this situation. [illegible] cooperation has been secured by DI/USAF and ATIC, and a [illegible], Dr. Robertson, and Mr. Durant of SI to ATIC is planned for Friday. It is hoped to organize the panel and undertake substantive scientific review of this subject within the next two to three weeks.

H. MARSHALL CHADWELL Assistant Director Scientific Intelligence

[omitted]

SEP 24 1952

MEMORANDUM FOR: Director of Central Intelligence

THROUGH : Deputy Director (Intelligence)

SUBJECT : Flying Saucers

1. Recently an inquiry was conducted by the Office of Scientific Intelligence to determine whether there are national security implications in the problem of "unidentified flying objects," i.e., flying saucers; whether adequate study and research is currently being directed to this problem in its relation to such national security implications; and what further investigation and research should be instituted, by whom, and under what aegis.

2. It was found that the only unit of Government currently studying the problem is the Directorate of Intelligence, USAF, which has charged the Air Technical Intelligence Center (ATIC) with responsibility for investigating the reports of sightings. At ATIC there is a group of three officers and two secretaries to which come, through official channels, all reports of sightings. This group conducts investigation of the reports, consulting as required with other Air Force and civilian technical personnel. A world-wide reporting system has been instituted and major Air Force Bases have been ordered to make interceptions of unidentified flying objects. The research is being conducted on a case basis and is designed to provide a satisfactory explanation of each individual sighting. ATIC has concluded an arrangement with Battelle Memorial Institute for the latter to establish a machine indexing system for official reports of sightings.

3. Since 1947, ATIC has received approximately 1500 official reports of sightings plus an enormous volume of letters, phone calls, and press reports. During July 1952 alone, official reports totaled 250. Of the 1500 reports, Air Force carries 20 percent as unexplained and of those received from January through July 1952 it carries 28 percent unexplained.

4. In its inquiry into this problem, a team from CIA's Office of Scientific Intelligence consulted with a representative of Air Force Special Studies Group; discussed the problem with those in charge of the Air Force Project at Wright-Patterson Air Force Base; reviewed a considerable volume of intelligence reports; checked the Soviet press and broadcast indices; and conferred with three CIA consultants, who have broad knowledge of the technical areas concerned.

5. It was found that the ATIC study is probably valid if the purpose is limited to a case-by-case explanation. However, that study does not solve the more fundamental aspects of the problem. These aspects are to determine definitely the nature of the various phenomena which are causing these sightings, and to discover means by which these causes, and their visual or electronic effects, may be identified immediately. The CIA consultants stated that these solutions would probably be found on the margins or just beyond the frontiers of our present knowledge in the fields of atmospheric, ionospheric, and extraterrestrial phenomena, with the added possibility that the present dispersal of nuclear waste products might also be a factor. They recommended that a study group be formed to perform three functions:

a. analyze and systematize the factors which constitute the fundamental problem;

b. determine the fields of fundamental science which must be investigated in order to reach an understanding of the phenomena involved; and

c. make recommendations for the initiation of appropriate research.

Dr. Julius A. Stratton, Vice President of the Massachusetts Institute of Technology, has indicated to CIA that such a group could be constituted at that Institute. Similarly, Project Lincoln, the Air Force's air defense project at MIT, could be charged with some of these responsibilities.

6. The flying saucer situation contains two elements of danger which, in a situation of international tension, have national security implications. These are:

a. Psychological - With world-wide sightings reported, it was found that, up to the time of the investigation, there had been in the Soviet press no report or comment, even satirical, on flying saucers, though Gromyko had made one humorous mention of the subject. With a State-controlled press, this could result only from an official policy decision. The question, therefore, arises as to whether or not these sightings:

(1) could be controlled,

(2) could be predicted, and

(3) could be used from a psychological warfare point of view, either offensively or defensively.

The public concern with the phenomena, which is reflected both in the United States press and in the pressure of inquiry upon the Air Force, indicates that a fair proportion of our population is mentally conditioned to the acceptance of the incredible. In this fact lies the potential for the touching-off of mass hysteria and panic.

b. Air Vulnerability - The United States Air Warning System will undoubtedly always depend upon a combination of radar screening and visual observation. The U.S.S.R. is credited with the present capability of delivering an air attack against the United States, yet at any given moment now, there may be current a dozen official unidentified sightings plus many unofficial ones. At any moment of attack, we are now in a position where we cannot, on an instant basis, distinguish hardware from phantom, and as tension mounts we will run the increasing risk of false alerts and the even greater danger of falsely identifying the real as phantom.

7. Both of these problems are primarily operational in nature but each contains readily apparent intelligence factors.

8. From an operational point of view, three actions are required:

a. Immediate steps should be taken to improve identification of both visual and electronic phantom so that, in the event of an attack, instant and positive identification of enemy planes or missiles can be made.

b. A study should be instituted to determine what, if any, utilization could be made of these phenomena by United States psychological warfare planners and what, if any, defenses should be planned in anticipation of Soviet attempts to utilize them.

c. In order to minimize risk of panic, a national policy should be established as to what should be told the public regarding the phenomena.

9. Other intelligence problems which require determination are:

a. The present level of Soviet knowledge regarding these phenomena.

b. Possible Soviet intentions and capabilities to utilize these phenomena to the detriment of United States security interests.

c. The reasons for silence in the Soviet press regarding flying saucers.

10. Additional research, differing in character and emphasis from that presently being performed by Air Force, will be required to meet the specific needs of both operations and intelligence. Intelligence responsibilities in this field as regards both collection and analysis can be discharged with maximum effectiveness only after much more is known regarding the exact nature of these phenomena.

11. I consider this problem to be of such importance that it should be brought to the attention of the National Security Council in order that a community-wide coordinated effort towards its solution may be initiated.

H M Chadwell

H. MARSHALL CHADWELL
Assistant Director
Scientific Intelligence

NMCC
THE NATIONAL MILITARY COMMAND CENTER
WASHINGTON, D.C. 20301

21 January 1976
0630 EST

MEMORANDUM FOR RECORD

Subject: Report of UFO - Cannon AFB NM

Reference: AFOC Phonecon 21055 EST Jan 76

The following information was received from the Air Force Operations Center at 0555 EST:

"Two UFOs are reported near the flight line at Cannon AFB, New Mexico. Security Police observing them reported the UFOs to be 25 yards in diameter, gold or silver in color with blue light on top, hole in the middle and red light on bottom. Air Force is checking with radar. Additionally, checking weather inversion data."

J.B. MORIN
Rear Admiral, USN
Deputy Director for
Operations, NMCC

SECRET (NOFORN) of 2 masters
(SECURITY INFORMATION when filled in)

Excerpts

SUPPLEMENT TO AF FORM 112

ORIGINATING AGENCY	REPORT NO.	PAGE		PAGES
US AIR ATTACHE	IR 193-55	2	of 9	

QUOTED below is the cable classified Top Secret which was sent to Hqs. USAF on 13 Oct 55. USAIRA control number is C-103 and text follows:

" INACT. TO: DINTA, WASH. DC. NOFORN. USAF handle as OPERATIONAL IMMEDIATE. USAF CRYPTO PASS TO CINCUSAFE AND USAIRA MOSCOW. THREE RELIABLE US OBSERVERS, SENATOR RICHARD RUSSELL, LT. COL. E.U. HATHAWAY, ARMY, MR. RUBEN EFRON, VISITED PRAGUE 12-13 OCT. ARRIVING DIRECT FROM KIEV, VIA BAKU, TIFLIS, DNIEPERPETROVSK, BLACK SEA AREA, AND REPORTED FOLLOWING TO USAIRA AND USARMA.: ON 4 OCT. 55 AT 1910 HOURS BETWEEN ATJATY AND ADZHIJABUL, TEN MINUTES BY RAIL AFTER DEPARTING ATJATY IN TRANS CAUCASUS REGION, TWO ROUND AND CIRCULAR UNCONVENTIONAL AIRCRAFT RESEMBLING FLYING DISCS OR FLYING SAUCERS WERE SEEN TAKING OFF ALMOST VERTICALLY ONE MINUTE APART. DISC AIRCRAFT ASCENDED NEAR DUSK WITH OUTER SURFACE REVOLVING SLOWLY TO RIGHT AND WITH TWO LIGHTS STATIONARY ON TOP NEAR MIDDLE PART. SPARKS OR FLAME SEEN COMING FROM AIRCRAFT. NO PROTRUSIONS SEEN ON AIRCRAFT WHICH PASSED OVER OBSERVERS' TRAIN. BOTH FLYING DISC AIRCRAFT ASCENDED RELATIVELY SLOWLY TO ABOUT 6000 FEET, THEN SPEED INCREASED SHARPLY IN HORIZONTAL FLIGHT BOTH ON NORTHERLY HEADING. FLYING ATTITUDE OF DISC REMAINED SAME DURING ASCENT AS IN CRUISE, LIKE A DISCUS IN FLIGHT. TWO OPERATING SEARCHLIGHTS POINTING ALMOST VERTICAL SEEN NEAR TAKEOFF AREA LOCATED ABOUT 1-2 MILES SOUTH OF RR LINE. AFTER SIGHTING SOVIET TRAINMEN BECAME EXCITED AND LOWERED CURTAINS AND REFUSED PERMISSION TO LOOK OUT WINDOWS. US OBSERVERS FIRMLY BELIEVE THESE UNCONVENTIONAL AIRCRAFT WERE GENUINE SAUCER OR DISC AIRCRAFT. USAIRA RATES INFO B-2. ON 9 OCT.55. AT DNIEPERPETROVSK AIRFIELD, HATHAWAY REPORTED

RECOMMEND COMPLETE DEBRIEFING OF RUSSELL GROUP UPON RETURN AND SUGGEST COMMENDATION FROM D/I FOR EFFORTS. RUSSELL GROUP DEPARTED PRAGUE ABOARD SWAISSAIR FOR ROME 13 OCT. (Signed) T.S.RYAN." 8c

On 12 Oct. 1955 at about 2145 hours, Sen. Russell, Lt. Col. E.U. Hathaway, U.S. Army staff officer assigned to Senate Armed Forces Committee, and Mr. Ruben Efron, Committee Consultant, arrived at Wilson (Hlavni) Station in Prague, having come direct from Kiev. Their rail route from Kiev brought them to COP, at the eastern border of Czechoslovakia, where they observed the RR gauge switching operation from the Russian broa gauge to the Czech standard guage. Upon arrival at the RR Wilson Station, the Russell group was met by the acting Chief of Mission, Mr. Harold Vedle-, and the USAIRA. We escorted the group to the US Residency where they were to spend the night. It was evident that they had seen much and had been to places in Russia and possibly in Czechoslovakia where US observers had no been, at least for a good many years. Sen. Russell stated that he had bee in Prague once before in 1927, and was anxious to see some familiar place After arrival at the Residency and dinner, Lt. Col. Hathaway expressed a desire to report something of the utmost importance to the USAIRA, "some you may not believe, but something that we've been told by your people ( ) doesn't exist." I suggested that we not discuss anything at the Residenc because of the absence of security precautions but suggested that we mee early the next morning in my office together with Col. Thomas Dooley , Army Attache. Lt. Col. Hathaway said he was anxious to report his obser and that he had witnesses, fortunately, in Sen. Russell and Mr. Efron.

We met at 0900 on 13 Oct. in the larger office of the Army Atta and proceeded with the debriefing amid adequate safeguards for talking. Present were: Lt. Col. Hathaway, Mr. Efron, Col. Dooley and myself. Col. Dooley and I took notes and provided paper for sketches. Sen. Russell was busy with the Chief of Mission and was unable to attend. Due to the departure time of the group, we were unable to spend more than one hour talking, the interview ending about 1000. Col. Hathaway did most of the explaining and answering with Mr. Efron supplementing and adding support.

Lt Col.Hathaway proved to be an excellent observer and Mr. Efron had kept detailed notes which he referred to for times and places.

Hathaway led off with "I doubt if you're going to believe this but we all saw it. Sen. Russell was the first to see this flying saucer and he called us to the window, and we both saw the second one (pointing to EFRON who nodded yes). We've been told for years that there isn't such a thing but all of us saw it, including Sen Russell. "It was emphasized that Sen. Russell saw the first flying saucer or flying disc ascend and pass over the train on a northerly course, taking off from the left side of the train's direction, which places the take-off area on the south side of the RR line on which they were travelling.

I stated that I don't disbelieve anything after having been in Czechoslovakia for 17 months. The following raw notes are quoted with my additional comments after:

1. "Two flying saucer type aircraft were seen between two railway station stops after we left BAKU."

2. "It was after we left ATJATY, we were there at 1900 and we saw the aircraft at 1910. The next place we saw was ADZHIJABUL." (Efrons notes.)

3. "They took off straight up and then the speed increased greatly as they moved straight ahead, horizontally, and disappeared to the right of the train." (Questioning revealed that the angle of ascent was not exactly "straight up" but rather in a slight arc just off the vertical line.)

4. "The whole object whirred and then levelled and zoomed off at very high speed." (Questioning revealed that the outer surface of the object revolved slowly in a clockwise direction or to the right, with the rate of ascent being relatively slow in comparison to the high speed which the object took off at when it reached altitude.)

5. " The take off was at an angle to about 2000 meters." (Both objects were said to have ascended almost vertically to an approximate altitude of 6000 feet before sharply increasing speed in level flight.)

6. "They were seen out of window on left side of train."

7. " Two searchlight were seen pointing at an angle near where the saucer took Off." (The angle was nearly vertical and evidently, I gathered, that the angle of one searchlight beam was nearly vertical approximating the arc which the disc ascended to 6000 feet, while the second searchlight beam was pointing at another spot. Lack of time prevented complete clarification of the searchlight beams. Dusk was falling at the time of sighting.)

8. "Some sparking or flame came out bottom as craft rose."

9. "After we saw the two discs, the Soviet trainmen became excited, closing curtains and telling us that we were not allowed to look out of windows." (The behavior of the trainmen was such as to indicate that the US passengers had seen something that they were not supposed to see.)

10. "Approximately one minute elapsed between the first and second takeoffs of the aircraft." (It was explained that Sen Russell had seen the

11. DELETED

12. "There were two lights towards the inside of the disc which remained stationary as the outer surface went around. " (Both agreed firmly on this point.) "The lights sat near the top of the disc." (If a line representing the diameter of the disc were divided into three segments, the lights would have been located at the two points of division between the middle segment and the two outside segments ie. see sketch drawn with aid of Mr Efron:

13. "The aircraft was circular." "The aircraft was round." "It resembled a flying saucer." "It seemed to be the shape of a discus, round and circular- revolving clockwise or to the right." (It was definitely round or at least circular in the eyes of these two observers, containing no protrusions or "sticks" or bulges. No estimate could be obtained from either observer re thickness or diameter.

14. " There was no noticable color." (It was stated that dusk prevented any color impressions.)

15. "After reaching 2000 meters, it whipped off at a great speed from our left to our right, or towards the north from the south." (Speed differential was very noticable between ascent and level flight speed.)

16. "We could see the take-off on the horizon to our left or south of out train."

17. "Outer part revolved slowly to right." (There seemed to be a different impression of the disc's movement while climbing and after assuming level flight, with the terms "revolving slowly" used for the climb and the term "whirring" for the cruising flight.

13. #"The disc rose in the same position as it was in when it sped away." The flying attitude of the flying disc was said to resemble a discus in flight.)

8E

USAIRA COMMENT: I believe that further debriefing of all three US observers in a more relaxed atmosphere and with more time would produce much more valuable technical details than the hurried interview above.

WARNING: This document contains information affecting the national defense of the United States within the meaning of the Espionage Laws, Title 18, U. S. C., Sections 793 and 794. Its transmission or the revelation of its contents in any manner to an unauthorized person is prohibited by law. It may not be reproduced in whole or in part, by other than United States Air Force Agencies, except by permission of the Director of Intelligence, USAF.

AF FORM 1 OCT 52 112a REPLACES AF FORM 112-PART II, 1 JUN 48, WHICH MAY BE USED. CLASSIFICATION (SECURITY INFORMATION When Filled in)

TOP SECRET

BARRY GOLDWATER
ARIZONA

COMMITTEES:
AERONAUTICAL AND SPACE SCIENCES
ARMED SERVICES
PREPAREDNESS INVESTIGATING SUBCOMMITTEE
TACTICAL AIR POWER SUBCOMMITTEE
NATIONAL STOCKPILE AND NAVAL PETROLEUM RESERVES SUBCOMMITTEE

United States Senate

WASHINGTON, D.C. 20510

March 28, 1975

Mr. Shlomo Arnon
U.C.L.A. Experimental College
308 Westwood Plaza
Los Angeles, California 90024

Dear Mr. Arnon:

The subject of UFOs is one that has interested me for some long time. About ten or twelve years ago I made an effort to find out what was in the building at Wright Patterson Air Force Base where the information is stored that has been collected by the Air Force, and I was understandably denied this request. It is still classified above Top Secret. I have, however, heard that there is a plan under way to release some, if not all, of this material in the near future. I'm just as anxious to see this material as you are, and I hope we will not have to wait too much longer.

Sincerely,

Barry Goldwater

Barry Goldwater

ROBERT F. KENNEDY
NEW YORK

United States Senate
WASHINGTON, D.C.

May 9, 1968

Mr. Gray Barker
Publisher, Saucer News
Box 2228
Clarksburg, West Virginia 26301

Dear Readers:

As you may know, I am a card carrying member of the Amalgamated Flying Saucers Association. Therefore, like many other people in our country I am interested in the phenomenon of flying saucers.

It is a fascinating subject that has initiated both scientific fiction fantasies and serious scientific research.

I watch with great interest all reports of unidentified flying objects, and I hope that some day we will know more about this intriguing subject.

Dr. Harlow Shapley, the prominent astronomer, has stated that there is a probability that there is other life in the universe.

I favor more research regarding this matter, and I hope that once and for all we can determine the true facts about flying saucers. Your magazine can stimulate much of the investigation and inquiry into this phenomenon through the publication of news and discussion material. This can be of great help in paving the way to a knowledge of one of the fascinating subjects of our contemporary world.

Sincerely,

Robert F. Kennedy

DEPARTMENT OF DEFENSE
JOINT CHIEFS OF STAFF
MESSAGE CENTER

RECEIVED
JUN -3 1980

VZCZCMLT565 ZYUW DIA RTS-2B 18134
MULT
ACTION
DIA:
DISTR
IADR(01) J5(02) J3:NMCC NIDS SECDEF(07) SECDEF: USOP(15)
ATSD:AE(01) ASD:PA&E(01) :DIA(20) NMIC
- CMC CC WASHINGTON DC
- CSAF WASHINGTON DC
- CNO WASHINGTON DC
- CSA WASHINGTON DC
- CIA WASHINGTON DC
- SECSTATE WASHINGTON DC
- NSA WASH DC
FILE
(047)

PE
366/03
374/00
378340
379/33
379/80

TRANSIT/1542115/1542207/000:52TOR1542204
DE RUESLMA #4888 1542115
ZNY CCCCC
R 022252Z JUN 80
FM USDAO LIMA PERU
TO RUEKJCS/DIA WASHDC
INFO RULPALJ/USCINCSO QUARRY HTS PN
RULPAFA/USAFSO HOWARD AFB PN
BT

345

SUBJ: IR 6 876 0146 80 (U)
THIS IS AN INFO REPORT, NOT FINALLY EVAL INTEL
1. (U) CTRY: PERU (PE)
2. TITLE (U) UFO SIGHTED IN PERU (U)
3. (U) DATE OF INFO: 800510
4. (U) ORIG: USDAO AIR LIMA PERU
5. (U) REQ REFS: Z-D13-PE030
6. (U) SOURCE: 6 876 0138. OFFICER IN THE PERUVIAN AIR FORCE WHO OBSERVED THE EVENT AND IS IN A POSITION TO BE PARTY TO CONVERSATION CONCERNING THE EVENT. SOURCE HAS REPORTED RELIABLY IN THE PAST.

7. __________ SUMMARY: SOURCE REPORTED THAT A UFO WAS SPOTTED ON TWO DIFFERENT OCCASIONS NEAR PERUVIAN AIR FORCE (FAP) BASE IN SOUTHERN PERU. THE FAP TRIED TO INTERCEPT AND DESTROY THE UFO, BUT WITHOUT SUCCESS.

PAGE 1 0013111T

DEPARTMENT OF DEFENSE
JOINT CHIEFS OF STAFF
MESSAGE CENTER

PAGE 2 ______________ 18134
8A. __________ DETAILS: SOURCE TOLD RO ABOUT THE SPOTTING OF AN
UNIDENTIFIED FLYING OBJECT IN THE VICINITY OF MARIANO MELGAR AIR
BASE, LA JOYA, PERU (16805S, 0715306W). SOURCE STATED THAT THE
VEHICLE WAS SPOTTED ON TWO DIFFERENT OCCASIONS. THE FIRST WAS
DURING THE MORNING HOURS OF 9 MAY 80, AND THE SECOND DURING
THE EARLY EVENING HOURS OF 10 MAY 80.
__________ SOURCE STATED THAT ON 9 MAY, WHILE A GROUP OF FAP
OFFICERS WERE IN FORMATION AT MARIANO MALGAR, THEY SPOTTED A
UFO THAT WAS ROUND IN SHAPE, HOVERING NEAR THE AIRFIELD. THE
AIR COMMANDER SCRAMBLED AN SU-22 AIRCRAFT TO MAKE AN
INTERCEPT. THE PILOT, ACCORDING TO A THIRD PARTY, INTERCEPTED
THE VEHICLE AND FIRED UPON IT AT VERY CLOSE RANGE WITHOUT
CAUSING ANY APPARENT DAMAGE. THE PILOT TRIED TO MAKE A
SECOND PASS ON THE VEHICLE, BUT THE UFO OUT-RAN THE SU-22.
__________ THE SECOND SIGHTING WAS DURING HOURS OF DARKNESS.
THE VEHICLE WAS LIGHTED. AGAIN AN SU-22 WAS SCRAMBLED, BUT THE
VEHICLE OUT-RAN THE AIRCRAFT.
8B. __________ ORIG CMTS: RO HAS HEARD DISCUSSION ABOUT THE
SIGHTING FROM OTHER SOURCES. APPARENTLY SOME VEHICLE WAS
SPOTTED, BUT ITS ORIGIN REMAINS UNKNOWN.
9. (U) PROJ NO: N/A
10. (U) COLL MGMT CODES: AB
11. (U) SPEC INST: NONE. DIRC: NO.
12. (U) PREP BY: NORMAN H. RUNGE, COL, AIRA
13. (U) APP BY: VAUGHN E. WILSON, CAPT, DATT, ALUSNA
14. (U) REQ EVAL: NO REL TO: NONE
15. (U) ENCL: N/A
16. (U) DIST BY ORIG: N/A

BT
#4888
ANNOTES
JAL 117

PAGE 2 00101111

NNNN
0222087

COMPLAINT FORM HQ IVOS

I ADMINISTRATIVE DATA

TITLE	DATE	TIME
KIRTLAND AFB, NM, 8 Aug - 3 Sep 80, Alleged Sigthings of Unidentified Aerial Lights in Restricted Test Range.	2 - 9 Sept 80	1200
	PLACE: AFOSI Det 1700, Kirtland AFB, NM	
	HOW RECEIVED: X IN PERSON / TELEPHONICALLY / IN WRITING	
	SOURCE AND EVALUATION: MAJOR ERNEST E. EDWARDS	
	RESIDENCE OR BUSINESS ADDRESS: Commander, 1608 SPS, Manzano Kirtland AFB, NM	PHONE: 4-7516
	CD 44 APPLIES	

II SUMMARY OF INFORMATION

REMARKS

1. On 2 Sept 80, SOURCE related on 8 Aug 80, three Security Policemen assigned to 1608 SPS, KAFB, NM, on duty inside the Manzano Weapons Storage Area sighted an unidentified light in the air that traveled from North to South over the Coyote Canyon area of the Department of Defense Restricted Test Range on KAFB, NM. The Security Policemen identified as: SSGT STEPHEN FERENZ, Area Supervisor, AIC MARTIN W. RIST and AMN ANTHONY D. FRAZIER, were later interviewed separately by SOURCE and all three related the same statement; At approximately 2350hrs., while on duty in Charlie Sector, East Side of Manzano, the three observed a very bright light in the sky approximately 3 miles North-North East of their position. The light traveled with great speed and stopped suddenly in the sky over Coyote Canyon. The three first thought the object was a helicopter, however, after observing the strange aerial maneuvers (stop and go), they felt a helicopter couldn't have performed such skills. The light landed in the Coyote Canyon area. Sometime later, three witnessed the light take off and leave proceeding straight up at a hight speed and disappear.

2. Central Security Control (CSC) inside Manzano, contacted Sandia Security, who conducts frequent building checks on two alarmed structures in the area. They advised that a patrol was already in the area and would investigate.

3. On 11 Aug 80, RUSS CURTIS, Sandia Security, advised that on 9 Aug 80, a Sandia Security Guard, (who wishes his name not be divulged for fear of harassment), related the following: At approximately 0020hrs., he was driving East on the Coyote Canyon access road on a routine building check of an alarmed structure . As he approached the structure he observed a bright light near the ground behind the structure. He also observed an object he first thought was a helicopter. But after driving closer, he observed a round disk shaped object. He attempted to radio for a back up patrol but his radio would not work. As he approached the object on foot armed with a shotgun, the object took off in a vertical direction at a high rate of speed. The guard was a former helicopter mechanic in the U.S. Army and stated the object he observed was not a helicopter.

4. SOURCE advised on 22 Aug 80, three other security policemen observed the same

DATE FORWARDED HQ AFOSI: HQ IVOS 10 Aug 80	AFOSI FORM 96 ATTACHED: ☐ YES ☐ NO
DATE: 9 Sept 80 — TYPED OR PRINTED NAME OF SPECIAL AGENT: RICHARD C. DOTY, SA	SIGNATURE: Richard C. Doty
DISTRICT FILE NO.: 8017893-0/22	DCH RESULTS: NEGATIVE / POSITIVE (See Attached)

AFOSI FORM 1 JUN 79 PREVIOUS EDITION WILL BE USED.

CONTINUED FROM COMPLAL F..M 1, DTD 9 Sept 80

aerial phenomena described by the first three. Again the object landed in Coyote Canyon. They did not see the object take off.

5. Coyote Canyon is part of a large restricted test range used by the Air Force Weapons Laboratory, Sandia Laboratories, Defense Nuclear Agency and the Department of Energy. The range was formerly patrolled by Sandia Security, however, they only conduct building checks there now.

6. On 10 Aug 80, a New Mexico State Patrolman sighted avaerial object land in the Manzano's between Belen and Albuquerque, NM. The Patrolman reported the sighting to the Kirtland AFB Command Post, who later referred the patrolman to the AFOSI Dist 17. AFOSI Dist 17 advised the patrolman to make a report through his own agency. On 11 Aug 80, the Kirtland Public Information office advised the patrolman the USAF no longer investigates such sightings unless they occur on an USAF base.

7. WRITER contacted all the agencies who utilized the test range and it was learned no aerial tests are conducted in the Coyote Canyon area. Only ground tests are conducted.

8. On 8 Sept 80, WRITER learned from Sandia Security that another Security Guard observed a object land near an alarmed structure sometime during the first week of August, but did not report it until just recently for fear of harassment.

9. The two alarmed structures located within the area contains HQ CR 44 material.

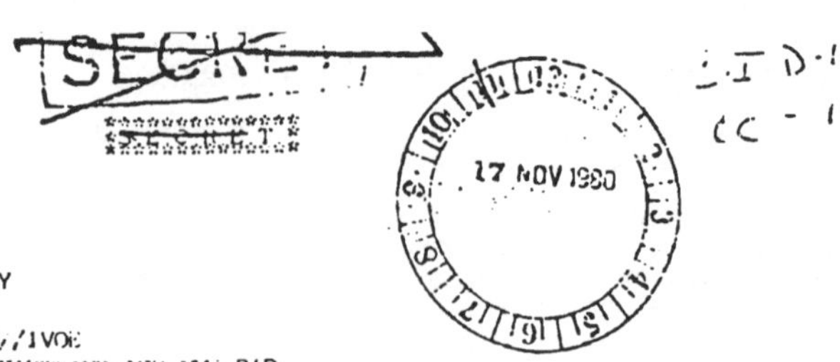

RTTEZYVW RUFLOJA9136
ZNY ~~SECRET~~
GT
SECRET FOR AFOSI ONLY
R 171130Z NOV 80
FM HQ AFOSI BOLLING AFB DC//IVOE
TO RUWTFBA AFOSI DIST 17 KIRTLAND AFB NM//BID
INFO 7602 AINTELG FT BELVOIR VA//INSR
~~SECRET~~ FOR AFOSI ONLY
REF: REQUEST FOR PHOTO IMAGERY INTERPRETATION YOUR MSG 292030Z OCT 80.
SUBJECT CASE NR: 8017D93-126 HQ CR 44
1. SUBJECT NEGATIVES/FILM WERE ANALYZED BY HQ IVT AND 7602 AINTELG, IT AND THE FOLLOWING RESULTS WERE FOUND:
A. NEGATIVE #1: DEPICTING C-5A AIRCRAFT ON APPROACH AND STREAKING UNIDENTIFIED AERIAL OBJECT IN LOWER RIGHT PORTION OF FILM. FILM FOUND TO BE UNALTERED. SIZE DIFFERENTIAL WAS NOT CONSISTENT WITH SIZE OF AIRCRAFT. CONCLUSION: INCONCLUSIVE
B. NEGATIVE #2; DEPICTING CYLINDER SHAPED UNIDENTIFIED AERIAL OBJECT IN UPPER LEFT PORTION OF PHOTO. FILM FOUND TO BE UNALTERED. FILM SHOWED OBJECT TO BE CONSISTENT WITH FIELD DEPH AND CONSISTENT WITH RELATIVE SIZE OF FIXED OBJECTS. CONCLUSION: LEGITIMATE NEGATIVE OF UNIDENTIFIED AERIAL OBJECT. BOLTON/REINFELD METHOD DID NOT REVEAL VISIBLE MARKINGS ON OBJECT.
C. NEGATIVE #3: DEPLICTING IRREGULAR SHAPED UNIDENTIFIED AERIAL OBJECT IN SEVEN FRAMES OF 8MM FILM. BECAUSE OF THE SIZE AND APPARENT SPEED OF OBJECT NO FURTHER CLASSIFICATION OR CONCLUSION COULD BE DRAWN. FILM SHOWN TO BE UNALTERED.
D. 34 INCHES OF 8MM FILM: DEPLICTING APPARENT COLORED OBJECT MOVING IN FRONT OF STILL CAMERA. FILM FOUND TO BE UNALTERED. SPECTROGRAPHY REVEALED COLORES TO BE BASIC PRISM FEATURES. DEPTH ANALYSIS REVEALED OBJECT TO BE WITHIN 152MM OF CAMERA. OBJECT WAS NOT CONSISTENT WITH RELATIVE SIZE OF FIXED OBJECTS OBSERVED FOR SEVERAL SECONDS IN FILM. CONCLUSION: INCONCLUSIVE.
E. ORIGINAL NEGATIVE DEPLICTING UNIDENTIFIED OBJECT. FILM FOUND TO BE UNALTERED. BECAUSE OF A LACK OF FIXED OBJECTS IN THE FILM, NO DEPTH ANALYSIS COULD BE PERFORMED. BOLTON, REINFELD METHOD REVEALED OBJECT TO BE SAUCER SHAPED, APPROXIMATE DIAMETER 37 FEET. OBJECT CONTAINED A TRILATERAL INSIGNIA ON THE LOWER PORTION OF OBJECT. CONCLUSION: LEGITIMATE NEGATIVE OF UNIDENTIFIED AERIAL OBJECT.
2. REF YOUR REQUEST FOR FURTHER INFORMATION REGARDING HQ CR 44, THE FOLLOWING IS PROVIDED: CAPT GRACE 7602 AINTELG, INS CONTACTED AND RELATED FOLLOWING: (S/WINTEL) USAF NO LONGER PUBLICLY ACTIVE IN UFO RESEARCH, HOWEVER USAF STILL HAS INTEREST IN ALL UFO SIGHTINGS OVER USAF INSTALLATION/TEST RANGES. SEVERAL OTHER GOVERNMENT AGENCIES, LEAD BY NASA, ACTIVELY INVESTIGATES LEGITIMATE SIGHTINGS THROUGH COVERT COVER. (S/WINTEL/FSA) ONE SUCH COVER IS UFO REPORTING CENTER, US COAST AND GEODETIC SURVEY, ROCKVILLE, MD 20852. NASA FILTERS RESULTS OF SIGHTINGS TO APPROPRIATE MILITARY DEPARTMENTS WITH INTEREST IN THAT PARTICULAR SIGHTING. THE OFFICIAL US GOVERNMENT POLICY AND RESULTS OF PROJECT AQUARIUS IS STILL CLASSIFIED TOP SECRET WITH NO DISSEMINATION OUTSIDE OFFICIAL INTELLIGENCE CHANNELS AND WITH RESTRICTED ACCESS TO "MJ TWELVE". CASE ON BENNEWITZ IS BEING MONITORED BY NASA, INS, WHO REQUEST ALL FUTURE EVIDENCE BE FORWARDED TO THEM THRU AFOSI, IVOE.
4. REF YOUR REQUEST FOR TECHNICAL ASSISTANCE. BECAUSE OF A CHANCE OF PUBLIC DISCLOSURE, NO KNOWLEDGEABLE PERSONNEL WITH SPA WILL BE PROVIDED. CONTINUE TO RECEIVE ASSISTANCE FROM INDIVIDUALS MENTIONED IN YOUR MESSAGE, MILLER, FUGATE. BECAUSE OF THE SENSITIVITY OF CASE, REQUEST THEY BE THOROUGHLY DEBRIEFED AT REGULAR INTERVALS.
BTS
HHIS
DOWNGRADE 17NOV2020

~~SECRET~~

PERSONNEL STATEMENT

FEDERAL AVIATION ADMINISTRATION
Anchorage Air Route Traffic Control Center

January 6, 1987

The following is a report concerning the incident to Japan Airlines Flight 1628 (JL1628) North of Fairbanks, Alaska on November 18, 1986 at 0218 UTC.

My name is Carl E. Henley (HC). I am employed as an Air Traffic Control Specialist by the Federal Aviation Administration at the Anchorage Air Route Traffic Control Center (ARTCC), Anchorage, Alaska.

During the period of 2030 UTC, November 18, 1986, to 0430 UTC, November 18, 1986 I was on duty in the Anchorage ARTCC. I was working the R/D15 position from 0156 UTC, November 18, 1986 to 0230 UTC, and the R15 position from 0230 UTC, November 18, 1986 to 0258 UTC, November 18, 1986.

I am making this statement to clarify certain points in my original statement dated November 19, 1986.

Ref paragraph 4:

I stated in paragraph four that several times I had several primary returns where JL1628 reported traffic; in actuality I observed three types of targets. I saw tentative radar targets which showed up as a (-) symbols. I saw (+) symbols that indicate radar only tracks. I also saw non run lenth targets which show up as a (.) symbols.

Additionally, I stated the traffic stayed with JL1628 through turns and descent, this information was what I received from JL 1628.

Carl E. Henley
Carl E. Henley
Air Traffic Control Specialist
Anchorage ARTCC

PERSONNEL STATEMENT

FEDERAL AVIATION ADMINISTRATION

Anchorage Air Route Traffic Control Center

The following is a report concerning the incident to aircraft JL1628 on November 18, 1986 at 0230 UTC.

My name is Carl E. Henley (HC) I am employed as an Air Traffic Control Specialist by the Federal Aviation Administration at the Anchorage Air Route Traffic Control Center, Anchorage, Alaska.

During the period of 2030 UTC, November 17, 1986, to 0430 UTC, November 18, 1986 I was on duty in the Anchorage ARTCC. I was working the D15 position from 0156 UTC, November 18, 1986 to 0230 UTC, November 18, 1986.

At approximately 0225Z while monitoring JL1628 on Sector 15 radar, the aircraft requested traffic information. I advised no traffic in his vicinity. The aircraft advised he had traffic 12 o'clock same altitude. I asked JL1628 if he would like higher/lower altitude and the pilot replied, negative. I checked with ROCC to see if they had military traffic in the area and to see if they had primary targets in the area. ROCC did have primary target in the same position JL1628 reported. Several times I had single primary returns where JL1628 reported traffic. JL1628 later requested a turn to heading 210°, I approved JL1628 to make deviations as necessary for traffic. The traffic stayed with JL1628 through turns and decent in the vicinity of FAI I requested JL1628 to make a right 360° turn to see if he could identify the aircraft, he lost contact momentarily, at which time I observed a primary target in the 6 o'clock position 5 miles. I then vectored UA69 northbound to FAI from ANC with his approval to see if he could identify the aircraft, he had contact with the JL1628 flight but reported no other traffic, by this time J11628 had lost contact with the traffic. Also a military C-130 southbound to EDF from EIL advised he had plenty of fuel and would take a look, I vectored him toward the flight and climbed him to FL240, he also had no contact.

Note: I requested JL1628 to identify the type or markings of the aircraft. He could not identify but reported white and yellow strobes. I requested the JL1628 to say flight conditions, he reported clear and no clouds.

Carl E. Henley

November 19, 1986

INFORMATION: ALERT REPORT

Director, AAL-1

Administrator

NOV.17, 1986, "SIGHTING": At 6:19 pm AST, JAL #1628 Cargo, B747, FL350 enroute to Tokyo via Reykjavik, Iceland, and Anchorage, reported observing lighted air traffic, in close proximity. Flight crew unable to determine shape but est. size, based on flashing yellow, amber, green, lights (no red lights) to be equal to B747. ARTCC controller advised him that there was no known air traffic, but did report intermittent radar targets. (Subsequent regeneration of radar tapes revealed no valid traffic data.)

Air crew sighting continued for over 350 miles until object left in eastern direction. Pilot also was able to view object using onboard color radar. US Air Force, Elmendorf AFB, reported having the JAL and an occasional primary target on ADC radar (military informing media that it was "clutter"). JAL pilot requested and performed 360-degree turn and object continued with him. UAL #69 and military C-130, volunteered to be vectored in attempt for visual sighting, both with negative reports.

JAL flight crew interviewed by FAA upon landing. Crew determined to be professional, rational. We have been coordinating with the military.

National and international news media inquiries mounting after inquiry by Kyodo News Service.

Don Keil

Franklin L. Cunningham

INSPECTION AND SURVEILLANCE RECORD

1. WORK ACTIVITY	2. UNITS	3. HOURS
INCIDENT		

4. NAME AND ADDRESS OF CARRIER, OPERATOR, AIRPORT, AGENCY, OR AIRMAN	5. CERTIFICATE NO. OR AIRCRAFT REGISTRATION MARK (No.)	6. RESULTS	7. FURTHER ACTION REQ.
		SATISFACTORY	NO
		UNSATISFACTORY (Explain in Item 8)	YES (Explain action in Item 8)

8. FINDINGS/RECOMMENDATIONS

J.A.L. B-747 CARGO FLT 1628 FROM ICELAND TO ANCHORAGE. CAPT. KENJU TERAUCHI. SPEED .84 MACH.
I received a call from Dick Powers concerning a JAL FLT which the CAPT. HAD STATED HE WAS being followed or shadowed.
I observed the A/C LAND ON R/W 6R AT 1820 HOURS NO OTHER A/C WAS NOTED. THE B-747 TAXIED TO INTL RAMP AREA. I INTERVIEWED CAPT. TERAUCHI & CREW of TWO (F/O & F/E) The CAPT. STATED THAT THIS WAS The 1ST Time Anything like this had happened to him. he STATED that approx. 5 NM After PASSING the Canadian/Alaskan Border at 35,000' Something Appeared 5 to 7 NM in front of the A/c it had lights 4 or 5 in a line (see drawings) and he said it was bigger than they were (B-747). At times this object would to the CAPT SIDE of the A/C (LEFT) Never the other side (Right). He referred to the dark side.— After passing the FAI Area he requested to fly parallel to course and this was granted. ~~over~~ page 2

(If more space is required, use reverse side)

9.	DATE	REGION AND DISTRICT OFFICE	INSPECTOR'S SIGNATURE
OPERATIONS	11/17/86	AAL-FSDO-63	[signature]
MAINTENANCE			
X AVIONICS			

FAA Form 3112 (8-70) ☆U.S. GOVERNMENT PRINTING OFFICE: 1982—571-36./313

INSPECTION AND SURVEILLANCE RECORD

1. WORK ACTIVITY		2. UNITS	3. HOURS
4. NAME AND ADDRESS OF CARRIER, OPERATOR, AIRPORT, AGENCY, OR AIRMAN	5. CERTIFICATE NO. OR AIRCRAFT REGISTRATION MARK (No.)	6. RESULTS	7. FURTHER ACTION REQ.
		SATISFACTORY	NO
		UNSATISFACTORY (Explain in Item 8)	YES (Explain action in Item 8)

8. FINDINGS/RECOMMENDATIONS

Page 2

when he turned to the right and flew parallel the object was gone. [In all cases the weather radar was also used to identify the object. and the 5 to 7 NM distance was taken from the radar display (20 NM range)]. They returned to course and the Capt said "There it was, as if it was waiting for me". At approx. Talkeetna Area the object took off to the east and was gone. A United Flt departed from Anc & was requested to check if they could see anything but it was gone before United got there. Nothing ~~[illegible]~~ different with the cargo except some expensive wine. The Capt. & crew were shook-up but professional. James Derry interviewed the crew at JAL Operations. Capt. Terauchi had asked ATC if they were picking up two targets and was told "just one". The total time was approx. 55 minutes. A new crew took the flight on to Tokoyo. Capt Terauchi & crew were to be in

(If more space is required, use reverse side) (Page 3)

OPERATIONS / MAINTENANCE / AVIONICS	DATE	REGION AND DISTRICT OFFICE	INSPECTOR'S SIGNATURE

FAA Form 3112 (8-70)

U.S. GOVERNMENT PRINTING OFFICE: 1982

INSPECTION AND SURVEILLANCE RECORD

WORK ACTIVITY		2. UNITS	3. HOURS
NAME AND ADDRESS OF CARRIER, OPERATOR, AIRPORT, AGENCY, OR AIRMAN	5. CERTIFICATE NO. OR AIRCRAFT REGISTRATION MARK (No.)	6. RESULTS SATISFACTORY UNSATISFACTORY (Explain in Item 8)	7. FURTHER ACTION REQ. NO YES (Explain action in Item 8)

FINDINGS/RECOMMENDATIONS

Anchorage for 3 days before any additional flights.
James Derry requested the tapes AND ANY OTHER info be SAVED.

PAGE:0011

INQUIRE=DOC10D
ITEM NO=00508802
ENVELOPE
CDSN = LGX391 MCN = 90089/26558 TOR = 900901048
RTTCZYUW RUEKJCS5049 0891251-CCCC--RUEALGX.
ZNY CCCCC
HEADER
R 301251Z MAR 90
FM JOINT STAFF WASHINGTON DC
INFO RUEADWD/OCSA WASHINGTON DC
RUENAAA/CNO WASHINGTON DC
RUEAHQA/CSAF WASHINGTON DC
RUEACMC/CMC WASHINGTON DC
RUEDADA/AFIS AMHS BOLLING AFB DC
RUFTAKA/CDR USAINTELCTRE HEIDELBERG GE
RUFGAID/USEUCOM AIDES VAIHINGEN GE
RUETIAQ/MPCFTGEORGEGMEADEMD
RUEAMCC/CMC CC WASHINGTON DC
RUEALGX/SAFE
R 301246Z MAR 90
FM
TO RUEKJCS/DIA WASHDC
INFO RUEKJCS/DIA WASHDC//DAT-7//
RUSNNOA/USCINCEUR VAIHINGEN GE//ECJ2-OC/ECJ2-JIC//
RUFGAID/USEUCOM AIDES VAIHINGEN GE
RHFQAAA/HQUSAFE RAMSTEIN AB GE//INOW/INO//
RHFPAAA/UTAIS RAMSTEIN AB GE//INRMH/INA//
RHDLCNE/CINCUSNAVEUR LONDON UK
RUFHNA/USDELMC BRUSSELS BE
RUFHNA/USMISSION USNATO
RUDOGHA/USNMR SHAPE BE
RUEAIIA/CIA WASHDC
RUFGAID/JICEUR VAIHINGEN GE
RUCBSAA/FICEURLANT NORFOLK VA
RUEKJCS/SECDEF WASHDC
RUEHC/SECSTATE WASHDC
RUEADWW/WHITEHOUSE WASHDC
RUFHBG/AMEMBASSY LUXEMBOURG
RUEATAC/CDRUSAITAC WASHDC
BT
CONTROLS
SECTION 01 OF 02 05049

SERIAL: (U) IIR 6 807 0136 90.

BODY
COUNTRY: (U) BELGIUM (BE).

SUBJ: IIR 6 807 0136 90/BELGIUM AND THE UFO ISSUE (U)

WARNING: (U) THIS IS AN INFORMATION REPORT, NOT FINALLY

PAGE:0012

EVALUATED INTELLIGENCE. REPORT CLASSIFIED

DEPARTMENT OF DEFENSE

DCI: (U) 900326.

REQS:

SOURCE: A- (U) LA DERNIER HEURE, 20 MAR, DAILY FRENCH LANGUAGE PAPER, CIRC 100,000; B- (U) LE SOIR, 26 MAR, DAILY FRENCH LANGUAGE PAPER, CIRC 213,000;

SUMMARY: (U) NUMEROUS UFO SIGHTINGS HAVE BEEN MADE IN BELGIUM SINCE NOV 89. THE CREDIBILITY OF SOME INDIVIDUALS MAKING THE REPORTS IS GOOD. SOME SIGHTINGS HAVE BEEN EXPLAINED BY NATURAL/MANMADE PHENOMENA, SOME HAVE NOT. INVESTIGATION BY THE BAF CONTINUES.

TEXT: 1. (U) NUMEROUS AND VARIOUS ACCOUNTS OF UFO SIGHTINGS HAVE SURFACED IN BELGIUM OVER THE PAST FEW MONTHS. THE CREDIBILITY OF THE OBSERVERS OF THE ALLEDGED EVENTS VARIES FROM THOSE WHO ARE UNSOPHISTICATED TO THOSE WHO ARE THE WELL EDUCATED AND PROMINENTLY PLACED.

2. (U) SOURCE A CITES MR LEON BRENIG, A 43 YEAR OLD PROFESSOR AT THE FREE UNIVERSIY OF BRUSSELS (PROMINENT) IN THE FIELD OF STATISTICS AND PHYSICS. HE CLAIMS TO HAVE TAKEN PICTURES OF THE PHENOMENA WHICH ARE STILL BEING DEVELOPED BUT WILL BE PUBLISHED BY THE BELGIAN SOCIETY FOR THE STUDY OF SPACE PHENOMENA IF THEY ARE OF GOOD QUALITY.

3. (U) MR BRENIG WAS DRIVING ON THE ARDENNES AUTOROUTE IN THE BEAUFAYS REGION EAST OF LIEGE, SUNDAY, 18 MARCH 1990 AT 2030 HOURS WHEN HE OBSERVED AN AIRBORNE OBJECT APPROACHING IN HIS DIRECTION FROM THE NORTH. IT WAS IN THE FORM OF A TRIANGLE ABOUT THE SIZE OF A PING-PONG BALL AND HAD A YELLOW LIGHT SURROUNDING IT WITH A REDDISH CENTER VARYING IN INTENSITY. ALTITUDE APPEARED TO BE 500 - 1000 METERS, MOVING AT A SLOW SPEED WITH NO SOUND. IT DID NOT MOVE OR BEHAVE LIKE AN AIRCRAFT.

4. (U) MR BRENIG CONTACTED A FRIEND VERY NEAR THE AREA WHO CAME OUT AND TOOK PICTURES OF IT WITH A ZOOM LENS AND 400 ASA FILM. BOTH INSISTED THE OBJECT COULD NOT BE AN AIRCRAFT OR HOLOGRAMME PROJECTION AS THE SKY WAS CLOUDLESS.

5. (U) THE SOURCE B ARTICLE WHICH DISCUSSES A BELGIAN TELEVISION INTERVIEW WITH COL WIL ((DEBROUWER)), CHIEF OF

PAGE:0013

OPERATIONS FOR THE BAF, MOST LIKELY WAS THE RESULT OF A FOLLOW-ON ACTION TAKEN BY MR BRENIG WHEN HE CONTACTED LTGEN ((TERRASSON)), COMMANDER, BELGIAN TACTICAL (OPERATIONAL) COMMAND. GEN TERRASSON CATEGORICALLY ELIMINATED ANY POSSIBLE BAF AIRCRAFT OR ENGINE TEST INVOLVEMENT WHICH COL DEBROUWER CONFIRMED DURING THE 25

ADMIN
BT

#5049

PAGE:0015

6. (U) DEBROUWER NOTED THE LARGE NUMBER OF REPORTED SIGHTINGS, PARTICULARLY IN NOV 89 IN THE LIEGE AREA AND THAT THE BAF AND MOD ARE TAKING THE ISSUE SERIOUSLY. BAF EXPERTS HAVE NOT BEEN ABLE TO EXPLAIN THE PHENOMENA EITHER.

7. (U) DEBROUWER SPECIFICALLY ADDRESSED THE POSSIBILITY OF THE OBJECTS BEING USAF B-2 OR F-117 STEALTH AIRCRAFT WHICH WOULD NOT APPEAR ON BELGIAN RADAR, BUT MIGHT BE SIGHTED VISUALLY IF THEY WERE OPERATING AT LOW ALTITUDE IN THE ARDENNES AREA. HE MADE IT QUITE CLEAR THAT NO USAF OVERFLIGHT REQUESTS HAD EVER BEEN RECEIVED FOR THIS TYPE MISSION AND THAT THE ALLEDGED OBSERVATIONS DID NOT CORRESPOND IN ANY WAY TO THE OBSERVABLE CHARACTERISTICS OF EITHER U.S. AIRCRAFT.

8. (U) MR BRENIG HAS SINCE ASSURED THE COMMUNITY THAT HE IS PERSONALLY ORGANIZING A NEW UFO OBSERVATION CAMPAIGN AND SPECIFICALLY REQUESTS THE HELP OF THE BELGIAN MOD.

9. RELATED A SIMILAR UFO SIGHTING WHICH APPARENTLY HAPPENED TO A BELGIAN AIR FORCE OFFICER IN THE SAME AREA NEAR LIEGE DURING NOVEMBER 89. THE OFFICER AD HIS WIFE WERE ALLEDGEDLY BLINDED BY A HUGE BRIGHT FLYING OBJECT AS THEY WERE DRIVING ON THE AUTOROUTE. THEY STOPPED THEIR CAR, BUT WERE SO FRIGHTENED THEY ABANDONED THE VEHICLE AND RAN INTO THE WOODS. THEY COULD NOT PROVIDE A DETAILED DESCRIPTION BUT WHATEVER IT WAS DEFINITELY APPEARED REAL TO THEM. UNDERLINED THEIR CREDIBILITY AS SOLID.

COMMENTS: 1. COMMENT. HE COULD PROVIDE VERY LITTLE CONCRETE INFORMAITON EXCEPT TO VERIFY THE LARGE VOLUME OF SIGHTINGS AND THE SIMILARITY OF SOME DURING NOV 89.

2. THE BAF HAS RULED SOME SIGHTINGS WERE CAUSED BY INVERSION LAYERS, LAZER BEAMS AND OTHER FORMS OF HIGH INTENSITY LIGHTING HITTING CLOUDS. BUT A REMARKABLE NUMBER OCCURRED ON CLEAR NIGHTS WITH NO OTHER EXPLAINABLE ACTIVITY NEARBY.

3. THE BAF IS CONCERNED TO A POINT ABOUT THE UFO ISSUE AND IS TAKING ACTION TO INVESTIGATE INFORMATION THEY HAVE. DOES ADMIT, HOWEVER, THAT HE IS NOT OPTIMISTIC ABOUT RESOLVING THE PROBLEM.

4. FIELD COMMENT. THE USAF DID CONFIRM TO THE BAF AND BELGIAN MOD THAT NO USAF STEALTH AIRCRAFT WERE ~~OPERATING~~ IN THE ARDENNES AREA DURING THE PERIODS IN

PAGE:0016

QUESTION. THIS WAS RELEASED TO THE BELGIAN PRESS AND RECEIVED WIDE DISSEMINATION.

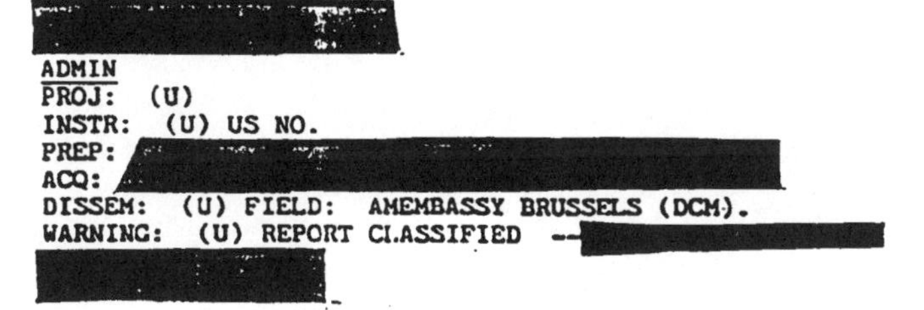

ADMIN
PROJ: (U)
INSTR: (U) US NO.
PREP:
ACQ:
DISSEM: (U) FIELD: AMEMBASSY BRUSSELS (DCM).
WARNING: (U) REPORT CLASSIFIED --

BT

#5049

DEPARTMENT OF THE AIR FORCE
HEADQUARTERS 81ST COMBAT SUPPORT GROUP (USAFE)
APO NEW YORK 09755

REPLY TO ATTN OF: CD

13 Jan 81

SUBJECT: Unexplained Lights

TO: RAF/CC

1. Early in the morning of 27 Dec 80 (approximately 0300L), two USAF security police patrolmen saw unusual lights outside the back gate at RAF Woodbridge. Thinking an aircraft might have crashed or been forced down, they called for permission to go outside the gate to investigate. The on-duty flight chief responded and allowed three patrolmen to proceed on foot. The individuals reported seeing a strange glowing object in the forest. The object was described as being metalic in appearance and triangular in shape, approximately two to three meters across the base and approximately two meters high. It illuminated the entire forest with a white light. The object itself had a pulsing red light on top and a bank(s) of blue lights underneath. The object was hovering or on legs. As the patrolmen approached the object, it maneuvered through the trees and disappeared. At this time the animals on a nearby farm went into a frenzy. The object was briefly sighted approximately an hour later near the back gate.

2. The next day, three depressions 1 1/2" deep and 7" in diameter were found where the object had been sighted on the ground. The following night (29 Dec 80) the area was checked for radiation. Beta/gamma readings of 0.1 milliroentgens were recorded with peak readings in the three depressions and near the center of the triangle formed by the depressions. A nearby tree had moderate (.05-.07) readings on the side of the tree toward the depressions.

3. Later in the night a red sun-like light was seen through the trees. It moved about and pulsed. At one point it appeared to throw off glowing particles and then broke into five separate white objects and then disappeared. Immediately thereafter, three star-like objects were noticed in the sky, two objects to the north and one to the south, all of which were about 10° off the horizon. The objects moved rapidly in sharp angular movements and displayed red, green and blue lights. The objects to the north appeared to be elliptical through an 8-12 power lens. They then turned to full circles. The objects to the north remained in the sky for an hour or more. The object to the south was visible for two or three hours and beamed down a stream of light from time to time. Numerous individuals, including the undersigned, witnessed the activities in paragraphs 2 and 3.

CHARLES I. HALT, Lt Col, USAF
Deputy Base Commander

Document #5

DEPARTMENT OF DEFENSE
JOINT CHIEFS OF STAFF
MESSAGE CENTER

PAGE 2 [redacted] 12843
12. (U) USDAO, TEHRAN, IRAN
13. (U) FRANK B. MCKENZIE, COL, USAF, DATT
14. (U) NA
15. [redacted] THIS REPORT FORWARDS INFORMATION CONCERNING THE SIGHTING OF AN UFO IN IRAN ON 19 SEPTEMBER 1976.

A. AT ABOUT 1230 AM ON 19 SEP 76 THE IMPERIDAL IRANIAN AIR FORCE (IIAF) COMMAND POST RECEIVED FOUR TELEPHONE CALLS FROM CITIZENS LIVING IN THE SHEMIRAN AREA OF TEHRAN SAYING THAT THEY HAD SEEN STRANGE OBJECTS IN THE SKY. SOME REPORTED A KIND OF BIRD-LIKE OBJECT WHILE OTHERS REPORTED A HELICOPTER WITH A LIGHT ON. THERE WERE NO HELICOPTERS AIRBORNE AT THAT TIME. THE COMMAND POST CALLED BG YOUSEFI, ASSISTANT DEPUTY COMMANDER OF OPERATIONS. AFTER HE TOLD THE CITIZEN IT WAS ONLY STARS AND HAD TALKED TO MEHRABAD TOWER HE DECIDED TO LOOK FOR HIMSELF. HE NOTICED AN OBJECT IN THE SKY SIMILAR TO A STAR BIGGER AND BRIGHTER. HE DECIDED TO SCRAMBLE AN F-4 FROM SHAHROKHI AFB TO INVESTIGATE.

B. AT 0130 HRS ON THE 19TH THE F-4 TOOK OFF AND PROCEEDED TO A POINT ABOUT 40 NM NORTH OF TEHRAN. DUE TO ITS BRILLIANCE THE OBJECT WAS EASILY VISIBLE FROM 70 MILES AWAY.
AS THE F-4 APPROACHED A RANGE OF 25 NM HE LOST ALL INSTRUMENTATION AND COMMUNICATIONS (UHF AND INTERCOM). HE BROKE OFF THE INTERCEPT AND HEADED BACK TO SHAHROKHI. WHEN THE F-4 TURNED AWAY FROM THE OBJECT AND APPARENTLY WAS NO LONGER A THREAT TO IT THE AIRCRAFT REGAINED ALL INSTRUMENTATION AND COMMUNICATIONS. AT 0140 HRS A SECOND F-4 WAS LAUNCHED. THE BACKSEATER ACQUIRED A RADAR LOCK ON AT 27 NM, 12 O'CLOCK HIGH POSITION WITH THE VC (RATE OF CLOSURE) AT 150 NMPH. AS THE RANGE DECREASED TO 25 NM THE OBJECT MOVED AWAY AT A SPEED THAT WAS VISIBLE ON THE RADAR SCOPE AND STAYED AT 25NM.

C. THE SIZE OF THE RADAR RETURN WAS COMPARABLE TO THAT OF A 707 TANKER. THE VISUAL SIZE OF THE OBJECT WAS DIFFICULT TO DISCERN BECAUSE OF ITS INTENSE BRILLIANCE. THE LIGHT THAT IT GAVE OFF WAS THAT OF FLASHING STROBE LIGHTS ARRANGED IN A RECTANGULAR PATTERN AND ALTERNATING BLUE, GREEN, RED AND ORANGE IN COLOR. THE SEQUENCE OF THE LIGHTS WAS SO FAST THAT ALL THE COLORS COULD BE SEEN AT ONCE. THE OBJECT AND THE PURSUING F-4 CONTINUED ON A COURSE TO THE SOUTH OF TEHRAN WHEN ANOTHER BRIGHTLY LIGHTED OBJECT, ESTIMATED TO BE ONE HALF TO ONE THIRD THE APPARENT SIZE OF THE MOON, CAME OUT OF THE ORIGINAL OBJECT. THIS SECOND OBJECT HEADED STRAIGHT TOWARD THE F-4 AT A VERY FAST RATE OF SPEED. THE PILOT ATTEMPTED TO FIRE AN AIM-9 MISSILE AT THE OBJECT BUT AT THAT

PAGE 2 [redacted] 00110101

57

PRIORITY

OCT1 MSG654 PAGE 02 267 0813

THAT THEY HAD SEEN STRANGE OBJECTS IN THE SKY. SOME REPORTED A KIND OF BIRD-LIKE OBJECT WHILE OTHERS REPORTED A HELICOPTER WITH A LIGHT ON. THERE WERE NO HELICOPTERS AIRBORNE AT THAT TIME. [redacted] AFTER HE TOLD THE CITIZEN IT WAS ONLY STARS AND HAD TALKED TO MEHRABAD TOWER HE DECIDED TO LOOK FOR HIMSELF. HE NOTICED AN OBJECT IN THE SKY SIMILAR TO A STAR BIGGER AND BRIGHTER. HE DECIDED TO SCRAMBLE AN F-4 FROM SHAHROKHI AFB TO INVESTIGATE.

B. AT 0130 HRS ON THE 19TH THE F-4 TOOK OFF AND PROCEEDED TO A POINT ABOUT 40 NM NORTH OF TEHRAN. DUE TO ITS BRILLIANCE THE OBJECT WAS EASILY VISIBLE FROM 70 MILES AWAY. AS THE F-4 APPROACHED A RANGE OF 25 NM HE LOST ALL INSTRUMENTATION AND COMMUNICATIONS (UHF AND INTERCOM). HE BROKE OFF THE INTERCEPT AND HEADED BACK TO SHAHROKHI. WHEN THE F-4 TURNED AWAY FROM THE OBJECT AND APPARENTLY WAS NO LONGER A THREAT TO IT THE AIRCRAFT REGAINED ALL INSTRUMENTATION AND COMMUNICATIONS. AT 0140 HRS A SECOND F-4 WAS LAUNCHED. THE BACKSEATER ACQUIRED A RADAR LOCK ON AT 27 NM. 12 O'CLOCK HIGH POSITION WITH THE VC (RATE OF CLOSURE) AT 150 NMPH. AS THE RANGE DECREASED TO 25 NM THE OBJECT MOVED AWAY AT A SPEED THAT WAS VISIBLE ON THE RADAR SCOPE AND STAYED AT 25NM

C. THE SIZE OF THE RADAR RETURN WAS COMPARABLE TO THAT OF A 707 TANKER. THE VISUAL SIZE OF THE OBJECT WAS DIFFICULT TO DISCERN BECAUSE OF ITS INTENSE BRILLIANCE. THE LIGHT THAT IT GAVE OFF WAS THAT OF FLASHING STROBE LIGHTS ARRANGED IN A RECTANGULAR PATTERN AND ALTERNATING BLUE, GREEN, RED AND ORANGE IN COLOR. THE SEQUENCE OF THE LIGHTS WAS SO FAST THAT ALL THE COLORS COULD BE SEEN AT ONCE. THE OBJECT AND THE PURSUING F-4 CONTINUED ON A COURSE TO THE SOUTH OF TEHRAN WHEN ANOTHER BRIGHTLY LIGHTED OBJECT, ESTIMATED TO BE ONE HALF TO ONE THIRD THE APPARENT SIZE OF THE MOON, CAME OUT OF THE ORIGINAL OBJECT. THIS SECOND OBJECT HEADED STRAIGHT TOWARD THE F-4 AT A VERY FAST RATE OF SPEED. THE PILOT ATTEMPTED TO FIRE AN AIM-9 MISSILE AT THE OBJECT BUT AT THAT INSTANT HIS WEAPONS CONTROL PANEL WENT OFF AND HE LOST ALL COMMUNICATIONS (UHF AND INTERPHONE). AT THIS POINT THE PILOT INITIATED A TURN AND NEGATIVE G DIVE TO GET AWAY. AS HE TURNED THE OBJEAZ FELL IN TRAIL AT WHAT APPEARED TO BE ABOUT 3-4 NM. AS HE CONTINUED IN HIS TURN AWAY FROM THE PRIMARY OBJECT THE SECOND OBJECT WENT TO THE INSIDE OF HIS TURN THEN RETURNED TO THE PRIMARY OBJECT FOR A PERFECT REJOIN.

D. SHORTLY AFTER THE SECOND OBJECT JOINED UP WITH THE PRIMARY OBJECT ANOTHER OBJECT APPEARED TO COME OUT OF THE

PRIORITY

58

PRIORITY   UNCLASSIFIED

DCT1   MS6654   PAGE 03 267 0813

OTHER SIDE OF THE PRIMARY OBJECT GOING STRAIGHT DOWN. AT A
GREAT RATE OF SPEED. THE F-4 CREW HAD REGAINED COMMUNICATIONS
AND THE WEAPONS CONTROL PANEL AND WATCHED THE OBJECT APPROACH
THE GROUND ANTICIPATING A LARGE EXPLOSION. THIS OBJECT APPEARED
TO COME TO REST GENTLY ON THE EARTH AND CAST A VERY BRIGHT
LIGHT OVER AN AREA OF ABOUT 2-3 KILOMETERS.
THE CREW DESCENDED FROM THEIR ALTITUDE OF 26M TO 15M AND
CONTINUED TO OBSERVE AND MARK THE OBJECT'S POSITION. THEY
HAD SOME DIFFICULTY IN ADJUSTING THEIR NIGHT VISIBILITY FOR
LANDING SO AFTER ORBITING MEHRABAD A FEW TIMES THEY WENT OUT
FOR A STRAIGHT IN LANDING. THERE WAS A LOT OF INTERFERENCE
ON THE UHF AND EACH TIME THEY PASSED THROUGH A MAG. BEARING
OF 150 DEGREE FROM EHRABAD THEY LOST THEIR COMMUNICATIONS (UHF
AND INTERPHONE) AND THE INS FLUCTUATED FROM 30 DEGREES - 50 DEGREES
THE ONE CIVIL AIRLINER THAT WAS APPROACHING MEHRABAD DURING THIS
SAME TIME EXPERIENCED COMMUNICATIONS FAILURE IN THE SAME
VICINITY (KILO ZULU) BUT DID NOT REPORT SEEING ANYTHING.
WHILE THE F-4 WAS ON A LONG FINAL APPROACH THE CREW NOTICED
ANOTHER CYLINDER SHAPED OBJECT (ABOUT THE SIZE OF A T-BIRD
AT 10M) WITH BRIGHT STEADY LIGHTS ON EACH END AND A FLASHER
IN THE MIDDLE. WHEN QUERIED THE TOWER STATED THERE WAS NO
OTHER KNOWN TRAFFIC IN THE AREA. DURING THE TIME THAT THE
OBJECT PASSED OVER THE F-4 THE TOWER DID NOT HAVE A VISUAL
ON IT BUT PICKED IT UP AFTER THE PILOT TOLD THEM TO LOOK
BETWEEN THE MOUNTAINS AND THE REFINERY.
E. DURING DAYLIGHT THE F-4 CREW WAS TAKEN OUT TO THE
AREA IN A HELICOPTER WHERE THE OBJECT APPARENTLY HAD LANDED.
NOTHING WAS NOTICED AT THE SPOT WHERE THEY THOUGHT THE OBJECT
LANDED (A DRY LAKE BED) BUT AS THEY CIRCLED OFF TO THE
WEST OF THE AREA THEY PICKED UP A VERY NOTICEABLE BEEPER
SIGNAL. AT THE POINT WHERE THE RETURN WAS THE LOUDEST WAS
A SMALL HOUSE WITH A GARDEN. THEY LANDED AND ASKED THE PEOPLE
WITHIN IF THEY HAD NOTICED ANYTHING STRANGE LAST NIGHT. THE
PEOPLE TALKED ABOUT A LOUD NOISE AND A VERY BRIGHT LIGHT
LIKE LIGHTENING. THE AIRCRAFT AND AREA WHERE THE OBJECT IS
BELWEVED TO HAVE LANDED ARE BEING CHECKED FOR POSSIBLE RADIATION

[redacted] MORE INFORMATION WILL BE
FORWARDED WHEN IT BECOMES AVAILABLE.
~~XGDS-2-31DEC2006~~
BT
#9712
PTCCZYUW RUEKJCS9712 2670810 0130-CCCC   2670814

PRIORITY

DEPARTMENT OF DEFENSE
JOINT CHIEFS OF STAFF
MESSAGE CENTER

PAGE 2 ████████ 12843
12. (U) USDAO, TEHRAN, IRAN
13. (U) FRANK B. MCKENZIE, COL, USAF, DATT
14. (U) NA
15. ███ THIS REPORT FORWARDS INFORMATION CONCERNING THE SIGHTING OF AN UFO IN IRAN ON 19 SEPTEMBER 1976.

A. AT ABOUT 1230 AM ON 19 SEP 76 THE IMPERIDAL IRANIAN AIR FORCE (IIAF) COMMAND POST RECEIVED FOUR TELEPHONE CALLS FROM CITIZENS LIVING IN THE SHEMIRAN AREA OF TEHRAN SAYING THAT THEY HAD SEEN STRANGE OBJECTS IN THE SKY. SOME REPORTED A KIND OF BIRD-LIKE OBJECT WHILE OTHERS REPORTED A HELICOPTER WITH A LIGHT ON. THERE WERE NO HELICOPTERS AIRBORNE AT THAT TIME. THE COMMAND POST CALLED BG YOUSEFI, ASSISTANT DEPUTY COMMANDER OF OPERATIONS. AFTER HE TOLD THE CITIZEN IT WAS ONLY STARS AND HAD TALKED TO MEHRABAD TOWER HE DECIDED TO LOOK FOR HIMSELF. HE NOTICED AN OBJECT IN THE SKY SIMILAR TO A STAR BIGGER AND BRIGHTER. HE DECIDED TO SCRAMBLE AN F-4 FROM SHAHROKHI AFB TO INVESTIGATE.

B. AT 0130 HRS ON THE 19TH THE F-4 TOOK OFF AND PROCEEDED TO A POINT ABOUT 40 NM NORTH OF TEHRAN. DUE TO ITS BRILLIANCE THE OBJECT WAS EASILY VISIBLE FROM 70 MILES AWAY. AS THE F-4 APPROACHED A RANGE OF 25 NM HE LOST ALL INSTRUMENTATION AND COMMUNICATIONS (UHF AND INTERCOM). HE BROKE OFF THE INTERCEPT AND HEADED BACK TO SHAHROKHI. WHEN THE F-4 TURNED AWAY FROM THE OBJECT AND APPARENTLY WAS NO LONGER A THREAT TO IT THE AIRCRAFT REGAINED ALL INSTRUMENTATION AND COMMUNICATIONS. AT 0140 HRS A SECOND F-4 WAS LAUNCHED. THE BACKSEATER ACQUIRED A RADAR LOCK ON AT 27 NM, 12 O'CLOCK HIGH POSITION WITH THE VC (RATE OF CLOSURE) AT 150 NMPH. AS THE RANGE DECREASED TO 25 NM THE OBJECT MOVED AWAY AT A SPEED THAT WAS VISIBLE ON THE RADAR SCOPE AND STAYED AT 25NM.

C. THE SIZE OF THE RADAR RETURN WAS COMPARABLE TO THAT OF A 707 TANKER. THE VISUAL SIZE OF THE OBJECT WAS DIFFICULT TO DISCERN BECAUSE OF ITS INTENSE BRILLIANCE. THE LIGHT THAT IT GAVE OFF WAS THAT OF FLASHING STROBE LIGHTS ARRANGED IN A RECTANGULAR PATTERN AND ALTERNATING BLUE, GREEN, RED AND ORANGE IN COLOR. THE SEQUENCE OF THE LIGHTS WAS SO FAST THAT ALL THE COLORS COULD BE SEEN AT ONCE. THE OBJECT AND THE PURSUING F-4 CONTINUED ON A COURSE TO THE SOUTH OF TEHRAN WHEN ANOTHER BRIGHTLY LIGHTED OBJECT, ESTIMATED TO BE ONE HALF TO ONE THIRD THE APPARENT SIZE OF THE MOON, CAME OUT OF THE ORIGINAL OBJECT. THIS SECOND OBJECT HEADED STRAIGHT TOWARD THE F-4 AT A VERY FAST RATE OF SPEED. THE PILOT ATTEMPTED TO FIRE AN AIM-9 MISSILE AT THE OBJECT BUT AT THAT

PAGE 2 ████████ 00110101

DEPARTMENT OF DEFENSE
JOINT CHIEFS OF STAFF
MESSAGE CENTER

PAGE 3 [redacted] 12043

INSTANT HIS WEAPONS CONTROL PANEL WENT OFF AND HE LOST ALL COMMUNICATIONS (UHF AND INTERPHONE). AT THIS POINT THE PILOT INITIATED A TURN AND NEGATIVE G DIVE TO GET AWAY. AS HE TURNED THE OBJEAZ FELL IN TRAIL AT WHAT APPEARED TO BE ABOUT 3-4 NM. AS HE CONTINUED IN HIS TURN AWAY FROM THE PRIMARY OBJECT THE SECOND OBJECT WENT TO THE INSIDE OF HIS TURN THEN RETURNED TO THE PRIMARY OBJECT FOR A PERFECT REJOIN.

D. SHORTLY AFTER THE SECOND OBJECT JOINED UP WITH THE PRIMARY OBJECT ANOTHER OBJECT APPEARED TO COME OUT OF THE OTHER SIDE OF THE PRIMARY OBJECT GOING STRAIGHT DOWN,AT A GREAT RATE OF SPEED. THE F-4 CREW HAD REGAINED COMMUNICATIONS AND THE WEAPONS CONTROL PANEL AND WATCHED THE OBJECT APPROACH THE GROUND ANTICIPATING A LARGE EXPLOSION. THIS OBJECT APPEARED TO COME TO REST GENTLY ON THE EARTH AND CAST A VERY BRIGHT LIGHT OVER AN AREA OF ABOUT 2-3 KILOMETERS.

THE CREW DESCENDED FROM THEIR ALTITUDE OF 26M TO 15M AND CONTINUED TO OBSERVE AND MARK THE OBJECT'S POSITION. THEY HAD SOME DIFFICULTY IN ADJUSTING THEIR NIGHT VISIBILITY FOR LANDING SO AFTER ORBITING MEHRABAD A FEW TIMES THEY WENT OUT FOR A STRAIGHT IN LANDING. THERE WAS A LOT OF INTERFERENCE ON THE UHF AND EACH TIME THEY PASSED THROUGH A MAG. BEARING OF 150 DEGREE FROM EHRABAD THEY LOST THEIR COMMUNICATIONS (UHF AND INTERPHONE) AND THE INS FLUCTUATED FROM 30 DEGREES - 50 DEGREES. THE ONE CIVIL AIRLINER THAT WAS APPROACHING MEHRABAD DURING THIS SAME TIME EXPERIENCED COMMUNICATIONS FAILURE IN THE SAME VICINITY (KILO ZULU) BUT DID NOT REPORT SEEING ANYTHING.

WHILE THE F-4 WAS ON A LONG FINAL APPROACH THE CREW NOTICED ANOTHER CYLINDER SHAPED OBJECT (ABOUT THE SIZE OF A T-BIRD AT 10M) WITH BRIGHT STEADY LIGHTS ON EACH END AND A FLASHER IN THE MIDDLE. WHEN QUERIED THE TOWER STATED THERE WAS NO OTHER KNOWN TRAFFIC IN THE AREA. DURING THE TIME THAT THE OBJECT PASSED OVER THE F-4 THE TOWER DID NOT HAVE A VISUAL ON IT BUT PICKED IT UP AFTER THE PILOT TOLD THEM TO LOOK BETWEEN THE MOUNTAINS AND THE REFINERY.

E. DURING DAYLIGHT THE F-4 CREW WAS TAKEN OUT TO THE AREA IN A HELICOPTER WHERE THE OBJECT APPARENTLY HAD LANDED. NOTHING WAS NOTICED AT THE SPOT WHERE THEY THOUGHT THE OBJECT LANDED (A DRY LAKE BED) BUT AS THEY CIRCLED OFF TO THE WEST OF THE AREA THEY PICKED UP A VERY NOTICEABLE BEEPER SIGNAL. AT THE POINT WHERE THE RETURN WAS THE LOUDEST WAS A SMALL HOUSE WITH A GARDEN. THEY LANDED AND ASKED THE PEOPLE WITHIN IF THEY HAD NOTICED ANYTHING STRANGE LAST NIGHT. THE PEOPLE TALKED ABOUT A LOUD NOISE AND A VERY BRIGHT LIGHT

PAGE 3 [redacted] 00110101

DEPARTMENT OF DEFENSE
JOINT CHIEFS OF STAFF
MESSAGE CENTER

PAGE 4 [redacted] 12843
LIKE LIGHTENING. THE AIRCRAFT AND AREA WHERE THE OBJECT IS
BELWEVED TO HAVE LANDED ARE BEING CHECKED FOR POSSIBLE RADIATION.
RO COMMENTS: [redacted] ACTUAL INFORMATION CONTAINED IN THIS REPORT
WAS OBTAINED FROM SOURCE IN CONVERSATION WITH A SUB-SOURCE, AND
IIAF PILOT OF ONE OF THE F-4S. MORE INFORMATION WILL BE
FORWARDED WHEN IT BECOMES AVAILABLE.
[redacted]
BT
#9575
ANNOTES
JEP 117

CENTRAL INTELLIGENCE AGENCY
INFORMATION FROM
FOREIGN DOCUMENTS OR RADIO BROADCASTS

REPORT NO. 00-W-23602

CD NO. --

COUNTRY Belgian Congo

SUBJECT Military; Scientific - Air

HOW PUBLISHED Daily newspaper

WHERE PUBLISHED Vienna

DATE PUBLISHED 29 Mar 1952

LANGUAGE German

DATE OF INFORMATION 1952

DATE DIST. 16 Aug 1952

NO. OF PAGES 2

SUPPLEMENT TO REPORT NO.

THIS IS UNEVALUATED INFORMATION

SOURCE Die Presse.

FLYING SAUCERS OVER BELGIAN CONGO URANIUM MINES

Fritz Sitte

Recently, two fiery disks were sighted over the uranium mines located in the southern part of the Belgian Congo in the Elisabethville district, east of the Luapula River which connects the Meru and Bangweolo lakes. The disks glided in elegant curves and changed their position many times, so that from below they sometimes appeared as plates, ovals, and simply lines. Suddenly, both disks hovered in one spot and then took off in a unique zigzag flight to the northeast. A penetrating hissing and buzzing sound was audible to the onlookers below. The whole performance lasted from 10 to 12 minutes.

Commander Pierre of the small Elisabethville airfield immediately set out in pursuit with a fighter plane. On his first approach he came within about 120 meters of one of the disks. According to his estimates, the "saucer" had a diameter of from 12 to 15 meters and was discus-shaped. The inner core remained absolutely still, and a knob coming out from the center and several small openings could plainly be seen. The outer rim was completely veiled in fire and must have had an enormous speed of rotation. The color of the metal was similar to that of aluminum.

The disks traveled in a precise and light manner, both vertically and horizontally. Changes in elevation from 800 to 1,000 meters could be accomplished in a few seconds; the disks often shot down to within 20 meters of the tree tops. Pierre did not regard it possible that the disk could be manned, since the irregular speed as well as the heat would make it impossible for a person to stay inside the stable core. Pierre had to give up pursuit after 15 minutes since both disks, with a loud whistling sound which he heard despite the noise of his own plane, disappeared in a straight line toward Lake Tanganyika. He estimated their speed at about 1,500 kilometers per hour.

Pierre is regarded as a dependable officer and a zealous flyer. He gave a detailed report to his superiors which, strangely enough, in many respects agreed with various results of research.

RELEASED 5/9/94

00-W-23602

The sketch below shows the construction principle of the "flying saucers." The captions are, in part, purely conjecture, based on reports by pilots who pursued the disks; in part, they were learned from secret research institutions. The central core contains the explosive (SP) and the installations for radar steerage (R). It has catapult knobs (KZ) and antennae (AN) as well as counter-pressure housing (GD). Around this core, a rim rotates which has jets (D) on its upper and lower side, plus fuel chambers (DB). The roller bearing is shown by the letter L. The launching occurs at a sharp angle in the manner of a discus throw; the revolutions per minute of the rim probably amount to 22,000. The jets on the bottom of the rim serve to propel the disk vertically upwards; lateral steerage results from switching on and off various jet groups.

[Appended sketch follows:]

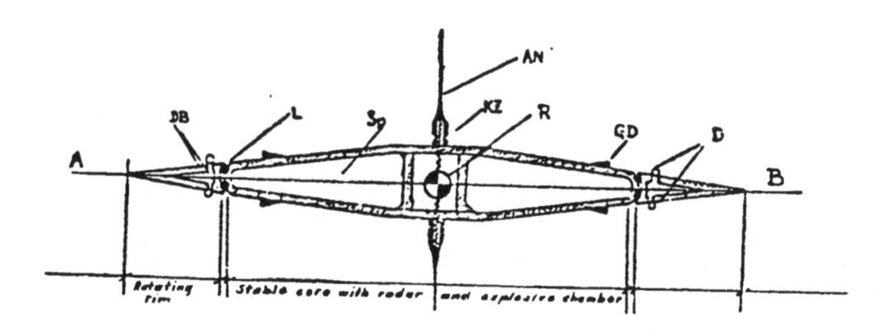

(Signed R. L. CLARK)
H. MARSHALL CHADWELL
Assistant Director
Scientific Intelligence

Enclosure - Tab A

Distribution:
Director - orig & 1
DD/I - 1
P&E/SI - 1
W&E/SI - 1
Opns/SI - 1
AD/SI - 2

OSI:RLC:FCD/mtw

(18 Dec 52)

TAB A

1. Motion Pictures, Tremonton, Utah

This case involves the sighting and photographing (Kodachrome film) of ten bright lights moving across the sky on 2 July 1952 in rough formation. Source is a Chief Photographer's Mate, USN, with 17 years photographic experience. The local time was 1110; weather conditions bright, clear, no clouds. Objects appeared to be "milling about" while traveling in a westerly direction across the sky. Source was driving along the road when the sighting occurred. He stopped the car and photographed the event with his personal camera. Toward the end of the sighting, one object separated from the rest and reversed course across the sky.

Status: ATIC Photographic Laboratory examination of the film resulted in following conclusions:

a. 10 objects, all alike in movement and size.

b. Decidedly improbable that they are birds or balloons.

c. Exact nature cannot be determined, because they are visible only as small spots of light. It can be deduced, however, that they are either non-spherical in shape and similar to bright metal in reflectance or else variably self-luminous. Objects which follow similar courses show similar brightness fluctuations which could be caused by their taking similar flight attitudes.

d. Apparently a coordination of movement to some extent among these objects. They seem to move in formations which are probably 3-dimensional in arrangement.

e. The movements suggest flight paths consisting of skew curves in space.

f. The single object which reversed course remained reasonably uniform in brightness. It followed a nearly straight line path with reasonable uniformity of motion at an angular velocity of about 2.1°/sec. (This is equivalent to the following speeds: 37 mph @500 yards; 75 mph @ 1000 yards; 373 mph @5000 yards; 750 mph @10,000 yards; etc.).

g. It would probably be extremely difficult to imitate this photography for fraudulent purposes.

This film is currently under examination by the U. S. Navy Photo Interpretation Laboratory, Anacostia. Estimated completion date: 15 January 1953.

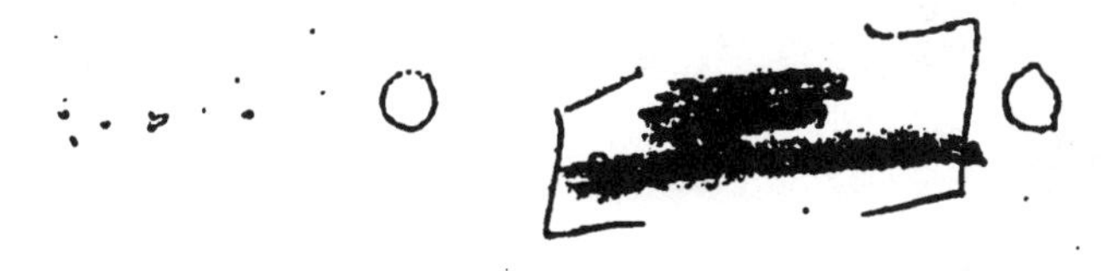

2. Bright Light sighted from Presque Isle and Limestone Air Force Bases, Maine

This sighting occurred the night of 10-11 October 1952 from 2300 to 0300 local time, by observers at the weather stations at these Air Force Bases. The description of the light was "circular orange object with four green lights nearby." Theodolite sightings of elevation and azimuth were obtained. Weather was clear.

Status: A comparison of observed azimuths and elevations of the supposed object with the calculated position and relative motion of the planet Jupiter leave little doubt that the observed object was actually Jupiter.

3. Reported Sightings of a Strange Object in Florida

This sighting was reported by a Boy Scoutmaster to have occurred at 2150 local time on 19 August 1952 near West Palm Beach, Florida. According to the story given, the source was driving along deserted road in his car, together with four Boy Scouts. Sighting a strange light, source stopped the car, cautioned the boys to wait, and entered the palmetto undergrowth alone. When he did not return in a few minutes, and witnessing some strange lights in the vicinity of the scoutmaster, the boys went for help, returning with a deputy sheriff. The scoutmaster appeared, badly frightened, slightly burned on the forearms. His story was that he had seen a large circular object about eight feet over his head which had released a "fire ball" which descended on him. He stated that he had thrown himself upon the ground and "blacked out." There were various other embroideries to the story. His cap was burned slightly and samples of grass taken from the immediate vicinity of the "sighting" differed strangely in appearance from samples 75 yards away.

Status: The background of the source indicates an unsavory personal reputation and criminal record, resulting in the belief that the report may have been an elaborate hoax. However, the unusual condition of the grass samples is currently unexplained. This fact, together with other aspects of the case, leave final determination in doubt at this time.

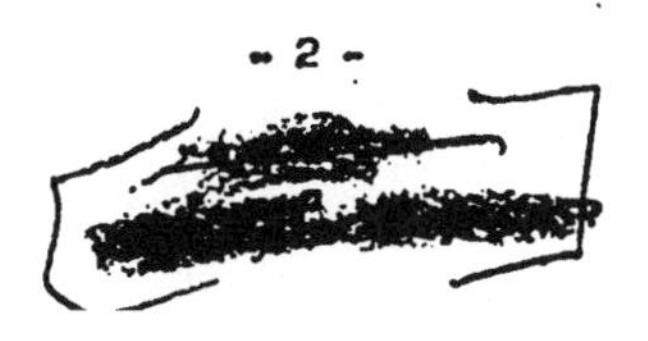

TITLE: INTERNATIONAL CONGRESS OF SPACE MEDICINE

DOCREFERENCE: [illegible]84876.
29JAN76, 2 PP

INFOLOCATION: MEXICO

INFODATE: 7509.

UNITED STATES SCIENTISTS BELIEVE THAT LOW MAGNETIC FIELD DO NOT HAVE A SERIOUS EFFECT ON ASTRONAUTS, BUT HIGH MAGNETIC FIELD, OSCILLATING MAGNETIC FIELD, AND ELECTROMAGNETIC FIELD CAN OR DO HAVE CONSIDERABLE EFFECT. THERE IS A THEORY THAT SUCH FIELD ARE CLOSELY ASSOCIATED WITH SUPERCONDUCTIVITY AT VERY LOW TEMPERATURES,

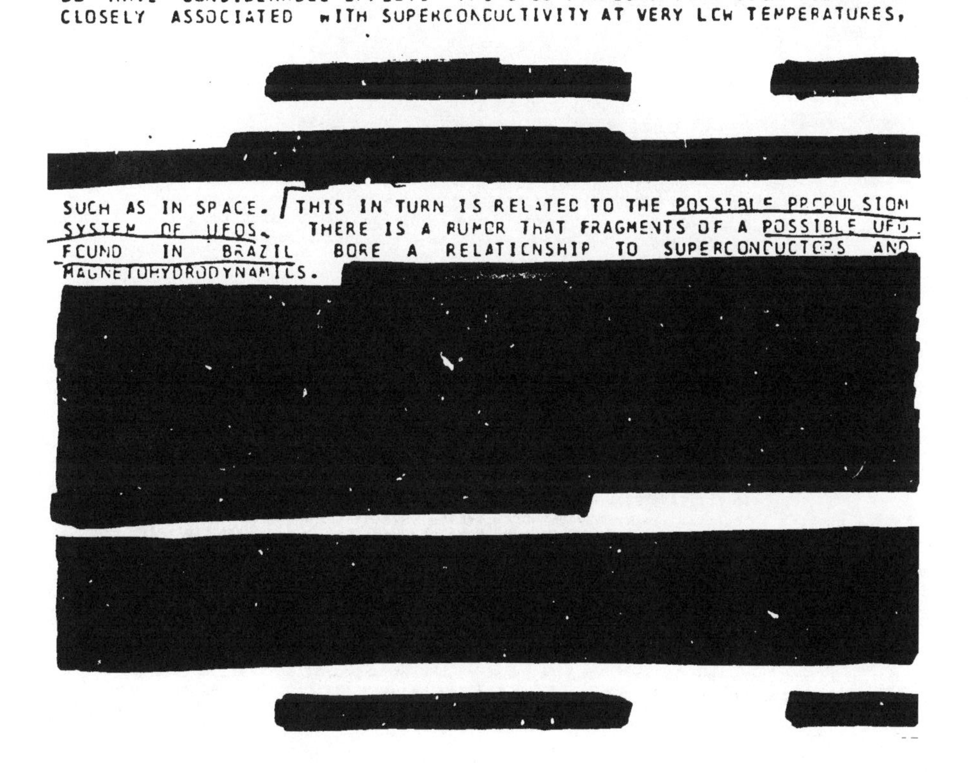

SUCH AS IN SPACE. THIS IN TURN IS RELATED TO THE POSSIBLE PROPULSION SYSTEM OF UFOS. THERE IS A RUMOR THAT FRAGMENTS OF A POSSIBLE UFO FOUND IN BRAZIL BORE A RELATIONSHIP TO SUPERCONDUCTORS AND MAGNETOHYDRODYNAMICS.

CENTRAL INTELLIGENCE AGENCY
INFORMATION FROM
FOREIGN DOCUMENTS OR RADIO BROADCASTS

REPORT NO. 00-W-29745

CD NO. 

COUNTRY	Sweden	DATE OF INFORMATION	1953
SUBJECT	Military - Unconventional aircraft		
HOW PUBLISHED	Daily newspaper	DATE DIST.	1 APR 1954
WHERE PUBLISHED	Stockholm	NO. OF PAGES	4
DATE PUBLISHED	18-20 Dec 1953		
LANGUAGE	Swedish	SUPPLEMENT TO REPORT NO.	

THIS IS UNEVALUATED INFORMATION

SOURCE Dagens Nyheter

VETERAN SWEDISH AIRMEN OBSERVE,
DESCRIBE DISK-SHAPED AIRCRAFT OVER SKAANE

[The information in this report was taken from three articles which appeared in the liberal Stockholm daily, Dagens Nyheter on 18, 19, and 20 December 1953. In the rendition of the first two articles (18 and 19 December), repetitious elements have been omitted. The third article is given in full.

Numbers in parentheses refer to appended sources.]

The chief pilot for Transair Airlines, Flight Captain Ulf Christiernsson, and his flight mechanic, Olle Johansson, reported that on the afternoon of 17 December 1953, while flying in a DC-3 over Skaane, they sighted a mysterious circular metal object flying in an opposite direction of them at a speed estimated at about the speed of sound. The airmen estimated that the object was about 10 meters in diameter.

Captain Christiernsson, at present employed by Transair in flying the morning [Stockholm] papers to southern Sweden, has very extensive air experience, having served as a volunteer with the RAF from 1942-1946, finishing his service with the rank of captain. He flew 30 missions against enemy territory from North Africa and Italy.

Captain Christiernsson made the following statement to Dagens Nyheter: "I do not doubt for an instant that it was not a jet plane. What I saw was a completely unorthodox, metallic, symmetric, round object which was unlike anything I have seen before. The mysterious object appeared suddenly on the air route traveled by all controlled air traffic between Bulltofta and Bromma airfields [at Malmö and Stockholm respectively]. I myself was en route to Bromma.

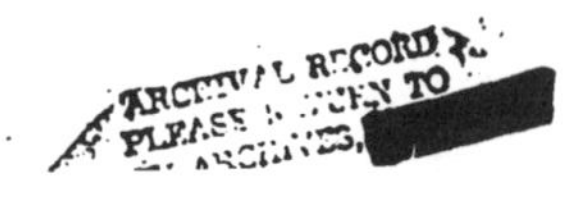

00-W-29745

Over Hässleholm, I saw an object -- on my right and obliquely in front of me, flying at a somewhat lower altitude -- which at first I thought to be a jet plane. The silhouette was thin and it approached me at a very high velocity. Olle Johansson and I have discussed the matter of its speed, and comparing its speed with, for example, that of the "Flying Barrels" [J-29], we have estimated the speed to be about that of sound. The whole business took place fantastically quickly, but I believe that I was able to see the object for 4 to 5 seconds.

"When the object got closer, I was able to ascertain that it was symmetric and metallic. It is very difficult to describe something that one has never seen before, but I would say that it looked like a flying lozenge. The object did not seem to have a crew, but seemed more to be a robot. When it passed under the wing [of the DC-3], I could no longer see it. The mechanic, who was able to observe it for five more seconds, confirms the fact that it was circular or possibly somewhat elliptical in form. At the time of the incident, we were flying at an altitude of 2,150 meters and the cloud ceiling was about 1,500 meters. Thus, the object should have been flying at an altitude of between 1,500 and 1,600 meters. We estimated the size to be about 10 meters in diameter. It left no exhaust or condensation trail.

"We are both absolutely convinced that it could not have been a meteor or other celestial phenomenon. We did not see any distinct light but were only able to see that the object had a metallic lustre. Immediately after the observation, we reported to F5 in Ljungbyhed and to the regional civil air security service at Bulltofta. The course of the object was south-southwest. The whole thing happened so quickly that we could not have managed to change course [and follow the object]..."

Olle Johansson's statement was as follows: "I was sitting forward in the right-hand seat of the pilot's cabin when Captain Christiernsson pointed to the object. What I saw was an ellipse with sharp outlines and something between silver and white in color. I saw it for about 10 seconds. It was approaching from the north in a direction opposite to ours, at a speed of about 1,200 kilometers per hour. It was flying entirely above the clouds. From Malmö northward, we were able to see the ground for only a few myriameters and after that there was a cloud covering all the way to Stockholm. We were flying at a speed of about 270 kilometers per hour. Ten minutes after the incident, we met an SAS (Scandinavian Airlines System) DC-4. Thereupon, we estimated the object's speed at about three times that of the DC-4. There seemed to be no flames or smoke trail from the object. Since we had the automatic pilot on, we had no chance to turn quickly enough to see where the object went."

The Defense Staff's short communique on the incident read as follows: "At 1457 hours on Thursday, the crew on a civilian commercial plane observed, in the vicinity of Hässleholm, an unknown object which moved at a high speed in a direction opposite to that of the plane. The object was viewed for 6 to 7 seconds. At the time of the incident, there was clear weather at the altitude at which the plane was flying. Because of the low cloud ceiling, the object could not have been seen from the ground. Within the knowledge of the Defense Staff, there was no Swedish plane in the area concerned at the time of the incident. Investigation continues."

Reports of "flying saucers" have arisen in both Europe and America on countless occasions in recent years but, according to a statement to Dagens Nyheter by a member of the Air Staff, these observations over Skaane can be termed the clearest and most detailed which heretofore have been made regarding mysterious, unknown aircraft.(1)

19 Jan 65

Case

Chief Petty Officer, Patuxent Naval Air Station, picked up on radar 3 consecutive trackings: December 19th 1964 between 3:15 and 3:30 P.M.

Initial sighting 2 objects 10 miles apart
2nd sighting picked up on screen 39 miles S.E. of Patuxent Naval Air Station travelir towards base at estimated speed of 6 thousand miles per hour. Lost it off screen abc 10 miles out of Patuxent.

3rd sighting on screen one UFO 8 miles N.E. of Patuxent which made 160° turn and dropped off screen. On same date about same time checked with an FAA station at XX Salisbury, Maryland which had picked up messages from U.S. Coast Guard reporting sightings of UFOs.

Based on radar beam data, altitude of UFOs estimated in range between XXXX 3000 to 25000 feet

APPROVED FOR RELEASE
DATE 16 Nov 78

#119

Office Memorandum • UNITED STATES GOVERNMENT

TO : Assistant Director, Scientific Intelligence DATE: 4 April 1958

FROM : Chief, Applied Science Division, SI

SUBJECT: Comments on Letters Dealing with Unidentified Flying Objects

REFERENCES: (1) Letter to Director, CIA, from Leon Davidson, dated 11 March 1958
(2) Letter to Director, CIA, from Donald E. Keyhoe, Director of National Investigations Committee on Aerial Phenomena

1. As a result of the action taken by the IAC on 4 December 1952 (IAC-M-90, Paragraph 3a), a Scientific Intelligence Advisory Panel was convened 14-18 January 1953. The panel consisted of the following scientists: H. P. Robertson, Luis W. Alvarez, Lloyd V. Berkner, S. A. Goudsmit, and Thornton Page. The panel concerned itself with the evaluation of any possible threat to National Security by unidentified flying objects. The panel issued a report dated 17 January 1953. This report was classified Secret.

2. The letters from Leon Davidson and Donald Keyhoe to the DCI concerned themselves primarily with Edward J. Ruppelt's book on Unidentified Flying Objects. At the time that the scientific panel met, Ruppelt was a Captain in the Air Force and attended the panel meetings. His book, however, is concerned with the identification of unidentified flying objects. Ruppelt's statements regarding the mission of the panel are in error. He has led the reader to believe the panel's mission was to identify the flying objects and to make recommendations on methods to further identify such objects. This is the basis for the apparent contradictions which arose during the Mike Wallace television interview. This is also the basis for Mr. Keyhoe's misgivings.

3. In late October 1957, Major James F. Byrne of AFCIN-X1A requested a declassified version of the panel report. This office contacted each member of the panel and an agreed upon, declassified version was written and sent to the Assistant Chief of Staff, Intelligence, Department of the Air Force on 20 December 1957. It was the decision of all the panel members and the CIA that while no member of the panel objected to the use of his name in connection with the declassified version, they desired that no connection of the panel members with CIA be disclosed.

SUBJECT: Comments on Letters Dealing with Unidentified Flying Objects

4. It is apparent from reading Mr. Davidson's letter that Mike Wallace had a copy of the scientific panel report. In addition, the association of CIA with the US Air Force in the selection of the panel was revealed during the television interview. Therefore, the panel members have been associated with CIA, contrary to their wishes and contrary to CIA's desires.

5. The real intent of the referenced letters is to obtain a copy of the panel report. In view of this, and of the above, it would be most expedient to send them the declassified version. In order to not reveal an association between the panel members and CIA, either the Air Force should answer the letters or we should make it plain to the recipients that we obtained the panel report from the Air Force.

6. Attached are copies of the declassified panel report.

W. E. LEXOW

Dr. Lloyd V. Berkner
President
Associated Universities, Incorporated
Room 6920
350 Fifth Avenue
New York 1, New York

Dear Lloyd:

You will recall in January 1953, we constituted a Scientific Advisory Panel on Unidentified Flying Objects with Drs. H. P. Robertson as Chairman, Samuel Goudsmit, Luis W. Alvarez, Thorton Page, and yourself as members. After its deliberation, the Panel reached two conclusions and made two recommendations which were included as Tab A of the report. Very recently, the Air Force has requested that the conclusions of this report be declassified so that they may be used in the press. A copy of the report is enclosed herewith for your information.

I have discussed this matter with Dr. Robertson and Dr. Goudsmit who agree that the conclusion contained in paragraph 2 and the recommendation contained in paragraph 4a can be declassified. But, they, as well as this Agency, will not agree to a declassification of the conclusion in paragraph 3 or the recommendation in paragraph 4b. It is our feeling that the association of the Panel with this Agency should not be disclosed; that paragraph 1 could be rewritten to eliminate this connection; and that the final six lines of paragraph 4 can stand as written.

I have queried the Air Force as to whether the names of the Panel members would be used. They have replied that names would be used only within official circles and would not be given to the press. But, as such information has a tendency at times to filter out, it should be recognized that, if approval is given for use of the names, they may well become common knowledge.

It would be very much appreciated if you could let me know as soon as possible what your reaction is to the Air Force declassification proposal; whether you agree with Dr. Robertson, Dr. Goudsmit and myself on limiting any declassification; and whether you would approve or disapprove the use of your name, granted that Agency connection with the Panel is withheld.

Very best regards.

Sincerely,

P.G. Strong

Philip G. Strong
Deputy Assistant Director

Enclosure
UFO Report (Secret)

23 February 1967

MEMORANDUM FOR THE RECORD

SUBJECT: Visit of Dr. Condon to NPIC, 20 February 1967

1. The U.S. Air Force has let a $300,000 contract to the University of Colorado to study reported UFO sightings. Brig. Gen. Edward B. Gillers, USAF, is senior Air Force contact and Dr. Thomas Rachford is senior Air Force Scientist on the project. The senior scientist from the University of Colorado is Dr. E.U. Condon.

2. On 20 February 1967 at 0915 Dr. Condon and four members of his investigative team visited NPIC. With Dr. Condon were Dr. Richard Lowe, University of Colorado, Dr. David Saunders, University of Colorado, Dr. William Price, Executive Director of AFRST, and Dr. Rachford, USAF. The purpose of this visit was to familiarize Dr. Condon and members of his team with selected photogrammetric and photographic analysis capabilities of NPIC.

3. The clearance level for the meeting was SECRET.

4. Upon arrival at NPIC, 0915, escorted the group to Mr. Lundahl's office. In the ensuing 10-15 minute discussion between Mr. Lundahl and Dr. Condon the following points were clearly established:

a. Any work performed by NPIC to assist Dr. Condon in his investigation will not be identified as work accomplished by CIA. Dr. Condon was advised by Mr. Lundahl to make no reference to CIA in regard to this work effort. Dr. Condon stated that if he felt it necessary to obtain an official CIA comment he would make a separate distinct entry into CIA not related to contacts he has with NPIC.

b. NPIC will not prepare any written comments, will not analyze information with the intent of drawing a conclusion, nor prepare written reports. NPIC personnel

SUBJECT: Visit of Dr. Condon to NPIC, 20 February 1967

will be available to assist Dr. Condon by performing work of a photogrammetric nature, such as attemptong to measure objects imaged on photographs that may be part of Dr. Condon's analysis. Work performed by NPIC will be strictly of a technical nature using services and equipment generally not available elsewhere.

5. Following this brief discussion in Mr. Lundahl's office the group adjourned to the conference room where a serics of briefings was presented to Dr. Condon and his group. Following a short introduction by the following briefings were presented:

a. General discussion of photogrammetry, including definition, terminology and, in general, what photogrammetry is and what it can do. presented this discussion.

b. followed with a presentation of the analysis he had been conducting on UFO photography furnished NPIC by Dr. Rachford. discussion was of a general nature and outlined the problems he had encountered because of lack of basic information, such as camera focal length, make of camera, unspecified enlargements, etc.

c. then gave a general discussion on the microdensitometer and its application to image analysis.

d. followed this with a presentation on isodensitometer experiments he has been conducting.

e. then escorted the group into the new clean area where they viewed and discussed the isodensitometer and the new Mann Microdensitometer.

f. Returning to the conference room, briefed the group on measuring instruments used in and followed by a general presentation on the success and failure had experienced in trying to measure c jects imaged on the second UFO project assigned Following this discussion then conducted the group into the instrument area where the Point Transfer Device, Mann 880 Comparator, the Benson-Lehner Plotter and the NRI were viewed by the group.

SUBJECT: Visit of Dr. Condon to NPIC, 20 February 1967

6. At about 1215 escorted the group back to Mr. Lundahl's office where a general discussion on UFOs ensued. At about 1235 the group adjourned to lunch and following lunch they left NPIC for a meeting with Brig.Gen Gillers at the pentagon.

7. Most all the discussion during the morning was of an unclassified nature dealing with primary basic fundamentals of photogrammetry, photographic analysis and problems related to the acquiring of enough information to conduct meaningful analyses.

16 May 1958

MEMORANDUM FOR RECORD

SUBJECT: Meeting with Air Force Personnel Concerning Scientific Advisory Panel Report on Unidentified Flying Objects, dated 17 January 1953 (Secret)

1. A meeting was convened this date with representatives of the Air Force to discuss what steps should be taken concerning the subject report in order to take care of inquiries such as the letters written by Mr. Leon Davidson. Mr. Davidson has been most insistent upon getting the entire report released. The full report is classified "Secret." A declassified version is available, a copy of which was given to Mr. Davidson.

2. The following personnel were at the meeting:

Mr. Philip G. Strong	DAD/C/SI, CIA
Major Joseph E. Boland	SAF LL-3
Major James F. Byrne	AFCIN-X1A
Major Lawrence J. Tacker	SAFIS
Dr. A. Francis Arcier	ATIC
Mr. George Cary	Legislative Counsel, CIA
Mr. W. E. Lexow	OSI, CIA

3. Paragraph 3 of the report cites examples of actions that could be taken by an enemy with possibly dangerous consequences to national security. This is the principal reason that the entire report cannot be declassified. This was agreed to in the meeting. In addition, it was pointed out by Mr. Strong that several of the panel members specifically requested that while they had no objection to their names being used in connection with the report, they did not want their names connected to the Central Intelligence Agency. So far it is believed that all connections between the panel members and CIA have been made by unofficial personnel.

4. In dealing specifically with Mr. Davidson it was agreed that Major Tacker would answer for the DCI at the same time that he was answering for the Air Forces. (Mr. Davidson sent a copy of his letter to Major Tacker to the DCI for a response.)

5. Mr. Strong pointed out that perhaps the best way to forestall any future inquiries along these lines was to put out a press release covering the subject of unidentified flying objects, utilizing the panel report as much as possible. Major Boland agreed

For translation, see next page.

Office Memorandum • UNITED STATES GOVERNMENT

TO: DIRECTOR, FBI DATE: March 22, 1950

FROM: GUY HOTTEL, SAC, WASHINGTON

SUBJECT: FLYING SAUCERS
INFORMATION CONCERNING

Flying Discs or Flying Saucers

The following information was furnished to SA [redacted] by [redacted]

An investigator for the Air Forces stated that three so-called flying saucers had been recovered in New Mexico. They were described as being circular in shape with raised centers, approximately 50 feet in diameter. Each one was occupied by three bodies of human shape but only 3 feet tall, dressed in metallic cloth of a very fine texture. Each body was bandaged in a manner similar to the blackout suits used by speed flyers and test pilots.

According to Mr. [redacted] informant, the saucers were found in New Mexico due to the fact that the Government has a very high-powered radar set-up in that area and it is believed the radar interferes with the controling mechanism of the saucers.

No further evaluation was attempted by SA [redacted] concerning the above.

RHK:VLM

Pertinent Parts Retyped For Readability

DATE: March 22, 1950

TO: DIRECTOR, FBI
FROM: GUY HOTTEL, SAC, WASHINGTON
SUBJECT: FLYING SAUCERS
INFORMATION CONCERNING

Flying Discs or Flying Saucers

The following information was furnished to ______

An investigator for the Air Force stated that three so-called flying saucers had been recovered in New Mexico. They were described as being circular in shape with raised centers, approximately 50 feet in diameter. Each one was occupied by three bodies of human shape but only 3 feet tall, dressed in metallic cloth of a very fine texture. Each body was bandaged in a manner similar to the black-out suits used by speed flyers and test pilots.

According to Mr. _____ informant, the saucers were found in New Mexico due to the fact that the Government had a very high-powered radar set-up in that area and it is believed the radar interfered with the controling mechanism of the saucers.

No further evaluation was attempted by SA_____x concerning the above.

RHK(?):VIM

PAGE:0025

INQUIRE=DOC3D
ITEM NO=00027685
CDS
C 04710RUEKJCS 5781 272201ZMCR 86-1004040 F I004710MIDB
S UPID
/ / FRP: , ,3, , , , ,

86 1004040 MCR PAGE 001 NC 1004040
TOR: 272201Z MAY 86 RUEKJCS 5781

HEADER
RR RUEAIIA
DE RUEKJCS #5781 1472010
ZNY CCCCC
R 272010Z MAY 86
FM JCS WASHINGTON DC
INFO RUEAIJU/NPIC WASHINGTON DC//IEG//
RUEALGX/SAFE
AIG 11881
R 272006Z MAY 86

TO RUEKJCS/DIA WASHDC//DC-4A/AT-5//
INFO RUEHRI/USDAO RIO DE JANEIRO
RUEAHQA/HQUSAF WASHDC//XOXXW/CVAI//
RUEAHQA/AFIS WASHDC
RUEOEHA/USCINCSO QUARRY HEIGHTS//SCJ2-I/BIOS//
BT
CONTROLS
05781

SERIAL: (U)

BODY
PASS: DIA PASS TO AIG 11881

COUNTRY: (U) BRAZIL (BR)

SUBJECT: /BAF HAS A CLOSE
ENCOUNTER OF THE FIRST KIND (U)

WARNING: (U) THIS IS AN INFO REPORT, NOT
FINALLY EVALUATED INTEL

DOI: (U) 860521

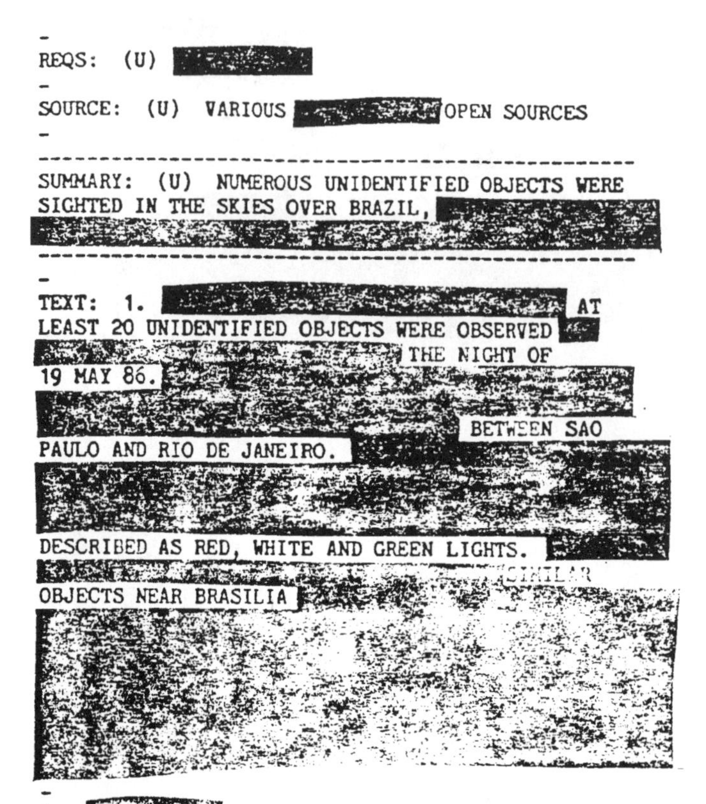

PAGE:0026

-
REQS: (U) [redacted]
-
SOURCE: (U) VARIOUS [redacted] OPEN SOURCES
-

SUMMARY: (U) NUMEROUS UNIDENTIFIED OBJECTS WERE SIGHTED IN THE SKIES OVER BRAZIL, [redacted]

-
TEXT: 1. [redacted] AT LEAST 20 UNIDENTIFIED OBJECTS WERE OBSERVED [redacted] THE NIGHT OF 19 MAY 86. [redacted] BETWEEN SAO PAULO AND RIO DE JANEIRO. [redacted] DESCRIBED AS RED, WHITE AND GREEN LIGHTS. [redacted] SIMILAR OBJECTS NEAR BRASILIA [redacted]
-
2. [redacted] THE AIR MINISTER IS QUOTED BY THE PRESS AS SAYING THERE WERE THREE GROUPS OF TARGETS ON THE GROUND RADAR AND THAT THE SCOPES OF THE AIRBORNE RADARS WERE SATURATED.
-

And They Say the Government is Not Interested in UFOs!

2 April, 1997

US Military Visitors

385th Signals Company, US Army Kuwait

Air Force Academy, Colorado Springs, CO

Air Force Institute of Technology, Wright-Patterson AFB, Ohio

Commander Naval Reserve Force, New Orleans, LA. CNRF.NOLA.NAVY. MIL

Defence Contract Management Command, Cleveland, Ohio

HQ Air Force Command Section, the Pentagon, Washington DC

HQ Air Force Personnel Center, Randolph AFB, San Antonio, TX

Joint Spectrum Center, Department of Defense, Annapolis, MD. Mission: to ensure the DoD's effective use of the electromagnetic spectrum in support of national security and military objectives.

Naval Air Systems Command HQ, Washington DC.

Naval Air Warfare Center, Aircraft Division, Indianapolis. Product Acquisition and Engineering.

Naval Aviation Department, North Island, San Diego.

Naval Sea Systems Command, Arlington, VA.Na

Naval Ship Systems Engineering Station (NAVSSES) and David Taylor Research Lab, Philadelphia.

Picatinny Arsenal, NJ. The Heart of the US Army's Armament and Munitions Research and Development Capability

Scott Air Force Base, Illinois, Home of the Air Force Communications Agency, Air Mobility Command, US Transport Command and USAF Military Affiliate Radio System

Space and Missile Systems Center, Los Angeles

Space and Naval Warfare Systems Command SPAWAR/ NCCOSC. Mission: to develop and acquire undersea surveillance systems, global weather and oceanographic forecasting systems and navigational systems to give the warfighter superior knowledge.

Supervisor of Shipbuilding, Conversion and Repair, US Navy, San Diego, CA.

US Army

US Army Communications-Electronics Command (CECOM), Research Development and Engineering Center (CERDEC), Ft. Monmouth, NJ., Night Vision and Electronic Sensors Directorate (NVESD)

US Army Corps of Engineers Construction Research Lab, Champaign, Illinois

US Army Corps of Engineers, Sacramento, CA

US Government Visitors

Argonne National Laboratory, Argonne, Illinois. Operated by the University of Chicago as part of the US Department of Energy's National Laboratory System.

Argonne National Laboratory, Corporate Information Center.

Argonne National Laboratory West, Idaho Falls, Idaho. Home of most of ANL's major nuclear reactor facilities.

Bonneville Power Administration

The Defence Mapping Agency, St. Louis, MO.Geospatial Information and Imagery Information.

Department of Energy

Department of Energy, Boeing Computer Services, Richland, WA.

Department of Energy, Nevada Test Site.

Department of the Treasury, US Govt.

Ernest Orlando Lawrence Berkeley National Laboratory, Berkeley, Ca. Operated by the University of California for the US Department of Energy. Research in advanced materials, biosciences, energy efficiency, detectors and accelerators.

Executive Office, the President, White House

Institute for Telecommunications Sciences, Research and Engineering Branch of the National Telecommunications and Information Administration.

Lawrence Livermore National Laboratory, Livermore, Ca. Operated by the University of California for the US Department of Energy. Focus is on global security, global ecology, and bioscience.

The Library of Congress

Los Alamos National Laboratory, Los Alamos, NM. Operated by the University of California for the US Department of Energy. Nuclear and advanced materials; nuclear weapons science and technology, nuclear science, beams and plasmas; complex experimentation and measurements; bioscience and biotechnology; earth and environmental sciences.

Los Alamos National Laboratory, Advanced Computing Laboratory

NASA Ames Research Center, Moffett Field, CA. In the heart of "Silicon Valley"

NASA Goddard Space Flight Center, Maryland, Northeast of Washington DC.

NASA Headquarters, Washington DC

NASA Jet Propulsion Laboratory, Pasadena, CA. Managed by the California Institute of Technology.

NASA John C.Stennis Space Center, Hancock County, MS. NASA'S Center of Excellence for Large Propulsion Systems Testing.

NASA Kennedy Space Center, Cape Canaveral, Fla.

NASA Langley Research Center, Hampton, VA.

NASA Lewis Research Center, Cleveland, Ohio.

NASA Johnson Space Center, Houston, TX.

NASA Tracking and Data Relay Satellite System, White Sands Complex, New Mexico.

National Institute of Environmental Health Sciences, Research Triangle Park, NC.

National Renewable Energy Laboratory

Oak Ridge National Laboratory - Defense Programs Organization and National Security Program Offices PM.ORNL.GOV

Oak Ridge National Laboratory

Oak Ridge National Laboratory Centers for Manufacturing Technology

Oak Ridge National Laboratory Chemical and Analytical Sciences Division

Office of Civilian Radioactive Waste Management, Yucca Mountain Project, Nevada

US Patent and Trademark Office

San Diego Data Processing Corp., US Govt.

Tennessee Valley Authority

The Salt River Project, Arizona. Major multipurpose project serving electric customers and water shareholders in the greater Phoenix area.

The Securities & Exchange Commission (SEC)

The US Senate

The Social Security Administration

US Department of Justice

US Environmental Protection Agency, Headquarters Administration. HQADMIN.EPA.GOV

US Environmental Protection Agency, Office of Research and Development, Atmospheric Environmental Research Lab, Air Engineering.

US Environmental Protection Agency, Corvallis, Oregon.

US Environmental Protection Agency, Region 5.

US Geological Survey

US Geological Survey, Computer Resources.

US House of Representatives

Aerospace Visitors

The Aerospace Corporation - the Integral Engineering arm for US National Security Space and Launch Systems Programs.

Allied Signal. An advanced technology and manufacturing company in the Fortune 100 and one of the 30 companies comprising the Dow Jones Industrial Average.

Boeing

Boeing Autonetics & Missile Systems Development Division

Honeywell Commercial Aviation Systems

Hughes Aircraft Company

Hughes Defense Communications, Sensors and Communications segment of Hughes Aircraft Co.

Lockheed Martin Missiles and Space.

McDonnell Douglas

Northrop-Grumman

Rocketdyne Division of Boeing North American Inc. Propulsion, Power Systems, Directed Energy and Imaging.

Rockwell Collins Avionics & Communications Division

TRW Space Park, Redondo Beach, CA. SP.TRW.COM.

Universal Analytics Inc., Structural Analysis for Aerospace and Nuclear industry.

Defense Contractors

AT&T Labs Research

Autometric Inc. Alexandria, Virginia. Remote Sensing, Spatial Information Production, Visualization, Image Processing and Analysis.

Bellcore (Bell Communications Research)

Bechtel

Booz Allen Hamilton, one of the world's largest management and technology consulting firms.

Cambridge Research Lab, Digital Equipment's Corporate Research and Advanced Development

Computer Sciences Corporation, ALMRS Project, Golden CO.

Cornell University, High Energy Particle Research Laboratory

Cray Research Inc.

Genentech, Inc.

General Electric

The Genetics Institute Inc.

Hewlett Packard

Hewlett Packard Engineering, Cupertino, CA.

Hewlett Packard Laboratories

Honeywell Inc.

Honeywell Solid States Electronics Center

IBM

IBM Microelectronics

IBM Networking

IBM RS 6000 Resource

Inktomi (Supercomputing)

Intel

Kodak

Lucent Technologies, Bell Labs Innovations

Motorola

National Semiconductor, Fairchild Division

Nuclear Physics Lab, University of Illinois at Urbana - Champaign

SAIC, Science Applications International Corporation, San Diego.

Stanford Linear Accelerator Center, funded by US Dept. of Energy

Sun Microsystems

Texas Instruments

Xerox Palo Alto Research

High Tech Visitors

ADE Corporation. Westwood, MA. Worldwide leader in the design, manufacture, marketing and metrology and inspection systems for the semiconductor wafer industry.

AG Communications Systems, Phoenix, AZ. Leader in development of intelligent networks.

Alza Corporation, Palo Alto, CA. Leader in development and commercialization of innovative pharmaceutical products using advanced drug delivery technologies.

AMD International. Global Supplier of Integrated Circuits. 1996 Revenue $1.6 billion.

Analogy, Inc., Beaverton, OR. World leader in analog, mixed-signal and mixed technology simulation.

Baxter International. Worldwide leader in technologies related to the blood and circulatory system.

Bull. International IT Group - Annual sales $4.7 billion.

Cisco Corp. (currently valued at $4bn)

LSI Logic, Computer Chip Makers

Micron Technology Inc.

Rockwell Semiconductor Systems

Silicon Graphics

Teradyne Inc., Boston, MA. World's largest supplier of ATE for the electronics and telecommunications industries.

Unisys

Wang

Other US Visitors

Aramco Services, Houston (Service Company for ARAMCO, Saudi Arabia) ARAMCO.COM.

ARCO

BASF Corp
British Petroleum (BP)
Chevron
Citibank
Consolidated Natural Gas Company, Pittsburgh
Disney
Dow Chemical
Houston Public Television
Minneapolis- St. Paul Star Tribune
Monsanto
The New York Time
PCS Health Systems. $11 billion in pharmaceutical care.
Project Vote Smart, who track the performance of over 13,000 political leaders
Rohm and Haas Co. One of the World's leading manufacturers of speciality chemicals and plastics. $4Bn. sales.
Schlumberger, an $8.9 billion worldwide leader in international Oilfield Services.
SETI
The Seattle Times
Texaco
Viacom
Wells Fargo Bank

Overseas Visitors (Selected)

The Astronomical Observatory, Brera, Italy
The Australian Broadcasting Corporation
The Australian Government, Dept. of Administrative Services
The Australian Ministry of Defence defence.gov.au
BHP. One of the world's largest diversified natural resources companies, headquartered in Australia.
Canadian Broadcasting Corporation
Center for Atmospheric Science, Cambridge University, UK.
Central Science Laboratory, UK Government. Crop research.
CERN, European Laboratory for Particle Physics, Geneva, Switzerland

Communications Research Laboratory, Ministry of Posts and Telecommunications, Japan

County Government of Hampshire, UK.

Credit Suisse Financial Products, UK.

CSIRO, Australia's Largest Government Research Agency.

The Czechoslovakian Army ISWG iswg.army.cz.

Department of Primary Industries, Queensland, Government of Australia

Faculty of Engineering, Universidad de Los Andes, Venezuela

Government of Malaysia

Government of New Zealand

Government of Northern Ireland

Government of South Africa

Hong Kong Internet Star

Institute for Nuclear Science, University of Mexico

Institute of Physics, Republic University, Montevideo, Uruguay

King Abdulaziz City for Science & Technology, Riyadh, Saudi Arabia

Mitsubishi Space Software, Japan

The National Electricity Commission, Mexico

Ontario Hydro, Canada. Mission: to make Ontario Hydro a leader in energy efficiency and sustainable development.

Physics Dept., University of Crete

South African Broadcasting Corporation

Tellabs Ltd., Shannon, Ireland

Trinity College, Dublin, Ireland - Math Dept.

The Venezuelan State Oil Company, PDVSA.

Note: Most University visitors worldwide have not been listed as there are so many from so many different countries.

A.J. Craddock
CSETI Web Administrator

CSETI—The Center for the Study of Extraterrestrial Intelligence

CSETI is a nonprofit tax-exempt research and educational organization with members worldwide.

Its primary goals are to:

- Establish a real-time diplomatic and research initiative to contact extraterrestrial civilizations, leading to a sustainable , peaceful and mutually beneficial relationship;
- Educate all sectors of human society about this subject in a credible and non-harmful manner.

The CSETI Project currently has working groups worldwide which are conducting research. The project is guided by an Advisory Board and International Director, Steven M. Greer, M.D. A senior diplomatic and research team known as the RMIT (Rapid Mobilization Investigative Team) responds to areas of significant apparent extraterrestrial activity and has successfully established contact with extraterrestrial spacecraft in the United States, England , Mexico and Belgium. This contact involves the coordinated signaling and vectoring of positively identified ET craft and the returned acknowledgment through similar signaling and near-landing events by those craft.

The Project also consists of an effort to educate all members of society about the Extraterrestrial issue. This aspect has consisted of talks and interviews by Dr. Greer in print media and on radio and television, providing briefing documents to members of the government and military in the US and abroad and meeting with government and military officials face to face for briefings and discussions.

You are invited to join this effort through membership in the organization, participation in trainings and workshops and/or financial donations to promote the continuation of the work.

Please see the membership form which follows or contact CSETI via: website: www.cseti.org

mail address: CSETI
P.O. Box 265
Crozet, VA 22932-0265

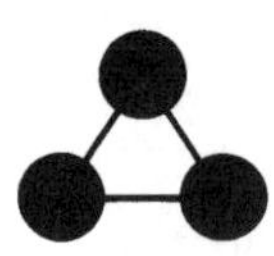

CSETI MEMBERSHIP

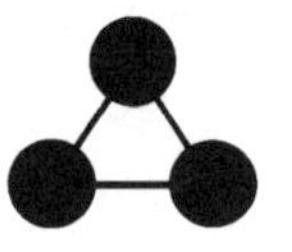

New Levels and Benefits!
Includes Special Members area of Web Site and Online Conferences with CSETI Director Dr. Steven Greer

We invite you to join CSETI or renew your membership at one of the following levels. Your membership supports our continued work in the efforts of disclosure and contact. All New Members receive a membership packet of articles and research reports.

Friend: $40 - $100 per year
(included with Working Group Training Kit and CSETI Ambassador to the Universe Training tuition) - Members receive access to members only section of the CSETI web site, which will have an online newsletter, special notices and news, and priority access to new research reports, Working Group reports and Position Papers written by Dr. Steven Greer. For at least $60 per year, members can receive a printed newsletter through the mail, upon request.

Subscriber: $9 per month ($108 per year) or higher
Member receives all of the above PLUS exclusive member access to online real time conferences with Dr. Steven Greer, CSETI director.

Benefactor: $500 to $9999 per year
Member receives Subscriber benefits plus 5 years of access to online real time conferences with Dr. Greer.

Lifetime Member: $10,000 or more donation
Member receives lifetime Subscriber benefits plus complementary fees for trainings and conferences.

** Check the CSETI web site at www.cseti.org or call us at one of the numbers below for more information on membership benefits and access to the members only areas. **

Membership form

Name (on credit card):	Date:
Address:	Email:
	Phone:
City/State/Zip Code:	Country:
New Membership or Renewal:	Member Level:
Circle one: Check or Visa or Master Card	Amount Enclosed:
Account #:	Expiration Date:

** Please Note - Your phone/email address is for our own internal records ONLY. They WILL NOT be sold to any outside organization. **

Send to:
CSETI
PO Box 4556
Largo, MD 20775 USA

or Fax credit card payments to:
1-800-633-2190 or 1-516-577-5433
or Email to: coordinator@cseti.org
or Call: 1-301-249-3915 or
1-888-ET-CSETI (1-888-382-7384)

Information re CSETI Trainings

Ambassadors to the Universe

Dr. Greer offers one day, two day and week long training sessions for those interested in contacting Extraterrestrial Intelligence (ETI). During these trainings, the participant is given the knowledge and experience to conduct real-time field research with ETI.

Depending on the length of the training, it will include.

- Philosophy and History of ET Contact
- Update on CSETI Project Starlight
- Consciousness Studies as they relate to ET communication and travel
- Training in Remote Viewing and Remote Vectoring
- Training in Coherent Thought Sequencing
- Discussion and practice of non-local forms of communication
- Night time field work practice

The week- long trainings are held in areas known to have sightings of ET Craft and Beings and are designed to give people the skills to form their own research groups . Reports included in section II will give an idea of some of the events which occur on the trainings and RMIT (Rapid Mobilization Investigative Team) field experiences. Although making contact cannot be guaranteed the week-long trainings almost always result in contact with Extraterrestrial Intelligence in physical or subtle forms.

If you would like information about upcoming trainings contact:

CSETI

P.O. Box 265 Crozet, VA 22932

or check our web site: <www.cseti.org>.

Steven M. Greer, M.D.

Dr. Greer is widely regarded as the world's foremost authority on the subject of extraterrestrial intelligence (ETI), and is the founder and international director of the Center for the Study of Extraterrestrial Intelligence (CSETI). A lifetime member of Alpha Omega Alpha, the nation's most prestigious medical honor society, Dr. Greer is an emergency physician and former chairman of the department of emergency medicine at Caldwell Memorial hospital.

Dr. Greer, as director of CSETI, has led research teams throughout the world investigating the existence of ETI and on several occasions has successfully established preliminary contact and communication with extraterrestrial spacecraft at close range. He has met with and provided briefings for senior members of government, military and intelligence operations in the United States and around the world, including senior CIA officials, Joint Chiefs of Staff, White House staff, senior members of Congress and congressional committees, senior United Nations leadership and diplomats, senior military officials in the United Kingdom and Europe and cabinet-level members of the Japanese government, among others.

Dr. Greer has been seen and heard by millions world-wide on shows such as the Larry King Show, CBS, the BBC, NTV in Japan, *Sightings* and *Encounters* TV programs in the U.S., the Armstrong Williams radio show and dozens of other TV and Radio programs.

He has addressed tens of thousands of people live at conferences and lectures around the world including the international convention of MENSA, the high-IQ group, the Institute of Noetic Sciences Board of Directors, and the Sierra Club.

He brings a unique combination of scientific knowledge, credibility, vision, humor and inspiration to his lectures. Dr. Greer. relies on first hand knowledge of extraterrestrial activity world wide, and has direct sources for information regarding covert operations dealing with the subject.

Supporters of his work are as diverse as Apollo astronaut, Dr. Edgar Mitchell, who walked on the moon in Apollo 14, to benefactor and philanthropist Laurance Rockefeller, to former British Ministry of Defense Head and five star admiral Lord Hill-Norton, to folk legend Burl Ives.

The scope of Dr. Greer's knowledge and experience permits him to address a virtually limitless diversity of audiences. He is able to relate the ETI subject to political and national security issues, consciousness studies, space exploration, the environment, religion and spirituality, world peace and disarmament issues, global transformation, new sciences, free energy, studies regarding our future and many other areas,

Dr. Greer is married. He and his wife, Emily, have four daughters and reside in the Charlottesville, VA area.